We Belong Dead:
Frankenstein on Film

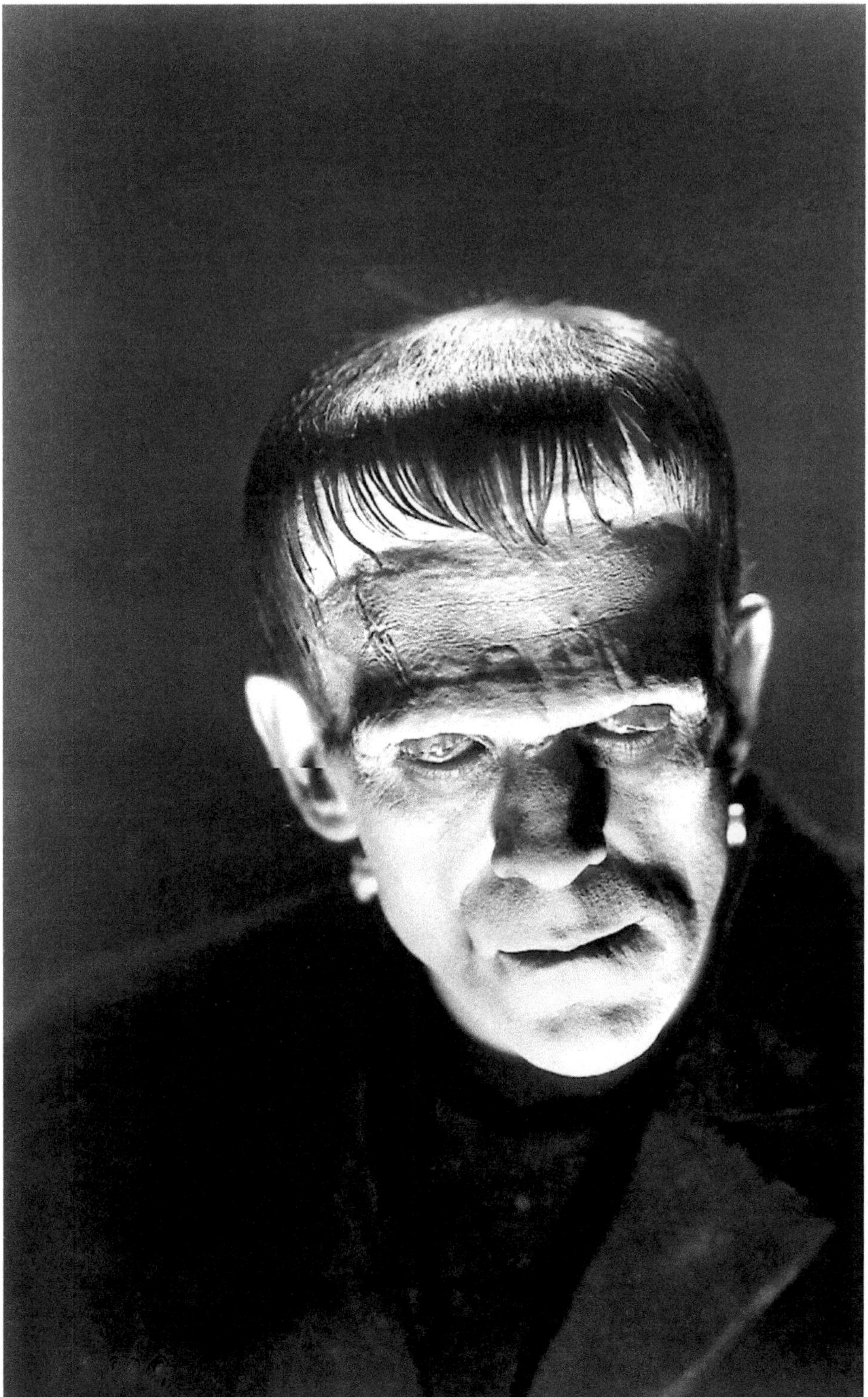

WE BELONG DEAD

FRANKESTEIN ON FILM

edited by
Gary J. Svehla
and
Susan Svehla

Luminary Press
Baltimore, Maryland

Interior and Cover Design: Susan Svehla
Copyright © 2005 Gary J. Svehla and Susan Svehla
Copyright © 1997 Gary J. Svehla and Susan Svehla

Without limiting the rights reserved under the copyright above, no part of this publication may be reproduced, stored in or introduced into a retrieval system, or transmitted, in any form, or by any means (electronic, mechanical, photocopying, recording, or otherwise), without the prior written permission of the copyright owners or the publishers of this book.

ISBN 1-887664-09-2
Library of Congress Catalog Card Number 97-76024
Manufactured in the United States of America
First Printing by Midnight Marquee Press, Inc., December, 1997
Revised Printing by Luminary Press an imprint of Midnight Marquee Press, Inc., May 2005

We are about to unfold the story of Frankenstein,
a man of science,
who sought to create a man after his own image—
without reckoning upon God.
It is one of the strangest tales ever told.
It deals with the two great mysteries of creation—
life and death.
I think it will thrill you.
It may shock you.
It might even... horrify you!
So, if any of you feel that you do not care
to subject your nerves to such a strain,
now is your chance to...
Well, we've warned you!
—Introduction to *Frankenstein*, Universal 1931

ROBERT DENIRO KENNETH BRANAGH
MARY SHELLEY'S
FRANKENSTEIN
BE WARNED
TRISTAR PICTURES WOWOW JAPAN SATELLITE BROADCASTING THE INDIEPROD COMPANY
AMERICAN ZOETROPE KENNETH BRANAGH "MARY SHELLEY'S FRANKENSTEIN"
TOM HULCE HELENA BONHAM CARTER AIDAN QUINN IAN HOLM JOHN CLEESE PATRICK DOYLE JAMES ACHESON
ANDREW MARCUS TIM HARVEY ROGER PRATT, B.S.C. KENNETH BRANAGH DAVID PARFITT
FRED FUCHS STEPH LADY FRANK DARABONT FRANCIS FORD COPPOLA JAMES V. HART JOHN VEITCH
KENNETH BRANAGH
NOVEMBER FOURTH
TRI STAR

Table of Contents

9	Introduction
13	**Frankenstein: The Early Years**
14	Mary Wollstonecraft Shelley by Gregory William Mank
17	Edison's *Frankenstein* by Frederick C. Wiebel, Jr.
28	**Frankenstein Becomes a "Universal" Legend**
30	Dysfunctional Family: The Universal Frankenstein Legacy by Gary J. Svehla
42	Universal Home Video Legacy Collection Frankenstein: The Legacy Collection by Gary J. Svehla
45	Frankenstein's Children: The Relationship of the Child to the Monster in the Frankenstein Films by John E. Parnum
70	*Frankenstein—Or, "My Heart Belongs to Daddy"* by Anthony Ambrogio
83	**Frankenstein Reanimated by Hammer Films**
84	The Evolution of Hammer's Baron Frankenstin by Gary J. Svehla
116	**What Hath God and Hollywood Wrought?**
117	*I Was a Teenage Frankenstein, Frankenstein 1970*, and *Frankenstein's Daughter* by Bryan Senn
132	*Frankenstein Meets the Spacemonster* by Don G. Smith
139	*Assignment Terror* by David H. Smith
150	*Blackenstein* by David H. Smith
160	*Lady Frankenstein* by David H. Smith
170	*The Screaming Dead* and *Erotic Rites of Frankenstein* by David H. Smith
183	**Frankenstein Invades American Homes**
184	*Frankenstein: The True Story* by Dennis Fischer
294	*Frankenstein*. TNT, 1993 by Arthur Joseph Lundquist
207	**The Modern Prometheus**
208	*Young Frankenstein* by Robert Alan Crick
221	*Frankenweenie* by Robert Alan Crick
230	Hollywood Tries to Reanimate Universal: The Bride& Van Helsing by Gary J. Svehla and Susan Svehla
236	*Gothic* by Arthur Joseph Lundquist
245	*Haunted Summer* by Arthur Joseph Lundquist
254	*Roger Corman's Frankenstein Unbound* by Arthur Joseph Lundquist
267	*Mary Shelley's Frankenstein* by Arthur Joseph Lundquist
283	*Frankenstein and Me* by Bryan Senn and Robert Tinnell

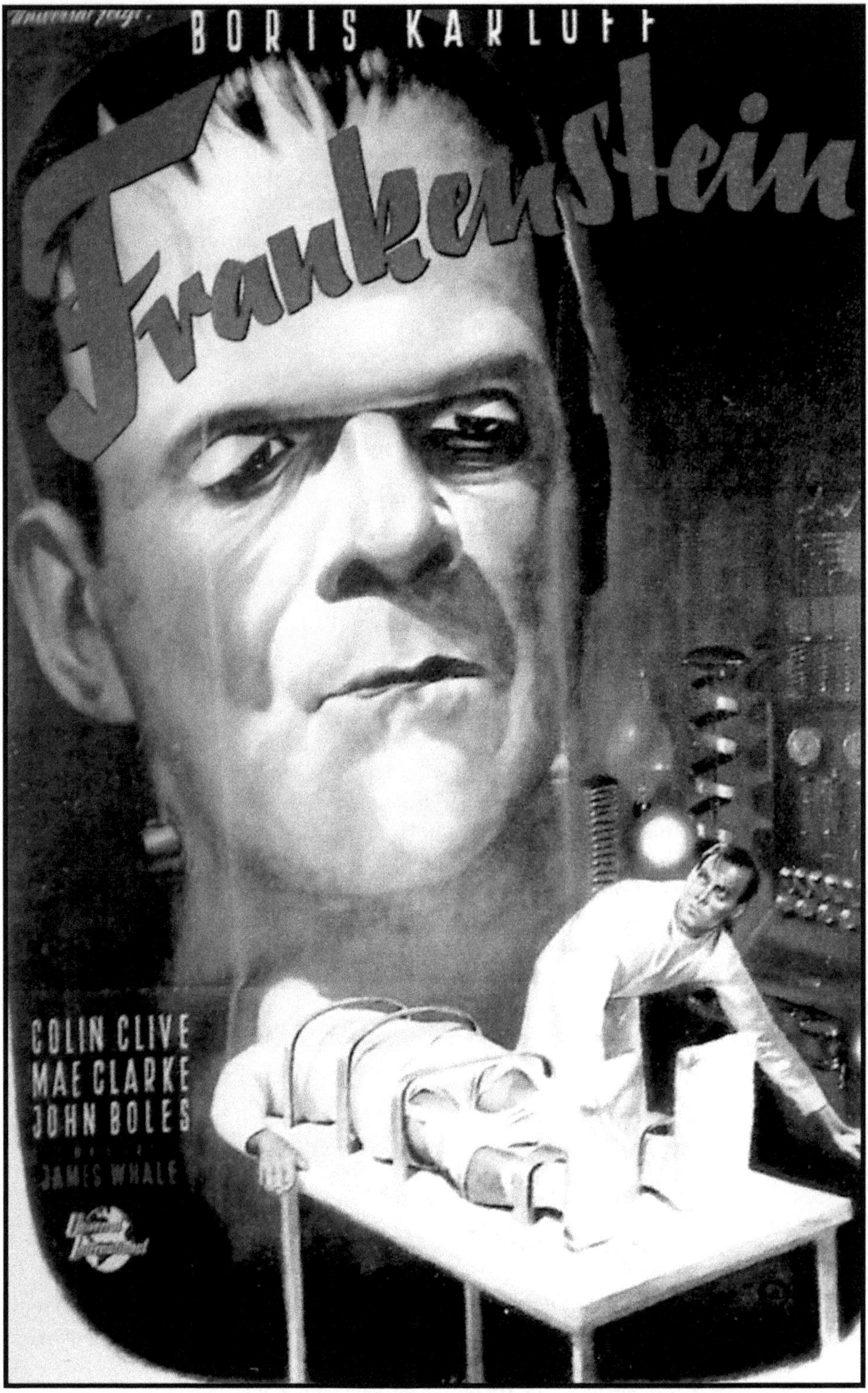
BORIS KARLOFF
Frankenstein
COLIN CLIVE
MAE CLARKE
JOHN BOLES
JAMES WHALE

INTRODUCTION

Young Mary Shelley, married to Percy Bysshe Shelley, one of the grand poets of England's Romantic movement, saw the publication of her immortal novel *Frankenstein* in 1818. She was only 19 years old.

The Romantics were not romantic in the "mushy" sense of traditional love poetry. Instead the Romantics were a youthful group of nonconformists who wrote lovingly of the past and the beauty to be found in purer, ancient times. The modern Industrial Revolution was progressing full-tilt in England and the Romantics saw such progress as a threat to the world's natural beauty and sanity. In a sense, they were the "hippies" of the late 18th century, who tried to get back into harmony with Mother Nature. They exhorted loving, respecting, and preserving the natural environment, all the while dabbling in sex and drugs.

The novel *Frankenstein* shows just how much can go wrong when the frightening new science disrupts the harmony of nature and God's great plan. The Romantics horror

Mary Shelley portrait by Reginald Easton circa 1820

was the horror of an uncomprehending industrial/scientific-charged society. They created a modern monster that ultimately turns against its creators, itself and everything in its wake.

But in the movies, the Frankenstein Monster became something radically different from Mary Shelley's vision of an intelligent and almost handsome creature, becoming something ugly, inhuman, grotesque, and quite simply monstrous. Yet at the same time, Frankenstein's Monster aroused sympathy in the heart of the terrified viewer when directed by artists such as James Whale, and Terence Fisher.

This book stands as a testament to the durability of Mary Shelley's original novel. The fact that today the name Frankenstein still elicits an immediate emotional response speaks of the universality of the Frankenstein mythos.

To a generation of baby boomers, we recall with fondness turning our TV antennas toward the dark heavens trying to pull in distant television channels to catch snowy glimpses of the classic Universal Frankenstein films of the 1930s on *Shock Theatre* or other late-night horror hosted festivities. The thrill of being able to stay up late, to sometimes watch all alone while all the other inhabitants of the household were sleeping, became something very special to me.

Growing up in the 1950s and 1960s, we saw the recreation of the Frankenstein myth rewritten first by England's Hammer Film Productions and later recast in science fiction terms, where even *The Thing* and *It! The Terror from Beyond Space* became variations on a theme: Frankenstein Monsters from outer space.

Frankenstein's Monster (*Frankenstein* [Universal, 1931] Boris Karloff and Ernest Thesinger), over the course of the 20th-century, became all things to all people.

Shuler Hensley as Frankenstein's Monster in *Van Helsing* (2004)

We watched during the decades of the 1970s and 1980s as filmmakers rediscovered *Frankenstein* and tried to retell the story, this time, truer to the original concept of Mary Shelley, adaptations that reconstructed our Universal visions of how a Frankenstein Monster should look, speak, and act. Most of us still prefer the Universal and Hammer versions, but once again *Frankenstein* became redefined for yet another generation.

Frankenstein's Monster, over the course of the 20th century, became all things to all people. He was the social outcast who still had redeeming qualities. He was the loner, the tortured outsider to whom most of us could relate. He was the symbol of fear and of death, the creature better off dead who still stalked the laboratories of egocentric science. He became the metaphor for science gone bad... he was the Dark Side before *Star Wars*. He became a symbol that life, no matter how pathetic, was always better than death.

Ted Cassidy as Lurch in *The Addams Family* (TV 1964-1966)

Fred Gwynne as Herman Munster

"Oh, it's you! For a moment you gave me quite a start."

An Addams Family cartoon from the pen of the wonderful Charles Addams. The cartoons would inspire the television series and later two films starring Raul Julia as Gomez Addams.

The Monster represented a creature who sometimes wanted to die but could not. The Monster became the mirror in which the movie viewer could view the cruelty of an insensitive society that both created and later abandoned its own abominations.

And within these pages, all the pieces of the jigsaw are repeatedly reassembled, each time recreating a different, finished puzzle, a puzzle that needs to be examined and explained. For each generation has the task of redefining its own Frankenstein Monster, recasting it as a reflection of all the horrors that each age lets loose upon an unsuspecting public. This book is by no means a complete listing of every *Frankenstein* film ever made. There are a number of very good books that have already done that. Rather it is a loving tribute to the Frankenstein Monster and the talented people who helped create him.

Whether we look at Frankenstein's Monster as the bogeyman, as metaphor, as kindred spirit, or as society's mirror, the fact remains that Mary Shelley knew not what she wrought during that haunted summer of 1816, and this volume is the latest effort in a relatively short line that tries to explain, looking at both cinema past and present, the meaning of Boris Karloff's immortal words from 1935's *Bride of Frankenstein*—"We belong dead!"
—Gary J. Svehla

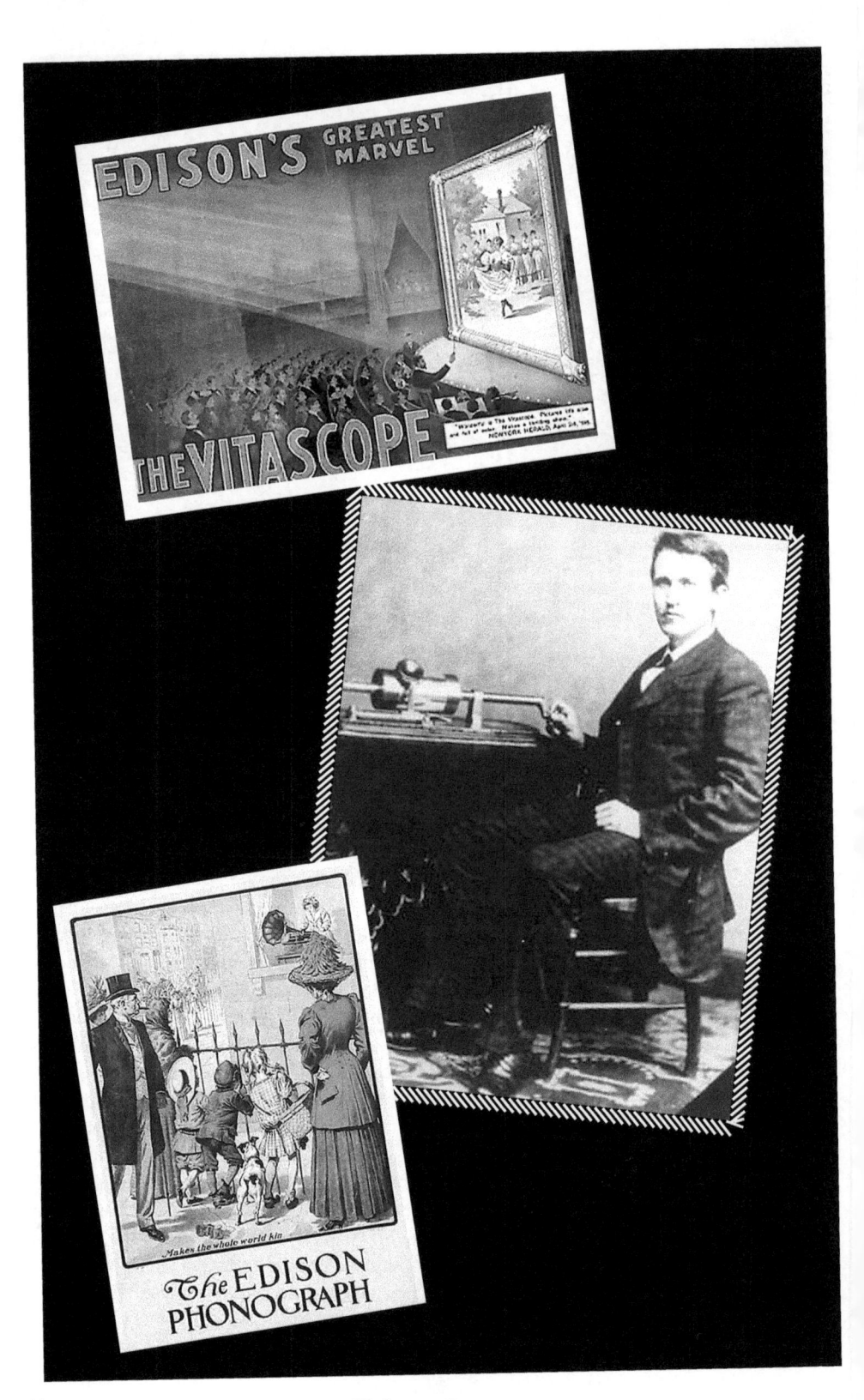

We Belong Dead

FRANKENSTEIN: THE EARLY YEARS

Believe it or not, the movies visited Mary Shelley's novel several times before the Universal classics of the 1930s. Films such as *Life Without Soul* and Thomas Edison's 1910 featurette helped to define the cinematic concept of the relationship between Dr. Frankenstein and the Monster he created in the lab, using ideas later incorporated into the Universal series. Edison's 1910 *Frankenstein* portrays the Monster as monstrosity, in many ways uglier than Jack P. Pierce's conception for actor Boris Karloff, which was created more than 20 years later.

In this section we first revisit Mary Shelley with a brief biography written by Gregory William Mank, whose landmark book, *It's Alive! The Classic Cinema Saga of Frankenstein*, published during the early 1980s, became the first serious text to examine *Frankenstein* on film. Other books followed—*Karloff and Lugosi, The Hollywood Hissables, Dwight Frye's Last Laugh*, etc.—as well as theatrical performances in regional theater including *Babes in Toyland* (as the evil Barnaby), *Lend Me a Tenor*, and *The Music Man*. Mank also wrote 11 production histories for the MagicImage Film Script series, licensed by Universal Pictures.

We then turn to the first classic adaptation of Shelley's novel, Edison's 1910 version. Long considered a lost film, fortunately, the 1910 version is now available on videocassette and DVD. Frederick C. Wiebel, Jr. is one of the people most responsible for keeping the Edison *Frankenstein* alive and in the public's eye. Wiebel, an artist and writer from Hagerstown, Maryland, has worked on restoring and scoring the Edison film, as well as touring the country giving lectures and presentations on the film at various film conventions and exhibitions including the National Institutes of Health's Library of Medicine's "Frankenstein: Penetrating the Secrets of Nature" (10/31/97-8/15/98) in Bethesda, Maryland; "Frankenstein Friday with Sara Karloff" (10/31/97) in New York City; and The Monster Bash (7/21/97) in Ligonier, Pennsylvania, where a rough-cut video version of the Edison *Frankenstein* was screened throughout the weekend. For information about Wiebel's self-published book on the 1910 *Frankenstein*, write: Frederick C. Wiebel, Jr., Fine Arts Studio, 136 E. Irvin Avenue, Hagerstown, MD 21742-3430.

Mary Wollstonecraft Shelley
by Gregory William Mank

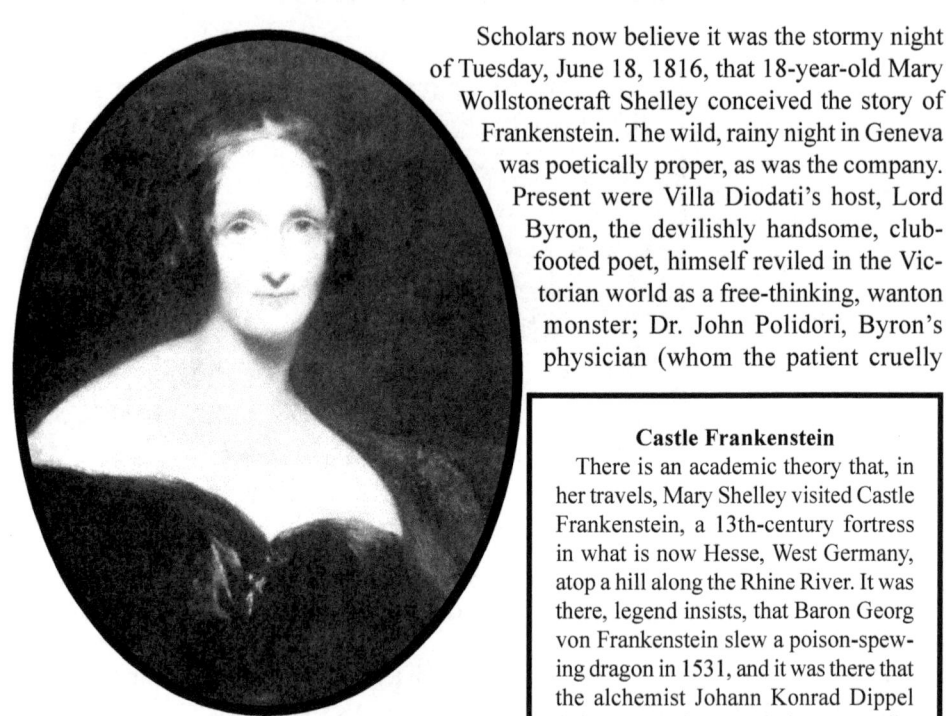

Scholars now believe it was the stormy night of Tuesday, June 18, 1816, that 18-year-old Mary Wollstonecraft Shelley conceived the story of Frankenstein. The wild, rainy night in Geneva was poetically proper, as was the company. Present were Villa Diodati's host, Lord Byron, the devilishly handsome, club-footed poet, himself reviled in the Victorian world as a free-thinking, wanton monster; Dr. John Polidori, Byron's physician (whom the patient cruelly

Portrait of Mary Shelley by Rothwell in 1841 from the National Portrait Gallery, London

Castle Frankenstein
There is an academic theory that, in her travels, Mary Shelley visited Castle Frankenstein, a 13th-century fortress in what is now Hesse, West Germany, atop a hill along the Rhine River. It was there, legend insists, that Baron Georg von Frankenstein slew a poison-spewing dragon in 1531, and it was there that the alchemist Johann Konrad Dippel (whose notoriety *might* have contributed to Mary's conception of Victor Frankenstein) began his life. The castle is a hotel today—popular with tourists who want to know where the Monster lived!—Gregory William Mank

The first page of Volume II of *Frankenstein* in Mary Shelley's handwriting

called "Polly-Dolly"), a whimpering would-be poet who kept vowing to commit suicide and finally did in 1921 by swallowing prussic acid; Claire Clairmont, Mary's half-sister, who was then pregnant with Byron's child Allegra; and there was Mary's lover, poet Percy Bysshe Shelley. They had fallen in love on the gravestone of Mary's mother, writer Mary Wollstonecraft, who had died giving birth to her. Shelley finally abandoned his wife Harriet (who later drowned herself) and two children for his soulful mistress. On May 3, 1816, accompanied by Claire Clairmont and their love child William, the couple fled England and began the "Grand Tour" of Europe.

It had been Byron's idea for each member of the little band to concoct a ghost story. Not only would Hollywood use her story for material, but her life would also influence several filmmakers including Ken Russell.

Lying awake in her bedroom at Villa Diodati, listening to the storm outside, Mary closed her eyes and saw in a vision (not a nightmare) the Monster Maker—and his Monster:

Mary Shelley portrait 1820 by Samuel John Stump

> ...I saw—with shut eyes, but acute mental vision—the pale student of unhallowed arts kneeling beside the thing he had put together. I saw the hideous phantasm of a man stretched out, and then, on the working of some powerful machine, show signs of life, and stir with an uneasy, half vital motion. Frightful must it be; for supremely frightful would be the effect of any human endeavor to mock the stupendous mechanism of the Creator of the world. His success would terrify the artist; he would rush away from his odious handiwork, horrorstricken...

Mary completed *Frankenstein* on April 17, 1817. Finding a publisher for this tale of blasphemy and horror was no easy task. It was the none-too-reputable firm of Lackington and Hughes that finally published *Frankenstein* (anonymously) on March 11, 1818. There was controversy indeed, and the *Quarterly Review* lambasted the book as "a tissue of horrible and disgusting absurdity."

Still, a classic had been born—a classic that would be the sole major literary achievement of Mary Shelley. Yet, when she died on February 1, 1851, treasuring the linen-wrapped heart of Shelley (who had wed her in 1818 and drowned in 1822), the long-respectable widow had the comfort of having created an immortal literary character.

The EDISON KINETOGRAM

VOL. 2   MARCH 15, 1910   No. 4

SCENE FROM
FRANKENSTEIN
FILM No. 6604

EDISON FILMS RELEASED FROM MARCH 16 TO 31 INCLUSIVE

Edison's
Frankenstein
by Frederick C. Wiebel, Jr.

Frankenstein was a highly successful novel that went through many adaptations for the stage shortly after its publication and by the end of the 19th century, it was also a magic lantern slide presentation before finally making it to the motion picture screen in 1910. It was through the production facilities of the Edison Manufacturing Company's movie studios in the Bronx, New York that Mary Shelley's creation first flickered into cinematic existence. Edison's *Frankenstein* is now considered by many to be the first "horror" film ever made, but at the time that appellation was never applied. It was simply released as a "dramatic" motion picture.

Thomas Alva Edison, the modern Prometheus and the prime mover behind the series of inventions that brought about commercial motion pictures, sent his agents and staff looking through the pages of classic literature in an effort to upgrade his films for a higher class of clientele and break open the foreign market with the uncopyrighted universal themes derived from literature. The story of Frankenstein was decided upon primarily because it possessed the necessary shock value that the studio perceived would draw thrill-seeking audiences under the guise of moral lessons painted on the screen with the photographic palette of special effects that only the new medium could provide.

The studio was counting on Dawley to recharge the unit and at the same time take great pains not to offend reformers of the day. Above: Charles Ogle as the Monster

Shortly after Frankenstein's (Augustus Phillips) arrival at college, he becomes absorbed in the mysteries of life and death. Courtesy Alois Dettlaff, Sr.

The year 1910 was the high water mark of the Nickelodeon movie theater era and also was the dawn of the golden age of silent films. The one-reel, 15-minute, feature-length movies were no longer relegated to filler spots in un-family-friendly Vaudeville theater programs, but were considered viable entertainment in their own right. Edison rejected the use of multi-reel films to tell a story, as he personally believed that longer films would cause severe eyestrain and lose the patience of a semi-literate audience.

By this time, Thomas Edison was not personally involved with the motion picture aspect of his many enterprises except to wield Napoleonic final approval over all productions and products released under his name. He relegated his time toward experimentation and developing the six-minute sound-on-cylinder synced films for his Kinetophone system. It has been suggested that Edison did want his company to film *Frankenstein,* but that can't be substantiated at this time. The film studio managers selected their top director and screenwriter, J. Searle Dawley, to handle the complicated "special" project. A director for the Edison Studios also acted like a producer in those days and performed all of the coordinating functions for the entire filming of the story. It was a difficult assignment, as Edison films had been severely attacked by critics and moral reform groups as inferior product; they constantly panned the films as dull, boring, vulgar, and cheap trash. Foreign distributors complained that Edison pictures were too "American" in their story lines and not did appeal to the European market.

J. Searle Dawley was chosen to direct *Frankenstein.*

18   We Belong Dead

Edison's properties department built a papier mâché dummy of the Monster, set fire to it, and filmed until it was reduced to ashes. Courtesy Alois Dettlaff, Sr.

A lot of money was poured into the recently upgraded studios in the Bronx and the executives were counting on Dawley to pull their productions out of the doldrums. He was instructed to take the utmost care in his handling of the writing and filming of the then-blasphemous novel and to take great pains not to offend the self-righteous reformers, yet still retain enough thrills for the general public. *Frankenstein* was perhaps perceived as a flagship to test these unstable waters, and also explore the world-wide market with a non-American story, particularly in England where its popularity was a guaranteed moneymaker. The studio backed its risky production to the limit with their best actors, the finest sets and costumes available, color tinting, trick photography, stirring music, and the necessary publicity needed to insure its success.

Frankenstein was featured with a photographic still of the Monster on the cover of the March 15, 1910 domestic edition of *The Kinetogram*, a bi-monthly Edison film release survey and also on the very first Edison film catalog ever offered in London. The studio's publicity writers went to great pains to emphasize the high moral tone offered in their principal release's production.

> To those familiar with Mrs. Shelley's story it will be evident that we have carefully omitted anything which might by any possibility shock any portion of an audience. In making the film the Edison Co. has carefully tried to eliminate all the actually repulsive situations and to concentrate its endeavors upon the mystic and psychological problems that are to be found in this weird tale. Wherever, therefore, the film differs from the original story it is purely with the idea of eliminating what would be repulsive to a moving picture audience.

To Frankenstein's horror, instead of creating a marvel of physical beauty and grace, there is unfolded before his eyes an awful, ghastly, abhorrent Monster.

J. Searle Dawley drew upon his immense background as a director and playwright for various New York City based theatrical stock companies to structure his photoplay, but added in the cinematic story telling effects he learned apprenticing under Edwin S. Porter, maker of *The Great Train Robbery* (1903), Edison's most successful film. Dawley condensed the essence of the overall story lines of the novel and incorporated some of the scenes and situations from R.B. Peake's 19th-century theatrical treatment *Presumption, or Fate of Frankenstein* with a heavy dose of Freud into his 14–plus-minute adaptation.

It was an established practice to print a complete story synopsis of each picture offered in the *Kinetogram* for the convenience of the film exchange buyers and to attract the attention of the movie theater operators who leased from them. A film exchange was very similar to a large video store of today, where a licensed theater member could rent three titles for $50 a day, which would be shown from eight o'clock in the morning till 12 midnight. A first-run feature was more expensive than an "older" film. Often competing theater owners would bid against each other for the more popular titles. Hundreds of movies were released each month by the various production companies with a Nickelodeon rotating programs two or three times a week, saving the weekend venue as the main attraction.

The Edison production was carefully described:

> Frankenstein, a young student, is seen bidding his sweetheart and father good-bye, as he is leaving home to enter a college in order to study the sciences. Shortly after his arrival at college he becomes absorbed in the mysteries of life and death to the extent of forgetting practically everything else. His great ambition is create a human being, and finally one night his dream is realized. He is convinced that he has found a way to create the most perfect human being that the world has ever seen. We see

his experiment commence and the development of it. To Frankenstein's horror, instead of creating a marvel of physical beauty and grace, there is unfolded before his eyes and before the audience an awful, ghastly, abhorrent Monster. As he realizes what he has done Frankenstein rushes from the room, only to have the misshapen Monster peer at him through the curtains of his bed. He falls fainting to the floor, where he is found by his servant, who revives him.

After a few weeks illness he returns home, a broken, weary man, but under the loving care of father and sweetheart he regains his health and strength and begins to take a less morbid view of life. His marriage is soon to take place. But one evening, while sitting in his library, he chances to glance in the mirror before him and sees the reflection of the Monster which has just opened the door of his room. All the terror of the past comes over him and, fearing lest his sweetheart should learn the truth, he bids the Monster conceal himself behind the curtain while he hurriedly induces his sweetheart, who then comes in, to stay only a moment. Then follows a strong, dramatic scene. The Monster, who is following his creator with the devotion of a dog, is insanely jealous of anyone else. He snatches from Frankenstein's coat the rose which his sweetheart has given him, and in the struggle throws Frankenstein to the floor. Here the Monster looks up and for the first time confronts his own reflection in the mirror. Appalled and horrified at his own image he flees in terror from the room. Not being able, however, to live apart from his creator, he again comes to the house on the wedding night and, searching for the cause of his jealousy, goes into the bride's room. Frankenstein coming into the main room hears a shriek of terror, which is followed a moment after by his bride rushing in and falling in a faint at his feet. The Monster then enters and after overpowering Frankenstein's feeble efforts by a slight exercise of his gigantic strength leaves the house.

The Monster, broken down by his unsuccessful attempts to be with his creator, enters the room, stands before a large mirror and holds out his arms entreatingly. Gradually the real Monster fades away, leaving only the image in the mirror. A moment later Frankenstein himself enters. As he stands directly before the mirror we are amazed to see the image of the Monster reflected instead of Frankenstein's own. Gradually, however, under the effect of love and his better nature, the Monster image fades and Frankenstein sees himself in his young manhood in the mirror. His bride joins him, and the film ends with their embrace, Frankenstein's mind now being relieved of the awful horror and which it has been laboring under for so long.

The creation of the Monster in the movie is far different from the book and the later film versions' assemblages of various corpse parts to be sparked into life by a bolt of lightning. It seems that Mr. Edison had no interest in promoting the fact that electricity could be the instrument in creating a monster. Dawley had to abandon science and rely more on Alchemy for his story. Dr. Frankenstein mixes a bunch of chemicals and powders together, throwing them into a caldron of steaming embryonic-type fluid, producing great billowing puffs of smoke.

It's assumed that the Monster's actor, Charles Ogle, created his own make-up. Courtesy MOMA

Charles Ogle portrait courtesy Frederick C. Wiebel

Then the Monster is created with "...some of the most remarkable photographic effects that have been attempted. The formation of the hideous Monster from the blazing chemicals of a huge caldron in Frankenstein's laboratory is probably the most weird, mystifying and fascinating scene ever shown on a film." Edison's properties department built a pápier maché dummy of the Monster, set fire to it, and filmed until it was reduced to a pile of ashes. When printed for the movie release, the frames were run backward causing the smoke and ash to swirl and reassemble into the creature. The sequence was tinted a fiery red and orange, giving a thrilling creation of the unsightly being. One sees a blackened skeleton assemble from out of thin air and bits of charred flesh creep across its blazing bones. Flames shoot out of the seared skull's eyes as the glowing Monster comes to life and starts to wave to the audience even before it is finished forming.

Cinematically speaking, the film is very straightforward. Dawley used no camera movement, close-ups, or weird angles to enhance the look of his filmed play but did apply subconscious, almost surreal story telling techniques. After its formation, the Monster seeks out its creator and emerges from Frankenstein's womb-like black bed curtains beckoning with its arms for a fatherly embrace. Of course this just causes Frankenstein to faint. Another clever Freudian device was the way in which Dawley uses a mirror to reflect and introduce the actors. The full-length looking glass takes up about one-third of the screen in the library scenes where a lot of the action takes place. We see Frankenstein sitting in a chair when he hears a knock at the door. In the mirror, the door opens and Elizabeth,

Frankenstein and the Monster fight over the unconscious Elizabeth (Mary Fuller). Courtesy Alois Dettlaff, Sr.

his bride-to-be, enters, while Frankenstein leans over the back of his chair and speaks to her "off-camera." When she leaves the room to make tea and Frankenstein's eyes follow her, we see the Monster open the door in the mirror to come in and meet its creator. This adds an unworldly element to the film that causes one to wonder if the Monster is real or just a figment of Dr. Frankenstein's dementia.

At the end of the feature, the Monster confronts its own mirrored image and disappears to remain in the mirror as Frankenstein observes its reflection instead of his own. But the power of love and positive thinking drives away the inner Monster of the id, leaving the doctor a good solid citizen. Dawley's principle of "There's only one story. Does the boy get the girl or doesn't he?" stands tall on virtuous territory with a novel 'happy ending' that never appears in the book.

For all of the moral tone expressed in the catalog publicity and the dampening down of the repulsiveness of the story, the Edison Studios certainly didn't apply any of that sentiment to the hideous creature staring out at us from the *Kinetogram* cover or the film itself.

It's assumed that the Monster's actor, Charles Ogle, created his own makeup, which was the custom of the day. It became the basis, minus the unruly mass of hair, for all of the Frankenstein movie Monsters to come. The triangular square-topped head, the high, sloping, scarred forehead and protruding Neolithic brow, the snarling mouth with twisting lips, and the blackened, sunken eyes all became standard enduring facial qualities for the decades and hundreds of movie treatments to come. Ogle also manufactured gloves with long, spidery fingers sprouting from bulging, veined hands with rotting bones popping out of the wrists. The Edison Monster more closely resembles Mary Shelley's description than most other treatments and looks more born of the charnel house than from a vat of steaming chemicals.

The Monster confronts his creator. Courtesy Alois Dettlaff, Sr.

Little is known about Charles Stanton Ogle. Edison publicity described him as "A giant in stature, Mr. Ogle attracts instant attention whenever he appears on the screen and from that moment never fails to hold it, and has a power that is not easily forgotten." However, he is barely remembered today. Born after the end of the Civil War on June 5, 1865, Ogle was raised with the purpose of following his father's footsteps in the ministry. But the acting bug had bitten him hard and he ran away with the circus and eventually pursued a career in the footlights of the New York stage. He became an Edison film stock company player in 1909, initially being paid five dollars a day, while making hundreds of their movies for over five years.

Ogle made his major impact working for Paramount Pictures in the 1920s, performing with such stars as Lon Chaney, Rudolph Valentino, Mary Pickford, Fatty Arbuckle, and Gloria Swanson in numerous Westerns, society farces, costume dramas, and anything else that was offered to him. He was a good solid character actor but rarely got leading roles and never again performed in a "horror" film. Ogle finished out his life in retirement, dying completely forgotten, as so many silent stars did, at the then ripe old age of 75 in Long Beach, California, on October 11, 1940. Today, Charles Ogle's sole claim to fame is that he was the first actor to portray the Frankenstein Monster on the screen.

Augustus Phillips played the lead role of Frankenstein and, though he performed in many pictures, very little is known about his personal life or career.

Mary Fuller was chosen to be the love interest and was the first real star attraction of the movies. Though she made over 300 short films, Ms. Fuller failed to adapt to multi-reel pictures and she quickly faded into obscurity by 1920. She later suffered a complete mental breakdown, spent the last 25 years of her life in an insane asylum, and is buried in an unmarked grave in Congressional Cemetery in Washington, D.C.

The production schedule for Edison's *Frankenstein* started January 17, 1910 and it was filmed over the next few days. It was released March 18, 1910 for a weekend premiere. This rush in production from filming to screening was typical of all Edison movies.

The photoplay initially got good reviews but was considered to be too weird and frightening by the general public. *Moving Picture World*, the leading trade publication of the time, said "... no film has ever been released that can surpass it in power to fascinate an audience. The scene in the laboratory in which the Monster seemed gradually to assume human semblance is probably the most remarkable ever committed to a film" (March 19, 1910).

"The formation of the Monster in the cauldron [sic] is a piece of photographic work which will rank with the best of its kind. The entire film is one that will create a new impression that the possibilities

By the release of the 1931 *Frankenstein*, Edison's version of *Frankenstein* had been almost forgotten.

of the motion picture in reproducing these stories are scarcely realized" (April 2, 1910).

Instead of creating a new film genre, the audience rejection literally stopped the horror film dead in its tracks. Some have reported that *Frankenstein* was banned outright in many communities and Edison was eventually forced to withdraw it from circulation.

The Edison Studios usually printed an average of 40 copies of each of their films, unless public demand was greater, or less. After their initial six-month run, the prints were returned to the laboratories and strip salvaged for their silver content. Fires in 1914 at the Bronx studio and at the Orange, New Jersey manufacturing plant destroyed most of the film prints and negatives held in storage.

By the time of the release of Universal's 1931 *Frankenstein* feature, the Edison film had been completely forgotten by the movie going public, and was to remain that way for over 50 years. However, when one views the film today there can be no doubt that the British director of Universal's production, James Whale, was directly influenced by it. The Edison film seems to have made more of a lasting impact in merry old England where audiences were accustomed to weird tales of horror and relished gory stories of the macabre.

When Universal Pictures had Jack Pierce first develop the Frankenstein Monster makeup for Bela Lugosi's rejected screen tests for their production of *Frankenstein*, Pierce obviously based it on Ogle's hairy portrait. Some have suggested that it was Lugosi himself who revived Ogle's Monster with his own designs. Pierce got his start in the movie business as a projectionist in 1910, possibly even screened Edison's *Frankenstein*, and eventually became the head of Universal's makeup department in 1926. Many have suggested that this initial Frankenstein Monster makeup was similar to previously filmed versions of *The Golem* (1920), but further renditions do not bear this out.

Director James Whale also had a hand in the makeup design, sketching the newly selected Karloff, whose features he found interesting and easily adaptable for the Monster. Whale once commented, "Boris Karloff's face has always fascinated me, and I made drawings of his head, and added sharp, bony ridges where I imagined the skin might have been joined." All this talk might have been good for the publicity department to run through the mills but one only has to look at Charles Ogle's interpretation of the Monster to see where the ideas really stemmed from. Surviving Universal test makeup photos show an Ogle-like, horizontally scarred, broad, flat forehead and heavily low-browed, triangular boxed cranium. They eventually moved the joining seam above the shortened hairline with tiny metal clamps. Some of the later publicity stills of Karloff show him in almost the same snarling pose as the one of Ogle that appears on *The Kinetogram* cover.

It's fun to speculate how Charles Ogle must have felt sitting in the audience, watching Universal's *Frankenstein* in 1931.

Some of the actions, scenes, characters, costumes, and sets from Edison's *Frankenstein* were retained or adapted by James Whale for Universal and incorporated in some of the sequels, as well. One suspects that Whale must have had a copy of the original film to consult. It's known that he studied and derived inspiration from other previously made horror movies such as *The Cabinet of Dr. Caligari* (1919), *The Golem* (1920), *Metropolis* (1926), and *The Magician* (1926).

It's fun to speculate how Charles Ogle must have felt sitting in the audience, watching Universal's *Frankenstein* two decades after he first brought the Monster to the screen. Thomas Edison never got to see the famous remake of his movie, for he died October 18, 1931, less than two months before the film was released.

One of the biggest differences between the two film versions is that Universal's *Frankenstein* was a monstrous success, being one of the top money grossers of 1932, whereas Edison's was doomed to obscurity. The Frankenstein Monster has come a long way to being accepted with open arms by the general public from the days when moviegoers rejected it, like Dr. Frankenstein did, when they couldn't face the disturbing scenes flickering from the Nickelodeons of 1910.

All memory of Edison's picture vanished like the unstable nitrate film stock used to capture it, turning to dust and scattering to the winds of time. In the early 1960s an amateur

The American Film Institute has declared Edison's *Frankenstein* as one of the top 10 culturally historical "lost" films.

film sleuth came across the *Kinetogram* cover photo of *Frankenstein* stored amongst the 4,000,000 documents preserved in the archives of the Edison National Historic Site in West Orange, New Jersey. The photo of the unnamed Ogle shortly began appearing in the pages of *Famous Monsters* and other popular magazines. By 1980, The American Film Institute declared Edison's *Frankenstein* one of the top 10 culturally historical "lost" films. Little did anyone realize that by an act of fate, the film miraculously survived, lying dormant in the Wisconsin basement of an eccentric film collector named Alois Dettlaff, Sr. who acquired it in the 1950s for a few dollars.

Generated interest in the film came to a head with the bicentennial of Mary Shelley's birth, August 30, 1797. For Halloween 1997 at least eight nationally broadcast television documentaries, many Associated Press wire services articles, several major exhibitions at libraries and museums, book releases, and even The United States Postal Service have promoted the Frankenstein Monster with many focusing on Charles Ogle's interpretation. Now with renewed interest in silent films and a marketability of Edison's *Frankenstein*, it is easily available to interested fans.

Once again, like the endlessly recycled Monsters that through the decades continually stomped across the screen, Edison's *Frankenstein* refuses to die. Charles Ogle was the first and is now the latest cinematic version of Mary Shelley's immortal creature to be released, or should we say, to escape. You just can't keep a good Monster down.

Frankenstein Becomes a "Universal" Legend

Mary Shelley owes more to Universal Pictures than Universal owes to Mary Shelley.

Simply stated, Universal borrowed a few themes and concepts from Mary Shelley's novel and recreated the novel in its own image, based in part upon the current *Frankenstein* stage productions of the day. But everyone's hand was in the soup, even original director Robert Florey who contributed to the screenplay before he was removed from the 1931 production and replaced by the eccentric James Whale. Whale was attracted by the novel's theme of isolation and rejection and the concept that society and its ways were sometimes evil, that we should pity those individuals that society chooses to reject. Universal cast Dr. Frankenstein in the guise of noble (yet slightly insane) artist, a rule-breaker who delights in challenging the dictates of society and of God, an egocentric genius who puts himself first before the needs of society.

Boris Karloff, using the inspiration of both makeup artist Jack P. Pierce and director Whale, crafted a performance that became uniquely his own, a vision very distant from Shelley's concept of the Monster, but a performance that still reigns supreme in the annals of Hollywood. Other performers played Frankenstein's Monster before Karloff, and many, many more recreated the role after him, but Karloff's performance has become the icon to which all the others are compared. And to be honest, no one has ever equaled, let alone surpassed, Karloff's performance.

The left-of-center James Whale fills his films with eccentric supporting casts that somehow became perfect in the quirky Whale universe: Dwight Frye as Fritz the Hunchback, later Karl; Colin Clive as the driven Henry Frankenstein; Ernest Thesiger as the devilish Dr. Pretorius; Una O'Connor as Minnie the Maid; E.E. Clive as the Burgomaster, etc.

After the pivotal classics *Frankenstein* (1931) and *Bride of Frankenstein* (1935), the only entries directed by James Whale, the Universal series became more formula driven as the series maintained and eventually went downhill, relegated to child-oriented B features in the 1940s. The emphasis in this section is upon the three major Universal entries, the third *Son of Frankenstein* (1939), directed by Rowland V. Lee becoming the final hurrah in a classic film series.

Gary J. Svehla sees the Universal *Frankenstein* series as representative of a dysfunctional family and he illustrates the symbolic nature of the Monster, showing why it became Everyman to the motion picture viewing audience. Svehla is editor and publisher of *Midnight Marquee* magazine, which he began at the age of 13, inspired by *Famous Monsters of Filmland*. Midnight Marquee is now in its 41st year and is published bi-annually. He has written extensively on classic horror films and hope to begin work on a film noir history after he retires from teaching high school English.

John E. Parnum, in his chapter, focuses on the relationship of the child to the Monster in the Frankenstein series, another way of viewing the mythos as family oriented. While Parnum focuses on the Universal series, he does stretch, mentioning how more recent films such as *Young Frankenstein* fit into the mold. Parnum was the former editor of *Cinemacabre*, one of the premier magazines on horror film published, and he maintained a huge horror film memorabilia collection, focused primarily around the Frankenstein Monster, at his home in Wayne, Pennsylvania. Sadly, John passed away in 2004 but we are happy his words and love of horror fils will live on at Midnight Marquee Press, Inc.

Art director Charles Hall and Electrical Effects designer Kenneth Strickfaden created the Universal *Frankenstein* sets, above the famed lab, which was later used by Mel Brooks for his loving Frankenstein tribute *Young Frankenstein*.

Anthony Ambrogio's chapter "*Frankenstein*—Or, 'My Heart Belongs to Daddy'" continues with the dysfunctional family theme whereby he focuses on the Universal Pictures Frankenstein entries. Anthony is a contributor to *Video Watchdog* and *Midnight Marquee*. His novel *Nuns Blood* was published in 1996. He lives in Detroit with his mystery writer wife Anca Vlasopolos and daughter Olivia.

Dysfunctional Family: The Universal Frankenstein Legacy

by Gary J. Svehla

Bela Lugosi might be the most revered horror personality of the century and his interpretation of Count Dracula from Universal's 1931 classic *Dracula* might be the king of the classic monsters, but I believe that Boris Karloff's interpretation of the Frankenstein Monster is the more important Universal monster icon.

And the reasons are not as apparent as one might think.

With his gaunt, skeletal appearance, his dead, sad eyes, his elongated arms, his stiff walk, and his terrifying groans, Boris Karloff's mime enactment of this ever-familiar fiend is the stuff of which classic movie performances are made. 1931's minimalist performance in *Frankenstein*—deadly serious and deathlike—led to 1935's more fully fleshed out, partially vocal interpretation of the dead man who walks again, uncomprehendingly, in *Bride of Frankenstein*. And while 1939's *Son of Frankenstein* featured Karloff's Frankenstein Monster more as a sideline advancing Basil Rathbone's interpretation of Dr. Frankenstein to star status and Bela Lugosi's supporting performance as crazed blacksmith Ygor to prominence, Karloff's Monster was still symbolically the star of the show.

But after so many years of in-depth, detailed film criticism, so many years of analyzing James Whale's and Rowland V. Lee's directing style and shining a light on so many star performances, what is left to discuss? For me, an analysis of how Boris Karloff transformed a potential one-trick-pony performance into a motion picture franchise, and why the Frankenstein Monster, as created by Karloff, became the most symbolically mythic and mesmeric of all the Universal monsters has never been successfully explained. Perhaps this chapter might shed a little more light on these two areas.

First of all, it must be noted that Universal's Frankenstein series became, artistically, the most significant horror film franchise because screenwriters such as Garrett Fort, Francis E. Faragoh, Robert Florey, John Balderston, and William Hurlbut did not idolize the Mary Shelley novel and instead only incorporated themes from the novel into the screenplay. The concept of the monster created from dead body parts reanimated with lightning, his body housing a defective, criminal brain, was solely the province of Universal. No beautiful-looking Adam here. Instead Boris Karloff created a unique sympathetic monster that has haunted the silver screen for over 60 years. And it is in those instances where the movies deviate from the source novel that the artistry of Universal (classic stories, inspired photography and direction, outstanding and unique performances, Gothic set design) comes to the forefront.

While Mary Shelley's novel deals primarily with the theme of abandonment (as do the Universal films), Universal wisely further develops this theme to depict one of cinema's first dysfunctional families, and the audience's ability to relate to such disharmony becomes the cornerstone upon which the Monster's personality is based.

For the time being, we will deal with the first two entries—*Frankenstein* and *Bride of Frankenstein*—both produced by Carl Laemmle's original Universal and directed by the

Boris Karloff as the Frankenstein Monster, used the inspiration of both makeup and a finely crafted performance to create the ultimate Monster, who to tis day still reigns supreme.

gifted James Whale. After these two movies, everything Universal presented in the Frankenstein mythos was a variation on a theme created here.

These original two Frankenstein movies bombard the audience with depictions of father/son relationships that have gone awry. We have the elder Baron Frankenstein concerned, as the wedding grows closer, that his son Henry (Colin Clive) is so obsessed with "another

We as an audience relate to Frankenstein's Monster (Karloff with Colin Clive and Dwight Frye) when he suffers torment at the hands of bullies and others who take unfair advantage.

woman" that he fears Henry's dalliance will destroy his relationship with fiancée Elizabeth. The Baron simply cannot accept the concept that it is Henry's scientific work that threatens the relationship, not another female.

We also have the father/son relationship between Henry and his devoted assistant Fritz (Dwight Frye), who is excited by the very same things that excite Henry, so he can be accepted by his protective mentor. The hunchback jumps into the grave as Henry is digging up the coffin at *Frankenstein*'s beginning and enthusiastically chimes, "Here it comes," as they lift the box upward. Later, when Henry tells Fritz to climb up the gallows pole to cut loose the corpse, the hunchback, afraid and horrified, shouts "no," but with more prodding agrees. It seems Fritz will do anything necessary to please the master/father figure.

Furthermore, we have the father/son relationship existing between Henry and his old professor from Goldstadt Medical College, Dr. Waldman (Edward Van Sloan), who taught at the college Henry abruptly left when his eccentric experiments involving fresh corpses led to suspicion. With gleeful intensity Henry tells his teacher "you were wrong" and excitedly tells Waldman how and why. A parallel relationship exists in *Bride of Frankenstein* when Dr. Pretorius (Henry's old professor from college) becomes the mentor and Victor the son/student.

Even the Burgomaster in *Bride* becomes father to the village's playful and fearful citizens. To reinforce this position, he all-knowingly utters: "You should thank your lucky stars they sent for me to safeguard life and property!"

And even Henry's adversary relationship with God is father/son based, with Henry daring to supersede the power of the creator by daring to steal the Father's secrets and use them to satisfy his own morbid curiosity.

And from these deteriorating father/son relationships come three-way triangles that threaten to destroy the titular or actual family.

For instance, in the original 1931 production, we see just how much the elder Baron is a creature of tradition. Before the wedding he lifts the glass cover of an ornamental tray that houses orange blossoms, which have been worn by Frankenstein grooms for three generations. Speaking to Henry, "Thirty years ago I placed this on your mother's head... in 30 years a youngster of yours will carry on this tradition."

While another woman does not threaten this relationship between Elizabeth and Henry, the obsessive nature of Henry's work does. His work figuratively becomes the "other woman" in the relationship. In *Bride of Frankenstein*, newlywed bride Elizabeth becomes immediately fearful and jealous of Dr. Pretorius, thinking Pretorius will once again ignite those ungodly passions which led to Henry's near death. So symbolically, Pretorius becomes "the other woman" to threaten Elizabeth's relationship with her husband.

While Fritz becomes the dutiful servant/assistant to Henry, Henry's increasing attention to his creation makes Fritz jealous; Fritz' abusive nature toward the Monster (tormenting him with whips and fire) may very well be a reflection of such jealousy.

All this leads up to the dysfunctional relationship existing between Henry and the Monster—first the all-attentive/obsessive Henry becomes bored with and neglectful of his "son," Henry's neglect allowing Fritz to torment the Monster and then Waldman to try to dissect it. Thus, the Monster feels unwanted, isolated, freakish, and desperately wants a friend of its own.

While the Frankenstein Monster might briefly haunt or terrify us, as it did audiences in the 1930s, the audience is much more likely to relate to the Monster's symbolic function as a rejected, isolated, unloved, innocent victim. And here is where the Monster becomes most mythic and ingrained in our psychological consciousness. This is where the Monster becomes the most important of all Universal monster icons.

I have come up with a list of eight reasons why we as an audience feel empathetic and even sympathetic toward Karloff's Monster, and by detailing roughly 20 sequences from the first two Universal Frankenstein movies, the Monster's ability to touch a universal nerve in its audience becomes clearly illuminated.

We as an audience relate to Frankenstein's Monster when it appears he suffers:
1. Frustration from learning (learning becomes an agent of the Monster's fear and rejection)
2. Loneliness caused by the feeling of being one of a kind
3. Torment at the hands of bullies and others who take unfair advantage
4. Alienation by being forced into a world he does not desire
5. Rejection reaching out to be part of the societal whole
6. the Awkwardness of being a stranger in an unknown body
7. abrupt Separation and Rejection at the hands of his "family"
8. Jealousy at being an inferior/defective copy of more perfect human beings

Simply stated, the universality of the Frankenstein Monster originates from the simple fact that he is like us at various moments in our lives: disconnected, alienated, frustrated, lonely, rejected, hated, awkward, jealous. Unfortunately, for the Monster, he is doomed to forever exist in this disparate, uncaring, negative abyss.

First, to illustrate Frustration from Learning, we have the initial appearance of the Monster from *Frankenstein* as he slowly backs through the door, turns around, and then we see a closeup of the Monster's face—dead half-closed eyes and stiff movements as it catatonically obeys commands. Sitting in a chair, the skylight opened, the Monster rises and

The sequence that best drives home the point of the loneliness of the Monster is from *Bride of Frankenstein* **when the Monster roams the foggy graveyard.**

looks upward, rising its bare arms skyward to grasp for the warming light. When the light source is turned off, the Monster thrusts its arms out pleadingly toward Henry.

"And now for our lesson," the blind Hermit intones from *Bride of Frankenstein*. In this very humorous yet warm sequence, the Monster learns the fundamentals of speech, what bread is, how wine is "good," how to shake the hand of a friend, why wood is good for the fire, and that even fire can be good (having already learned fear of fire at the end of a burning torch and at the hands of the villagers in *Frankenstein*). The Hermit states, "There is good and there is bad." However, the lesson abruptly ends when the Monster is taught fear and rejection when two lost, intruding woodsmen (one of them John Carradine) abruptly invade the Hermit's cabin, see the Monster, are startled, and in the ensuing shuffle burn the cabin down. The Monster learns that there is good and bad, but unfortunately for him, bad always seems to be the end result of all his lessons.

Second, to represent Loneliness Caused by the Feeling of Being One of a Kind, we are reminded of the conclusion of *Frankenstein* when the Monster, trapped in the burning windmill, screams and wails like a cornered animal, never understanding fully why its actions resulted in so much scorn. As the Monster panics, trying to evade the flames and crumbling beams of wood, he ultimately becomes pinned under a falling timber, moaning in pain. Here we see a creation, who never asked to be born, cruelly hunted down and savagely slaughtered in such a way that if he were an animal, the mistreatment would surely be protested by today's animal rights groups.

Similarly, at the beginning of *Bride of Frankenstein*, with Maria's parents searching the burned out mill for evidence of the Monster's bones, Hans falls through the weakened flooring to the flooded area below. There the Monster stirs, having survived the flaming inferno,

In *Bride of Frankenstein* Karl (Dwight Frye) torments the Monster, but the Monster quickly grabs him and throws the screaming man from the tower.

and he savagely attacks and drowns Hans. Hans' wife, thinking she is extending her hand to her husband, instead gives a leg-up to the Monster. As she screams, he throws her, like a ragdoll, to her death. Interestingly, the Monster's extended arm and hand are mistaken by Hans' wife as the beloved arm of her husband, and only when she sees the full form of the Monster does she panic and scream. In other words, the Monster is almost human enough to be mistaken for the real thing, but once recognized, he is seen as the Grendel in a society of Beowulfs and is made the outcast simply because of his size and ugly countenance.

Symbolically, the sequence that best drives home the point of the loneliness of the Monster is the wonderfully symbolic sequence from *Bride of Frankenstein* when the Monster roams the foggy graveyard, stumbing past various statues and gravemarkers, savagely knocking over one such marker leading to the crypt below. There he eyes the coffin of his bride-to-be. Such a sequence illustrates the Monster's recognition of himself as a creature separate from living human beings; he sees himself as a creature of the night, of the graveyard, of the dead. Sadly, all his peers, like himself, are dead, but they are motionless and uncommunicative. He, also dead, lives and has the ability to express his loneliness as a solitary member of his kind.

Third, to portray his Torment at the Hands of Bullies and Others who take Unfair Advantage from *Frankenstein*, we have the jealous and twisted assistant Fritz, who tortures the Monster with his snapping whip and cruel-tempered flaming torch. The Monster, when confronted with such torture, yelps and moans, tries to escape and hide, and even Henry orders Fritz "to leave it alone," but the sadistic assistant only continues his torment until the Monster ultimately slays his tormentor.

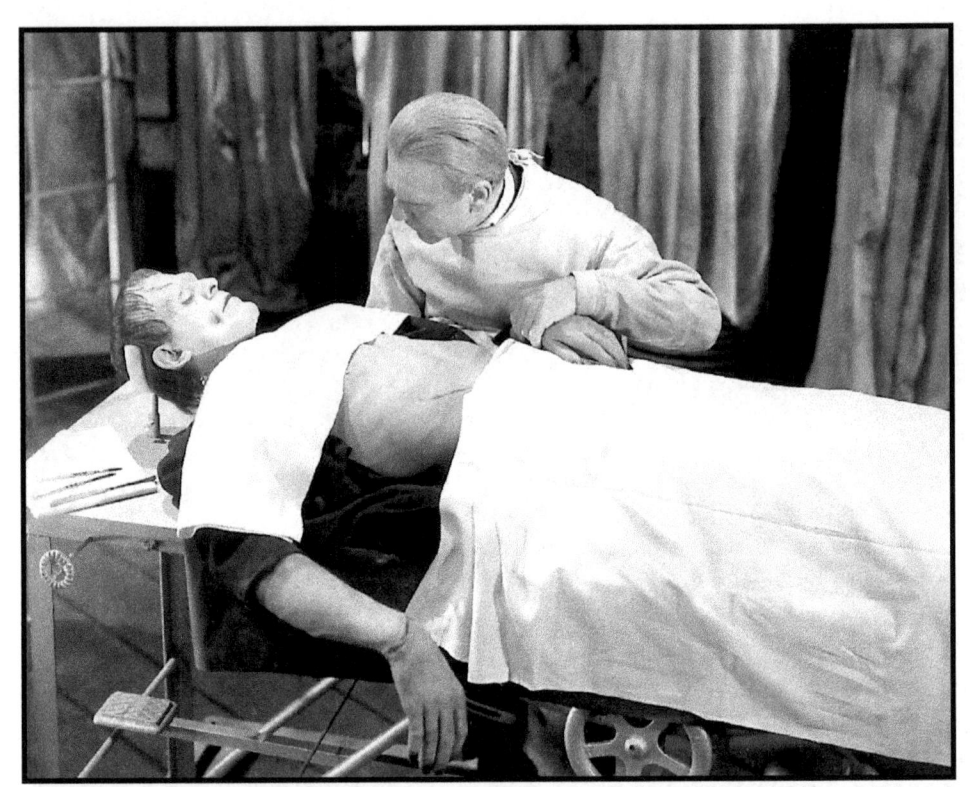

In *Frankenstein*, when the Monster lies awaiting dissection at the hands of Dr. Waldman (Edward Van Sloan), Karloff has been robbed of all his humanity.

In an obvious copy of this sequence, *Bride of Frankenstein* features a quick, unmotivated parallel sequence again with the Monster and Dwight Frye (now as Karl) atop the watchtower. Outside as the storm rages, Karl torments the Monster with his fiery torch, but the Monster quickly grabs him and throws him screaming off the side of the tower.

Finally, in *Bride of Frankenstein*, the Monster is chased by the village mob (formed by the fatherly Burgomaster) through the woods, up rocky hills, where he tries to hide from the hunting dogs in hot pursuit. Soon he is captured by the mob, who pelt him with thrown objects, tie him to a long log in a obvious Christ crucifixion stance, and thrust him into a hay-lined horse drawn cart, a pitchfork holding his head motionless. Returning to town, he is cruelly carried downward to an underground dungeon where he is chained to a huge wooden chair that reduces his motion to twitches and blinks.

Fourth, to observe the Monster's Alienation Being Forced into a World It Does Not Desire, we only have to look again at the initial Monster sequence from *Frankenstein*, Karloff enters the room backwards, soon to be exposed to the bright rays of light; he moves so tentatively that the performance draws strength from the simple fact that we are observing a terrified creature who does not feel part of the environment into which he has been thrown. His gaunt features, emphasizing his elongated arms, dead eyes, and stiff motion, make the audience terribly aware that this creature does not belong in our world and does not wish to be here.

Later, when the Monster lies supine on the surgical table, awaiting dissection at the hands of eminent Dr. Waldman, Karloff has been robbed of all his humanity, now he is simply a specimen awaiting to be disassembled, appendage by appendage, organ by organ, at the hands of science. Truly, the Monster has been reduced to the level of a failed experiment, the evidence of which is about to be erased without emotion or concern. However, when Waldman leans closer to the extended corpse, the Monster's arm slowly rises behind the unknowing doctor, the hand first grabbing the neck and soon the throat. This experiment refuses to be simply erased!

The Monster's Alienation can also be seen in the conclusion of *Frankenstein*, in the old windmill, as Henry tries to flee from the Monster, but the Monster pursues its creator, struggling to subdue his symbolic "father" who no longer has any need for his "son." The Monster, in rage from hatred and anger because he was forced into a world in which he does not belong—a world where even his creator rejects him. The Monster tosses Henry off the side of the windmill, almost certainly to his death. The Monster's face, after he thinks he has "killed" Henry, is panicked and fearful—his face is like that of a child who did something horribly wrong and instantly regrets the action. It is this face the villagers see as they set the windmill ablaze.

Finally, *Bride of Frankenstein'a* underground crypt sequence—beginning with the Monster roaming the fog-shrouded graveyard, passing assorted markers—best illustrates the Monster's alienation. Stumbling across Dr. Pretorius' picnic—candles, a skull, food, and wine on a tablecloth covered casket—Pretorius bids the Monster welcome, offering the fiend some wine (in fact Pretorius is the first person to treat the Monster as a human being, with politeness and kindness). "You make man like me?" the Monster asks, but Pretorius answers matter-of-factly, "No, woman... friend for you!" The Monster smiles "I want friend, like me... made me—from dead. I love dead, hate living." To which Pretorius responds, "You're wise in your generation." Sadly, the Monster is now able to verbalize his alienation and realizes that he is one of a kind, an aberration of nature. And his only desire is to have a mate similar to himself. Everyone in the audience can relate to such a simple urge.

Fifth, Rejection Reaching Out to be Part of the Societal Whole can be witnessed in the Little Maria sequence in *Frankenstein* when Maria herself is at first rejected by her own father. "Won't you stay and play with me, Father?" "I'm too busy," the soon-to-depart father replies. Emerging from the bushes as soon as her father leaves, Maria introduces herself to the Monster, without an ounce of fear, requesting, "Will you play with me?" Moving to the water's edge, Maria tells the Monster: "You have those [flowers], I'll have these... I can make a boat, see how mine float." The Monster, enthralled, giggles and smiles. It is only when he innocently picks up Maria and throws her into the water, to see how she will float, and she sinks and drowns, that the Monster panics and runs away.

In a similar idyllic sequence in *Bride of Frankenstein*, the Monster is roaming a beautiful woods when he comes upon a stream, bends down and drinks. When he sees his own reflection, he uses his hand to cause ripples in the water to break up the image. A beautiful young shepherdess approaches with her sheep, sees the Monster from a bluff overlooking the stream, screams, and falls in. The Monster sympathetically pulls her out, saving her life, but as she revives, she screams "don't touch me" alerting nearby hunters who fire and hit the Monster in the arm. Simply because the Monster is different—bigger and uglier—he is immediately rejected. It seems only Dr. Pretorius is willing to give the Monster the time of day.

Sixth, to display the Awkwardness of Being a Stranger in an Awkward Body, we turn to the Hermit sequence in *Bride of Frankenstein*. Smiling when hearing sweet violin music, the Monster at first watches and then bursts in on the Blind Hermit, who warmly greets the Monster. Sensing the Monster is hurt, he immediately sits him down near the warm fire. The Hermit sees the Monster as a gift from God: both are afflicted (one cannot speak, the other cannot see) and are in need of a friend. The Monster's awkward frustrations over trying to grunt out verbal communication, trying to eat from a bowl, struggling to do the simple little tasks that most human beings can perform effortlessly, only shows how the Monster is uncomfortable with its own body.

The initial sequences in *Frankenstein*, showing the Monster's slow, stiff movement, the rigidity of using his hands and arms, his hunched-over stance when trying to learn to walk, all equally illustrate the fact that this adult body houses the consciousness of a newborn where every motion and sound emitted displays the awkwardness of being a stranger in a new body.

Seventh, the Abrupt Separation and Rejection at the Hands of his Family can first be traced in the conclusion of *Frankenstein* when the search party led by Henry, now working with society against his own creation, scours the hills to track down the Monster. As Henry becomes separated from his own search party, who call out his name, the Monster silently watches Henry come closer. Torch in hand, monster-maker confronts Monster and they, all alone, briefly stare each other down. Quickly the Monster grabs the hated torch and a struggle ensues. The Monster knocks his symbolic father unconscious and drags him off toward the windmill.

In *Bride of Frankenstein* the Monster encounters society's tribe of rejects, the Gypsies, who symbolically are as much out of the loop as the Monster. When he tries to raid their campfire in search of some food, he burns his hands, screams out in pain, and is then run off by them. Symbolically, during those times he is surrounded by other rejects, instead of forming a bond together, he is still rejected and becomes an outcast to the outcasts.

Finding a friend in Dr. Pretorius, the Monster is quick to do his bidding, displaying loyalty to the sole person who seemingly accepts him. In a pivotal sequence when Pretorius is trying to persuade Victor to continue his experiments, of which Victor wants no part, Pretorius brings in the Monster who orders Victor to "sit down" and tells his creator "you must do it." When Henry tells Pretorius he won't discuss the situation while the Monster is present, Pretorius sends the Monster to kidnap Elizabeth to add leverage to his position.

Later in the laboratory, after Victor agrees to continue his experiments on the promise that Elizabeth is safe and will be returned unharmed when the experiment is finished, the Monster becomes a stern taskmaster, ordering Victor to work nonstop, to never take a break. Only when Pretorius drugs the Monster's drink does Henry get any peace of mind, let alone rest.

Eighth, the Monster's Jealousy at being an Inferior/Defective Copy of More Perfect Human Beings can be witnessed in *Frankenstein* in the sequence where Victor locks Elizabeth in the bedroom on their wedding day, for her own protection. Upon first hearing the grunts of the Monster, Elizabeth nervously stalks her bedroom as the audience sees the Monster approach via the back bedroom window. Unknown to Elizabeth, the Monster enters the bedroom and silently stares at her from behind, the audience on the verge of yelling "Turn around you damn fool!" In a highly symbolic shot, the unconscious Elizabeth falls, quite suggestively, sprawled in her bridal gown over the edge of her bed. The Monster leaves and she moans "Don't let it come in here" when she is finally rescued. In other words, Victor has created a flawed pseudo-human being, and the fact that the Monster attacks Victor's bride-to-be on their wedding date suggests that Victor has someone of his own kind to share his life with, but the Monster can only be reminded that he is one of a kind.

Perhaps the Monster's jealousy can best be illustrated at the conclusion of *Bride of Frankenstein* when the Monster first meets his intended bride. Unfortunately, the Bride is blatantly attracted to Henry, and clutches and huddles at his side, in obvious fear of the

Monster. When the Monster appears, he is smiling with friendly outstretched hands, muttering "friend," in an almost pleading manner. But she screams and hugs Henry. The Monster growls, more in frustration than as a threat, takes the Bride's hand, and gently pats it. But for the second time she screams bloody murder. "She hates me," the Monster declares, "like others." Now realizing that he will always be the rejected one, even by others made just like he was, he clutches that all too obvious lever that will blow them all to atoms. Realizing the importance of love, he allows Henry and Elizabeth to escape— "You go," but to Pretorius he glumly states, "We belong dead!" and as the Bride hisses, the Monster pulls the lever, blowing up the watchtower.

Son of Frankenstein **relegated Boris Karloff's Frankenstein Monster (pictured with Basil Rathbone) to bench-warming status.**

Four years later, under new management, the "new" Universal inaugurated the second wave of American horror cinema with *Son of Frankenstein*, a movie that increased the budget for this third Frankenstein production; boosted the star power by adding Basil Rathbone (as son Wolf von Frankenstein), Bela Lugosi (as crippled blacksmith Ygor), and Lionel Atwill (as artificial-armed Inspector Krogh); but relegated Boris Karloff's Frankenstein Monster to bench-warming status (with the exception of a few stellar sequences). The inspired director James Whale is gone, replaced by Rowland V. Lee who rewrote the script daily, the final story bearing little resemblance to Willis C. Cooper's screenplay.

All the criticisms of the 1940s Frankenstein films' Monsters (portrayed by Lon Chaney, Bela Lugosi, and Glenn Strange), concerning the Monster's character-less automaton function, originated in this production. True, unlike the later productions whereby the comatose creature is reactivated to die only minutes later, Karloff does spend the second half of the film in an animated state, but significant appearances are few and far between.

Reduced to a sideshow attraction in his own movie, Karloff's Monster is formulaic and less artistically rendered making the New Universal production appear more like product in a successful franchise. The father/son relationship (and even the triangle) continues with Wolf being cast as the son of Henry, but Wolf is described by Ygor as being the "brother" to the Monster, apparently referring to the fact that both are sons of Frankenstein. Ygor becomes the third wheel in the relationship between Monster and monster-reviver (Wolf) because Ygor wants to control the Monster and is jealous of the power that Wolf has over his reanimated creation. In another sense, the ever-protective Inspector Krogh becomes the father figure to Wolf, ensuring that the irate villagers do not commit acts of violence against the survivor to the house of Frankenstein that they hate so much. So much for symbolic subtlety.

The Monster's early sequences are artistic dead weight, with the hulking fiend's inanimate state of consciousness presenting the feared Monster as a comatose lump. The first significant sequence with the Monster occurs in the lab where the Monster first places its hand on Wolf's shoulder and then rubs its maker's face. The Monster registers a confused expression, but when he examines his own features in the large laboratory mirror and looks at the handsome Wolf, the audience can readily see that once again the Monster is noticing its own deficiencies. The Monster is repulsed by his features, he growls and holds his pleading outstretched arms toward Wolf. This revisits the theme of the Monster's Loneliness caused by the Feeling of Being One of a Kind.

But even the Monster's murder sequences, as he is used by Ygor to kill two of the jurors who sentenced him to hang, are pedestrian at best. In the first sequence the Monster is seen slowly moving among the misty rocks lying beyond the road. The Monster's body extends onto the roadway hanging on to a tree as his victim rides by. The fiend grabs the victim by the neck and places his unconscious body under the wheels of his own cart, crushing the poor man's legs and chest. In the second murder sequence, the Monster, seen as a black silhouette, approaches his seated victim from behind and suddenly bangs the man on the head, apparently killing him instantly.

The next significant sequence featuring the Monster occurs after Wolf has shot Ygor (who tried to attack the doctor with a hammer) to death. Alone in the lab, the Monster quietly approaches the fallen Ygor, slowly climbing the laboratory steps to find his friend. The Monster falls to his knees and huddles over the body of Ygor, prodding the corpse with his hands. The Monster sobs and moans as he realizes the fate of the blacksmith. Seeing blood on his one hand, the Monster screams out in pain, his heart broken, and he glumly carries the body back to Ygor's bedroom and deposits the corpse on the bed. With a sad face and watery eyes, the Monster screams one more time and storms out in anger. (Shades of the Abrupt Separation and Rejection at the Hands of his Family.) Returning to the lab, the fiend has a temper tantrum and throws expensive equipment into the sulfur pit below. Suddenly finding a book of fairy tales (belonging to Wolf's son Peter), the Monster smiles as his mind hatches a new plan.

In the Monster's final important sequence, he sneaks via back passageways into sleeping Peter's bedroom, his sudden appearance causing the housekeeper to faint. In a tender visual sequence, the huge Monster leads the innocent Peter by the hand up toward the laboratory, revenge the obvious reason for the kidnapping. (Here the theme of feeling Jealousy for Being an Inferior/Defective Copy of more Perfect Human Beings can be witnessed.) However, the Monster is so kind, gentle, and nurturing, that the one sequence where the Monster momentarily considers throwing the baby into the sulfur pit instead of lifting him up the ladder is the only lingering indication that the Monster intends to do harm to the child. The child, once up the ladder, extends his own hand to help the Monster up. Even after Inspector Krogh enters the lab with his men, guns blazing, his artificial arm ripped off by the Monster, the creature gently holds the child wedged underneath his one foot as Wolf swings down from above, knocking the Monster into the sulfur pit to his scalding death.

Karloff, unhappy that the Monster spoke in *Bride of Frankenstein*, demanded that the Monster be returned to his former mute status, but where the Monster came to vivid, stark life in the original 1931 production, here, in *Son*, Karloff is mostly reduced to lumbering loafer status. A few sequences remind us of the greatness of his former performances, but generally, because of insensitive direction and lack of a well formulated script, Karloff becomes the very one-dimensional Monster he feared the role had degenerated into during the production of *Bride of Frankenstein*.

Boris Karloff's Frankenstein Monster has touched a common nerve with seven generations of movie fans because he represents so many things to so many people. Simply put, he becomes Everyone. His relationship to his creator represents the poor, pathetic victim in a typically dysfunctional family. His isolation, loneliness, and lack of love ring true with all of us at one time or another. His awkwardness, the sense that the Monster is a stranger to his own body, appeals to the lifelong adolescent in all of us, for all of us have felt self-conscious of our own body at various points in our life. All of us, because we all have crosses to bear, have felt anger, frustration, and rage, psychologically if not physically, and have wanted to mindlessly strike out simply to express our too-long suppressed feelings. And Frankenstein's Monster represents that defective, flawed human being residing in all of us. Who hasn't felt abandoned, mistreated, unloved, abused, ugly, lonely at some point in our lives? And the Monster reminds us that even he can be sympathetic, misunderstood, and finally worthy of receiving love. No other Universal Monster quite represents such appeal, and it is this immediate human connection that makes Karloff's Frankenstein Monster a mirror image of how so many of us really perceive ourselves.

When Hollywood was selling the concept that any member of the audience could be John Wayne, Clark Gable, or Cary Grant, the audience always realized the truth: most of us felt more closely assigned with Frankenstein's Monster. There's a symbol for the human condition that stands the test of time!

Universal Home Video Legacy Collection
Frankenstein: The Legacy Collection
by Gary J. Svehla

Frankenstein: 4.0; *Bride of Frankenstein*: 4.0;
Son of Frankenstein: 3.5; *Ghost of Frankenstein*: 3.0; *House of Frankenstein*: 3.0

For fans of classic horror movies, the three new box sets of Universal's classic monster movies are to die for. First, yes, all of these movies have been formerly available on DVD, but I wanted to make the case that Universal monster collectors would do well by purchasing the new box set. Although this book is dedicated to Frankenstein, we'll cheat a little and discuss the entire Legacy Collection, because if you're reading this book, we know you love all the monsters, not just Frankenstein's Monster.

First of all, let's discuss the packaging. True, we do not get individual poster art of each movie, but the title depictions of Frankenstein's Monster, The Wolf Man and Dracula are superb graphic designs. Each gatefold box easily slides out of the slipcase which features a transparent panel on the front that allows the dominant monster in the set to be seen, but the transparent panel has a spooky background setting into which the face of the monster is perfectly framed. Inside the slipcase is a one page glossy insert, one side advertising all three box sets, the other detailing (short description with cast and credits) all four or five films contained in each box set. Then we have the expensive looking gatefold DVD case, the front containing the cover monster painting and title, the back containing sepia photos with a detailed description of what is found on disc 1 (always one sided) and what is found on disc 2 (front side and back side). Then when we open the gatefold, we are hit with a panoramic two page sepia photo spread from the movie (a key scene such as the laboratory creation sequence from Frankenstein, the underground crypt sequence with Bela Lugosi as Dracula near his coffin and Claude Rains confronting his son Larry Talbot) housing the two DVDs included in the package. A defining quote from the movie runs along the bottom edge of the inside gatefold. The packaging is extremely impressive and has that expensive "we care" look.

Okay, okay, you agree that the packaging is impressive, but why splurge if we already own the movies? Fine, here's more to consider. Each box set, containing four or five movies (The Wolf Man Box only contains four films), sells for $25 street price at Best Buy (on sale for $20). That rounds out to be $4-$5 per film. But all the extras from previous releases are included, and a marvelous new documentary appears in each box (and each documentary is different for each box set).

First let's examine the *Frankenstein: The Legacy Collection* box set. We get audio commentary on *Frankenstein* and *Bride of Frankenstein*, trailers, *Boo!* a short film, poster and photo archives for *Frankenstein* and *Bride of Frankenstein* and two documentaries. But what is new is the remastered soundtracks on some of the movies which eliminate most of the hiss, pops, crackles and feature a less end-high tinny soundtrack (such remastering is advertised on all three box sets). I have not yet had the time to compare sound between older and newer versions of these movies, but the sound has a heavy bottom and sounds very clean. Unfortunately, the censored grunts and groans of the dying Bela Lugosi from *Dracula*, restored to laserdisc, are once again missing from the soundtrack here. Also a negative splice near the end of the credits for *Frankenstein Meets the Wolf Man*, resulting in an audible, annoying pop, still has not been repaired digitally. But what is new are documentaries hosted by writer/director Stephen Sommers whose new film *Van Helsing* rethinks the original Universal monsters for a new generation. Each documentary in each box focuses on Frankenstein's Monster, The Wolf Man or Dracula. The documentary has on-screen interviews with not only Sommers but members of the cast of *Van Helsing* as well (Kate Beckinsale, Hugh Jackman, etc.) and features impressive montages from all the Universal classics plus footage from *Van Helsing*. As Sommers enthusiastically makes clear, his wish in making *Van Helsing* was to demonstrate that he loved these classic Universal movies.

Dracula: The Legacy Collection box set offers the option of hearing the original minimal *Dracula* musical score or easily switching to the recently-composed Philip Glass score performed by the Kronos Quartet. We also have the *Dracula* Stephen Sommers documentary. Lupita Tovar introduces the Spanish version of *Dracula*, and we have the documentary, *The Road to Dracula*. David J. Skal provides auditory commentary to the original *Dracula*. And we have a poster and still gallery.

Finally, *The Wolf Man: The Legacy Collection* box set offers the third and final new Stephen Sommers documentary, this time focusing on lycanthropy. A documentary, *Monster by Moonlight*, appears. Author Tom Weaver provides auditory commentary for *The Wolf Man*.

So, besides getting each movie for at most $5.00, Universal has included all the older extras of insightful and carefully executed documentaries, audio commentaries, poster and still galleries, remastered soundtracks and new documentaries featuring a tie-in to *Van Helsing*. And each collection is housed in attractively designed gatefold boxes that fit inside slipcases.

Still not convinced?????

Here's two more reasons to purchase. The print and soundtrack to *House of Dracula*, first time on DVD, is outstanding. The print barely features a mark and the contrast creates true blacks and subtle shades of gray. Most fans consider *House of Dracula* to be perhaps the worst of the monster rally B productions and feel it is inferior to *House of Frankenstein*. What *House of Frankenstein* has is Boris Karloff, but his performance is totally lethargic with J. Carrol Naish stealing the show. John Carradine is good, as is Chaney, Jr., with teenaged Elena Verdugo submitting a fresh performance. But the movie is segmented into parts—the traveling circus, Count Dracula, the Wolf Man and returning Frankenstein's Monster to full potency. For me the film is poorly paced and disappoints. However, *House of Dracula*, directed by Erle C. Kenton, is darker and more shadowy. The plot is fully integrated as one story and Onslow Stevens does a better mad scientist than Karloff did in *House of Frankenstein* (playing a sympathetic Jekyll-Hyde performance). John Carradine is just as effective a Count Dracula here, as is Lon Chaney, Jr. as Larry Talbot/The Wolf Man. For me *House of Dracula* is the black sheep of the Universal horror factory and its restoration with perfect picture and sound allows fresh evaluations. Don't get me wrong, *House of Dracula* is a B programmer so it does suffer from the same flaws as Universal's other B productions, but I just happen to consider it vastly superior to the generally over-praised *House of Frankenstein*.

Also, the bane of the originally released Universal horror film DVDs has been the subpar print of *Bride of Frankenstein*. Many writers have already pointed out that the laserdisc release was superior in many ways to the well-worn and soft (with less than perfect contrast) DVD release, and most people consider *Bride of Frankenstein* to be the hallmark release of the monster legacy series. However, unannounced, the DVD print of *Bride of Frankenstein* has been quietly upgraded and the result is amazing. Just put in the old DVD release and compare it to this new Legacy box set release. Yes, if one were to quibble, of course one could find flaws in the original source material, and *Bride of Frankenstein* does cry out for the type of restoration accorded *Vertigo* and *Singin' in the Rain*. But the upgraded print provided by Universal is vastly superior to the older DVD print and *Bride of Frankenstein* can once again be seen for the eccentric classic it most certainly is.

Finally, if sales warrant (here's the third and final reason to buy these box sets), Universal intends to perhaps provide Legacy box sets to the Mummy movies, the Creature movies and perhaps other Universal titles that never appeared on DVD. Isn't it about time for *The Black Cat, The Raven* and *The Invisible Ray* to hit DVD!!!! If sales dictate Universal might bring out any number of cherished horror classics (and not just classic releases). So even if you think you have everything included in these three box sets, well, think again. Just like memorable dining experiences that we pay for many times throughout our lifetimes, buying these cherished cinematic classics a second or third time is not insane. I expect to buy them again without complaint, but Universal, please just bring out some new titles as well!

FRANKENSTEIN'S CHILDREN
The Relationship of the Child to the Monster in the Frankenstein Films

by John E. Parnum

When Universal released director James Whale's *Frankenstein* on November 21, 1931, the trade magazine *Motion Picture Herald* carried a review by Leo Meehan, who was obviously greatly disturbed by the film. Meehan described how women left the theater trembling, men exhausted, and how he certainly would let no child of his sit through the movie. Meehan bemoaned, "And I won't forgive Junior Laemmle or James Whale for permitting the Monster to drown a little girl before my very eyes. That job should come out before the picture is released. It is too dreadfully brutal, no matter what the story calls for. It carries gruesomeness and cruelty just a little beyond reason or necessity."

Perhaps Mr. Meehan never read the classic tale by Mary Shelley upon which the film was based, where the Monster's first murder is the deliberate strangulation of Victor Frankenstein's younger brother William. Mary's decision to kill off the young boy may have stemmed from the fear of her own child, William, dying at an early age; she had already lost a first baby who was born prematurely and had died in two weeks. As it turned out, her William died three and a half years later, after the publication of *Frankenstein*. Yet even today, writers relate passionately to the deaths of their children: Stephen King admitted how *Pet Sematary* was the most difficult book he had ever written, since he related it to what he would do if his own children died.

Portrait of William Shelley by Aemilia Curran

The Child as a Victim of the Monster

In Ms. Shelley's Gothic tale of horror, the author piles one injustice after another upon Victor's creation, so that in due time it comes to hate its maker. Upon awakening one day in the countryside, the Monster sees a beautiful child running toward it. It realizes that the boy may be too young to be frightened by its deformity and that it could capture him and educate him to be his friend. (Perhaps Mary remembered Percy Shelley's desire to retire from the world and educate a five-year-old girl, or knew that her father, William Godwin, as a bachelor failed in his attempt to raise a 12-year-old second cousin.) But William is terrified and the Monster seizes him to placate him. Screaming, the boy threatens to tell his father, and the Monster informs him that he will never see his father again. Still, William protests, claiming that his father, M. Frankenstein, will punish him. When the Monster hears the name Frankenstein, his rage is incited: "You belong then to my enemy—to him towards

In 1986, the censored scene of Frankenstein tossing little Maria into the lake was found and restored to videotape and laser disc copies of *Frankenstein.*

whom I have sworn eternal revenge; you will be my first victim." After strangling the boy, the Monster's "heart swelled with exultation and hellish triumph," and he knew that the act would hurt Victor and "carry despair to him, and a thousand other miseries shall torment and destroy him." I wonder what Leo Meehan would have thought had James Whale filmed the scene as Mary Shelley had written it.

The scene as Whale filmed it is one of tenderness and sensitivity. We have left the brooding watchtower where Henry (no longer the Victor of Shelley's novel) Frankenstein (Colin Clive) infused life into his patched-together corpse (Boris Karloff). The setting is one of idyllic beauty, a lake with mountains in the background and little Maria (Marilyn Harris), holding a kitten, watching her father Ludwig (Michael Mark) cut wood by a small cottage. The father tells his daughter he must go check his traps and when he returns he will take her to the village. The child asks him if he won't stay and play with her, but he says he's too busy and she should play with her kitten instead. He kisses her goodbye and they wave to each other. As originally written, scripters Garrett Fort and Francis Edwards Faragoh had Maria asking her mother to stay and play with her. Whoever decided to use the other parent made a wise choice: the Monster had been abandoned back in the watchtower by Henry, who left him to be dissected by his former teacher Dr. Waldman (Edward Van Sloan). Maria has been temporarily abandoned by Ludwig. So the Monster and the little girl have a common connection between them: they have been left alone by their fathers.

The Monster has throttled Waldman and escaped from the watchtower. When it stumbles upon Maria, she is sitting by that picturesque lake, picking daisies and still holding her kitten. At first she is startled by the Creature's appearance, but as it moves toward her she introduces herself and asks if it will play with her. She takes its hand, leads it to the shore, and gives it a flower. The Monster smells the daisy and smiles. It is happy for the first time. She gives it more flowers and tosses some of hers into the water, commenting on how they float like a boat. The Monster joins in her game, but after it has thrown all of its daisies into the lake, it becomes confused. Thinking that the flowers looked so beautiful in the water, it reaches for her. Perhaps she too will look beautiful floating in the lake. As it lifts her roughly in the air, Maria screams, "No! You're hurting me! No!" And it tosses her in. She surfaces once, makes a brief gasp, and then sinks beneath the water as the Monster tries to reach for her. The Monster is confused as it stumbles into the woods. Its demeanor is one of sorrow (it has lost its only friend), guilt, and anger (at itself and perhaps even at little Maria for leaving it). It is a credit to Karloff's acting that he was able to bring off these conflicting emotions so credibly.

For many years the scene of Maria's death were missing from the film, although the scene of her father carrying her body into the village were left intact.

Unfortunately, for a long time, movie audiences and TV watchers never saw Karloff's remorseful reaction scene. Perhaps critic Leo Meehan's review was read by Management at Universal, because soon after the movie's release, the scene was cut. Ironically, the censoring involved only the Monster tossing Maria into the lake and his resulting anguish—the scene ending with the Monster reaching for the little girl. The next time we see her is when her father carries her limp bedraggled body into the village. The censors, in their wisdom, now suggested to the audience an even more sinister implication: the Monster may have sexually attacked Maria. Trailers for *Frankenstein* compounded the problem: "When this dead hand moves, the Monster created by a man they called mad is turned loose to... prey upon the innocence of children," narrated as the Monster and Maria walk toward the lake. Of course, neither the scene as originally filmed nor as later censored would affect today's hardened audiences accustomed to Freddy Krueger's bloody violence toward teens. Now, on the other hand, if the Monster threw Maria's kitten into the water, that would be a surefire way to incur the wrath of the ever-growing animal rights groups.

In 1986, the censored scene was found and restored to videotape and laser disc. As Wesley Holt related in a laser disc review of *Frankenstein* in *Filmfax*, Dave Oakden of Universal proudly announced that the company retrieved an original nitrate negative from its vaults to produce an excellent fine-grain print, which did not include the censored scene. That was found "in a 35mm fine grain dupe print that was in England. Since we had no choice but to use this in this particular scene, it has a higher-contrast look to it than the rest of our restoration...." Now everyone can see the scene that R.H.W. Dillard in his chapter "Even a Man Who Is Pure at Heart: Poetry and Danger in the Horror Film" from *Man and the Movies* (W.R. Robinson, editor) calls "the essence of the film." He points out, "that moaning figure thrashing through the hanging bows of a willow tree... black and ugly, a creature of death and darkness, he is as innocent and wounded as we all are. He is fallen, and the remainder of the film carries him on down that dark descent."

In shooting Maria's drowning, Whale wanted Karloff to throw Maria (Marilyn Harris) overhandedly into the lake. Karloff disagreed, saying it should be done as written.

Ivan Butler in all three editions of his *Horror in the Cinema* concurs with Dillard: "The scene, which could have been so sentimental and embarrassing, is handled with such restraint by Whale and played with such sympathy by Karloff, that no falsity mars it. Karloff's final departure, wringing his hands in agony of dawning comprehension, is as moving a moment as any on the screen." So much for critic Leo Meehan. Ivan Butler does make one totally uncalled-for observation. He claims that "Whale had the subtlety to choose an ugly little girl (with, alas, an even uglier accent), which added pathos to the episode." The script describes Maria as a "pretty little child of about seven," not an ugly one which Marilyn Harris certainly was not. Perhaps "plain" would be a more appropriate word, and that's the character Harris is playing, a woodcutter's child in simple clothes. "Ugliness" describes some of the actual events that took place during the filming of the sequence.

James Whale possessed a rather sadistic streak. Feeling that Karloff, an ex–truck driver, was far beneath him, he made the actor endure many unnecessary takes, carrying Colin Clive over his shoulder up the hill to the climactic windmill scene. In shooting Maria's drowning, he wanted Karloff to throw her overhandedly into the lake. Karloff disagreed, saying that was a violent act, and it should be done the way the script was written: "Kneeling, he places the little girl on the surface of the water—an expectant smile on his face again as though he were expecting her to float." But Whale was used to getting his way. As described in Gregory W. Mank's Production Background in the *Universal Filmscript Series: Frankenstein* (Philip J. Riley, editor), "The company sided with Karloff.... 'This was the nearest the Monster came to having a soul.' But James Whale... responded, 'The death has to take place.' 'He fumbled for words as he tried to convey why to us,' said Karloff, 'because in a strange way we were all very hostile about it. He couldn't just bully us into acceptance. Then he said, 'You see, it's all part of the ritual.' " Apparently a compromise was reached since in the film Karloff throws the child into the water with an underhanded toss.

If Whale's demands seem cruel, they in no way match those of Marilyn's sadistic and selfish mother, one of the most heartless stage mothers of all time. Greg Mank, who interviewed Marilyn, relates in the *Filmscript Series* how after Maria is thrown into the lake, Marilyn's mother shouted from the shore, "Throw her in again. Farther!" Although Marilyn had hurt her back, Whale promised her anything if she would do another take. Since Marilyn's mother kept her on a strict diet, the little girl begged Whale for a dozen hard-boiled eggs. Karloff tossed her in again, and Whale, out of the goodness of his heart, gave her two dozen. Marilyn told Mank that her mother was furious "that I hadn't asked for something like a bicycle." Other horror tales of child abuse abound in Mank's Production Notes.

In a production shot from *Young Frankenstein*, Peter Boyle as the Monster and Anne Beesley prepare for the "What-shall-we-throw-into-the-water-now?" scene.

On the lighter side, the 1974 Mel Brooks parody *Young Frankenstein* pokes fun at the first three Universal Frankenstein films. Naturally, one of the scenes spoofed is the little girl, now named Helga, and her flowers. Helga sits by a well, dropping daisies down the abyss, and singing in an irritating voice "Oh, I love my pretty little flowers." We wonder how Brooks will handle the obviously ominous sequence as the Monster (Peter Boyle with zippers instead of bolts in the neck) approaches the child. Helga, played bratishly by Anne Beesley and looking much like Patty McCormack in *The Bad Seed*, has the upper hand from the start. When Helga says, "Oh dear, nothing left. What shall we throw in now?" the Monster looks directly at the audience and leers knowingly. In the meantime, Helga's parents argue about their daughter's whereabouts after having carefully tucked her into bed, concerned the Monster is on the loose. But the games have thankfully shifted to the seesaw. Helga, sitting on the lower side of the seesaw, orders the Monster to "Sit down!"—a takeoff on Colin Clive's instruction to the Monster in the original *Frankenstein*. Of course, when he does, he catapults Helga through the upstairs window into her bed. The parents look in on their daughter and smile at each other in relief. It's all silly fluff, but still holds up well these days.

The Monster (Boris Karloff), pleading for acceptance, is rejected again by some terrified schoolchildren in *Bride of Frankenstein*.

The child encounter in *Bride of Frankenstein* is of a much more sinister nature. Even though we do not see Freida's murder, there is none of the innocence that was implied in *Frankenstein*. The Monster (Karloff, again), having been hunted, tormented, and imprisoned, has broken out of his dungeon and is terrorizing the countryside. William Hurlbut's screenplay, adapted from his and John Balderston's story, describes several brief examples of the mayhem the Monster has wrought. The first has a group of women scurrying into the safety of a cottage. One of the women looks around wildly for her daughter: "Where is Freida?" The scene shifts to the entrance of the village church. A group of children in their first communion dresses are exiting. The mother runs to them and repeats, "Where is Freida?" A child with flowers in her hand replies, "She just left... Oh, look!" Script: "They all rush forward to a patch of white behind one of the tombstones where the body of poor Freida lies. We do not see the child but the expression of frozen horror on the faces of the mother and the children... tells only too plainly that the Monster has passed that way." The concluding shot of the mother carrying the bloody body of her daughter, with dangling head, and the frightened children weeping hysterically was cut from the final print, although a still photo exists to verify its actual shooting.

We will never know the details of how Freida died. It does not seem likely that the Monster murdered her in cold blood, given its previous encounter with little Maria in *Frankenstein*. Perhaps as it was charging down the road, Freida stepped in front of it and the resulting collision hurled the child into the air, dashing her to the ground. Perhaps it even felt remorse over the accident; a second child killed because of its ineptitude could cause even greater guilt. We know that it still possesses sensitivity; it earlier rescued a shepherdess from drowning, only to be rewarded by being shot at. And later it enjoys a short respite from its tormentors when it is befriended by the blind hermit (O. P. Heggie). Maybe it was Karl (Dwight Frye) who killed Freida. In a subplot that was cut from the release print, Karl (Dr. Pretorius's grave-robbing assistant) murders his miserly Uncle and Auntie Glutz for their hoarded savings, certain that the crime would be blamed on the Monster. Might little Freida have witnessed the deed, with Karl then forced to kill her?

A later encounter with children in *Bride of Frankenstein* seems also to vindicate the Monster. When the Monster is forced to flee the hermit's burning hut, it staggers

The Monster's relationship with Frankenstein's son Peter is the most complex of the series in Universal's *Son of Frankenstein*.

into the woods calling for its friend. A group of schoolchildren are walking down a path as the Monster emerges from the bushes. It waves its hands gently in a friendly gesture that implies a pleading for understanding. The children, of course, flee in terror. This brief cry for sympathy might negate any horrendous deed implied earlier in the script.

Karloff's last foray as the Frankenstein Monster was in the 1939 *Son of Frankenstein* and his relationship with his creator's grandson, Peter, is the most complex of the three films. Henry has died, passing on his estate, his belongings, and his secrets of life and death to his son Baron Wolf von Frankenstein (Basil Rathbone), who moves into the castle one rainy night with his wife and son Peter, much to the consternation of the villagers who fear he will follow in his father's footsteps. They're right, of course, and as the advertisements proclaimed: "After 20 Years! The mania of the monster-maker... passing from father to son... unleashed a new juggernaut of destruction upon the world!" Yes, Karloff's Monster is revived, but before we can explore its relationship with Wolf's son Peter (Donnie Dunagan), we must first look at an incident that occurred several decades before.

Inspector Krogh (played with distinction by Lionel Atwill in immaculate uniform and wooden arm) arrives at Wolf's surrealistically designed estate to offer protection to the family from the unfriendly villagers. When Wolf defends his father's reputation and asks the inspector if he knows of even one criminal act his father's creation committed, or if he ever even saw him, the inspector replies: "The most vivid recollection of my life. I was but a child at the time, about the age of your own son, Herr Baron. The Monster had escaped and was ravaging the countryside—killing, maiming, terrorizing. One night he burst into our house. My father took a gun and fired at him. The savage brute sent him crashing to a

Inspector Krogh (Lionel Atwill) asks Peter Frankenstein (Donnie Dunagan) about the giant who pays him nightly visits in *Son of Frankenstein*.

corner. Then grabbed me by the arm. One doesn't easily forget, Herr Baron, an arm torn out by the roots!" He slaps the wooded arm to his side and tells Wolf that his ambition was to have been a soldier: "But for this, I, who command seven gendarmes in a little mountain village, might have been a general!"

Now, in addition to eliciting sympathy for Krogh and providing some shocking black humor for the climax of the film, this self-pitying speech also serves to instill an aura of fear in the audience as to the unrelenting destructiveness of the Monster. But *Son* was written by a different screenwriter, Willis Cooper, who may or may not have been familiar with the character of the Monster in the previous films. On top of that, director Rowland V. Lee threw out much of what Cooper had written and made up segments as filming took place. Further defense of the Monster's deed comes when you realize that Krogh's father had just shot at him. Maybe the young Krogh was retaliating against the Monster and it grabbed him in self defense. A little boy is a fragile thing and a Monster sometimes doesn't realize its own brute strength. At any rate, when the Monster establishes a relationship with Peter Frankenstein, it is a gentle one until the climax, when intent turns nasty, but is redeemed by the kindness of a child's innocence.

Wolf is first made aware that his son has encountered the Monster during the aforementioned visit by Krogh. Earlier, while exploring the ruins of his father's laboratory he meets the broken-necked blacksmith Ygor (Bela Lugosi), who leads him to the comatose Monster. In hoping to redeem his father, Wolf, assisted by his butler Benson (Edgar Norton), tries unsuccessfully to restore strength to the Monster. So Wolf is doubly shocked during Krogh's visit when his son Peter announces that a giant has paid him a visit during the night. "A giant come in here and woke me up," the child stammers. His nursemaid Amelia (Emma Dunn) laughs: "A giant? What an imagination!" Peter corrects her: "No, Amelia, it wasn't

In the climax of *Son of Frankenstein*, the Monster (Boris Karloff) rips off the wooden arm of Inspector Krogh and pins Peter Frankenstein to the floor.

my imagination. A giant come here—and woke me up. And I got up, he had ahold of my arm." Inspector Krogh touches his own wooden arm with fearful recollection.

When Wolf asks Peter if he chased him away with his gun, the boy smiles. "Oh, no. He's a nice giant. I gave him my picture book and then he went away. Are there many giants around here?" Krogh looks sternly at Wolf: "Only one that I ever heard of." "That must be him then," the boy says innocently.

Wolf takes his son to his room and asks him about the "elephants and tigers" he had been hunting. And then about the giant. Peter admits that he just made up the elephants and tigers, but that the giant was real. And when Wolf asks his son what the giant looked like, the boy stretches out his arms and does the Monster strut. "He's a great big man with a hairy coat on, and he walks like this." Wolf realizes with mixed emotions that his father's creation walks again. He rushes to the laboratory and indeed sees that his efforts to restore the Monster have been successful.

It is important to understand that Peter is a Frankenstein: He is inquisitive like his father and grandfather. He wants to know what the ugly stuffed animal trophy on the wall is and is told it's a boar. "Like Aunt Fanny," the kid quips in the film's lame attempt at humor. He is brave for a child of four or five; he likes to hunt "elephants and tigers." And when Amelia and his mother Elsa (Josephine Hutchinson) prepare him for bed one stormy night, Amelia offers to close the curtains to shield him from the lightning; Peter protests: "Oh, please don't, 'cause I like the lightning." Elsa tells Amelia, "His father's taught him never to be afraid; and he isn't!" So it is this innocent bravado that perhaps attracts the Monster to the little boy. Like little Maria, the child does not fear it. And like little Maria, the boy has been good to it: Maria offering it flowers and companionship; Peter giving it his book of fairy tales.

The young (Maria and Peter) and the disabled (the blind hermit) have been the creature's only friends. But will the tragic accident by the lake be repeated in this new relationship? The Monster has lost everyone it has ever loved: Maria, the hermit, and its one hope for a fulfilling happy future—the bride whom Henry created for it and who spurned it.

But we must not forget evil Ygor, who has also befriended the Monster. This is a different kind of relationship, one more like a dog to its master. "He does things for me," the blacksmith tells Wolf. And indeed it does, like killing off the jurors who once sentenced Ygor to be hanged. And at Ygor's command, it murders Benson so there will be one less person who knows the Monster lives. But in serving Ygor, it has become more like a robot, a senseless thing devoid of the emotions it displayed in the first two films, causing Karloff to quit the role after this film; there was nothing more he could give to the character.

After more villagers are murdered by the Monster, Inspector Krogh returns to the Frankenstein castle to protect the family from mob violence. He visits Peter in his room. "Has the giant paid you any more visits?" he asks, and the boy replies, "Yes." "He's a great big fellow, I imagine. So big he can hardly get through that door?" Peter tells Krogh that he doesn't come through the door and the inspector asks how he gets in. "Oh, through the wall.... Over there." Krogh is puzzled and asks the boy, "You're not afraid of him at all, are you Peter?" The lad replies, "Oh, no. He's a nice giant. He gave me a watch. Would you like to see it?" The watch belongs to Benson, who has been missing for several days. Later, when Peter is out of the room, Krogh returns and discovers a sliding pillar leading to a secret passage, where the policeman discovers Benson's body.

In the meantime, Wolf has shot Ygor in self defense. When the Monster discovers the blacksmith's body, it is furious, displaying for one of the few times in the film an emotional anguish instead of brute senselessness. In a rage, it destroys the lab equipment and comes upon Peter's book of fairy tales. With a cruel snarl it rips the book in half and storms off through the myriad of passageways to Peter's room. It awakens the boy and takes his hand, leading him back through the secret passage. The walkway leads to an active sulfur pit, but at the end there is a ladder up the side of the pit that rises to Frankenstein's laboratory. When the Monster and Peter arrive at the edge of the pit, the creature picks the boy up and raises him above his head as if to throw him in the pit. But then he does a curious thing: he places Peter on the rung of the ladder and the boy climbs to the top where he emerges in the lab. Did the Monster feel that its revenge against Wolf would be more devastating if it threw Peter into the boiling sulfur from the top of the pit? Or was the whole act a "cheat" by director Lee to instill horror and suspense in the audience?

When Peter climbs out at the top, he extends his hand to help his friend. "Here we are," he exclaims innocently. The Monster, startled by the boy's courteousness, has a change of heart, if indeed its mission was to destroy Peter, who then leads it across the cluttered floor. At this moment Krogh and Wolf arrive. Krogh fires at the Monster, who rips off the Inspector's wooden arm and waves it wildly in the air. Seeing that his son is pinned under the Monster's foot, Wolf swings across the lab on a chain and knocks the creature into the boiling sulfur. He then picks up his son and together they kneel at the edge of the pit, watching the boy's friend baked alive... a traumatizing event that would, under ordinary circumstances, ensure Peter many years of therapy with a shrink. And perhaps that is the reason why Peter von Frankenstein never appeared in future Universal *Frankenstein* films to carry on "the mania of the monster making."

In the original script that Lee threw out, the relationship between Wolf's son and the Monster is hardly one of compassion. Angry that Wolf has failed to make him a "friend," the Monster kidnaps the boy and prepares to remove his brain. Through a ruse, Wolf distracts the creature and then stabs it. An army of soldiers finish off the job by machine-gunning the Monster, who falls into a watery pit. The Inspector then drops a hand grenade into the pit, blowing the Monster to pieces. As filmed by Lee, *Son of Frankenstein* keeps the horrific thrills without damaging the child/Monster relationship, a quality that enhanced James Whale's original.

Director Lee was impressed with actor Donnie Dunagan and cast him in two additional films. Audiences and critics were not so charitable. Though the kid had a cute head of curly blond hair, his whining is quite irritating, and because of his inexperience, he muffs many of his lines. In *Universal Horrors* by Tom Weaver and John and Michael Brunas, it's noted that the San Antonio actor's "charms undoubtedly outweighed his talents. As Peter, Donnie is amateurish and camera-conscious." Blackie Seymour, in his Pentagram Review of *Son* in *Classic Images*, Number 213, refers to Donnie as "not exactly a heart-stealer." The most blistering criticism of the boy comes from Bryan Senn in *MonsterScene*, Number 4: "What cannot be excused, however, is the obnoxious performance of little Donnie Dunagan as Wolf's son Peter. His screeching 'Well Hello' and constant baby talk are grating and intrusive. Director Lee should have toned down this little hellion and saved us all some auditory aggravation." In Lee's *Tower of London*, released later that year, Karloff, as the club-footed executioner Mord, does get the opportunity to murder Dunagan, who portrays Baby Prince Richard—an act that *Son of Frankenstein* audiences might not have objected to at all.

Peter gives the Monster is given a book of fairy tales in *Son of Frankenstein*.

Thus, in the first three Universal *Frankenstein* films, the Monster established a somewhat sympathetic friendship toward children, in which fate turned the relationship at times to tragedy—certainly a more pleasant situation than in the classic 1818 tale. Interestingly enough, when Kenneth Branagh filmed his version, *Mary Shelley's Frankenstein*, in 1994, the Monster's encounter with Victor's little brother William is strangely sterile. We get brief glimpses of little William (Charles Wyn-Davie) picnicking on a mountain with Victor (Branagh) and his fiancée Elizabeth (Helena Bonham Carter) as they harness lightning from a sudden summer storm, or of William happily riding on the shoulders of his father (Ian Holm) while Victor is away at medical school. He is a beautiful child, about as close to Mary Shelley's concept of William as has been portrayed on the screen.

The Creature (Robert De Niro), having undergone the usual torments bestowed upon monsters, takes refuge near a cottage where a young family ekes out a modest living as farmers. The mother and father (Joana Roth and Mark Hadfield) have two small children, Maggie (Sasha Hanau) and Thomas (Joseph England), whom they school at home when they are not tilling their crops. A blind grandfather (Richard Briers) lives with them. The Creature secretly learns from the children's lessons, and it returns the favor by surreptitiously doing heavy chores. Since their mysterious benefactor is unknown to them, the grandfather tells Maggie that it is the Spirit of the Forest. Later, while the parents are out, an unsympathetic landlord (Alfred Bell) arrives and grabs Maggie by the face. When the grandfather comes to her aid, this nasty man assaults him also. Maggie flees into the forest, not realizing the Creature has come to her grandfather's rescue. The Creature then chats amicably with the old man as Maggie returns with her parents, who wrongly assume the Creature was the one terrorizing the family. The father then beats the Creature mercilessly until it is forced to flee. Little Maggie, first intrigued by the idea of the Spirit of the Forest giving them gifts, has inadvertently caused it pain and rejection, simply because she innocently forgot to mention that it was the landlord who had attacked them.

The Creature, filled with rejection and hate, vows revenge on its creator, and sets out for the Frankenstein estate in Geneva (it has learned about his beginnings from Victor's diary, left in an overcoat he stole). Elizabeth has also arrived at the home and William (now played by an older Ryan Smith) admires her locket, which contains a picture of Victor. He playfully snatches it and runs off into the woods. The screenplay by Steph Lady and Frank Darabont details William's encounter with the Creature as follows: "William comes into view of the pond. There's a figure sitting half-concealed among the tall reeds, gazing off across the water and playing his delicate wind instrument with oddly pleasing dissonance.... William draws close, curious, not wanting to intrude but listening to the music. The figure in the reeds still hasn't noticed him...." Once again, in innocence of childhood there is no fear, and it is not until the Creature turns, stares at him, and starts toward him that the boy runs away. But the boy's fear of the Creature is because he was caught spying upon it and not due to its repulsiveness. In his flight, William drops the locket, which the Creature retrieves and opens. It gazes upon the face of his creator and intones: "Frankenstein!"

The details of William's murder take place offscreen. We learn that the Creature hides the locket on a friend of the family, Justine (Trevyn McDowell), who is blamed for the crime and later hanged by an angry mob. For the first time in a Frankenstein film, a child's murder is committed in a premeditated act of vengeance. And while De Niro does a remarkable job of generating sympathy for his Creature, it is this cold-blooded murder of an innocent child that might prompt us to excuse Leo Meehan's chastisement of Universal's original *Frankenstein*.

The Monster in the Role of a Child

Why has the Monster gotten along so well with small children? We have seen how innocence and the lack of fear have played integral parts in establishing a compatible relationship. But perhaps, and most important of all, the Monster develops a rapport with the younger set because he himself is newly born. While physically mature, it has the mentality of a child and is treated as such by both its creator and the children it encounters. When Frankenstein introduces his creation to Dr. Waldman in the 1931 film, Karloff's Monster walks through the door backwards, not yet having learned social graces. Frankenstein commands the Monster to "Sit down!" like a stern father to a child. (Four years later in *Bride of Frankenstein*, the Monster is able to return the statement in the encounter with its creator when it demands that Henry make him a mate.) Henry opens the skylight to reveal daylight to the Monster for the first time and it stretches its arms out toward the sunlight like a child reaching for a new toy. When the Monster joins Maria in floating the daisies like toy boats in the lake, it is as innocent and honest as any child making friends for the first time.

The Monster also has the fears that many children possess. Experience has taught it to shun the hostile mob, much like a child will go out of his way to avoid the school bullies. The Monster, tormented by Frankenstein's torch-wielding assistant, fears fire, just as children fear the physical punishment of spanking from a parent. In *Bride of Frankenstein*, the Monster's short idyllic life with the blind hermit is a childhood learning experience, with the hermit teaching it to talk and helping it to overcome its fear of fire. The Monster cajoling the hermit to play a tune on his fiddle is as natural as if it were coaxing a parent to read a bedtime story. And all the while, it bounces its hands like a child of four or five. It gets the opportunity for some light reading in *Son of Frankenstein* when Peter gives it the book of fairy tales. But its childishness does not always mean it is docile. Like a hyperactive child or like one who does not get his way, this kid sometimes turns nasty.

When a double bill reissue of *Bride of Frankenstein* and *Son of Frankenstein* appeared at our repertory theater, my imagination visualized the latter with a baby flat-topped Monster terrorizing the villagers rather than the son of the doctor to which the title referred. Perhaps if I had seen the companion film *Bride of Frankenstein* at a preview before its initial release (though I wasn't even born yet), I would have indeed seen the baby Monster of my imagination. When Dr. Pretorius (Ernest Thesiger) invites Henry to see his own experiments, he opens a sarcophagus and produces six glass bottles containing miniature figures of a queen, king, archbishop, devil, ballerina, and mermaid. In a seventh bottle is a creature that was an in-joke reference to James Whale's original *Frankenstein*, but was cut from the final release print as too silly or too macabre. It was a baby in a high chair, played by young actor Billy Barty made up to resemble an infant Boris Karloff, pulling the petals off a daisy. Pretorius remarks: "I think this baby will grow into something worth watching." Considering Pretorius's explanation of how he grew his experiments from human seed (are we talking about sperm here?), the idea of a baby Monster is indeed repellently intriguing. Only a long-shot of Barty waving from the high chair with the other creatures exists in prints today.

The concept of the Monster as a child has been a popular one in many cinematic versions of the classic tale, from the 1973 four-hour television adaptation *Frankenstein: The True Story*, with Michael Sarrazin as the creature, to the 1977 Swedish/Irish production *Victor Frankenstein* with Per Oscarsson as the Monster. It even exists in the last in the Universal series, *Abbott and Costello Meet Frankenstein*, when the Monster suddenly bumps into Lou Costello and it throws its hands in the air and gives a startled grunt. Dracula has to reassure Glenn Strange's hulking creature: "Don't be afraid; he won't hurt you." Dracula exerts a hypnotic influence over the Monster, reducing the brute to childish obedience. Even Costello refers to the Monster as "Junior."

The most dramatic Monster/child relationship occurs in the third Universal sequel, *The Ghost of Frankenstein* (1942), as Lon Chaney,

Foreign *A&C Meet Frankenstein* poster

Determined to have his brain placed in the head of Cloestine (Janet Ann Gallow), the Monster (Lon Chaney, Jr.) challenges Ludwig (Sir Cedric Hardwicke) and his daughter Elsa (Evelyn Ankers) in *The Ghost of Frankenstein*.

Jr. steps into Karloff's boots and demands a brain transplant using the little girl's brain. With the miraculously restored Ygor freeing the Monster from the hardened sulfur pit, the two make their way to Vasaria where Henry Frankenstein's second son, Ludwig, runs a sanitarium. In the village, the Monster stops to watch a group of children. Little Cloestine (four-year-old Janet Ann Gallow) is playing with a ball on a string. Three boys decide they will torment the child and one of them runs over and kicks the ball high in the air, where the string snarls on a chimney. When the Monster walks toward them, the boys flee in terror. Cloestine walks timidly away from the Monster, an action probably instilled by a parent's warning about never running from a dog or it will chase you. Then she stops and turns bravely to face the Monster. "Hello. Are you a giant?" She examines its huge hands. Recognizing the cruelty Cloestine has just experienced, it reaches down to lift her as the camera shoots up from her perspective and then down from the Monster's—an action that not only exaggerates the difference in size of the players, but serves to unite them in a bonding friendship. Cradled in its arm, Cloestine asks, "Can you get my ball?" and points to the chimney. "Way up there."

By this time, a crowd has gathered. As the Monster carries Cloestine up the steps, a villager intervenes and the Monster knocks him to the street. A second villager aims a rifle but is stopped by Cloestine's father, Herr Hussman (Olaf Hytten), who is afraid he'll hit the little girl. A third villager approaches the Monster on the rooftop, but is sent crashing to the ground. The Monster retrieves the ball and gives it to Cloestine as her father calls up to her: "Cloestine. Ask your friend to bring you down, dear. Tell him no one will hurt him." Cloestine complies with her father's request: "Take me down; my daddy says no one will hurt you." Reluctantly, the Monster hands Cloestine over to Hussman, but as they hasten away, the Monster, who probably didn't realize he was going to be separated from his little friend, starts after them. The police pounce on him to Ygor's ignored protests.

Since the Monster is considered a madman, the Prosecutor Eric Ernst (Ralph Bellamy) requests the presence of Ludwig Frankenstein (Sir Cedric Hardwicke) at the hearing to establish the Monster's insanity. The courtroom is packed with villagers who watch Eric unsuccessfully interrogate the chained Monster. A group of children stand in the doorway watching the proceedings; among them is Cloestine. When Eric's questions get no answers, the Magistrate (Holmes Herbert) says that he's heard that the little Hussman girl has a certain influence on the prisoner. "Perhaps if she talked with him, we might learn his identity." Herr Hussman protests, but the magistrate argues, "He did her no harm and some attempt must be made to establish his identity." Cloestine has walked to the front of the court and takes the Monster's hand as she asks its name and where it lives. The Monster smiles at Cloestine as she asks "Won't you tell us?" Ludwig enters and Eric takes Cloestine away. The Monster smiles at Ludwig, but when Frankenstein rejects it, the Creature snaps its chains and rampages out of the court.

Eventually the Monster ends up at the sanitarium, and Ludwig decides to replace the Monster's criminal brain with Dr. Kettering's (Barton Yarborough), Ludwig's brilliant assistant, who had been killed earlier by the Monster. Old Ygor asks an appalled Ludwig to give the Monster his [Ygor's] brain. The Monster, however, has its own idea for a replacement. One night, it steals into the Hussman house to kidnap Cloestine. In her bedroom,

Chaney played the Frankenstein Monster as an unfeeling brute in *The Ghost of Frankenstein*.

Cloestine smiles at the Monster as it lifts her out of her bed. Pausing at a night table, it also takes Cloestine's ball, the toy that brought them together, but unknowingly knocks over a lamp as it exits the room. The lamp falls to the floor and bursts into flames.

Back at the sanitarium, as Ygor bribes Ludwig's other assistant Dr. Bohmer (Lionel Atwill) to transplant his brain, the Monster arrives with Cloestine. Bohmer is furious with Ygor for letting the Monster kidnap the little girl. Ygor argues with the Monster that an operation on Cloestine would kill the child. "You wouldn't want to hurt your little friend?" He describes what he and Bohmer are planning: "...Ygor has a better idea. You will see. You will have the brain of your friend Ygor. Tonight, my brain will be your brain. Tonight, Ygor will die for you!" The Monster is not impressed. It opens a door to search for Ludwig, and when Ygor tries to hold him back, it crushes the blacksmith between the door and the wall. It seems that now Cloestine is dearer to the Monster than old Ygor.

The Monster carries Cloestine to the living room where Ludwig is being confronted by his daughter Elsa (Evelyn Ankers) about the ethics of brain transplants and his harboring of the Monster that her boyfriend, Eric, has been searching for. The Monster holds Cloestine out to them—like an offering—and places its fingers across the little girl's forehead, then against its own. Elsa is horrified: "He wants the brain of that child!" Elsa is wrong, of course. The Monster, as portrayed by Chaney, is a dumb brute, but certainly has the sense to know that if Cloestine's brain is put into its skull, it will cease to exist. So its demands must be that *its* brain be put into Cloestine's head. It will no longer then be the repulsive thing that has frightened villagers for two generations. It will achieve a pedophilic means to an end in which the union is not sexual, but rather an immature desire to be one with the child who has shown it kindness.

Cloestine pleads to be taken home and Elsa reaches for the child. The Monster is about to strike her when Ludwig intervenes, bravely standing his ground until the creature hands Cloestine over to him. Ludwig gives the child to Elsa and gets them out of the room as he tempts the Monster into his lab with Cloestine's ball. As written by W. Scott Darling, the script added a more meaningful exchange as Ludwig reassures the Monster, "Your little friend will be waiting for you. Do you understand?" The Monster mutters something in a pleading manner. Ludwig then instructs the Monster: "Then do exactly as I tell you. Trust me." The screenplay describes what happens next: "The Monster stares at Frankenstein, apparently understanding the friendly voice more than the words. Then slowly it raises its hand toward Frankenstein, who does not move back, but remains facing the Monster with a radiant smile. It puts its hand on Frankenstein's shoulder, taps it lightly in a gesture of trust. Frankenstein reacts as if he has won a struggle."

In the end, however, the embittered Bohmer does indeed see that Ygor's brain ends up in the Monster, with disastrous results. Ygor's blood type is different from that of the Monster, who goes blind and destroys the laboratory. As fire races through the sanitarium, Eric and Elsa hand over Cloestine to her father, who has arrived leading the requisite mob scene.

Chaney played the part with little sensitivity, certainly less than Karloff in any of his three appearances. It is doubtful that Chaney could have generated sincere sympathy for his relationship with Cloestine, since he played the part as such an unfeeling brute. And that's a shame, since Darling created some very tender moments between the Monster and Cloestine. As written originally, when the Monster enters the little girl's bedroom, it knocks a music box off a table and it plays a tune. Cloestine awakens and smiles at the Monster. "A sob of joy comes over from the Monster... with its head moving from side to side in joy and little sounds of pleasure, it lumbers up to the bedside.... Cloestine, still unafraid of the Monster, smiles as it reaches and almost reverently touches her head, running its fingers through her hair." The little girl holds a one-sided conversation with the Monster: "I thought I was dreaming... You must hide, or run away. They're trying to catch you.... Everyone's afraid of you—but me." Then she hears the bizarre notes from Ygor's pipe. She is alarmed but convinces herself as the Monster picks her up in its arms: "I'm not frightened."

Chaney, with the exception of a slight smile, forgoes any of these interactions with Cloestine. It's too bad, since this is what gives the Monster its humanity and redeems it from the horrible crimes it has committed. Karloff said after *Son of Frankenstein* that he would no longer play the part since the Monster was becoming "a comic prop in the last act." Cynthia Lindsay related Karloff's objections in *Dear Boris* (Alfred A. Knopf, New York, 1975, page 59): "'I could see the writing on the wall,' he said, 'as to what was going to happen to the character of the Monster. There is just so much you can develop in a part of that nature, and it was a case of diminishing returns.'" Karloff was right, of course, but wouldn't it have been interesting to see how he would have handled the child/Monster relationship in *The Ghost of Frankenstein*? It would have been a relationship certainly more important and sensitive than his encounters with Peter in *Son of Frankenstein* and certainly more fulfilling than his brief moment of happiness with Maria.

Perhaps for a minute we should consider the Tim Burton 1984 black-and-white short *Frankenweenie,* in which the "Monster" is a dog named Sparky and the "scientist" is his owner, a young lad named Victor Frankenstein (Barret Oliver). Burton filmed this tribute to the original Karloff *Frankenstein* for Walt Disney Studios, which shelved the movie when it garnered a PG rating because mothers at a preview screening objected to the film's macabre humor, fearing their children might imitate the boy in putting together their own mad lab and bringing a family pet back to life. It wasn't until Burton directed some top money-making, highly acclaimed hits that Disney decided to release the 27-minute black comedy on videotape.

As young Victor tosses a ball to Sparky, a rather ugly but faithful bull terrier (originally a dachshund was to be used—hence the name Frankenweenie), the ball rolls into the street and Sparky, chasing it, is run over and killed. Victor, inspired by a scientific school experiment, retrieves his pet from a stylized cemetery right out of the 1931 *Frankenstein*'s grisly opening set and builds a modified laboratory in his attic to bring Sparky back to life. Revived, the poor animal is uglier still, with patchwork stitches and the mandatory bolts in its neck. During its journeys around the neighborhood it frightens the residents, who take on all the hostilities of a real *Frankenstein* film mob. They even chase the critter to an abandoned miniature golf course where, with Victor, it takes refuge in a small-scale windmill. Their feelings are reversed when Sparky rescues Victor from the burning structure at the sacrifice of his own life. But the neighbors compassionately unite by starting their cars and, with lots of jumper cables, revive Sparky, who trots off with a French poodle wearing a familiar Elsa Lanchester hairdo.

Cute. But what is important here is that once again, the "Monster" is benevolent to a child, and the child reciprocates, even though adults consider the creature hostile and ugly. The prejudices of maturity are stripped by a child's innocence and love. It is perhaps the first time that a Frankenstein shows undying adoration for his creation, unless you consider Sting's selfish obsession with his female creation (Jennifer Beals) in *The Bride* (1985).

The Monster as a Victim of the Child

We have observed how the child has been a victim of the Monster, sometimes through a blameless accident. But what is more fascinating is that at times the Monster has been destroyed by a child's innocent act. The story of the Golem is based on Jewish folk tales about a creature made of clay who was brought to life by a rabbi to save his city from spoilers. The creature, however, becomes a rampaging monster. Some scholars have written that Mary Shelley may indeed have been familiar with the legend, and that this, along with her fear for her little William's fragility, may have played an important part in her creative process while writing *Frankenstein*. Certainly James Whale and his scriptwriters were influenced by the 1920 version titled *Der Golem: Wie Er in die Welt Kam* when creating the sequence of the Monster's encounter with little Maria. In describing this scene in "The Stage and Film Children of Frankenstein: A Survey" in *The Endurance of Frankenstein* (George Levine and U.C. Knoepflmacher, editors), Albert J. Lavalley writes: "The incident with the child and the flower is probably drawn from *The Golem*..., but it also evokes the momentary compassion for little William in the novel, which paralyzes the Monster before the need for revenge asserts itself."

Filmed several times previously in Germany by Paul Wegener (who also starred as the creature of clay), the 1920 version, *The Golem: How He Came into the World*, with a script by Henrik Galeen, was the first time the Monster was conquered by a child. It had been brought to life by Rabbi Low and his assistant Famulus, who recited a magic word from a book on sorcery and then placed that word in an amulet star on the Golem's chest. The climax of the film is described in Arnold L. Goldsmith's *The Golem Remembered*.

A little girl offers an apple to the fearsome Monster of Clay (Paul Wegener), a good deed that ultimately brings about the destruction of *The Golem*.

He relates how scriptwriter Galeen solved the problem of destroying this seemingly indestructible monster by creating "... a strikingly effective scene for which the audience has been prepared by the Golem's earlier interest in children. Reappearing at the city gates, the Golem watches the children at play in the bright sunlight with flowers in their hair. In a symbolic act intended to bring this sunlight and joyous activity into the dark, stale ghetto, he uses his brute strength to tear down the city gates. The children flee in terror, but one girl remains." Notice how the desire for sunlight precedes Karloff's reaching for the skylight in *Frankenstein*, and how all the children but little Cloestine flee from Chaney's Monster in *The Ghost of Frankenstein*.

Goldsmith continues: "She stands there crying as the Golem smiles at her gently. When she offers him an apple, he picks her up and holds her in his arms. Fascinated by the amulet on his chest, this blonde Aryan beauty removes it, thus reducing the giant man to a lifeless statue." Similarly, isn't it the children in the Universal *Frankenstein* series who ultimately cause the Monster's destruction? Little Maria's drowning so angers the villagers that they are incited to mob violence and burn the Monster in the windmill. The schoolchildren the Monster encounters in *Bride of Frankenstein* may have pointed the mob to the cemetery where the Monster meets Dr. Pretorius, who aids Henry in creating the mate who spurns it. In *Son of Frankenstein*, isn't it the book of fairy tales that Peter gave to the Monster that sparks it to kidnap the little boy and meet a fiery end in the sulfur pit? And in *The Ghost of Frankenstein*, even though it is the wrong blood type that destroys Chaney's Monster, it is

Herr Hussman who, not having found the bones of his daughter in their burned-down home, incites the mob to storm Frankenstein's sanitarium.

In 1957, Hammer Films of England remade the first of many of the Universal classics, for the first time in blood-curdling color. The studio's initial contribution was *The Curse of Frankenstein*, with Peter Cushing as the infamous baron, and for that time, the film set a tradition at Hammer for excessive gore and bloodletting. So it seems odd that, in the penchant for gruesomeness in the six Peter Cushing *Frankenstein*s (the series followed the exploits of the baron, rather than the Creature), only the first—*The Curse of Frankenstein*—involved an encounter between the Monster and a child, and a rather oblique one at that. A blind man (Fred Johnson) and his grandson (Claude Kingston) walk in the woods. As the old man rests, the little boy kneels down by a lake to pick mushrooms, a scene reminiscent of Whale's *Frankenstein*. Christopher Lee's Creature murders the grandfather senselessly. We see the boy leaving the lake and running back to where he left his grandfather. That's it. We cannot even be sure that a second murder took place except that there is a knapsack of mushrooms lying on the ground.

Far more interesting is the encounter with a child in the 1970 *Curse* remake *Horror of Frankenstein*. Ralph Bates replaced Cushing in this subpar tongue-in-cheek, serio-comic version (a severed hand gives Victor the finger when he charges it with electricity). Victor's creation this time is played as a childlike brute by David Prowse (later of Darth Vader fame). Victor even condescends to reward it with a patronizing "Good boy!" One night it ventures into a cottage and awakens a sleeping girl. Her screams bring her father from the woods, and he finds his daughter on the floor crying, "He hurt me; nasty Monster!" He picks her up and carries her outside where he meets Victor searching for the Monster. He tells Victor, who shows little sympathy for the child, that the Monster is headed back to the castle.

The creature is indeed back at Frankenstein's digs where it attacks Elizabeth (Veronica Carlson). Victor arrives in time and simply asks the Monster, "What on earth do you think you're doing?" He admonishes his creation: "Well, you've really got yourself in trouble this time. What we've got to do now is to make sure you don't get *me* into trouble, too." He approaches the monster with a gigantic syringe, and the thing backs away. "Don't be such a baby. It's only going to make you sleep."

The police arrive and the father and little girl wander aimlessly into the castle. The child fidgets constantly with Victor's lab equipment. She is unpleasant and, in the words of Ivan Butler when he assessed Carol Jeayes, "an ugly child," so obnoxious that we almost wish that Prowse had done away with her back at the cottage. "Stay away from that, little girl," Victor admonishes. "Sir, kindly keep your child under control!" As Victor offers lame explanations to Elizabeth's account of the Monster's attack on her, the little girl releases a lever, which sends gallons of acid into a large sarcophagus-shaped lead vat. Victor turns pale. The police leave to get a search warrant. As the father and the ugly little girl leave, she reveals, "It was quite a nice Monster, really." Victor stares sadly into the acid vat as two boots rise to the surface. Victor's handiwork has gone down the drain, thanks to the curiosity of a little girl who unknowingly has vindicated all the children the Monster has harmed over the years.

But it is an unsatisfactory climax to a rather uninteresting and tedious film. Matthew Bradshaw in *Cult Movies*, #12, complains: "All this leads up to one of the most disappointing endings I've ever seen. The Monster is done in by sheer chance, leaving Victor with an 'Oh, well, guess I'll just start again' look on his face. No big finale, the story just stops, and save for the destruction of the Monster, little is resolved. The viewer is left to wonder, what was the point of the previous 91 minutes?"

Predating Branagh's *Mary Shelley's Frankenstein* by a year was the TNT cable production directed by David Wickes, who claimed that his version was the first to be faithful to the book. As Mark Salisbury reported in *Fangoria*, #123, Wickes insisted "Nobody's ever done the novel.... It was written in 1818 and is a serious work of literature—all about cloning and genetic engineering, very topical.... The novel hasn't been famous all these years because it's no good. So since nobody's ever really done it, I decided it was time to do so."

But despite Wickes' claim that he was the first to film Mary Shelley's story, there are some important discrepancies. The Monster, played sympathetically by Randy Quaid, has his beginnings as a full grown body, curled up in a fetal position in a tank of "embryonic fluid," and cloned from Victor's own body, bringing a touch of 20th-century science fiction to the Gothic tale. Frankenstein (Patrick Bergin) regretfully reflects on his abandoned creation, "That was his first encounter with the human race. Like a child with no one to guide him. No one to help. And the guilt was mine—all mine."

Quaid remains benevolent for a good part of the production. The Monster observes some children playing by a mountain stream, and is happy. One of the youngsters, Amy (Amanda Quaid), sees it, and, startled by its ugliness, falls into the torrent. The Monster plunges in after her, carries her to the shore, and caresses her wet hair. It is shot by a hunter and is swept over the falls.

Even this does not sour the Creature against the human race. It secretly watches Elizabeth, Justine, and William picking flowers. William (Timothy Stark) is much older than Shelley described him and certainly not the curly-haired blond cherub from Branagh's film. He is also a liaison between Justine and Henry Clavel, delivering love letters they write to each other. One night, the Monster musters his courage and brings a flower to Justine (Jacinta Mulcahy) who flees the house in terror. When the Monster goes after her to proclaim his friendliness, William, with another love message, rides up on a horse. The animal is startled by the Monster, rears up, and throws William, who is crushed under the horse. Justine claims the "Devil killed William," goes mad, and kills herself. Victor, of course, blames his creation, but later relents to the Creature's request for a mate. He actually clones his fiancée Elizabeth (Fiona Gilles). With his destruction of the "Bride," Victor continues the tradition that turns the monster into a creature of anger and hate and leads to that final, fatal confrontation at the North Pole. The Monster has been destroyed because a horse accidentally fell on a young boy, setting in motion a series of fateful events leading to the tragic conclusion.

An early television adaptation of *Frankenstein* (January 18, 1952) cast Lon Chaney, Jr. as the Monster and John Newland as Victor in a *Tales of Tomorrow* episode. The Monster encounters William in the playroom, grabs the boy when the lad calls it ugly, holds him in front of a mirror, and sees that it is indeed ugly. The boy escapes but Victor later uses him as bait to lure the Monster back into the lab, where he electrocutes the creature. This was at a time when television performances were "live," and Chaney, inebriated during the performance, thinking it was a dress rehearsal, cursed at his mistakes. As Don Smith tells us in his biography of Chaney, Jr., "so mortified was Chaney upon learning of his error that it took him several weeks to recover emotionally."

And it is probably best if we forget this production also.

On the lighter side, in 1981 Fred Dekker directed *The Monster Squad*, a kind of Little Rascals Meet Frankenstein—a charming tribute to those Universal creature features. Dekker, along with screenwriter Shane Black, involved a bunch of 12-year-olds in tracking down Dracula, Frankenstein's Monster, the Wolf Man, the Mummy, and the Creature from the Black Lagoon, who suddenly pop up in a little southern town trying to retrieve an ancient amulet that controls the balance between good and evil. The kids all belong to a club and since they really believe in monsters, they're the only ones who can save the world. The sister of one of the boys, five-year-old Phoebe, keeps trying unsuccessfully to join their monster club, and it is she who makes friends with the Monster (played sympathetically by Tom Noonan), the only creature not out to wreak havoc. In Les Paul Robley's article "Creating a Vortex for Monster Squad" in the December 1987 *American Cinematographer*, the author writes: "Dekker said there's a real sense of pathos to him, for like the misunderstood Monster in Shelley's novel, all he wants is to be like others. He finds friends in children."

The Monster (Tom Noonan) finds a friend in Phoebe (Ashley Bank) and the child/Monster relationship comes full circle in *The Monster Squad*.

Phoebe (Ashley Bank) encounters the Monster in the woods and later introduces it to the boys, who flee in terror. She tenderly holds the hand of the Monster, who smiles at the quaking members of the Monster Squad. "It's OK, guys; he's friends with us. Come on. Don't be chickenshit." Sweet music plays in the background. This naturally gets Phoebe into the Squad. As they sit around the clubhouse debating whether they should break the tradition of admitting an adult, the Monster sits on the floor content to pet Phoebe's stuffed puppy dog. When they leave, the Monster is startled by a Frankenstein Monster mask. "Scary," it intones, and they walk off into the sunset.

The Monster warns the group that Dracula wants them dead because they know about the magic amulet. Still, they invade Dracula's mansion in the swamps, but the Monster is booby-trapped and pinned under heavy timbers. "He died to help us," says Sean (André Gower), the leader of the club. They steal the amulet and head for a showdown with the monsters in the town square. There, they receive the help of their "scary old German guy" friend (Leonardo Cimno) and the necessary virgin—one of the boys' sister (Lisa Fuller)—who must recite the incantation that will open a hole into limbo where dwells a vortex-whirlwind that will swallow the forces of evil forever. The police intervene and are badly defeated by Dracula and his cohorts. It appears that the "virgin" may not have been qualified to recite the verse—she admits she "did it" with her current boyfriend, but didn't think he counted.

Scary German guy points to little Phoebe and says, "She can recite the incantation!" Phoebe is halfway through the verse when Dracula grabs her by the neck.

Just at that moment, the Frankenstein Monster arrives in time to save Phoebe. It tears into Dracula, who drops the little girl, now free to finish the incantation. A giant vortex forms in the night sky as the Monster holds Phoebe's hand and smiles sadly at her. The monsters, and anything that is not nailed down, are slowly pulled into the nefarious whirlpool. The Monster, who has been holding onto Phoebe behind a park bench, is sucked away from her. "Don't go; don't go away!" the little girl cries. The departing monster calls out to her: "Phoebe. Phoebe. Bye..." In a selfless gesture of farewell, Phoebe throws her rag puppy dog to it, knowing that it will ease the pain of loneliness of whatever damnation the Monster is bound for. It clasps the dog to its chest and vanishes into the swirling black hole.

Melanie Pitts in her uncharitable review in the *Village Voice* complained: "As for *The Monster Squad*, subject me to *Ilsa, She-Wolf of the SS*, cut off my toes with toenail clippers, blind me with a curling iron, but don't make me watch Frankenstein get sucked into the vortex while waving and smiling and clutching a stuffed puppy dog. I can't take it." In my opinion, this assessment is for the "Pitts," and perhaps it would have been kinder to bring back *Motion Picture Herald* reviewer Leo Meehan to see what he thought of the little girl causing the Monster to be drowned in the inky blackness of the whirlpool. It is a scene that chokes me up every time I view it. Here is the fitting reverse of James Whale's *Frankenstein*. The innocence of the Monster causing Maria's accidental death has come full circle with Phoebe unwittingly bringing about her Monster's demise. It is a tragic gesture where love and friendship are abruptly ended through an unintentional act by the participants in each film. What redeems Phoebe is that she gives up her rag dog, throwing it to the drowning Monster like a life preserver. Isn't it a shame that Karloff's Monster couldn't have saved the drowning Maria by throwing her a rope or a branch?

We Are All Lonely Monsters

In 1973, an award-winning Spanish film made the rounds of the art houses where it garnered praises for its director, Victor Erice, and its child star, Ana Torrent, who portrayed young Ana, obsessed with finding the spirit of the Frankenstein Monster. In the October 3 issue of *Variety*, the reviewer called *El Espiritu de la Colmena* (*The Spirit of the Beehive*) a "sensitive, beautifully wrought film" and said that its director "must be reckoned as one of the most talented in Spanish filmdom."

This haunting film of childhood fears and loneliness takes place in a small Castilian village in 1940, just after the Spanish Civil War. A traveling film exhibitor brings a print of the 1931 *Frankenstein* to show the poverty-stricken villagers. In the audience is Ana and her older sister Isabel (Isabel Telleria). They watch in awe the Edward Van Sloan prologue, warning the audience of the terrors to come. When the scene between the Monster and Maria is shown, a look of apprehension comes over the children's faces, but Ana's is relieved when Maria gives the Monster the daisies. Then, later, as Maria's father carries his

Ana (Ana Torrent) and Isabel (Isabel Telleria) get a lesson on mushrooms from their father (Fernando Fernan Gomez) in *The Spirit of the Beehive*.

daughter's lifeless corpse through the streets, Ana asks her sister, "Isabel, why did he kill her?" Isabel, undoubtedly as stunned as Ana, puts her off by saying: "I'll tell you later."

That night as the children lie in bed, Ana asks Isabel again why the Monster killed Maria and why they killed it later. Isabel replies: "They didn't kill him or the little girl... because in the movies everything is a lie. It's a trick. And, besides, I've seen him alive." When Ana wants to know where, Isabel invents a fanciful answer. "In a place I know near the village. Other people can't see him. He only goes out at night." Ana wants to know if it's a ghost and Isabel tells her it's a spirit. "Spirits have no body. That's why he can't be killed." Ana argues that in the movie it had arms and feet and everything, to which Isabel imaginatively replies, "That's when he puts on his disguise to go out." When Ana wants to know how her sister talked to the Monster, Isabel explains, "I've already told you. He's a spirit. But if you're a friend of his, you can talk to him whenever you want. You close your eyes and you call to him: 'It's me, Ana. It's me, Ana.'"

Downstairs they hear footsteps. It is their father Fernando (Fernando Fernan Gomez), a bee keeper, pacing in the night as he broods over Maeterlinck's philosophical work, *The Life of the Bees*. When he finally retires to bed in the wee hours, his wife, Teresa (Teresa Gimpera), feigns sleep and thinks about a lost, perhaps imaginary, lover who does not reply to the many letters she mails.

One afternoon, Isabel takes Ana to a deserted shed on the Castilian plains where she claims the Monster lives. They see a giant footprint in the hardened mud and Ana places her own foot in it. It is twice as big as hers. In a contrasting scene, their father, in one of his few attentions to his children, takes them into the woods and gives them a lecture on poisonous mushrooms, one example of which he crushes under his boot.

Death is a constant puzzle for the little Ana. One day Isabel cruelly pretends to be dead. As Ana tries to get her sister to talk and show signs of life, Isabel lies motionless. Ana goes for help, but nobody is around. When she returns, her sister is gone. Then Isabel sneaks up on Ana with a large garden glove that resembles a Monster's hand and frightens her little sister.

Ana visits the shed again, this time alone, and discovers an army deserter (Juan Margallo) hiding there. Like the little girl in *The Golem*, she offers him an apple. Just as the spirit of the bee rests in her father's hives, just as the spirit of the mother's lover is captured in her photo album, and just as the power of a locomotive is trapped in the tracks when Ana puts her ear to the rails, so too does the little girl think that the spirit of the Monster lives in the fugitive.

The next day she returns with more food and her father's overcoat. His watch, with his initials on it, is concealed in the pocket. She tends to the deserter's wounded foot. After she leaves, soldiers arrive, machine-gun the fugitive, and transport his body to the auditorium, placing it under the movie screen where the villagers had watched *Frankenstein*. When Ana realizes that something has happened to her friend, she runs to the shed. Meanwhile, the coat and watch, having been identified as Ana's father's, are returned to him, and he takes off after his daughter. As Ana stares at the puddle of blood on the floor of the shed, her father appears in the doorway. The frightened child runs away.

The Spirit of the Beehive **is a poetic, atmospheric film dealing with childhood fantasies and family relationships. Pictured is Jose Villasante as the Monster.**

That night, the villagers, resembling a mob scene from *Frankenstein*, fan out with dogs and lanterns to search for the missing Ana. In the darkness, she looks at her reflection in a lake and sees the face of the Frankenstein Monster replace her own. The Monster (Jose Villasante) appears and kneels down beside her. As it reaches out to her, Ana closes her eyes.

The little girl is found safe the next morning, but in a state of shock. The mother complains to the doctor (Miguel Picazo) that her daughter doesn't recognize them; it's as if she and her husband didn't exist, which, of course, has been the situation all along. The doctor tells Teresa that Ana will gradually forget and what's important is that their daughter is alive. Isabel visits her sister's bedside and the roles are reversed. Now it is Ana in a deathlike coma who is not speaking to Isabel.

That night Ana recovers and walks to her window. From the balcony, she looks out into the dark night. She recalls her sister's words: "If you are a friend of his, you can talk to him whenever you want to. You close your eyes and call him." Ana shuts her eyes and whispers: "It's me, Ana. It's me, Ana." In the distance we hear the lonely whistle of a train answering her.

The Spirit of the Beehive is a poetic, atmospheric film dealing with childhood fantasies and family relationships. It is a film in which Charles Michener in his review in *Newsweek* finds the "characters cling to dreams with the driven tenacity of bees to the honeycomb." He also states that director "Erice brings together all of the film's themes and images into a dramatic metaphor that seems to stand for the historical struggles of Spain itself—the struggle of generosity in a land of harsh necessities, of artistic creation in a repressed society, of life, in other words, against death."

But the most powerful theme in the film is that of loneliness—and what that loneliness can do to a person. Fernando, obsessed with his bees and his books, is set apart from the rest of his family. Teresa is so lonely from lack of affection that she seeks solace from an imaginary lover. The children, on their own, are companions to each other, but when Isabel plays the nasty prank on Ana, the younger sister must look elsewhere for love. Ana finds a kindred spirit in the fugitive, who himself is isolated from friends as he hides alone in the shed. And when he is gone, she must seek out the Monster of her imagination as a fulfillment for friendship.

So too do the Monster and the children of the *Frankenstein* films seek out each other for love. Karloff's classic Monster encounters Maria, left alone to play by herself, and a beautiful but short friendship develops. Peter Frankenstein, cursed by the family name, has no village playmates and is left alone to "hunt elephants and tigers" and seek out the company of one lonely giant. Cloestine, tormented by the village bullies, is naturally drawn to the Giant who can change life's little injustices for her. Phoebe, who so wants to be a member of her brother's club, recognizes the benevolence of the Monster and uses it as a means to an end. And the Monster itself, always alone because of its ugliness, seeks out the innocence of children, not to prey upon them as the misleading ads proclaimed, but as a method of achieving its humanity.

It is this humanity that has dignified the *Frankenstein* films throughout the decades. When there is no encounter with a child, the Monster remains a brute, devoid of feelings and compassion, like Lugosi's Monster in *Frankenstein Meets the Wolf Man*, or Glenn Strange's in *House of Frankenstein* and *House of Dracula*. In the lesser films, the Monster is a stomping automaton, an unstoppable killing machine. Put a child in the picture, and the Monster regains its humanity. But isn't that what it's all about anyway? When compassion is lost—like Wolf's and Ludwig's total disregard for their family's safety, like Patrick Bergin's Victor who abandons his benevolent creation, like soldiers gunning down a defenseless fugitive in a shed—then humanity is also lost. And we all become Monsters in the end.

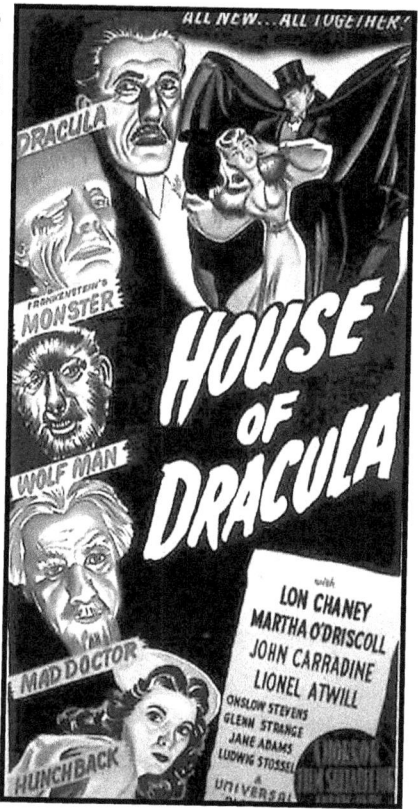

Frankenstein—
Or, "My Heart Belongs To Daddy"
by Anthony Ambrogio

On its most immediate level, the novel *Frankenstein* explores the consequences of a creator/parent's refusal to accept his parental responsibilities. Repulsed by his "ugly baby," Frankenstein abandons it minutes after it stirs. His desertion precipitates the tragedy that afterwards befalls him and the Monster and that occupies the bulk of the book. The creature's miraculous creation is merely Mary Shelley's starting point. She barely concerns herself with the actual creation process, which she describes in a few vague paragraphs. (Perhaps modesty or social convention prevented her from elaborating. However, as a woman, with the potential for creating life within her—having already been a mother twice—Shelley could afford to take the miracle of childbirth as a given and concentrate on its aftermath.)

Colin Clive as Frankenstein in Universal's 1931 film

In contrast, the cinema—that male-dominated medium—is fascinated by Mary Shelley's idea of *man*-made creation and concentrates almost wholly on that. Making the Monster is the center and core of the movie *Frankenstein* (1931): The process, shown in detail, occupies nearly half of the film's running time. *Frankenstein*'s director, James Whale, and its screenwriters—all men—converted Shelley's almost classical tragedy into something for the boys, a "men-only" tale, a male fantasy of birth without women.

1. Why Do You Think They Call It a *Labor*atory?

The movie's Henry Frankenstein (Colin Clive) gives his Monster life with his own hands, all by himself. His project to confer life upon dead tissue is literally "his baby": "That body... has never lived," he tells his former mentor, Prof. Waldman (Edward Van Sloan) about the soon-to-be-animated corpse. "*I* created it..." At the culmination of his labor, Frankenstein takes his greatest pains; he throws switches, raises the body to meet the lightning that will jolt it to life, and generally plays obstetrician to his own conception. When the body is lowered and its arm moves, proving that Frankenstein has endowed it with life, his exultation is as great as any new mother's—"It's alive; it's alive," he rejoices hysterically—and his friend Victor (John Boles) and Waldman must restrain him in his ecstasy.

The restored video version also partly includes Henry's apt comparison, "In the name of God, now I know what it feels like to *be* God!"—apt because Genesis is a male fantasy, too: God, the Supreme Father, creates His son Adam with His own hands, in His own image. Like God, Frankenstein is the only other male ever to give birth without women.[1]

2. Bringing up Baby

Frankenstein frequently alludes to his creation's newborn state and to the fact that the newly (re-)formed Monster is like a child and must be taught like one.[2] Our initial view of the creature erect—when it shambles in backward—confirms this impression of an overgrown toddler who hasn't yet mastered proper coordination. It turns around and, for the first time, in a series of close-ups, we see its face—a face only a father/mother like Frankenstein could love (because he made it; because it is *his* face, too, as explained in Section 4).

With infinite patience, proud parent Frankenstein guides his creation to a chair and sits it down, happy to show skeptical Waldman what an obedient, clever child he has. (Because of the film's different emphasis, Frankenstein's paternal attitude toward his creature here differs dramatically from his fearful attitude in the book.)

Frankenstein's display does not impress Waldman. He remains convinced of the truth of his earlier pronouncement to Henry: "You have created a Monster, and it will destroy you."[3] Now Waldman cautions Henry about infant-overstimulation, warning that the creature's reward for performing so well in front of company—its first exposure to the light—is over-exciting it.

Brandishing a torch, Frankenstein's deformed assistant, Fritz (Dwight Frye), interrupts the lesson. The Monster panics, forcing Waldman and Frankenstein to subdue it. This first onscreen representation of the film's violent sibling rivalry both cuts short the scientists' debate about creature-rearing (Waldman believes that it proves his position) and effectively terminates the Monster's education and any hope of ever civilizing it.

3. "Dad Always Liked You Best!" (Gives New Meaning to "Carrying a Torch")

In the film's first half, Frankenstein is brusque with the childlike Fritz, curtly ordering him about and immediately losing patience if Fritz fails to meet his expectations. (Like an anxious, expectant parent, Frankenstein is nervous about his second child's imminent birth and thus short-tempered with his pseudo-first child.) Despite this mistreatment, the dwarf remains loyal to Frankenstein. Obviously starved for affection, he is happy to receive *any* attention.

Frankenstein does exhibit brief flashes of kindness toward Fritz—e.g., he gently tells him not to be afraid of the sewn-together tissue he's about to animate and praises Fritz's contribution to the effort ("Here's the final touch: the brain you stole, Fritz"). Frankenstein is like the pregnant mother who realizes she's been short with her child and tries to make amends by including him in the birthing process. Thus, Frankenstein and Fritz's relationship is very much that of parent and child, father and son.

As far as Fritz is concerned, that relationship is terminated when the other child, the Monster, arrives and displaces Fritz in his father's affections. This displacement was probably inevitable: after all, Fritz is at best Frankenstein's "adopted son"; the Monster is Henry's "flesh and blood"—conceived of and borne by him. Probably also inevitably, Fritz develops a classic case of jealousy toward his new "brother." Perhaps his earlier bungling of the normal and abnormal brains he stole was a manifestation of his then-unconscious desire to hurt this interloper. Now he constantly torments the creature, whipping him and shoving torches in its face.

Frankenstein (Colin Clive) and Fritz's (Dwight Frye) relationship is very much that of parent and child, father, and son in *Frankenstein*.

Torches become significant symbols in *Frankenstein*. Naturally, the Monster fears them because they burn it, but these pain-bestowing, sticks also represent parental power to it, the torch being akin to the lightning that gave it life. Not surprisingly, the Monster's "older brother," Fritz, wields a torch—clumsily—in an effort both to imitate his father and to put down his father's favorite. Of course, he fails.

Frankenstein, as might be expected, initially fares better with his torch. After the Monster has hanged Fritz, Frankenstein manages, with a torch, to keep the creature at bay long enough for Waldman to sedate it.[4] Later, however, after the Monster's escape and visit to Frankenstein's bride (the significance of which is discussed in Section 6), Frankenstein's torch proves totally ineffectual when he confronts the creature on the mountain top.

Fritz's sadistic treatment of the creature leads to his death at the Monster's hands. "He hated Fritz. Fritz always tormented him," neglectful parent Frankenstein admits—or realizes—too late. And, later, after his collapse, he concedes, "It's all my fault." So he reluctantly acquiesces when Waldman insists that the creature be dismantled. The dissection fails; the creature escapes, and its fleeting, fumbling taste of freedom ultimately leads to its destruction by the villagers (who trap it in a windmill and set fire to it—with torches).

4. Like Father, Like Son (and I'm Not Kidding)

Frankenstein himself figures prominently in his creature's ultimate destruction. Initially, he abdicates his responsibility, leaving the creature's euthanasia to Waldman, which results in Waldman's murder and the Monster's escape. (At his wedding reception, Frankenstein's guests toast him and wish for "A son to the house of Frankenstein," little knowing that

In the end, Frankenstein acknowledges his responsibility and leads a search party after the Monster (Boris Karloff) in *Frankenstein*.

there already *is* a son to the house of Frankenstein—the Monster, who at that moment is roaming the hills, committing mayhem—en route *to* the house of Frankenstein.) In the end, Frankenstein acknowledges his responsibility and leads a search party after the Monster. He—alone—finds his creation. The duo—creator and created, father and son—stand poised for a moment, and then, after a brief, lopsided struggle, the Monster overpowers Frankenstein and carries him away. (It is indicative of *Frankenstein*'s male nature that the hero—and not the heroine—is carried off by the Monster.)

The finale in the old windmill (and a thematic, architectural counterpart to Frankenstein's tower laboratory) provides a variation on this creator-creation stand-off and illustrates that the two are one: Arthur Edeson's camera shows us the pair separated by the squeaking wheel of one of the mill's gears. Frankenstein peers through the revolving vertical spokes. There is an abrupt, imperceptible cut—matched to the movement of the spokes—and Frankenstein's face is replaced by, becomes, the Monster's.

This identification is significant, for the best horror films are those in which good and evil emanate from the same source, in which the menace cannot be destroyed without the hero being destroyed too, so that—as in classical tragedy (e.g., *Oedipus Rex*)—the viewer experiences a catharsis, both pity and terror.[5] Since Frankenstein is identified with his creation, since the one partakes so much of the other and had its being in and from the other, good and evil do emanate from the same source in this film, as in classical tragedy. (Similar to *Oedipus Rex*, and as in Freud's Oedipus complex, the son tries to do away with, to replace, his father in *Frankenstein*.)

The movie's logic, then, would seem to require that Frankenstein perish with his creation in the burning windmill (as Waldman's prophecy, "You have created a Monster, and it will destroy you," suggested). And the Monster certainly seems to destroy Frankenstein, tossing him onto one of the spinning windmill blades, from which he crashes down to earth. But the film tacks on an ending at odds with this classically tragic resolution, appending a happy, boy-girl reunion to it, showing Frankenstein recuperating peacefully at home in bed with his fiancée by his side. Thus, the cinema Frankenstein (unlike his novelistic counterpart) escapes paying for his sin against nature, his peculiar parthenogenesis, his far-from-immaculate conception.

5. Man, Woman, Birth, Death, Infinity

This one-parent birth, precluding the female and making the male both father and mother, is the movie's real deep, dark secret, the real meaning of that old chestnut about men tampering with things best left alone. That "moral" is never voiced in the movie proper—just as it is never voiced in the novel proper. It's only mentioned in the prologue spoken by Edward Van Sloan (which was added to the film after its completion)—just as it's only mentioned in the novel's preface, which Shelley added to the book 13 years after its first publication, when she herself had become "proper" and religious.

While it has the appearance of blasphemy, Frankenstein's sin is not against God. God doesn't seem to mind Frankenstein's presumption, for He makes no effort to chastise him. Divine justice doesn't punish Henry; Henry isn't punished at all. Only in the sense that *Frankenstein* (and its sequels) illustrates the error of man's attempt to usurp nature's—woman's—function through unnatural childbirth (by showing that such conception always results in a monstrosity) can it be said to mete out punishment to its protagonist.

In the film, Henry realizes the error of his ways, his tragic flaw, and rectifies it—making amends by destroying his abnormal creation and then settling down with his fiancée. He could still appropriately meet his tragic fate in the windmill, but Universal—apparently deciding that Frankenstein's love for a good woman was enough not only to redeem his soul but to save his life—lets him live.

6. Frankenstein Created Woman

The love of a good woman plays a significant but muted role throughout the Universal *Frankenstein* series, increasing in importance as the Monster's role diminishes. Women in *Frankenstein* and its sequels remain in the background, for the most part, serving as emblems—reminders of normal sexual relations and proper propagation—to Henry and to all the male experimenters who follow in his footsteps.

The only substantial female role in *Frankenstein* is that of Elizabeth, Frankenstein's fiancée, played by Mae Clarke, who, earlier in 1931, got a grapefruit in her face from James Cagney in *Public Enemy*. Her situation in *Frankenstein* is only marginally better. Essentially passive, Elizabeth initiates only one action: She shows Victor a disturbing letter from Henry, which convinces Victor to seek Prof. Waldman's aid, and she proves herself concerned and independent enough to accompany Victor in his quest and persuasive enough to enlist Waldman's help.

Elizabeth's first scene with Victor suggests the possibility of a love triangle. He makes timorous advances, which she (somewhat regretfully) rejects, remaining loyal to Henry. Neither ever broaches the subject again, but, toward the movie's end, when Frankenstein goes out to do what he must and destroy the Monster, he tells Victor, "I leave Elizabeth in your care, whatever happens. Do you understand? In your care."—suggesting that Frankenstein was originally intended to meet his doom and that this was his oblique attempt to

Elizabeth (Mae Clarke pictured with Colin Clive) in the 1931 *Frankenstein* does just as little in the novel, but there her presence has greater thematic significance.

give his blessing to a Victor-Elizabeth union at picture's close. Instead, Universal opted for the ending that keeps Henry and Elizabeth together.[6]

Throughout the film, Elizabeth is important for what she represents to Henry. He grants Victor and Waldman entrance to his tower laboratory only because she's with them. Her presence briefly recalls him to his former self and reminds him of normal relationships, normal sex. However, once they're all inside that phallic tower—an exclusively male symbol—her influence diminishes, and Frankenstein goes on with his experiment.

Elizabeth does little else—can't do much else—in the film. She, with Victor, fails to dissuade Baron Frankenstein (Frederick Kerr) from looking for his son; she shares one short scene with Henry when he's recuperating from his harrowing tower adventure, trying to erase his lurid memories by cheering him with thoughts of their forthcoming marriage (normal sex); and finally (except for our brief glimpse of her reunion with Henry at the end), she appears in the wedding scenes—where she is menaced by the Monster.

Elizabeth does just as little in the novel, but there her presence has greater thematic significance. Prof. Anca Vlasopolos has convincingly argued that Frankenstein mistakenly regards his fiancée as his sister, and that all his actions, including the Monster's creation, are attempts to avoid incest.[7] This certainly makes Elizabeth and the marriage more central to the book than they seem to be to the movie, where Henry suffers from no such delusion. Also, in the book, the Monster's menacing of Elizabeth assumes a certain importance by analogy: in the novel, Frankenstein agrees to give the Monster a mate, but then reneges. After

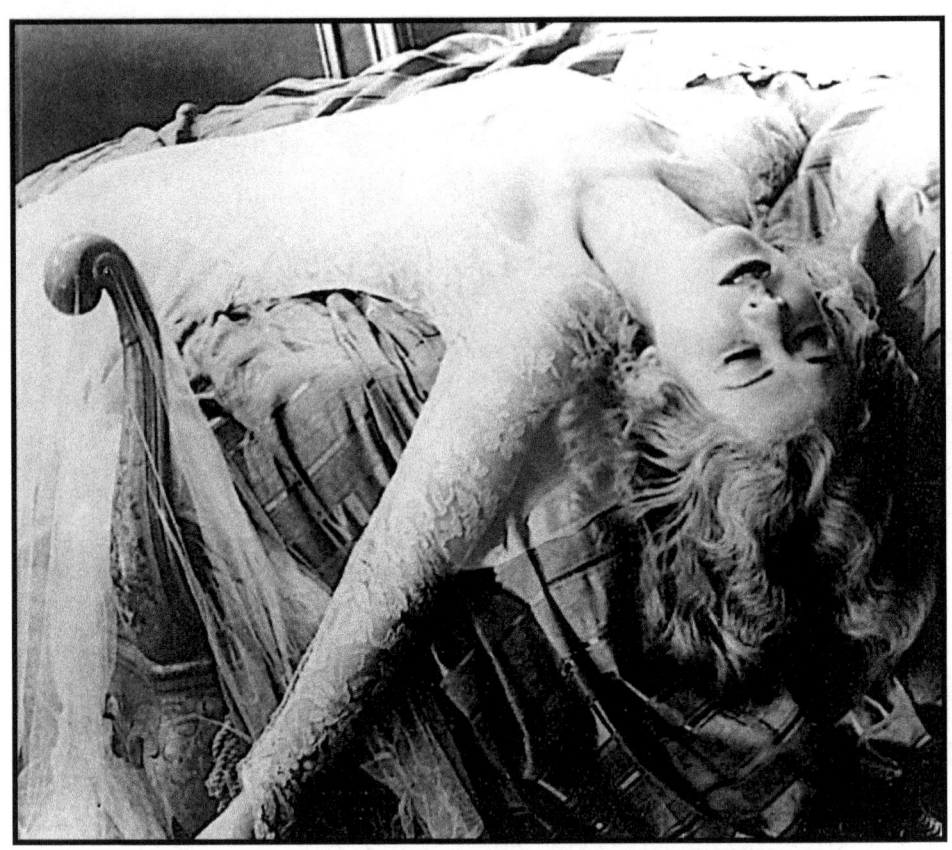

Has Elizabeth been the victim of an offscreen rape in *Frankenstein*?

he half-assembles but then destroys the Monster's intended, his articulate creation vows, "I'll be with you on your wedding night," and makes good this threat, strangling Elizabeth the evening she's married, wreaking his version of Old Testament vengeance: a bride for a bride. In the movie, the Monster is with Henry on his wedding day, too, but at first glance his attack on Elizabeth seems arbitrary, apparently lacking the strong motivation it has in the book.

Most viewers don't look for motivation in monsters' assaults. (Audiences expect monsters to menace people, particularly heroines, as a matter of course.) However, in the film, the Monster's menacing of Elizabeth is not so arbitrary as it seems—not if we realize that she is a pawn in the movie's Oedipal conflict. There is a psychosexual reason for his attack—a reason related to the movie's male, father-son theme.

The creature, almost by instinct, makes its way to its creator's home (and bride). At the first sign of trouble, Frankenstein locks his new wife in their bedroom and pockets the key (another phallic symbol). But his son, the Monster, gets in anyway and advances upon the helpless, trapped female. What happens behind that closed door in the time it takes Frankenstein to hear Elizabeth's screams, rush back, fumble with the key, and unbar the door, only to find the Monster gone and Elizabeth half-conscious, sprawled on the bed—in the manner, significantly, of Fuselli's central figure in his painting "The Nightmare"? "Keep it away! Don't let it come here!" she cries in shock. Does virginal blood now stain Elizabeth's once-white wedding gown? Has she been the victim of an offscreen rape?[8] Has the Monster committed the jealous, pseudo-Oedipal act of violating his recently acquired "step-mother"? The likely answer to these three questions is "Yes."

Note that this attack reawakens Henry's sense of responsibility, spurs his resolve to destroy this offspring who threatens to usurp his functions—who already has usurped Frankenstein's function with his bride (as their subsequent mountain-top confrontation confirms: The Monster easily brushes aside his father's impotent torch, demonstrating the son's superior sexuality, masculinity).

Why is the scene as shown so indirect, then? Did the filmmakers fail to realize the episode's implications and thus not emphasize them? Or were they only too aware of those implications—and did they thus purposely mute them for fear of censorship? Considering Universal's other purposeful mutings (e.g., Van Sloan's added prologue and the cut scenes of Henry comparing himself to God and the Monster drowning little Maria [Marilyn Harris][9]), all indications suggest that Whale and company knew very well what this scene signified.

7. In Comedy, There Is Truth (Not to Mention Lots of Laughs)

Various comic renditions of *Frankenstein* prove my assertions. Since parodies and lampoons grossly exaggerate for humorous effect, they often unwittingly but far more explicitly reveal a theme that the original only subtly implies. For example, the musical comedy *I'm Sorry, the Bridge is Out, You'll Have to Spend the Night* featured a Dr. Frankenstein whose "main objective was getting a suitable brain for his nearly brainless Monster for the sole reason of having someone to call him 'Daddy.' "[10] This one-line joke reveals the essence of the filmic Frankenstein myth.

8. This Explanation May Be Wilder Than You Think, But It Brooks No Denial

Even more revealing than an obscure, short-lived West Coast play like *I'm Sorry...* (filmed as the equally obscure *Frankenstein Sings...The Movie* [1994]) is the well-known screen comedy *Young Frankenstein* (1974).[11] Scripted by its director, Mel Brooks, and star, Gene Wilder, it is a loving, respectful parody of the Karloff Frankenstein films.

To simulate the look of the Universal series, Brooks secured Kenneth Strickfaden's actual scientific apparati from the 1931 *Frankenstein* for use in his laboratory sequences and commissioned Dale Hennesy (Art Director for *Fantastic Voyage* [1966] and *Sleeper* [1973]) to design a properly expressionistic castle, which cinematographer Gerald Hirschfeld shot in black and white, often in the deep-focused, low-ceilinged manner that John Mescall and George Robinson filmed *Bride* and *Son of Frankenstein* respectively. Complementing this pictorial accuracy and decorative authenticity is Brooks' almost exact duplication—*without parodistic intent*—of key scenes from the earlier *Frankenstein*s. The "birth" of the Monster (Peter Boyle) in *Young Frankenstein* parallels Karloff's Monster's in the original, sometimes shot for shot, action for action, right down to the creature's first movements—the initially imperceptible, then ever-increasing twitching of the fingers of its right hand after it has been exposed to the life-giving lightning. Perhaps if *Young Frankenstein* weren't quite this loving and respectful, it would be even funnier than it is.[12]

But maybe *Young Frankenstein* couldn't help it; perhaps it is so loving and respectful in spite of itself. Reviewer Jay Cocks noted:

> The Shelley story ought to have turned wormy by this time from virtually constant exposure. It is, however, still a powerful myth. One good measure of its resiliency is that even when Brooks is lampooning it, the story remains compelling, nearly inviolate. When Gene Wilder's Dr.

In a comic reversal, daddy (Gene Wilder) climbs upon sonny (Peter Boyle) boy's knee and hugs him affectionately in *Young Frankenstein*.

>Frankenstein tries to zap life into a grotesque, inanimate form, the movie goes serious despite itself. The myth is better, more involving than the joke being made about it.[13]

As Cocks also remarked, once young Frankenstein stumbles upon his grandfather's notes, *How I Did It* (Wilder and Brooks' gag title for Frankenstein's *Secrets of Life and Death* in the Universal series), "he is quickly seduced... by the siren call of Victor's madness"; he cannot resist the temptation to imitate his ancestor, just as Henry Frankenstein's descendants and admirers in every subsequent Universal entry cannot resist the temptation to reanimate the Monster. The allure of male conception, the ability to boast "I made it all by myself," is too great for any of these men to resist.[14]

This seriousness in spite of itself to which Cocks refers is tellingly revealed in one scene of *Young Frankenstein* that begins comically enough. Frankenstein enters his Monster's cell, ordering his assistants not to open the door, no matter what. Naturally, once he gets in and confronts the brute, he wants out, but his loyal assistants, faithfully following his first instructions, ignore his pleas. Thus, out of self-preservation at first, Frankenstein attempts to appease his creation, telling it what a good, fine boy he is. As the Monster succumbs to this flattery, Frankenstein begins to believe it himself (after all, this *is* his child) and soon, in a comic reversal, daddy climbs upon sonny boy's knee and hugs him affectionately. So far, so funny—while at the same time a revealing demonstration of the *Frankenstein* father-son theme.

But the scene ends on a completely serious note. Frankenstein's assistants finally decide to see if he's still alive. "Dr. Fronckenshteen! Are you all right?" they call. They call him "Fronckenshteen" because, up to now he's insisted on this mispronunciation to dissociate himself from his "mad" forebears. But, now, he replies, with fierce pride, in near hysteria, "My... name... is... *Frankenstein*!" This assertion is too earnest to be comic; I've never heard an audience laugh at it, and I don't think it was meant as a joke. Parenthood does strange things to people; acknowledging his paternity, Frankenstein is not about to disown his child or deny his heritage.

9. A Double Bill: He Done Her Wrong plus Oedi-Pals at Last

Young Frankenstein repeats the misogynistic pattern of the Karloff films. The movie's three female leads, while not kept in the background quite so much as their Universal counterparts, have mostly thankless roles and suffer from male chauvinistic treatment. As Inga, Frankenstein's lab assistant (and, later, paramour), Teri Garr has the most screen time, but it's spent playing the usual dumb-blonde part. As the sinister housekeeper, Frau Blucher (horses whinny fearfully at the very mention of her name), Cloris Leachman fares better; she initiates two important actions—getting young Frankenstein interested in his ancestor's experiments and allowing the just-created Monster to escape—but then she practically disappears from the film, and has perhaps only two more lines of dialogue.

Even though Frankenstein's fiancée, Elizabeth (Madeline Kahn), only briefly appears at the beginning and doesn't return 'til the end, she is the most important woman in *Young Frankenstein* (and the one most shabbily treated). Wilder and Brooks' comic handling of her character makes explicit that subtle implication in the original.

Abducted by the Monster, Elizabeth cowers up at him, wondering what it is going to do with her. It leers down at her, knowing what it is going to do with her. And then it rapes her (with the "enormous schwanzstucker" to which Inga made incredulous reference when the Monster was still on the drawing board). *Young Frankenstein* reveals onscreen what must have occurred behind closed doors in the 1931 *Frankenstein*, overtly depicting Frankenstein's Oedipal nightmare—the monstrous son asserting sexual rights over its father's woman.

If this weren't a comedy and if Frankenstein hadn't already fallen for Inga anyway, what would be even more nightmarish for Frankenstein about this rape is that Elizabeth *enjoys* it.[15] It's bad enough for the father to fear that his son might make advances toward his wife; it's much worse if she responds and prefers the son. But, since *Young Frankenstein* is a comedy, its Oedipal conflicts work themselves out.

In *Bride*, after Frankenstein and Pretorius succeed in creating a mate (Elsa Lanchester) for the Monster, it is clear that she prefers the creator to his creation.

For one thing, Frankenstein doesn't love Elizabeth any more; he's transferred his affections to Inga, so he doesn't feel that the Monster is cutting in on his territory. Therefore, at the film's conclusion, he can even magnanimously submit to a transfer operation to give his creation some of his personality and intelligence, rendering the Monster benevolent, articulate, and no longer a threat to humankind. The transfer makes Frankenstein more of an actual father to the creature, because now, in an unorthodox way, the Monster directly partakes of Frankenstein's "heredity."

Both Frankenstein and his creation settle down with their respective brides, Inga and Elizabeth (whose sexual experiences with the Monster have turned her into a replica of Elsa Lanchester's Bride of Frankenstein, complete with electric-shock hairdo), and, in the last scene, the audience and Inga learn that, during the transfer, Frankenstein gained something from his "son"—the famous phallus. In Oedipal terms, this is a symbolic castration of the son by the father, a castration whereby the son doesn't get hurt but the father gets satisfaction. There now exists a golden mean between parent and child, each sharing attributes of the other, so the already faded Oedipal conflict is resolved. In this respect, in its happy dénouement, *Young Frankenstein* is practically unique. Only the Universal series' *Bride of Frankenstein* (in other respects more misogynistic than *Frankenstein*) offers a similar, very brief reconciliation and understanding between creator and creation.

10. Electricity + Electra + Atrocity = Electratrocity

In *Bride*, after Frankenstein and the perverse, misogynistic, obviously sexually aberrant Dr. Pretorius (Ernest Thesiger) succeed in creating a mate for the Monster, it becomes

The torch-carrying crowd sets fire to the windmill in *Frankenstein*.

painfully clear that she prefers the creator to his creation, the father to the son. Repulsed by her half-brother because she finds him ugly and frightening, the creature's intended mate is led, by her aesthetic sense, to embrace another form of incest: Running from the Monster, she runs straight into Frankenstein's arms.

It stands to Freudian reason that the daughter should gravitate toward her father, preferring him over any other man. The Monster seems to realize this, at least on an intuitive level (after all, a similar impulse drove him to Frankenstein's bride in the previous film), and it knows its conjugal relationship is doomed. It had wanted "a girl just like the girl who married dear old dad," but such a girl, it discovers, is only interested in dad.

"She hate me," the Monster tells his creator, too tactful or embarrassed to mention the Oedipal rest of the matter. An unspoken bond of understanding and compassion forms between the pair; Henry would like to assure his forlorn Monster that it is not so, but he knows that the ever-retreating, never-to-be bride who clings to him would belie his words, so he can give the creature no comfort, only mute sympathy. The Monster is resigned, however: "She hate me," it repeats, "like others." Its hand falls on the laboratory's phallically erect suicide switch; it ignores Pretorius' terror-stricken pleas, "Look out for that lever! You'll blow us all to atoms!"

At that moment, Elizabeth (here played by Valerie Hobson) appears at the window of the locked laboratory door, calling to Henry. Frankenstein urges her to save herself before the Monster pulls the switch. "I can't leave them!" he tells her. But the Monster hesitates; it sees what its father and its father's wife have together and knows now that it cannot duplicate that relationship (although it has tried to—with Elizabeth in the first film and with her substitute here). "Yes," it contradicts Henry in an emotion-choked voice: "Go! You live! Go!" It accepts Henry and Elizabeth's relationship—its Oedipal conflict is resolved (as it is in the Mel Brooks parody)—and it can allow its creator to escape with his wife.

As for Pretorius, who cannot ever be a partner in a normal heterosexual relationship, the Monster cuts short his attempted departure with these famous last words: "You stay! We belong dead." And, after one final, longing look at its intended mate, it throws the switch, returning Pretorius to the elements with which the movie's imagery has associated him—hell (as the devil) and death—returning itself and its mate to the dead. Earlier, in their encounter in the sepulcher, the Monster told Pretorius that it hated the living and loved the dead, and now—in an orgasmic explosion that bursts the phallic tower, destroying it completely—it achieves in death the only consummation possible with its "bride" (sardonically so labeled by Pretorius after her animation, while wedding bells pealed ironically over the soundtrack).

The destruction of a phallic structure (the tower, the windmill) at the finale of the first two *Frankenstein* films signals a return to and reaffirmation of normal human relationships and childbirth in an otherwise male-obsessed, male-engendering world—at least until the phallic male fantasy rears its ugly head in the series' next entry.

Frankenstein Reanimated by Hammer Films

More than 20 years after the Universal heyday, England's family oriented Hammer Film Productions became the only other movie production company to create a serious ongoing film series based upon Mary Shelley's *Frankenstein*. And while Hammer's efforts were even more limited by time and budget than the Universal product, they were destined to be viewed as inferior variations on a theme. However, the Hammer efforts thrilled the generation raised during the 1950s and 1960s because we now had a modern Frankenstein vision to call our own.

And Hammer's efforts were always unique and generally did not rely upon the Universal mythos (the one exception, *The Evil of Frankenstein*, is covered in this section): Hammer added color and visceral violence to the mix, Hammer emphasized the character of Monster-maker Baron Frankenstein (a superb series of performances by Peter Cushing) over the Monster, and Hammer explored themes that were taboo during the 1930s—sexuality, soul transference and spirituality, insanity, etc.

While Hammer never produced a movie with the creativity and vision of *Frankenstein* or *Bride of Frankenstein*, Hammer can proudly boast that they furthered the thematic concepts with superb productions such as *The Curse of Frankenstein, Revenge of Frankenstein* and *Frankenstein Must Be Destroyed*. Even the lesser Frankenstein productions—*The Evil of Frankenstein, Frankenstein Created Woman*—provided thrills and a solid night's entertainment. For the betterment of all, Hammer kept the name of Frankenstein vital for almost another 20 years.

In this section Gary J. Svehla examines the evolution of Doctor Frankenstein or Baron Frankenstein as he was known at Hammer Films. The wonderful Peter Cushing, the kindest of men created a Frankenstein many times more evil than his Creation.

Peter Cushing

The Evolution of Hammer's Baron Frankenstein
by Gary J. Svehla

After making their mark upon the world of science fiction cinema with the Quatermass series (*The Creeping Unknown* and *Enemy from Space*) and *X, The Unknown*, Hammer Film Productions decided to now try to reinvent the cinematic world of Gothic horrors made so popular by Universal Studios during the 1930s, this time by adding deep saturated doses of color and English gentility.

When *The Curse of Frankenstein* was released upon American shores in 1957, Hammer had hit its financial and creative stride with a franchise series that would stretch well into the 1970s. Curse of Frankenstein began the collaboration between Hammer superstars Peter Cushing and Christopher Lee, teaming the acting team with director Terence Fisher and screenwriter Jimmy Sangster for the first time.

Since the Hammer Frankenstein series has been analyzed to death in print, my focus here is not upon the merits or meaning of the series, it is not to contrast Freddie Francis' directorial style to Terence Fisher's. It is not to compare the relative creative opulence of the studio (utilizing minimal budgets for maximum results), its sets and budgets, during the Bray Studio period, compared to its more expensive but generic look toward the end. It

With *The Curse of Frankenstein*, Hammer created a franchise series that would stretch will into the 1970s.

is not even to compare the Hammer series to the Universal series.

No, the focus of this chapter is to document the evolution of what I consider to be the quintessential Mary Shelley as well as Hammer character, Baron Victor Frankenstein, Peter Cushing's supreme cinematic triumph and obviously the characterization of his career, as portrayed in six films produced by the studio between 1956-1974. By focusing upon Peter Cushing's performances in each of the series' entries, we see not necessarily the betterment of the series over the years, but we see the metamorphosis of Peter Cushing's Baron Frankenstein into a classic movie role that stands the test of time, a persona so much a part of his humanity that Cushing often transcended the limitations of the scripts and budgets to produce a *tour de force* performance in each of the Hammer entries. Artistically, Peter Cushing's Baron is one of the principle reasons why the reputation of Hammer has transcended the "B" horror market. Let us examine why.

Belgian poster for *The Curse of Frankenstein*

"I always had a brilliant intellect!"
THE CURSE OF FRANKENSTEIN
[1957; Screenplay by Jimmy Sangster; Directed by Terence Fisher]

Jimmy Sangster's script immediately establishes the emphasis in the Hammer series upon the character of monster-creator Baron Victor Frankenstein, instead of focusing upon the Monster, as Universal did 25 years earlier. However, the script of *The Curse of Frankenstein* spends too much time recasting the dominant elements from the Universal series (the obsessiveness of the doctor, the conflict between monster-creator and assistant, the blind hermit in the woods sequence, the damaged brain, the climax occurring on the eve of the Baron's wedding, the interference caused by the doctor's fiancé, etc.) that it seems afraid to break out of this set pattern (although Universal's copyright for the Karloff make-up caused Phil Leakey to concoct a new monstrous look for Christopher Lee's Creature). Indeed, as written, the script casts the role of Baron Frankenstein as an almost one-dimensional obsessed scientist who dares to defy society's rules and the laws of nature. But Peter Cushing struggles to make the role so much more.

The script cleverly tells its story in flashbacks, a priest coming to visit the Baron in prison before his execution. Addressing the priest, the Baron Frankenstein states he asked

Cushing, as the Baron, is always serious and works intensely in his laboratory in *The Curse of Frankenstein*.

for him because, "I could think of nobody else... people trust you. Just listen. Tell me you'll stay!" The Baron's aristocracy begins to take over as his tone changes from gentle pleading to one of demand, as he firmly planting his hand upon the priest's shoulder—soon both hands are clutching his neck. Threatening to leave the presence of this lunatic, the priest receives an apology from the Baron, "I won't forget myself again. I always had a brilliant intellect..." and tells of his childhood "where it all began."

As rewritten in the Hammer canon, Baron Victor Frankenstein lost his father at age five and there gained his title. Ten years later, his mother dies and Victor inherits the family fortune. An aunt who is dependent upon the mother's monthly check to support herself and her daughter, Elizabeth, is concerned that the young Baron will discontinue this financial support. It is also understood that the young Elizabeth, the Baron's cousin, will someday wed the Baron. The Baron gladly agrees to continue the financial support. But what he needs now is a tutor to feed his ever inquisitive mind. Thus, enters Paul Krempe (Robert Urquhart), a man who is surprised that the teenaged Baron is conducting his own affairs with such sophistication. In voice over, the Baron confides that Paul was "an admirable tutor" but that he learned all Paul had to teach in only two years. Cocky, self-assured, arrogant are phrases which categorize our earliest looks at the Baron.

Paul and his student work intensely in the Frankenstein laboratory bringing life to a dead dog. Here the Baron's obsessive one-dimensionality is made clear by Cushing's intense performance. While working, Cushing is always serious, he feverishly looks down at gauges, waves demandingly for Paul to cut off the machinery at a precise second, wipes his brow with his handkerchief. His blue eyes widen as he listens for the reanimated heartbeat of the now revived dog. Smiling for the first time, he exclaims, "Paul, it's alive. We've done it!" Cushing's energetic eccentricity makes the Baron's inquisitive nature crystal clear. But it is this linear obsession which dominates Cushing's performance throughout.

The differences between pupil and tutor soon become clear. Paul, wishing to present their findings to a scientific board meeting the next month, is immediately shot down. "We won't! We mustn't share it yet. We must move on to the next stage!" This attitude becomes an essential quirk in the Baron's character; as in Shakespeare's universe it will become the Baron's tragic flaw. Once he has conquered knowledge at one level, instead of publishing or presenting his findings to his medical peers, the Baron simply wishes to immediately proceed to the second stage. In other words, instead of putting his scientific knowledge to practical use, he has an insatiable thirst to move onward, to explore the unknown for its own intrinsic sense, rather than to benefit humanity. Thus his quest is more neurotic than self-satisfying—he obviously does not enjoy his accomplishments at any stage. He must constantly move onward. He is a driven man.

The Baron announces to Paul it is not enough to bring the dead back to life; thus his goal: "We must create a human being!" When Paul protests calling such work a "revolt against nature," the Baron counters with the ironic, "Paul, you haven't shown scruples up 'til now!" The manner in which Cushing delivers this line, a slight all-knowing smile on his face, that evil glint in his eye, transforms the up-to-now one-dimensional character to new levels of insight. Throughout the movie, Cushing delivers similar lines with the same gusto. Looking at the rotting corpse snatched from the gallows, the Baron gazes at the huge hands and states, "Clod-hopping. No wonder he was a robber. He couldn't do anything else!" After cutting off the rotting head and thinking about replacing the hands, the Baron tells Paul, "Let him rest in peace, while he can!" Soon Paul refuses to aid the Baron in his experiments claiming moral outrage. However, he does not leave the house because of another primary interest.

It seems the sudden, unexpected arrival of cousin Elizabeth (Hazel Court) complicates matters. She tells Paul (who at first she mistakes for the Baron), "I've come to live with Victor," announcing her mother's recent death. The Baron plans to proceed with his experiments even with the presence of Elizabeth, and Paul's obvious attraction to Elizabeth establishes him as her great protector. Elizabeth, unable to care financially for herself, only too well understands the ramifications of her pre-arranged marriage to the Baron and his wealth.

However, the Baron is already engaged in another affair, passionately kissing Justine (Valerie Gaunt),

Hazel Court as Elizabeth

the household maid, who herself has her sights set on the Baron. She is more than a little threatened by the presence of Elizabeth in the household and states she is tired of meeting the Baron in dark corridors. The Baron is smart enough to see through this ruse. "What makes you think I'd marry you!" And in another double-entendre orders, "See to her [Elizabeth's] every need as thoroughly as you've seen to mine." Cushing embellishes these lines with nuance of a sly sexual nature. He is saddled by the script that tries to keep his performance one-dimensional, but he tries to bring something special to the role. It seems Cushing utilizes every opportunity he can to imbue his character with underlying motives or nuance that deviate from the literal translation of the script.

The Baron toys with Paul's outrage by pretending he could continue with his unnatural work alone. "This will end in evil," Paul proclaims. The calm Baron responds, "Oh, I just rob a few bodies, but what doctor has not done that? How will we ever learn... My creature will be born with a lifetime of knowledge." But that leads to the question of a brain, and the Baron desires the brain of a great intellect.

Naughty maid Justine (Valerie Gaunt) meets a bad end in The Curse of Frankenstein.

Enter brilliant Professor Bernstein, the gracious dinner guest who is sadistically pushed off the balcony to his death. Referring to the earlier quirk in the Baron's personality, the wise old professor warns that scientists are "too concerned with discovery" and grow bored so easily that they too soon "go back into the darkness" of discovery instead of using that new-found knowledge to help mankind. Reinforcing Elizabeth's fear that the Baron spends entirely too much time in his laboratory, the Professor states that time slips away until "one is too old to enjoy life."

After the murder of Bernstein, Paul sees the Baron open the professor's coffin and remove his brain, stating, "I can stop you from using his brain." The Baron nonchalantly replies, "Why? He has no further use for it!" After a struggle, whereby the brain is injured, the Baron showing his violent rage screams, "Get out of here, get out!!!" Thus, Cushing's performance gravitates from aristocratic self-control, with an air of arrogance, to one of unhinged temper tantrums of uncontrolled anger and frustration.

Paul tries to warn Elizabeth one more time. She shows no inclination to leave, instead asking are you saying Victor is "wicked or insane?" Paul hits the nail on the head by saying, "Neither. He can't see the consequences, he's so wrapped up in his experiments!"

But the Baron, frustrated in working alone, pleads with Paul to again help him. "I want you to help me. I'd thought I could work it myself—I can't." But the arrogance and aristocratic insolence returns: "You will help me Paul, whatever you say!" Paul agrees to help if the Baron promises to destroy his creation after he proves his experiments. The Baron agrees. But by manner of Cushing's delivery, the viewer can almost imagine the crossed finger held secretly behind the Baron's back.

Cushing portrays a throttled victim better than anyone else on screen.

In his laboratory the Baron confronts the bandaged monster. He is promptly picked up off the ground by his neck. The Monster tries to choke the life out of the insignificant human. Cushing, who portrays a throttled victim better than anyone else on screen, plays the strangulated, bug-eyed, semi-conscious victim to the hilt. He will repeat this same physical talent in *Horror of Dracula*, *The Mummy*, and *Brides of Dracula*. After being rescued, the Baron, wild-eyed, shouts, "I did it Paul!"

The Creature escapes into the woods, confronts a blind hermit, and is shot to death by the eager-to-destroy Paul. Together they bury the corpse. "I don't think I will ever forgive you for what you've done, Paul!" says the Baron.

The exhumed corpse is seen hanging from a hook suspended in the Baron's laboratory. With grim, quiet determination, the Baron obsesses and whispers, "I will give you life again."

Justine confronts the Baron with news that she is pregnant and that "you promised to marry me." To which the Baron only insensitively laughs. "Pick any man in the village, it's probably him [the father]! Get back to your work!" he callously orders. When Justine threatens to expose the Baron to the authorities, the Baron grows intense and serious, "Proof, that's what authorities want!" He then orders her out of the house by morning.

Of course to get proof, she must investigate the laboratory and the small storage room in back of the lab. There, the reanimated Creature lies in wait as the conniving Baron follows her—closing and locking the door once she enters that storage room. Hearing her screams the Baron records an unnerving look of absolute relief. Formerly seen as simply being obsessed and committed to science for its own sake, the Baron is now revealed to be callous, evil, and manipulative. He murders in cold blood to save his own prestigious reputation.

Eager to now outrage Paul by showing him his revived patchwork creature, the Baron demonstrates to Paul that his Creature now obeys by responding to short commands like sit down and stop. Paul insults the Baron by asking, "Is this your creature of superior intellect?" The Baron, outraged and defensive, responds, "There you see the result of your handiwork. This is your fault Paul (referring to the bullet in the head that Paul fired). You won't win Paul. I will carry on, get another brain, and then another!!!"

This being the final straw, Paul threatens to go to the authorities. But the Baron counters with, "You're as much a part of this as I am." And based upon his upcoming actions, Paul does indeed understand the truth of these words.

The Creature escapes from the lab, stalks the rooftop, and lumbers toward the innocent Elizabeth on the eve of her wedding night ("We're not sentimental young lovers," the Baron reminds Elizabeth earlier that evening.). Frantically racing to rescue his bride-to-be, the Baron gets a pistol from a glass case and fires at the monster who lunges at Elizabeth. Unfortunately, the bullet finds Elizabeth (who survives) and the Creature approaches an uncharacteristically cowardly Baron who whines, "Get away from me" as he throws a lamp igniting the Creature into a blazing inferno. The pain-riddled Creature falls through the skylight into the acid bath below. The Baron is arrested for the murder.

While Elizabeth waits outside, Paul visits the Baron in jail as the priest looks on. The Baron, eyes wide and excited, is eager for Paul to validate his incredible story. Paul stands by mute, refusing to lift a finger to confirm the facts. The Baron sensing Paul's real motive for refusing to help, suddenly lunges at his former childhood tutor and tries to strangle him, "Paul, you've got to save me. I'll make you..." The Baron's arrogance returns one final time. Paul, by refusing to confirm the truth, allows the Baron to be seen as a simple insane murderer who must now face the guillotine. Outside Paul returns to the waiting arms of Elizabeth. As the Baron must now realize, Paul may have committed the most vile, evil act of the movie by remaining silent so that the Baron will be out of the way so that he can have Elizabeth all to himself.

Top: The Monster (Lee) attacks his creator (Cushing).

Bottom: Frankenstein torches his creation at the finale of *The Curse of Frankenstein*.

Thus, sticking to a script which revamps the 1931 Universal script rather than returning to Mary Shelley's original novel, Peter Cushing creates a distinct persona of the obsessed, aristocratic, and arrogant Baron. As enacted in *The Curse of Frankenstein*, Cushing's Baron is depicted as ruthless, self-serving, and emotionally cold. He is truly a one-dimensional villain, a true "mad" scientist oblivious to those around him. Only in the film's final minutes do we feel a glimmer of sympathy for the Baron because Paul's actions are ultimately even more evil than the Baron's.

"He cuts 'em up, alive!"
THE REVENGE OF FRANKENSTEIN
[1958; Screenplay by Jimmy Sangster; Directed by Terence Fisher]

After the success of *The Curse of Frankenstein* and *Horror of Dracula*, sequels were inevitable. However, Hammer's sequel to *Curse* was superior in every way, simply because screenwriter Jimmy Sangster felt free of the Universal Pictures' formula and created his own version of the *Frankenstein* mythos. Also, the sequel was better able to embellish the character of the Baron, and actor Peter Cushing was, as always, enthusiastic to reveal far more of the subtleties inherent in the mad doctor's inner soul. Thus, while the first *Frankenstein* collaboration between Fisher, Sangster, and Cushing was creatively stilted and confining, this first sequel allows each of these gifted artists the opportunity to let down their hair, creatively.

While the Baron was primarily obsessed, aristocratic, and cruel in the original entry, here the Baron displays the compassion which is necessary for the audience to care about his character (since he is the returning icon, not the Creature). Having escaped the gallows, the Baron's conspirators execute and bury the priest in his place. Going incognito, the Baron moves to another village and assumes the identity of one Dr. Stein, a mysterious doctor distrusted by the town's Medical Council but loved by its citizenry. It seems Stein, a loner, refuses to join the Council. As one member intones with a degree of agitation, "Three years ago, when he first came, no one here heard of him, no one knew his background. Now he is the most popular doctor...who steals patients from us!" The verdict: Dr. Stein must be made to join this elite group.

Dr. Stein has become doctor to the upper class as he attends to patients such as the Countess and her daughter. The reticent yet lovely daughter is manipulated by

Frankenstein faces the hangman's noose at the end of *Curse*, but manages to escape for *Revenge.*

mother who insists the girl is ill. Mother complains she has "no vitality" and orders the doctor to "overhaul" her. Complaining of palpitations and dizziness, she desires the doctor to listen to her daughter's heart by placing his ear against her bosom. "You are a man, you can do a great deal for her. I have money..." The Countess' implications are crystal clear.

The doctor uses money earned in this manner to finance a Poor Hospital for the underprivileged and needy, more often inhabited by criminal elements. There the Baron is seemingly sympathetic to the needs of the underclass yet his true nature cleverly shines through. Examining a patient and inspecting his tattooed arm, the doctor announces, "You have to have it off." The arm is seemingly healthy, but the Baron is readying the perfect body to once again create life and this is the arm of a pickpocket, a man whose fingers are nimble and especially skilled. The doctor's advice after breaking the grim news to his distressed patient, "Find another trade or use your other hand!" The Baron's cruel humor is still intact. The haughty members of the Medical Counsel, an investigative group of three, are shocked by the squalor in this free clinic. One intones, "The stench is enough to kill me." The Baron is wise enough to realize that craving off the limbs of the rich would not get him far, but who really cares about the needs of the underprivileged? His seemingly humanitarian efforts are in reality self-serving and cruel. But this time the Baron is unable to operate as himself, so he must create a gentile and highly cultured persona, the external personality of a dashing, almost romantic god of science.

His plan is to reward the paralyzed crippled assistant Karl by transferring his brain into his new unborn body, thus curing Karl of his physical infirmaries. The Baron is forced to take Dr. Hans Kleve (Francis Matthews) into his confidence as the young doctor, a member of the Council, recognizes Dr. Stein as Baron Frankenstein from having attended the funeral of the late Dr. Bernstein. Hans' motives are honorable, "I am in search of knowledge. I want to be the pupil of the finest medical brain in the world." The Baron, flattered by such devotion, replies, "I am not an easy man to work for. I wonder if I can trust you... Uncertainty is part of life!" Showing his young student his former wine garden laboratory located in the cellar of a building, young Hans slightly trips as the duo go down the steps. "It would be a pity to loose you!" The intent here is ambiguous: does the Baron feel backmailed and manipulated or does he welcome the opportunity to become a tutor to another inquisitive mind much like Paul Krempe was once his tutor. The Baron lectures Hans gleefully as resident "professor" showing him disembodied eyes and hands floating in beakers and bottles, sharing his proud secrets with his eager student. Thus, another kind side of the Baron is revealed.

As he reveals the inner demons which fuel his passion to continue his experiments, the Baron, greatly distressed, cries, "I made it to be perfect. If it wasn't damaged, the name of Frankenstein, my work, would be considered a genius of science! I swore I would have my revenge!" Then showing him the big secret behind the curtain in his lab, the upright bandaged body of the future Creature (Michael Gwynn), the Baron beams with pride, "This is something I am proud of... this time he is perfect!"

Once basic change occurs in the Baron's character: now in public view as Dr. Stein, he now hides his sarcasm and criticism under the cloak of polite manners. His tongue is just as critical but subtle and thinly veiled. For instance, when the Council members confront the Baron and tell him they have elected to have him join their prestigious order, the Baron displays his loathing for them. One Council member introduces himself, "I am the President of the Medical Council." To which the Baron responds, "Congratulations," smiling politely. Once he is offered the opportunity to join the medical group, the Baron turns angry and vicious. He claims when he first came to this town to set up his practice three years

Revenge's token woman Eunice Gayson attracts the interest of Richard Wordsworth in *The Revenge of Frankenstein*.

ago, he was met "with firm resistance" by the Council whose sole purpose, according to the Baron, is to "eliminate competition." Insisting he has "grown accustomed to working alone" and that he "enjoys it," he rebukes their oppressive invitation.

The Baron, except for his occasional sexual fling in *The Curse of Frankenstein*, is married to his work and has little time nor patience for women. The obnoxious female in this chapter is named Margaret (Eunice Gayson), the daughter of the town minister who insists she volunteer her time by working in the Poor Hospital. The Baron dare not insult the minister, a leading citizen, so he must put up with her intrusions. But he makes his intentions perfectly clear to her, "Margaret, I must ask you to keep out of the ward when I'm on duty." Here wonderful Richard Wordsworth (the victim of *The Creeping Unknown*) plays the sweeper, sort of the titular leader of the underprivileged hospital patients, who is always eager to impress Margaret. Warning her, "He cuts 'em up, alive! Brought a new one in the other day. Locked up in the attic; I have a master key!"

This "new one" is the latest creation of Frankenstein, the result of the brain transplant between poor physically-challenged Karl and the new unborn bits-and-pieces "perfect" body. As the Baron told Hans, Karl is "a very sound brain in that unfortunate body." The Baron's warning, "The brain will take time to adjust to the new body—this is only the beginning of our work!" If the brain is jarred or damaged before it has time to heal, the personality of the kindly Karl will change. These same experiments, attempted only upon chimp Otto earlier, resulted in the vegetarian chimp resorting to cannibalism: eating meat, against its natural nature.

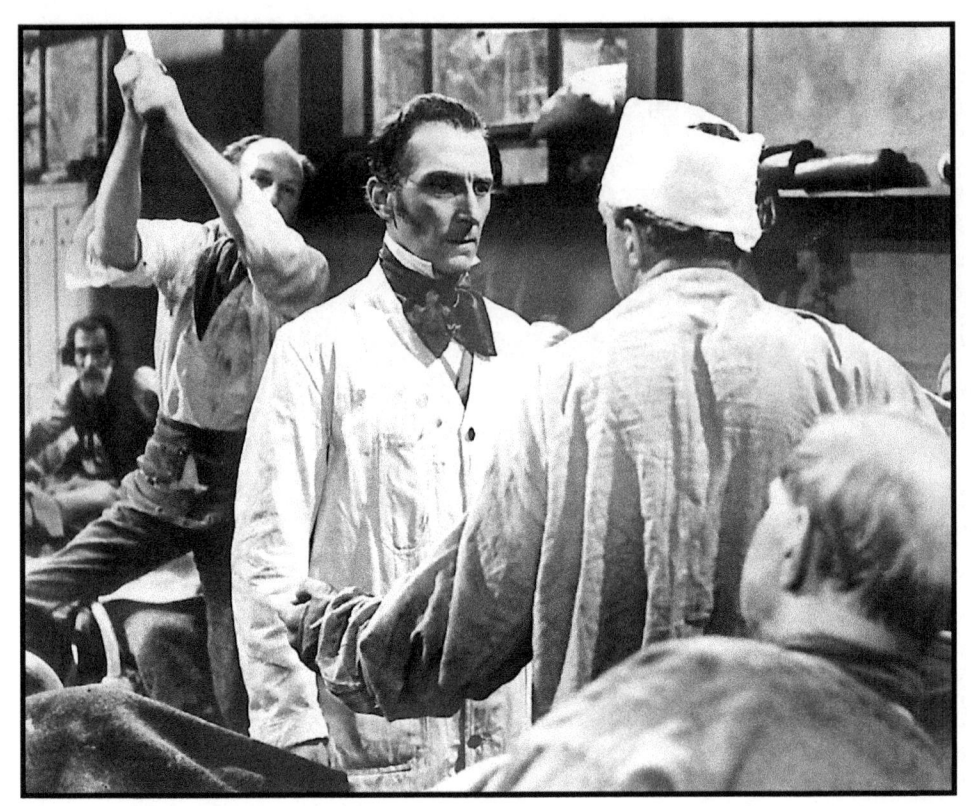

The formerly loved and trusted Baron's true plot is discovered by the enraged patients, who beat him to the point of death.

Of course, such is to be the fate of reborn Karl when the naïve Margaret, given the key to the locked bedroom door, allows the still-healing human release from his restraints, which allows him to get dressed and flee. Unfortunately, assistant Hans needlessly frightens Karl by telling him of the Baron's future plans, putting Karl and his old body on display for the scientific world to study. Once free, the first thing Karl does is return to the laboratory where he burns his old body. He is discovered and is sadistically pummeled by the janitor. After repeated blows to the face and head, Karl turns monstrous and chokes the bully to death. But the damage has been done. The Baron and Hans discover their experiment has flown the coup, Hans questions, "How did he undo the straps?" The Baron, challenging the limited thinking of his assistant, yells "Why, always why!!!" But Hans tells the Baron he told Karl of the Baron's future plans, the Baron immediately understanding the psychological implications, retorts with his customary, "You fool!" Then the Baron aggressively states, "Sooner or later he'd need my help. Go back to the ward. Do as I tell you!"

Later attending a society party, at the invitation of the Countess and her daughter, the Baron and Hans are introduced and the Baron smiles and turns on the charm as only Dr. Stein can. The drooling, crippled maniac that Karl has become crashes through the French windows and, recognizing Dr. Stein, blows his cover by holding the partygoers spellbound, "Frankenstein! Frankenstein!!! Help me!" after which he collapses and dies.

The war between Dr. Stein and the Medical Council now escalates with the announcement that Dr. Stein is in actuality Dr. Victor Frankenstein. As one Council member mutters, "This is the chance we have been waiting for!"

Hans, afraid for the Baron's life, pleads with him to flee town, to start afresh somewhere else. But the Baron's pride won't allow him to run away. After being "ordered" to appear before the Medical Council, the Baron plays his innocence by lying through his teeth, all with customary believability and expertise. "Gentlemen, I deny it absolutely. There are dozens of Frankensteins. I am a Frankenstein. But I did not want to be handicapped by that name so I changed it... I think a little proof instead of a lot of gossip would be advantageous."

However, returning to his Poor Ward, the Baron is greeted with utter silence, looks of hatred, and suspicious eyes from those patients, who had previously loved and trusted the good doctor. The Baron inquires of one patient, "How's the head?" The man replies, "Keep your murdering hands off me, Frankenstein. Murderer! Murderer!!" Bottles fly at the Baron—flung by unknown hands behind him. He is knocked unconscious when a wooden crutch beans him over the head, again from behind. Then the mob of patients swarm around the bloodied Baron kicking and stomping him to near death. Hans intervenes and carries the broken, lifeless body back to the laboratory.

"Hans, it's no good... You know what to do!!" the Baron desperately states.

Conveniently, the Baron has stitched together an exact replica of himself, ready for a brain transfer in the event that he needed a new body (complete with tattooed arm no less). During the middle of the operation when the police and members of the Council arrive, Hans produces the dead body of the original Baron to the satisfaction of all. "The body must be buried in unhallowed ground!" Once they leave, Hans continues the operation, "Pray heaven I have the skill to do this."

The scene changes to London as the mobile camera enters the clinic of one Dr. Franck, the now mustachioed Peter Cushing, once again dressed debonairly, he places a flower in his lapel. Opening the door to his study, he turns on his charm and welcomes the latest aristocratic patients. The Baron to Hans, "You are an excellent pupil. This scar will hardly show."

In *Curse* Cushing was all pout and attitude. His character was consistent and clearly defined, unchanging, the same above as below the surface. Cushing's genius and exuberance elevated his performance well beyond a mad stereotype, but as written, the script limited his ability to expand upon the characterization. Here, in *Revenge*, Jimmy Sangster's much-improved script allows Peter Cushing the latitude to subtlety expand upon the Baron's character. We have the Baron pretending to be either Dr. Stein or Dr. Franck, respected, polite, and mannerly member of affluent English society. But underneath the surface, we have a not quite so mad scientist who still believes the ends justify the means. A doctor who devotes his time to the free clinic for the poor, seemingly out of a sense of humanity but in reality out of the need to dissect and amputate perfectly healthy subjects for their body

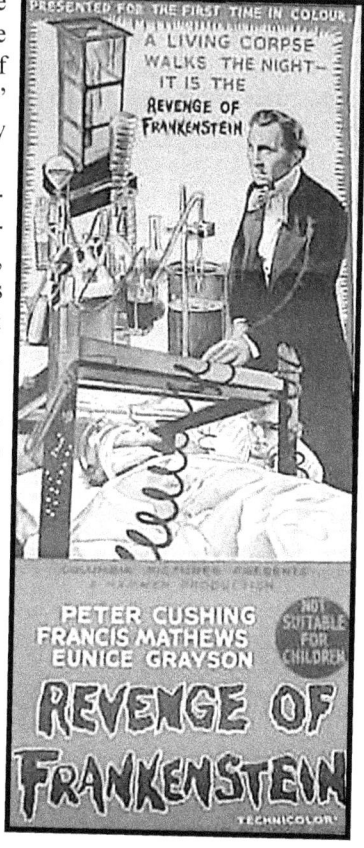

Australian poster for *The Revenge of Frankenstein*, notice the misspelling of Eunice Gayson's name.

parts. The Baron loathes humanity both in the larger sense (he hates the pomposity of the Medical Council, the status quo dictators of the norms of society) and the smaller sense (his disdain for Margaret, his manipulation of the Countess, the cruel mutilation of the tattooed-armed patient). Instead of immediately telegraphing his every thought and impulse, the more subtle character of the Baron is revealed through exposing and contrasting his false (debonair) external self to his true (cruel and heartless) internal self. At last, with *The Revenge of Frankenstein*, the character of Baron Frankenstein was coming into its own.

"Why can't they ever leave me alone!"
THE EVIL OF FRANKENSTEIN
[1964; Screenplay by John Elder (Anthony Hinds); Directed by Freddie Francis]

The image of Baron Frankenstein near the end of Hammer's *The Evil of Frankenstein* casts Peter Cushing in dashing Indiana Jones-style grandeur. After escaping cleverly from prison by tricking the prison guard, Cushing steals a horsedrawn carriage, and using a whip to motivate the horse, rides the carriage standing up, the wind blowing through his disheveled hair. Is this the image of villain?

Earlier, returning to his family chateau after 10 years in exile, the Baron becomes outraged to learn that all his family heirlooms, furniture, carpets, etc. have been cleared out and apparently sold. Later seeing his ring on the Burgomaster's finger, the Baron causes quite a scene in a local pub by yelling for the police to "arrest that man!" while his new assistant Hans (this time played by Sandor Eles) spirits the fugitive scientist out of harm's way.

Later that evening, the Baron triumphantly invades the elegant Burgomaster's home, seething with frustration over the fact that he himself is in desperate need of money for his research and that the above-the-law Burgomaster is living in high style off ill-gotten gains. "I've come for my property... my ring!" Looking around the home, the Baron's eyes bug half way out of his head as he sees half his possessions here! "My desk, my carpet—even my bed!" which at the moment is occupied by the Burgomaster's wife, a buxomy blonde who seems more than a little "in the mood." In dashing rogue hero style, the Baron escapes from the bedroom by tying a blanket to the end of the brass bed climbing rapidly outside the window, stopping momentarily to give the Burgomaster's sexy wife an all-knowing wink.

Yes, the image of the Baron has changed remarkably since his last incarnation. The screenplays by Jimmy Sangster have been replaced by John Elder's, and director Terence Fisher has been replaced by former cinematographer Freddie Francis (supposedly Hammer was upset at Fisher since his last Hammer horror, *The Phantom of the Opera*, was not a smash hit). Compared to the original conception of the Baron in *Curse*, Cushing here plays an outlaw hero where all authority figures surrounding him are more loathsome and despicable than he ever was. Sure the Baron dabbles in dead bodies and grave stealing, but ethically this is small potatoes compared to the grand larceny of the Burgomaster and the abuse of power dictated by the Chief of Police. The bottom line is that the Baron is a man of dignity and determination.

And if the Burgomaster and Chief of Police aren't villain enough, enter Zoltan (Peter Woodthrope), the greedy, maniacal hypnotist. After the Baron reanimates his pathetic (both from the viewpoint of makeup execution and character) Monster (this was the first Hammer Frankenstein film released by Universal, so for the first time the Monster could dare to approximate Karloff's Monster concept), the Baron disappointedly discovers that the

Baron Frankenstein and Hans (Sandor Eles) once again reanimate the Monster in *The Evil of Frankenstein.*

Creature's brain has been so damaged that he needs the help of the hypnotist to reach the Creature's subconscious to bring him back. The manipulative Zoltan realizes the power he can wield if he keeps the Monster under his own control and not under the Baron's. Threatening to leave the creature in a dormant state, the Baron, against Hans' wishes, agrees to Zoltan's terms.

Of course, Zoltan, who has just been run out of town by the Chief of Police, wants a little old-fashioned revenge and this allows him to put the Monster under his direct control. At night he sends the fiend out to steal gold and kill his enemies. For the first time Hammer's resurrected "Creature" becomes a zombified killing machine, who under direct command of the evil Zoltan, blindly maims and destroys in the stereotypical Monster manner.

Unlike the more imaginative Jimmy Sangster who was moving the series further and further away from the Universal 1940s' image of the Monster, John Elder embraced all the weak qualities of both the Hammer and Universal series to meld this, the most disappointing of the entire Cushing series. However, Cushing's Baron Frankenstein has been fine-tuned by the enthusiastic thespian to the point that his characterization no longer needs direction or an effective script. Cushing's Baron brilliantly survives the transition to a new (inferior) director and script writer. And instead of portraying the insidious villain, Cushing's Baron here becomes the self-sacrificing hero.

Peter Cushing, as the underdog, misunderstood man of scientist, gains the sympathy of the audience from the opening reel. The film's best sequence, a pre-credits prelude, involves the mourning for a recently dead peasant, laid out on a large wooden table at dusk.

Zoltan (Peter Woodthrope) becomes the main villain, rather than the Baron or Monster (Kiwi Kingston), of *The Evil of Frankenstein*.

Suddenly, a large window near the table flies open, the raging wind instantly blowing out the illuminating candles near the body. Suddenly, mysteriously, someone pulls the body across the table swiftly out the window. We then see the smiling face of a graverobber, throwing the corpse over his shoulder, quickly arriving at the laboratory of Baron Frankenstein. The graverobber tells the Baron the obvious, that he has brought a body for his research, to which Cushing dryly states, "So I've observed... and so will half the county if you don't get it inside!" During the movie's credits the physically intense Baron removes the corpse's heart declaring, "He doesn't have any more use for it" (paralleling a similar line from *Curse*).

Frankenstein orders the much younger and more virile assistant Hans to "start the wheel," the youth grunts and strains to physically start the huge wheel turning. Hans has no luck until the Baron almost pushes him out of the way and, utilizing all his strength, gets the wheel spinning mostly by his own power and force of will. The movie quickly establishes the Baron as a man of dedication, perseverance, and strength, values that movie heroes frequently display.

And to firmly establish the Baron's heroic underdog image, in the midst of his experiment the laboratory is invaded by the county priest, a stereotypical "hell and brimstone" variety clergyman. "Get rid of them Hans." However, the priest and his mob storm the lab, the priest yelling words of blasphemy and damnation, using a cane to break beakers and lab tanks, one containing the recently rejuvenated human heart. Baron Frankenstein, with a look of outrage, cries, "You realize you are trespassing, you are interrupting my work."

Seeing the damage already done, the Baron has to be physically restrained by Hans. "Destroyed! They always destroy everything!"

The Elder screenplay even establishes the priest as symbolizing the blind hatred and fear inherent in the members of society who destroy what they do not understand, assuming new knowledge to be evil knowledge. For a change we see the priest as villain and scientist/explorer as rogue hero. And actor Peter Cushing seems energized by this ever-evolving complexity.

Throughout *The Evil of Frankenstein*, the Baron constantly states,"Anything that doesn't conform... they have to destroy. They haven't beaten me. I won't let them beat me!!!" Sadly, at movie's end, after the Baron's chateau explodes, the Baron apparently dead inside, Hans bemoans, "They beat him after all."

Zoltan (Peter Woodthrope) becomes the movie's chief villain (one of a wide variety of villains) by virtue of his manipulative and self-centered urges. Both the Baron and Zoltan are ostracized from the community, but Zoltan is a profiteer, thief, and ultimately a murderer while the Baron displays loftier virtues. The Baron here is displayed as a man of honor and dignity. After forcing the Baron to accept his deal that only Zoltan controls the Monster, Zoltan extends his hand and says, "Let's shake on it." Frankenstein, disdaining the opportunist hypnotist, simply replies, "No need... I've given my word."

At the film's explosive climax, after Zoltan is savagely speared by the Monster and dies, the Creature drinks a bottle of chloroform, becoming violently ill, catching the chateau on fire. The Baron immediately tries to attend to the needs of the Creature telling Hans and the mute servant girl to "get away from here." Displaying the best aspects of the self-sacrificing hero, the Baron wishes to save the young innocents and would rather die in the fiery inferno rather than see his creation suffer or harm anyone. One of Cushing's final sequences involves the dashing scientist swinging Errol Flynn style across his lab on a chain, contradicting the standard image of mad scientist as a crotchety old man who toddles around the laboratory. No, as *The Evil of Frankenstein* establishes, the Baron, formerly the evil monster maker, is here shown to be the romantic, charismatic monster destroyer and ultimately the film's hero.

"Bodies are easy to come by, souls are not!"
—FRANKENSTEIN CREATED WOMAN
[1966; Screenplay by John Elder (Anthony Hinds); Directed by Terence Fisher]

Continuing with a screenplay by John Elder and returning Terence Fisher to the director's chair, *Frankenstein Created Woman* is an improvement over *The Evil of Frankenstein*, boasting one of the most off-beat scenarios of the entire series; John Elder, following the lead of Jimmy Sangster, creates a story which moves far beyond the Universal mythos, his major failing the first time around. Unfortunately, while the aging Peter Cushing looks wonderful as the Baron, his character has been reduced once again to being one dimensional and his screen time has also been clipped.

For the first time in the series, the subplot, this time involves the love relationship between a deformed girl, Christina (Susan Denberg), and the Baron's assistant, Hans (this time played by Robert Morris). It details how Hans (the son of a guillotined murderer) is framed for the murder of Christina's father by three rich louts and overrides the Baron's tale. While the story is novel, creating a strong sense of pathos, it leaves little for the Baron and his new doctor/assistant Dr. Hertz (sympathetically played by Thorley Walters in one of his best roles) to do except restore the executed Han's soul into the resurrected Christi-

The Baron ponders the mysteries of the soul in *Frankenstein Created Woman*.

na's body (now recreated as a blonde centerfold playmate) and watch as the soul of Hans, commanding the actions of Christina, seeks revenge on the three louts who never paid for the murder of Christina's father.

This entry does contain some wonderful sequences with the Baron, especially the film's novel beginning which establishes Baron Frankenstein as the continually resurrected star of the series (unlike the Universal series where the Monster was constantly being reborn). Here, in a tense sequence, Dr. Hertz is counting down the minutes until exactly one hour has passed. The elderly, dazed doctor yells for a drink from young assistant Hans, who hands Hertz the entire bottle. Suddenly, the ice chamber door is opened and a huge metal coffin is wheeled out onto a conveyor rack. The crate lid is opened to reveal the deathlike, crystalized Baron Frankenstein. Quickly, wires are attached to the Baron and then to a huge metal grid overhead. Electrical charges are blasted into the Baron, quickly reviving the scientist who had been dead for one hour. "See Hans, he's alive," Hertz proudly announces. Smelling salts bring the frozen doctor to consciousness.

"Of course I'm alive. For one whole hour I was dead. It was an hour, wasn't it? Why has my soul remained... why!"

In a dramatic twist of convention, the Baron is literally resurrected—brought back from the dead in the film's first few minutes. By now, with this fourth entry in Hammer's Frankenstein series, it has been established that Cushing's Baron is the entire motivation for the films.

Once again the quaint town and its close-minded citizens become the villains, the enemy of the man of science. "He's some sort of monster in league with the devil himself,"

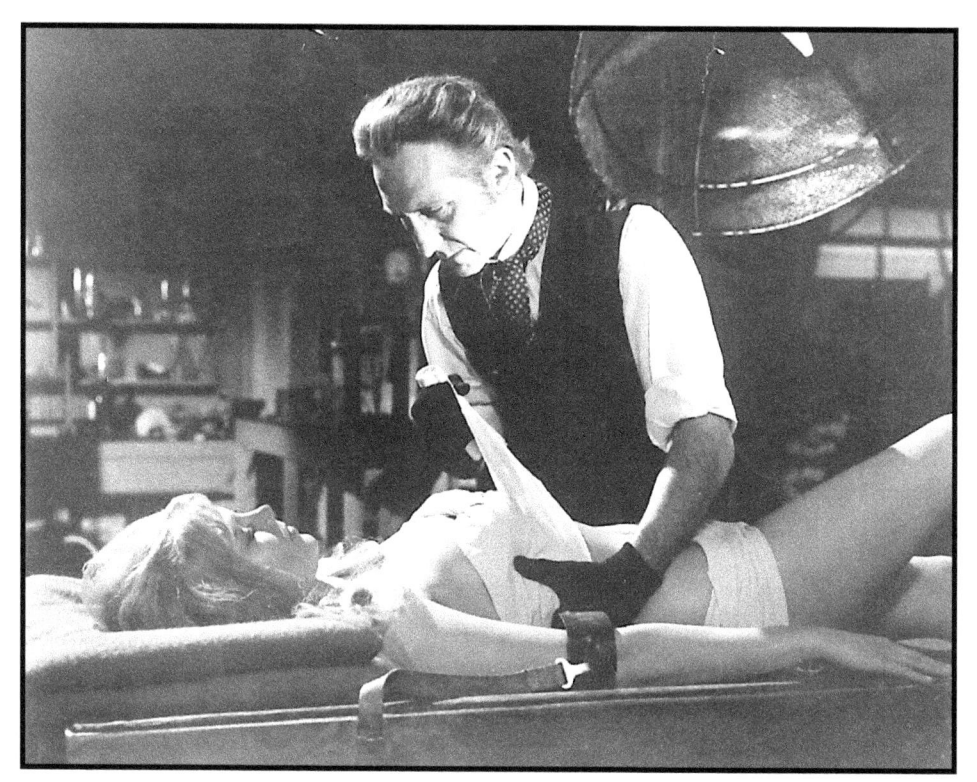

This Frankenstein Creature is the dishy Susan Denberg who seeks revenge on those who mistreated her before she was beautiful.

a citizen proclaims. Hans, who defends the Baron and his work, responds, "If it is a choice between him and they, I would pick him every time."

The other more visible villains are three rich young punks, sons of the elite of the community, who spend all their time dressed as fancy dandies drinking, partying and yet somehow they always come up short when it is time to pay their bill. The arrogance and callowness of the rich elite make this *Frankenstein* entry very class conscious. The Baron and Hertz are shown to be poorer than poor (with all their available cash going into the cost of their scientific apparatus) failing to even come up with the money needed to buy a simple bottle of champagne—the Baron sends Hans to the local Inn to tell the landlord to put the champagne on his account. Later journeying to the pub for a meal, the Baron cleverly tells one of the louts who has been wounded in a knife fight with Hans—who had been protecting the honor of Christina—that Dr. Hertz will render first-aid for a "slight charge," just enough to pay for the meal. The Baron, who was depicted as the epitome of aristocratic arrogance in the premiere entry, is now reduced to being one of the common folk to contrast his noble endeavors to the shallowness of the rich elite.

Unfortunately, Cushing's Baron here resembles Sherlock Holmes (Rathbone style) and Walter's Dr. Hertz resembles Dr. Watson (Nigel Bruce's doddering old fool). The wizened Baron is very impatient with those ordinary people who fail to immediately comprehend his work. "Haven't you grasped anything I've been doing these last six months?" to which the diligent, dedicated Dr. Hertz humbly responds that he is just a drunken old muddle-head. But the truth remains that the Baron's hands have been damaged (a possible tie-in to the explosive finale to *The Evil of Frankenstein*?), a fact made clear by the black gloves the Baron wears. When carrying a coffin later in the film, the Baron grunts and grimaces in pain. Earlier, while working in the lab, the Baron is unable to twist a dial and needs assistance. During the all-important surgery, Hertz admits, "The hands were mine; the skill was his!" While Cushing is constantly reminding the kindly Dr. Hertz what he doesn't know and how ignorant he is, the fact remains that the Baron depends upon Hertz's medical skills and steady hands to carry out all his work. And the Baron's cold, cruel self-centeredness makes Hertz all the more lovable.

The Baron still has authority problems in *Frankenstein Created Woman*.

When his young assistant Hans is on trial for a murder he did not commit, Cushing speaks on his behalf in court, politely compassionate yet looking annoyingly at his watch as if precious time is being wasted. "I am a doctor of medicine, law, psychics," and when he is accused of witchcraft, declares that he would have a degree in that too if one were offered. When the court sarcastically accuses him of being a clever man, the Baron proudly retorts, "Yes I am." The Baron quickly sputters out that Hans has been "trustworthy, diligent, quick-witted," etc. and that as a scientist he would conclude, "it is extremely unlikely that he could commit murder." When countered with the question: "Impossible?", the Baron glumly responds, "No, not impossible."

As soon as Hans is convicted on circumstantial evidence, instead of mourning the fact, the Baron is almost exuberant, "This is our chance!" To which Dr. Hertz asks, "Is it right?" To which the Baron states, "What is right" explaining he plans to capture Han's soul in his apparatus. As he cheerfully tells Hertz, "Bodies are easy to come by, souls are not!"

The Baron's theory is a simple one: that the human soul doesn't leave the body at the instant of death. If the soul can be contained while the body is repaired, the soul and body can later be united after the body has been "fixed." The arrogant doctor declares, "This is not supposition, it's a fact!" to which he finally summarizes, "I have conquered death!" The Baron's ego has not seen this amount of inflation since *The Curse of Frankenstein*.

When the Hans/Christina Creature murders two of the young louts who framed Hans for the murder of Christina's father, the town begins to suspect that the Baron's witchcraft is behind this violent murder spree. "Is this why you interrupt my work! For this fantasy!!" When the police announce they might have to take steps, the Baron indignantly responds, "You mean you will burn me!" Instantly calming himself, he now speaks to reason. "What can I do to convince you that you are wrong... How can I make you understand? The murderer will strike again unless I get to her first... It seems you beheaded the wrong man!" The police respond, "You take us for fools!" to which the Baron quickly and honestly says, "Yes!!!"

During the 1960s, the elderly Baron's disdain for authority made him a hero to the youth who purchased the tickets. Today, his pompous self-importance seems less heroic.

Yet, even with all his pomposity and posturing, the audience still sides with the often too demanding Baron.

In an abrupt finale, the Baron once again utilizing a horse-drawn carriage to catch up to the murdering Christina/Hans creature (she carries the head of her decapitated lover in her hat box and his spirit gives her murderous commands), the Baron arrives a moment too late, finding the stabbed-to-death corpse of the third hoodlum as Christina is told by the head that she can now rest, which means a suicidal leap into a raging river. The Baron slowly walks away in disgust.

While Cushing's performance is kinetic, verbally sharp, and comfortable (for the Baron must now seem to Cushing like an old pair of broken-in slippers), the script once again lessens his importance and reduces his characterization to a one-dimensional stereotype. At least *The Evil of Frankenstein*, a far inferior film, kept the Baron front and center and pivotal to the story. Here, in *Frankenstein Created Woman* we once again yearn for the complexities of character which the last three entries introduced and developed.

"Stupidity does bring out the worst in me!"
FRANKENSTEIN MUST BE DESTROYED
[1969; Screenplay by Bert Batt (from an original story by producer Anthony Nelson Keys and Batt); Directed by Terence Fisher]

After two screenplays by Jimmy Sangster where Baron Frankenstein's character was primarily evil and two screenplays by John Elder whereby the virtuous and heroic qualities of the character emerge, now the screenplay by Bert Batt invigorates the series with Hammer's finest *Frankenstein* script yet. Developing Sangster's conception of Baron Frankenstein rather than Elder's, Bert Batt restores the Baron as an inherently evil personality, a person more loathsome than Karloff's Frankenstein Monster could ever hope to be. And finally, Hammer has the budget to produce an "A" quality production, again directed by Terence Fisher, which features Peter Cushing in practically every scene, the major flaw with *Frankenstein Created Woman*. Many consider *Frankenstein Must Be Destroyed* to be the finest entry in the series, and while some may still prefer *Revenge of Frankenstein*, this production highlights Hammer at its creative peak.

Just as the James Bond films became famous for pre-credit sequences which had little to do with the ensuing movie, Hammer here has fun with resurrecting Baron Frankenstein one more time. The movie unfurls with a closeup on another hat box (a carryover image from *Created Woman*) and another ghastly decapitation. Frankenstein's subterranean laboratory is broken into (a reference to the lab in *Revenge of Frankenstein*). He gasps as he sees an "unborn" body hanging suspended in a glass case (another reference to *Revenge*), the intruder is surprised by the sudden appearance of a horrible looking fiend who carries the hat box containing the severed head. The two struggle, damaging the lab in the process, until the thief runs off. Suddenly, the fiend pulls the fake rubber mask from his face, reveal-

The Baron is at his most evil in *Frankenstein Must Be Destroyed*.

ing the dashing features of Peter Cushing. Once again, this rather silly premise of having the Baron wear a Halloween mask as camouflage when committing murder becomes a strong visual image to introduce the returning Baron, almost intended as a wink to fans of the Hammer series.

But from this point, the film becomes very somber and ultimately depressing, establishing a far darker, realistic tone to this entry.

The youth interest is supplied by handsome Simon Ward (Dr. Karl Holst) and lovely Veronica Carlson (Anna), pawns in the manipulative game of Frankenstein. Fleeing his laboratory at the film's beginning, the Baron rents a room at the boarding house of Anna, single, who runs the establishment alone, using all her money to pay for expensive hospital bills for her critically ill mother. Financial help comes from Dr. Holst, Anna's fiancé, who claims, "Illegal drugs are one market where money does not dry up." In charge of drugs at the mental hospital where he works, Holst changes the records to hide his illegal activity, all the profit going to pay for Anna's mother's medical expenses.

Unfortunately, the Baron overhears this conversation while he is just outside the front door. Holst, inside, realizes he dropped a box of cocaine on the doorstep, now conveniently found by the Baron who, smiling politely, returns the box to Holst. "I found this on your doorstep... it's cocaine, isn't it?" Holtz and Anna excuse themselves, but the Baron charges to the door, turns, and declares, "Neither of you are going anywhere tonight. Both of you are involved in very illegal business!" The young doctor thinks the Baron wants blackmail money, but instead, he announces "I want your help."

The first favor immediately occurs when the Baron has Anna eject all four of the guests staying in the boarding house. The night before, the tenants were describing the Baron as "damn surly" and as one who hardly ever manages to say one word to the others. Enter the Baron who immediately goes to his own corner of the parlour sitting at a desk with his back to the others. They discuss "the worst madman of the decade, Dr. Frederick Brandt" who five years earlier caused "such a furor" in the medical world with the "devilish notion" of transplanting brains. They also mention another doctor who shared the same idea, Baron Frankenstein from Bohemia. "Ran him out of his country as well." Both are referred to as "the devil's disciples."

The Baron, listening to all this talk, calmly and politely interjects, "Excuse me, I didn't know you were doctors!" The tenants immediately announce they are not. "Ah, I thought you knew what you were talking about... stupidity brings out the worst in me... fools like you." The pompous guests all express outrage and declare their new guest to be extremely rude. Debating the use of the word "progress" as the Baron uses it, the Baron draws a parallel for them. "Man is given to invention and experiment. If that were not true, we would still be eating in caves, stringing bones about the floor, and wiping our fingers on animal skins. In fact, your lapels do look kind of greasy... Good night!!" Of course the Baron cannot continue his experiments with these closed-minded gentlemen around.

When the Baron announces who he really is, Karl Holst proclaims, "I thought the world has seen the last of you!" And then the Baron announces his plans: to rescue Dr. Brandt from the mental hospital, cure his insanity, and learn Brandt's theories on transplanting the human brain, the work of which the Baron admits has progressed further than his own. And since Karl works as a doctor in the hospital, the Baron needs his assistance to supply floor plans, supply entrance to rooms, and aid in sedating other patients during the kidnapping.

The Baron's self-professed righteous cause is preserving the brains of the great minds of the world. He claims their bodies get sick and die, the bodies are buried and rot while the mind is at the peak of its development. Brain transplants would allow the bodies to be fixed and the brain to be returned, just as his theory of capturing the human soul while the body was being repaired was established in the last entry.

Of course, after the kidnapping of Brandt from the hospital, Brandt suffers a heart attack and will die unless the Baron transplants his brain into a new body immediately; the ideal choice is one Dr. Richter, one of the chief doctors who works in the mental hospital. Karl realizes one life would have to be sacrificed: "That would be murder!" The Baron, smiling, states, "You're used to that by now." (referring to Karl's earlier murder of an elderly night watchman in the drug supply storage room).

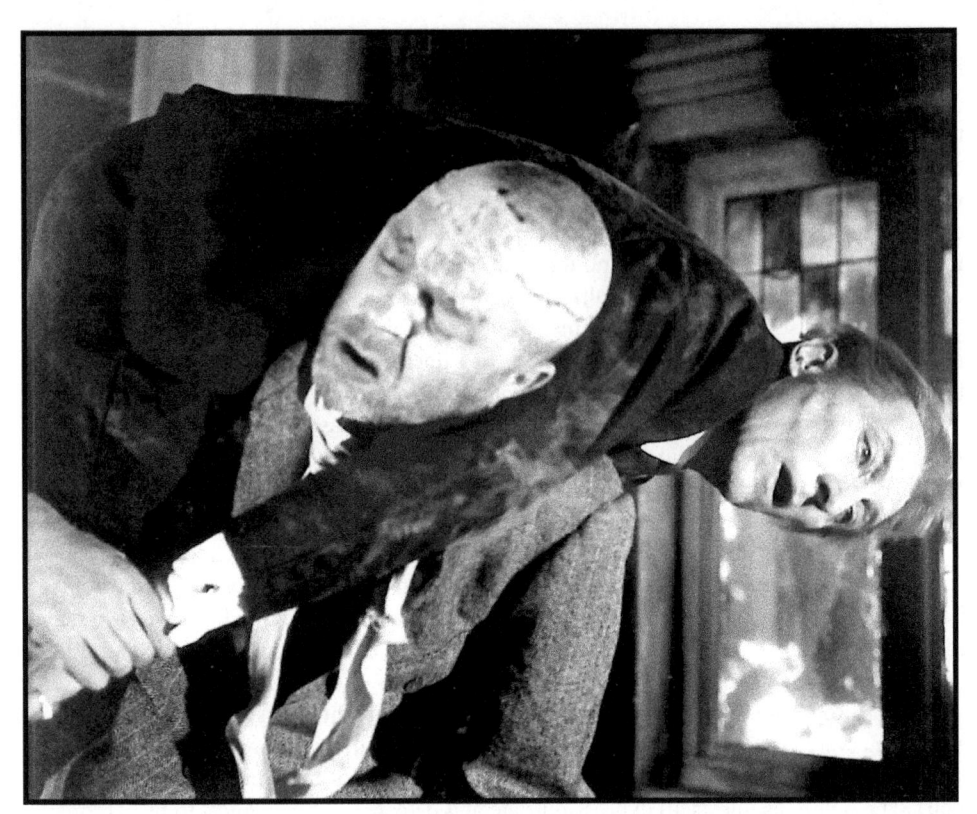

The Creature (Freddie Jones), unhappy with being reborn, has plans for a fitting end for the Baron.

Very interesting is Frankenstein's relationship to the beautiful Anna, a person the Baron seems to enjoy terrifying. Assisting the Baron in examining Brandt after he is first kidnapped, Anna is cleaning up the superficial cuts on his face as the doctor listens to Brandt's heart. Finishing up and walking away, the Baron screams at her, "I'm not done yet!" Constantly, throughout the movie, the Baron demands that Anna make him coffee. But Karl claims the Baron does not need Anna and demands he let her go, but he calmly counters, "I need her—to make coffee." The ultimate outrage occurs when Anna is preparing for bed in her room, her sensuous form silhouetted under her nightgown by the lamp light as the Baron passes by her room and stops. "Please leave my room," she implores. The Baron locks the door from the inside, and she demands firmly that he give her the key, holding her robe up to cover her scantily clad figure. He holds out his hand with the key in it, but as Anna pensively approaches him, he throws the key on the bed, to which she races. There the Baron animalistically attacks Anna, ripping apart the back of her gown, throwing her down on the bed, he on top of her. As the passive Anna squirms and screams, the Baron cruelly satisfies his sexual appetite.

The Baron's debonair and outwardly aristocratic attitude, always calm and under control when interacting in public, sometimes less controlled internally or when around people such as Holtz who know the real personality, can best be seen in the sequence involving Brandt's wife recognizing the Baron on the streets as he buys a flower for his coat lapel. Following Frankenstein to the boarding house, she knocks on the door and inquires, "Is Baron Frankenstein staying here?" Thinking cleverly and rapidly on his feet, the smiling and charming scientist breaks to the front door and states, "It was my intention to call on you this evening. Your husband is here. It was the only way I had to save him," referring to the fact that if he had asked to experiment on her husband, she would have definitely denied him access.

Taking this woman who has been in contact with the police seemingly into his confidence, he continues, "It was within my power to help him. He's downstairs––he is safe." The Baron, very accommodating, very helpful, leads Mrs. Brandt into the cellar and shows her the bandaged form of her husband (unknown to her, his brain now in another man's body). There the Baron allows her to ask her husband questions which he can answer with a simple yes or no using his left hand. The Baron smiles, "He's cured!" Showing Mrs. Brandt upstairs, he insists, "You must never speak of this to anyone. You may come here anytime to visit. In one week you and he can begin a new life."

Dr. Karl Holtz (Simon Ward) unwillingly helps the Baron operate on Richter/Brandt.

Showing the satisfied Mrs. Brandt to the front door and slowly closing the door behind her, the Baron frantically turns and shouts, "Pack! We're leaving." In other words, we once again see the difference between the cultured gentleman persona which the Baron easily assumes and the cutthroat, manipulative, cold persona within. And Cushing plays this ambiguity with such craft and energy.

Several sequences throughout the movie show the majestic Baron sitting most elegantly in his padded chair, smoking a cigar, snipping on delicate cup of tea/coffee, propped up in front of the fireplace. Contrasted to this elite comfort, being waited on hand and foot by Karl and mostly Anna, the beast in the Baron, lurking just below the surface, often emerges showing his savage side. Karl plans to escape by stealing a carriage from the stables, the Baron mysteriously appears and says, "What are you doing, Karl!" The two immediately fight, and while the Baron must be twice as old as the youthful Karl, the physically adept Baron wins the slugfest. Anna, inside, is confronted by the now conscious and freely walking Richter/Brandt creature. In fear, wielding a scalpel, Anna stabs the misunderstood resurrected man and, in a daze, sits on the stairs holding the bloody instrument. Returning, the Baron hears from Anna's own lips what she has done (the stab wound was not severe) and in immediate rage plunges the knife into Anna's lower chest killing her instantly. Never has the evil of the Baron been delivered quite so callously and in such a cold manner.

At the film's again fiery climax, the disappointed Brandt, not happy with being reborn in another man's body, plots a fitting end for the Baron. Pulling out his notes which he realizes is the Baron's only reason for keeping him alive, he places the papers on his desk and places oil lamps all around the house pouring kerosene throughout. Once the Baron arrives, Brandt plays a game of cat and mouse, "I fancy I am the spider and you are the fly," setting the house ablaze and challenging the Baron to find the room where the papers are before everything goes up in smoke. Just barely finding the brain transplant notes in time, racing frantically out of the house, the Baron is tripped by the just-arriving avenging Karl who is struck unconscious by Brandt who drags the Baron, kicking and screaming, back into the flaming inferno to both their supposed deaths.

In sharp contrast to the dignified, eccentric yet highly likeable Baron of the John Elder scripted movies, Bert Batt reconstructs Baron Victor Frankenstein as a pompous, self-centered, manipulative, cruel bastard, a role performed brilliantly by Peter Cushing. Many Hammer fans sometimes wish the Hammer series had ended here on this artistic high note, but one more Frankenstein film was to follow, the final film directed by the aging Terence Fisher.

Ten days! If I've succeeded, every sacrifice would have been worthwhile!"
FRANKENSTEIN AND THE MONSTER FROM HELL
[1974; Screenplay by John Elder (Anthony Hinds); Directed by Terence Fisher]

By the mid-1970s, Peter Cushing looked older than his years, his body too thin, his face hollow and gaunt, obviously wearing a curly-haired wig for his final performance as the Baron. And while the aging Terence Fisher would never again direct another film (he would die in 1976), this also spelled the final major performance for Peter Cushing in a Hammer Film. And while most critics easily dismiss this film's importance, it is a wonderful, fitting finale to an important series.

Once again John Elder (Anthony Hinds) submits the screenplay, his finest entry in the series, again returning the Baron to more sympathetic, heroic proportions, although not the dashing romantic hero of *Evil* nor the one-dimensional obsessive seeker of knowledge of *Created Woman*. John Elder finally got the complexities of the Baron right, submitting a script that allows Peter Cushing to add a new dimension to his faithful old friend the Baron. And while Hammer's faltering budget was beginning to show somewhat, Terence Fisher mounted a wonderful production with a creepy asylum set and superior acting by even the bit players. Though unjustly maligned and viewed as fluff when compared to *Must Be Destroyed*, *Frankenstein and the Monster From Hell* is one of the best entries in the series, both from the point of view of overall story, acting, and Cushing's always impressive

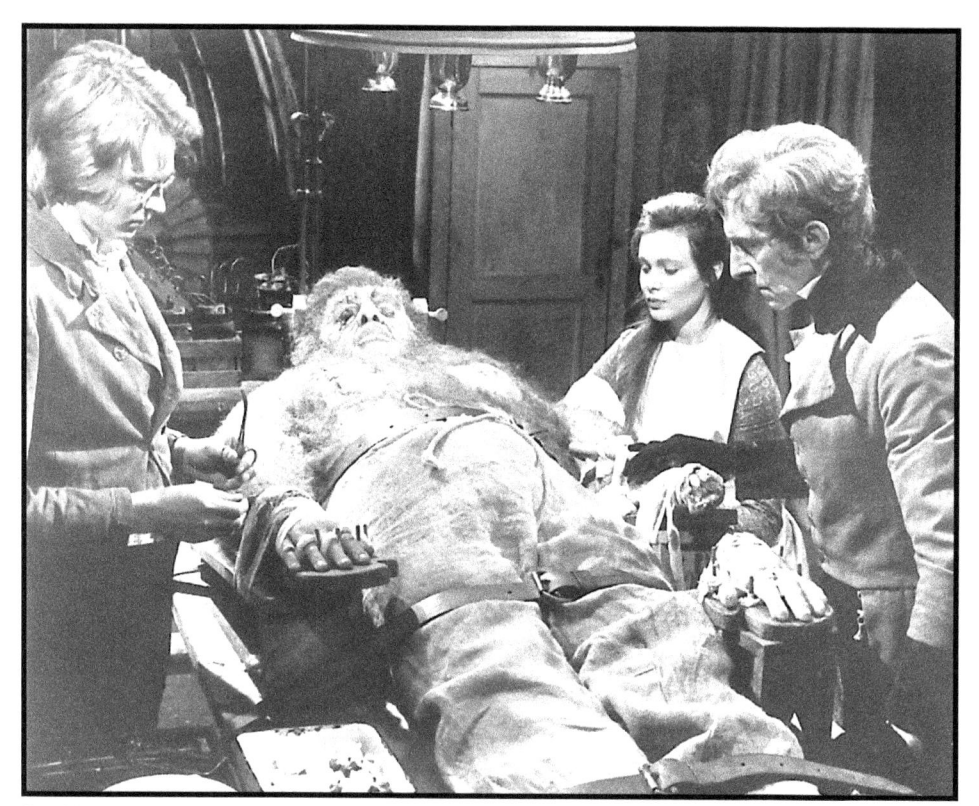

Dr. Simon Helder (Shane Briant) and Sarah (Madeline Smith) operate on the Monster (David Prowse) in *Frankenstein and the Monster from Hell*.

performance. The film is only compromised by the horrible makeup of the Monster (here played by Dave Prowse) which rivals the ineptness of the monster in *Evil*.

By this time the Baron's work has been published and copied by eager apprentices, in this case Dr. Simon Helder (Shane Briant), a man who pays for corpses from graverobbers. Unfortunately, the police are able to trace these nefarious affairs to Helder's home laboratory where a policeman finds the stolen corpse and a jar of human eyeballs. Panicking, the officer spills the eyes to the disgust of the doctor—"You bloody fool. If only you could appreciate the difficulty in getting specimens like these!" Calmly admitting he plans to "stitch them [body parts] together to create a new man," the doctor is arrested for "sorcery" and sentenced by a lenient judge to five years in the State Asylum for the Criminally Insane. Young Helder protests, "I am a doctor, you know. I've been involved in research... for the good of mankind," but the judge is not impressed reminding the young doctor that he sentenced, years ago, a Baron Frankenstein to the same asylum for similar offenses. At this point Simon's eyes light up.

Arriving at the medieval appearing asylum, the cruel guards give the cooperative surgeon an "initiation" whereby he is bathed with a fire hose which bloodies him and knocks him unconscious. As all the inmates stand around enjoying this sadistic entertainment, the festivities are brought to a somber conclusion by the sudden appearance of the resident physician at the asylum, Baron Victor Frankenstein!

"Go back to your rooms. It's all over. Quietly, don't rush." To the guards, he snaps in a firmer tone, "You will follow me... " The Baron quickly leads them to the office of

The Monster's brain is replaced with the brain of a musical genius.

the Asylum Director, a quirky, nervous sort who talks too much as though to hide his insecurity. At this point the Baron catches the Director with a half-dressed girl, obviously an inmate with whom he has been having intimate relations. "Don't act like an animal toward my patients!" the Baron yells. "If that happens again, I'll leave this place. The Baron is dead, remember? As resident doctor I can leave." Demanding the Director reprimand the guards for their cruelty, the Director immediately obeys the Baron's demands—Frankenstein is obviously running the place, a fitting metaphor for the lunatics taking over the asylum. The Baron complains to the Director that he has been unable to pick up his special medical supplies because past bills have not been paid. The Director agrees to rectify the situation immediately—after the Baron reminds him that the asylum's budget for library books does not include rare collector's items such as the ones on the Director's desk. It is apparent that the clever Baron has dug up enough dirt on the Director that he can now call the shots. After at first refusing the brandy the Director offers, the Baron now says, "I'll take that brandy." The Director, smiling, assumes the Baron will drink with him here in his office. "No, I'll take it with me. I have work to do!!" the Baron snaps.

The Baron and his female assistant Sarah, a mute girl called the Angel by the inmates because of her charitable, nurselike nature, sees to Simon's wounds. Helder of course recognizes the Baron and announces that he has read his published works and has been trying to duplicate his experiments, without much success. The Baron needs an assistant to carry out the demands of attending to the needs of the inmates because he requires "more time to devote... to my own private work" and immediately forces the Director to sign the papers making the Simon his new assistant with all privileges. As the Baron tells the Director, "He is no more insane than you or I" and the irony here is that both men, the Baron and Director, are of questionable mental health. The two main points the Baron stresses to Simon is that the Baron is dead, buried in the courtyard out back, and that before he passed on, "the Baron collected some notes on how this establishment is run" putting him in a position of power. At the asylum, the Baron is known as Dr. Carl Victor.

The Baron makes the medical rounds with Simon telling the young apprentice that these will be his duties tomorrow. We meet a man who is standing against his cell wall with his arms outstretched, who believes he is God. The Baron declares, "He's not the first man, nor will he be the last man, who thinks he is God." Of course the obvious analogy to the Baron makes the viewer question the so-called genius or insanity of the Baron. The Baron points out a corridor which leads to a speical section. He explains that these are his very special patients that he will continue to care for himself. The first cell is empty, the thick metal bars twisted and torn. The Baron claims the inmate committed suicide by jumping 30 feet and still refused to die. The Baron notes his "pure animal strength," calling the inmate a "throwback, more animal than human." Then they call upon the Professor, a man who loves playing and composing music for the violin. He composed a song called "The Angel" for Sarah whom he claims "is more beautiful than music." A student of pure mathematical theory, formulas are sprawled all over the walls, he claims math is "almost as beautiful as this one here," referring to Sarah. The Baron calls the Professor a genius, but claims when roused he becomes as savage as a cat (and has savagely attacked the Director in the past). Another inmate curves beautiful statues, one of an angel he gives to Sarah (the Angel). "See those hands...Would you think it possible for those hands to do this sort of work!" the Baron announces to Simon. Slowly it becomes apparent that the Baron uses patients in his special ward, much like his Free Ward in *The Revenge of Frankenstein*, as a reserve for body parts needed in future experiments. However, he subtlety disguises this fact for some time. Fisher's direction of the individual inmates is interesting and a highlight of the film. The twisted turnabout of having the anti-societal Baron running the insane asylum, his position of power juxtaposed to all the kindly, misunderstood, and sympathetic "lunatics" locked inside, as well as the obviously perverted and unbalanced Director, who is but the Baron's pawn, is more than just a tad ironic. Elder's script seeks to have the audience question the concept of insanity as well as who in the asylum really is insane; the answer is neither easy nor obvious.

Simon, discovering a secret entrance by which Sarah exits, enters to find a beastly monster contained in a locked steel cell. Obviously the man who fell 30 feet to his death did not stay dead. He also notices the hands of the sculptor have been crudely sewed to the monstrous hairy limbs of this "throwback." The Baron proudly declares, when Simon notices these hands, "It is an accomplished fact, something I hope you appreciate."

Speechless, Simon slowly utters, "I've heard you were a brilliant surgeon," to which the Baron answers, "I was, still am, in here" pointing to his head. Still wearing the black gloves from the last John Elder scripted *Created Woman*, the Baron slowly peels off the gloves to reveal burned, deformed hands. "They were burned in the interest of science." Thus, Sarah's crude surgery accounts for the piecemeal monster before them. Simon excitedly announces he is not just a doctor but a surgeon, and for the first time in a long while, the Baron's eyes light up.

During an operation which Simon performs, the elder teacher watches Simon like a hawk ("No, never use a dirty instrument!") and is impressed as new eyes are added to his Creation. At the conclusion the Baron, with an air of anticipation about him, says, "In one hour we will see!" To which Simon smiles and retorts, "Let us hope it is he who sees!" For the first time, the Baron repeats the obvious joke, laughing out loud. "I like that!" Thus, a very human, low-key moment erupts from the formerly rigid, humorless Baron. Little touches such as this one add a layer of humanity to the stuffy old Baron's character.

The only thing left, as the Baron declares, is a brain, "preferably the brain of a genius." Simon immediately fears that the Baron intends to kill the kindly old professor for his brain. "I'm not a murderer, Simon," the Baron indignantly utters. However, the next morning the Professor is found dead, having hanged himself with his violin strings. The Baron coolly proclaims, "The question of a brain has been settled." Only later does Simon find a medical record note in the Professor's violin case which claims the Professor is "incurable." Simon obviously understands why the Baron allowed the note to fall within reach of the professor. The Baron defends himself stating, "I was unable to cure him—could you!!! Then... he was incurable." Thus technically the Baron is correct when he stated he wasn't a murderer, but he is guilty of orchestrating the ultimate depression which led the Professor to kill himself, bringing the same practical results as cold-blooded murder would have produced.

Unfortunately, although the brain transplant is successful, the desired results are not. The Baron Frankenstein of Bert Batt's *Must Be Destroyed* script would never share credit or act humbly, but the Baron of Elder's script is quite willing to give credit where due. Immediately after the operation, the Baron states, "Simon, thank you! Ten days... If I've succeeded, every sacrifice would have been worthwhile." To which Simon says, "You've done it!" To which the Baron corrects, "No, we've done it, the three of us," even crediting Sarah. However, during the Monster's convalescence, the beast becomes frustrated while groping for his violin which he smashes in his depression. The Baron loses patience demanding, "You must learn to use them [his hands]. You will learn. You must practice coordination!"

Finally, the Baron admits defeat claiming, "We failed, Simon. At least I failed... the body is rejecting the brain; the man will become a cabbage and die." Simon tells the Baron he must be patient. Soon the Monster reverts to his old brain mentality (before the transplant), picking up shattered pieces of glass which he uses as a weapon (something the Professor never did). Once when Simon is being threatened by the glass wielding fiend, the Baron, in classic Cushing style, smashes a bottle of sleeping gas into a cloak, jumps onto a table, and dives onto the monster's back. He pulls the cloak over the Monster's head, rendering the fiend unconscious as it struggles to throw the pest from his shoulders as a rodeo bronco tries to throw his rider. At over 60 years of age, Cushing still displays his kinetic vigor of old.

"We were both right and wrong. The body is taking over the brain... there is still a way to succeed!" the Baron proclaims. His bizarre plan is to "capture the essence of the man, that a new version of the man is born." This will be carried out by mating the monster with Sarah, an idea which does not please Simon. Simon warns, "You cannot divorce science from humanity," displaying the fact that Simon is a youthful mirror image of the Baron, but a mirror image with a soul and conscience, the tragic flaw missing in the Baron's character. Adding sexist drivel, the Baron declares, "Her real function as a woman could be fulfilled." The Baron warns Simon, "Don't do anything stupid." Of course he, the concerned protector of Sarah, does.

Attempting to stab and destroy the beast before it savages its beauty, Simon is momentarily distracted by the Angel herself. The Monster grabs his wrist and escapes. The Director and inmates see the fiend digging up graves in the courtyard, apparently having a desire to see where his second-hand body parts originated. After killing the Director by slitting his throat with a broken piece of glass, the monster slowly ambles down into the lower inmate cell area. The guards fire and the Monster doubles over in pain, the sympathetic

The Baron never accepts defeat and plans to begin again after his Creature is destroyed by the inmates.

Angel offering her out-stretched hand for support. However, the inmates fearing that Sarah will be harmed, brutally attack and kill the beast. Entering the scene, the wounded Baron takes control. "Silence! Go back to your rooms. It's all over now. All over." Turning to the guards, he smugly utters, "Now you can use your hose. Make this place clean."

The final sequence is impressive, displaying a very energetic and invigorated Baron speaking to Simon. "We have a lot of work. Too much reliance on surgery, not enough on bio-chemistry. He was of no more use to us or himself. This was the best thing that could have happened. But next time! We shall start afresh!!!" With that twinkle in the eye and hope in the future, the Baron, having only lost one small battle, prepares to win the war. Never discouraged, never defeated, he eagerly prepares to begin his work anew. Unfortunately, Hammer never continues the series but at least the final screen appearance of Baron Frankenstein displays exultation and childlike enthusiasm at the thought of continuing his work, no matter how realistic these goals may be.

Peter Cushing was more than the ace up Hammer's sleeve; he was, quite simply the entire *Frankenstein* franchise.

For somehow, this final impression of Cushing as the Baron is sad. By now everyone in the theater realizes that the show is over for the Baron, that the escape of the Monster, the murder of the Director, and the spectacle observed by the inmates themselves cannot be easily swept under the carpet and forgotten, as the Baron assumes it can. The jig is obviously up. Investigations would expose the obvious fact that an inmate is running the asylum and that the Baron's secret position of power would be exposed. Even though he earlier threatened to simply walk out and leave the asylum, and now he expresses a similar desire to continue his work, the fact remains that the Baron, no matter how clever he might be, is reacting in an unrealistic manner. In basic terms, intelligent or not, much like the kindly Professor whose violent rages got him locked away forever in an asylum cell, the Baron is obviously insane and acts out a dream fantasy. After a lifetime of fighting society and its confining, conservative mores and laws, the combatant Baron has finally cracked under the pressure. No longer viewed as cruel nor cold-blooded (at least as the earlier Bert Batt script depicted him), the Baron finally becomes an object of our pity, a sad, pathetic broken man who never achieves his cherished goals of a lifetime. On this note, the Hammer series concludes.

We must always bear in mind that the Hammer *Frankenstein* series was never concocted as a continuing series from its conception. Hammer Films, much like Val Lewton films decades before, were sold on titles, star appeal, and monster/name recognition. Just as lack of continuity often marred the Christopher Lee *Dracula* films, the *Frankenstein/Cushing* series only contained one constant—Peter Cushing. The screenplays revolved between Jimmy Sangster, John Elder, and Bert Batt. The director in five films was Terence Fisher, but Freddie Francis directed the fourth entry. Thus, when speaking of the evolving character of Baron Victor Frankenstein (aka Dr. Franck, Dr. Stein, Dr. Victor, etc.), we are not speaking of one artistic vision written and directed by the same team or same person. Instead, we are speaking of the dedication and vision of one talented thespian to imbue craft, caring, and passion into a "B" film characterization that rises far above and beyond the parameters of low-budget filmmaking. Working with a variety of writers, more than one director, constantly changing casts, weaker or stronger scripts, the talents of Peter Cushing shine brightly and serve as a unifying artistic beacon which merges all the disparate components of the series into a unified whole. No small feat!

Cushing brilliantly deals with the Baron's aristocracy and single-minded determination of Jimmy Sangster's initial script; the dichotomy of character inherent in Sangster's second entry (whereby the gentile public-persona Baron is contrasted to the actual self-serving butcher of the underprivileged in *The Revenge of Frankenstein*); Sangster's vision of the Baron as dashing romantic hero or obsessive (yet somehow lovable nonetheless), self-absorbed scientist; Bert Batt's conception of the Baron as someone ultimately evil and cold-bloodedly cruel, committing whatever acts necessary to achieve his goals; and John Elder's final script whereby the Baron, obviously out of touch with reality, eagerly looks forward to the continuation of his work even though his ruse of being the resident doctor at the State Insane Asylum has been exposed. The one constant force which melds all these contrasting elements together is Peter Cushing, an actor who spent his entire career proving that low-budget movie acting, while not Shakespeare, could be just as serious, emotional, expansive, and ultimately moving. Cushing, playing the Baron as a hero or as the personification of pure evil, made the viewer care about his character and respond accordingly. Baron Victor Frankenstein's many personas—murderer; dashing romantic hero of the boudoir, lecturer on the stupidity of the common citizen, were made coherent, consistent, and believable by Peter Cushing—even if the opposing and oftentimes contrasting character changes in each successive script did not. For one rare time, an acting talent solidified the artistic vision of a movie series much more so than did even the writers, producers, and directors involved. Meshing separate pieces from different puzzles, to use an analogy, the superlative talents of Peter Cushing allowed him to create a cohesive whole, an artistic vision that satisfied, where everything somehow fit, amazing as this might sound. He forged this vision by the sheer determination of talent and will. Peter Cushing was more than the ace up Hammer's sleeve; he was, quite simply, the entire franchise.

What Hath God and Hollywood Wrought?

The decades of the 1950s, 1960s, and 1970s produced many sensitive, serious, and artistic retoolings of Mary Shelley's *Frankenstein*. Unfortunately, the Frankenstein Monster became a universally recognized icon, a hero of young people everywhere, and therefore the opportunity arose to exploit the Monster as well as the themes and concepts of the novel.

Exploitation is not always a bad thing. Once the Frankenstein concept was retooled for teen oriented productions such as *I Was a Teenage Frankenstein, Frankenstein's Daughter*, and *Frankenstein Meets the Spacemonster*, the Monster became more than just a movie or literary character. Frankenstein's creation become an American commodity, an institution whose name and image could be marketed and sold for profit. The Frankenstein Monster jumped off dusty library shelves to become a brand name.

The tragic Monster, created by an English teenager, was now connecting with teenagers around the world. Japan's Toho created *Frankenstein Conquered the World*, while Europe boasted *The Erotic Rites of Frankenstein, The Screaming Dead, Assignment Terror*, etc. Mary Shelley's Monster even managed to find his way into the black exploitation movie craze of the late 1960s and 1970s with *Blackenstein*.

Rebellious teens around the world were intrigued by the exploits of the Frankenstein Monster, who had now been cast in so many different formats and directions that even Mary Shelley would be hard pressed to recognize her creation. Few of these young fans had read the original novel. Beginning in the 1950s, Frankenstein and his Monster became more a product of the movies than of literature. It would take another 20 years before the literary roots were rediscovered.

Bryan Senn contributes an affectionate look at the exploitation gems of the 1950s. Senn lives in Washington state with his young son, Dominic, and his wife, Gina Beretta, who holds a Ph.D. in *murder* (criminology, actually). When not trying to stay on Gina's good side, he managed to finish several books including *Fantastic Cinema Subject Guide* (co-authored with John Johnson), *Golden Horrors*, and *Drums O' Terror: Voodoo in the Cinema*.

David H. Smith contributes the bulk of the chapters in this section and has the unenviable task of finding merit in the world's worst *Frankenstein* movies. But Smith relishes his role as defender of the nadir, for his entire film writing career consists of unearthing those neglected, despised, and technically deficient rejects of the cinema. Smith lives with his wife Lynn and son in South Florida and contributes to Midnight Marquee Press and magazine.

Don G. Smith also contributes to this section, with a chapter on *Frankenstein Meets the Space-monster*.

The REAL "Curse of Frankenstein,"
or, America's No-Budget Answer to Hammer's Horror

I Was a Teenage Frankenstein, Frankenstein 1970, and *Frankenstein's Daughter*

by Bryan Senn

Throughout most of the 1950s, all things Frankenstein became conspicuous solely by their absence. After Universal's 1948 comedic send-off *Abbott and Costello Meet Frankenstein*, the Monster lay dormant for nearly a decade... until a small British film studio decided to branch out from their black-and-white adaptations of radio dramas into the realm of Gothic horror—Gothic *color* horror, that is. When Hammer's *The Curse of Frankenstein* hit American shores in 1957, its huge financial success produced a tidal wave of excitement among the smaller, independent American film companies. Though the majors held their collective noses and stayed away from such a grisly (and offensive—according to the pontificating critics of the day) topic, several more adventurous filmmakers decided to temporarily leave off the Big Bugs and Invading Aliens then flooding the drive-in screens to see if they could hang ten on this new Frankenstein wave.

First up (though producer Herman Cohen would never admit to being galvanized into action by the Hammer film) was AIP's *I Was a Teenage Frankenstein*. Soon after, in rapid succession, came Allied Artists' *Frankenstein 1970* and Astor Pictures' *Frankenstein's Daughter*. In typical quick-buck fashion, all three of these productions eschewed their model's period setting, Gothic trappings, and expensive color film stock (a few standing castle sets in *Frankenstein 1970* and *one minute* of color at the climax of *Teenage Frankenstein* notwithstanding) to create cheap, "modern," teen-targeted tellings of the Frankenstein tale.

The first Hollywood Frankenstein of the decade (and the best as it turned out—though that seems like faint praise indeed considering the competition) was aimed squarely at the juvenile market. As a follow-up to the ultra-successful *I Was a Teenage Werewolf*, *I Was a Teenage Frankenstein* unfortunately fell well short of its predecessor. Thanks to a sensitive script and an intense, sympathetic performance from Michael Landon in the title role, *Teenage Werewolf* rose above its puerile title to present an engrossing (if outlandish) tale of teenage angst disguised as lycanthropic rampage. *I Was a Teenage Frankenstein*, however, truly lived *down* to its absurd appellation.

Professor Frankenstein (Whit Bissell), a guest lecturer from England, has set up shop in a small American college town. Apart from collecting his lecture fees, the real reason he's here is to "assemble a human being using parts and organs from different cadavers" (as he informs his astonished colleague). Duping local medico Dr. Karlton (Robert Burton) into becoming his assistant, Frankenstein does just that—by stealing teenage body parts from a fatal car crash. In his locked basement lab, Frankenstein and Karlton construct a perfect physical specimen (Gary Conway), "a teenage marvel" (as Frankenstein labels him). There's just one hitch, however; the "marvel's" face looks like it's been in a road accident (unsurprising, since it *has*). Frankenstein controls his creation (who pumps iron, whines about not being able to go out among people, and even cries) by promising it a new face. After a few troublesome moments, such as when the monster sneaks out of its basement abode and accidentally kills a beautiful girl, or when Frankenstein disposes of his nosy fiancée by having his creation dump her into the lab's handy alligator pit, the doctor takes his teen titan out to lover's lane to procure a new face. Decapitating a local lothario, Frankenstein grafts the handsome countenance onto his creation, and the experiment is complete. With the good Professor's visa about to run out, however, he must get his triumph over to his native England to continue his work. To this end, he plans to disassemble the lad, pack the pieces into crates, and reassemble him once he gets home (thereby avoiding all that annoying passport and immigration red tape). But the creature becomes suspicious and finally turns on its master, sending Frankenstein to the same gruesome fate as his fiancée. When the police arrive, the JD/monster backs away from the cops—right into a nasty bank of equipment that electrocutes the poor creature.

From its inception, *I Was a Teenage Frankenstein* was a rush job, even more so than the usual low-budget feature. An influential Texas exhibitor named R.J. O'Donnell, disgruntled with the higher percentages demanded by the majors, offered AIP the plum playdate of Thanksgiving Week if they could supply a suitable double-feature for his large theater chain.

So with the deal made on Labor Day, producer Herman Cohen started work on *I Was a Teenage Frankenstein* and its co-feature *Blood of Dracula*, which were shot back to back. "Both *Frankenstein* and *Blood of Dracula* were written and put in front of the camera in only four weeks, in order to make that Thanksgiving date," stated Cohen. "And there was a shortage of money at the time. So I had to really, really cut down."

I Was a Teenage Frankenstein obviously suffered from this lack of time and money, though even with more of both one seriously doubts it would have turned out much better given the filmmakers involved. Director Herbert Strock makes no attempt to build any atmosphere, giving *Teenage Frankenstein* the same listless treatment he awarded the rest of his boring genre filmography: *Gog* (1954), *Blood of Dracula* (1957*), How to Make a Monster* (1958), *The Devil's Messenger* (1961), *The Crawling Hand* (1963), and *Monster* (1979). While *Teenage Frankenstein* may be the best of the bunch, that says little when its competition consists of dreary dreck like *Gog* and *The Crawling Hand*. For *Teenage Frankenstein* Strock shoots in a dull, straightforward manner (as usual), relying on Philip Scheer's outlandish road-pizza makeup, a few gruesome props, and 83 seconds of color footage to wring whatever dubious "thrills" can be found in Aben Kandel and Herman Cohen's absurd screenplay. (Kandel and Cohen showed how little enthusiasm they felt for their work by hiding behind the pseudonym "Kenneth Langtry.") Strock's cause isn't helped by set decorator Tom Oliphant's cheap, mundane lab equipment, Leslie Thomas' nondescript Motel-6–style interiors, and cinematographer Lothrop Worth's penchant for over-bright, flat lighting.

Kandel and Cohen's script, though containing more than its fair share of dull stretches, admittedly sports some unintentionally entertaining incongruities and amusing dialogue. For instance, when Frankenstein needs to dispose of unwanted body parts (or unwanted fiancées for that matter), he simply opens a secret panel in his basement and drops them down a chute. "I have a very interesting final resting place for bones and tissues I'll never need," he tells his wondering assistant as we're shown a large alligator consuming his unwanted bundle. While most people make do with your standard garbage disposal, Dr. F. possesses a unique "gator-disposal" in *his* bungalow. (He must have searched far and wide to find a rental house with just the right watery gator pit in the cellar!) Whit Bissell himself seemed nonplussed at this *Better Homes and Gardens* nightmare. "It was never explained how I got that alligator pit into my house," marveled the actor, "but you didn't have to explain things like that in those days."

According to Herman Cohen, at least one aspect of this gator-gaff proved gruesomely authentic. "We got the alligator from the Buena Park Alligator Farm," reported Cohen, "and it was an alligator that they had brought in from Texas. There it was owned by a guy that owned a roadside inn in a small town outside of Dallas. He would hire a waitress who had no family, he would swing with her and what have you, and then when he got tired of her, he would throw her in a pool in his basement where he had this alligator! That alligator had killed about *seven women*!"

In addition to such amusing anomalies, the screenplay is simply littered with ridiculous and highly quotable dialogue. "In this laboratory there is no death until I declare it so!" exclaims a grandiose Frankenstein to his timid assistant. Well! After animating his creature, Frankenstein insists he possesses the ability to speak: "With all the surgical skill and vital rays lavished on him, he should talk like a—like a congressman in a filibuster." And, who, of course, can forget that oft (mis)quoted gem: "Speak! You've got a civil tongue in your head. I *know* you have because I sewed it back myself."

For the feminists in the audience, the script offers some highly hissable lines like, "You know perfectly well that science has proved conclusively that in all forms of life the female pursues the male," and "Isn't that the way of women—make us poor men suffer for *their* blunders."

As well as covering the burning themes of life, death, the battle of the sexes, and the disposal of unwanted limbs and organs, the screenplay also tackles the dreaded Generation Gap. Though he himself sits squarely on the stodgy shoulders of middle age, Professor Frankenstein seemingly takes the youthful side of this age-old conflict. "I shall use only the ingredients of youth," he proclaims, "not the worn-out body inhabited by an overtaxed brain...*only in youth* is there any hope for the salvation of mankind." Just how old is Dr. F. anyway (and how "overtaxed" is *his* brain)? But one can excuse a little pandering if it gets your target audience to buy more tickets. "I believe that teenagers are misunderstood by adults," remarked Cohen, "whether they be teachers or parents or what have you. I knew that teenagers would like that kind of story. With *I Was a Teenage Werewolf*, the kids in the theater were crying when he was killed. The same thing with *Teenage Frankenstein*. Somebody wants love, somebody is ugly, somebody doesn't fit in, somebody is an introvert, somebody has a father and mother divorced." While using Frankenstein as the mouthpiece of the young, however, Kandel and Cohen also cast him in the contradictory light of an unbending, authoritarian parent who goes so far as to make his child/creation call him "sir." The horror!

By far the two greatest assets possessed by *Teenage Frankenstein* are the authoritative playing of Whit Bissell as Professor Frankenstein and the impressive makeup atop Gary Conway's buffed frame. While the monster's kisser looks more than a little like a novice sculptor's rejected high school project, the crazy-quilt ridges of skin, bulging eye, and wild tufts of hair make it an immediately recognizable (though not quite convincing) icon for cheesy 1950s gruesomeness.

Whit Bissell is one of those character actors whose face is readily familiar but whose name seems to elude the memory. A frequent supporting player both in films and on television for over three decades, *I Was a Teenage Frankenstein* gave this capable and underrated actor one of his rare starring roles. And Bissell makes the most of the rather low-grade material given him here. He comes off as a reasonable man of science—rational, even likable. In fact he seems the aggrieved party at the film's beginning when one of his colleagues ridicules his theories. Bissell keeps his head, however, and rather than ranting in the usual mad-scientist manner, he answers the barbs coolly and calmly. Bissell makes Professor Frankenstein into a calculating, purposeful man who'll let nothing so petty as morals or humanity stand in the way of his work. Though he seems to have some small feeling for his dutiful fiancée, he has no compunction about throwing her to the lions (or in this case a hungry gator) when she gets in the way of his experiment. "He's a charming guy, a marvelous actor," praised Cohen. "He's so professional, and I liked him in every way. He was just perfect for the part." Bissell was a regular in 1950s sci-fi, and his steadying presence enhanced such films as *Lost Continent* (1951), *Creature from the Black Lagoon* (1954), *Target Earth* (1954), *Invasion of the Body Snatchers* (1956), *I Was a Teenage Werewolf* (1957), *Monster on the Campus* (1958), and *The Time Machine* (1960).

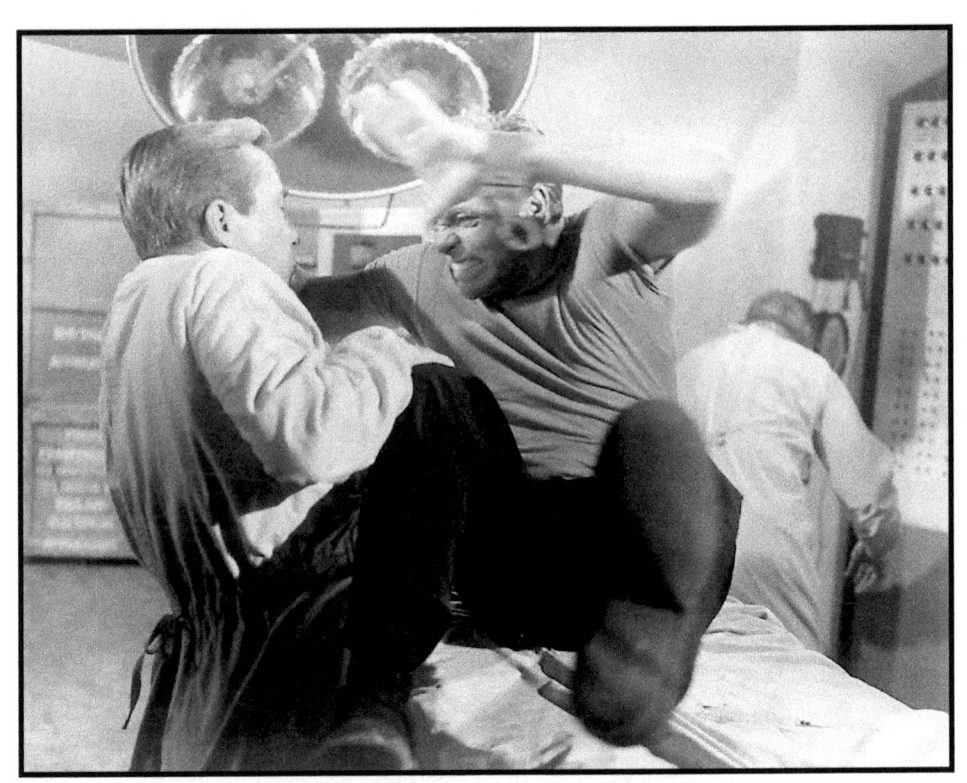

To play the "teenage marvel," producer Cohen chose a 20-year-old UCLA art student named Gareth Carmody (Gary Conway), seen here attacking Whit Bissell.

To play the "teenage marvel," producer Herman Cohen chose a 20-year-old UCLA art student named Gareth Carmody because, said Cohen, "He was physically and dramatically right for the part. You know, Teenage Frankenstein had to have a good body." Carmody fit the bill well enough, and provided both the right physique and an appropriately bewildered demeanor. "Cohen had a gimmick for *Teenage Frankenstein*," recalled the actor on how he landed the role. "He was looking for a teenager—the ideal teenager. They were going to search across the country, one of those deals. I got it because I was around; I was just there and somebody said, 'I think this guy could be what you're looking for.' I didn't seek it out. It kind of came to me." Apart from having to hide his handsome face under the uncomfortably heavy makeup for most of the picture, Carmody had to give up his name as well. Cohen insisted on changing the first-time actor's name, reasoning, "I thought ['Gareth Carmody'] was just too classy." Carmody had no objections to using a new moniker. "When I did *Teenage Frankenstein*, I thought I was going to do this as a joke," explained the actor. "I just felt that it was not really consistent with my own attitude of being an artist. So I thought it would be appropriate to change my name to something else. Gareth is my real name, but I was always called Gary, so that was no big switch. And Conway was the name of my grandmother's father. I inherited it, so to speak. I've always felt a little bit put out, because I thought I'd be Gary Conway only one or two times. I didn't know that it would follow me all the way along the line."

When the sparks fly (literally) at the film's climax when the teenage monster awkwardly backs into the bank of equipment, the black and white film suddenly bursts into full color. "At that time," recounted producer Herman Cohen, "I thought that was quite inventive. We couldn't afford to make the picture in color, so I came up with the idea, and I talked Jim Nicholson [co-president of AIP] into letting me spend a few extra bucks." To Cohen's credit, this unexpected change does add a certain excitement to the rather contrived climax. And the monster's makeup actually looks better (and more realistic) in color, its sickly fleshy hues and brown matted hair adding a genuine ghastliness lacking in the black-and-white footage. (Note: While the creature has his new, normal face during this scene, the picture ends with a close-up of the monster's ugly visage as Dr. Karlton tells the police, "You should have seen his face!").

Something else that gives *Teenage Frankenstein* a leg up on its competition (so to speak) is some rather shocking footage of a severed limb. "I remember when we had Whit Bissell use the electric saw to cut off the leg," recalled director Herbert L. Strock, "what I did was use the *sound* of the saw hitting the bone and you *felt* that it went through the bone—you never saw it. And then we lifted this phony leg through the scene. I remember when the censors ran this picture, they were furious. I had to run it again and explain to them that my effect was great—they loved the effect—but I did *not* show the leg being cut off, which they insisted I did." While certainly not in the best of taste, this grisly and effective bit (with the bloody leg's raw end facing toward the camera in all its gory glory) certainly remains memorable.

I Was a Teenage Frankenstein garnered some downright favorable reviews—at least in terms of the juvenile/horror market. *The Hollywood Reporter* opined that it was "intelligently and imaginatively done... [T]here is enough of genuine frightfulness to satisfy any fan of these presentations." *Harrison's Reports* concurred: "There is plentiful action and, even though it is just so much claptrap, it ought to satisfy the undiscriminating movie-goers [re: teenagers] who enjoy such pictures." The loftier *New York Times* critic, however, went into a convoluted tirade on "the mass social sickness euphemistically termed 'juvenile delinquency.'" Of the picture itself, the reviewer merely noted that "the film warrants little attention."

The next vehicle to cruise down the Frankenstein freeway proved even less appealing than *Teenage Frankenstein*. Updating the Frankenstein legend with atomic reactors and the original monster himself, Boris Karloff (playing the doctor this time), may have sounded like a good idea at the time, but *Frankenstein 1970* falls flat on its Franken-face.

"[*Frankenstein 1970*] was made because we had a three-picture deal with Karloff," related producer Aubrey Schenck. "We had to pay him $30,000 whether we used him in a picture or not. So we went to the guys at Allied Artists—they wanted pictures—and we made it quickly for them. It was like a pick-up deal. I think we made it for $110,000 [director Howard Koch put the figure at $105,000]. They paid us $250,000 for it—an outright buy."

In the film, Karloff plays a present day (or at least 1970 as the title would have us believe) Baron Frankenstein, a victim of torture at the hands of an unspecified (i.e., Nazi) regime. (Note: The original script was called *Frankenstein 1960* [just two years in advance of its 1958 release]; since nothing is ever made of its "futuristic" setting, it's anybody's guess why the filmmakers ultimately added another decade to their title.) As the last of the Frankenstein line, Karloff still inhabits the old family castle, where he has built an ultramodern laboratory in a secret room under the crypt with plans to make a new, improved version of his infamous ancestral monster. For this he needs an atomic reactor (apparently the tried and true method of using plain old lightning proved too archaic for him). For financial reasons, he allows a pesky TV crew to use his castle as the background for their

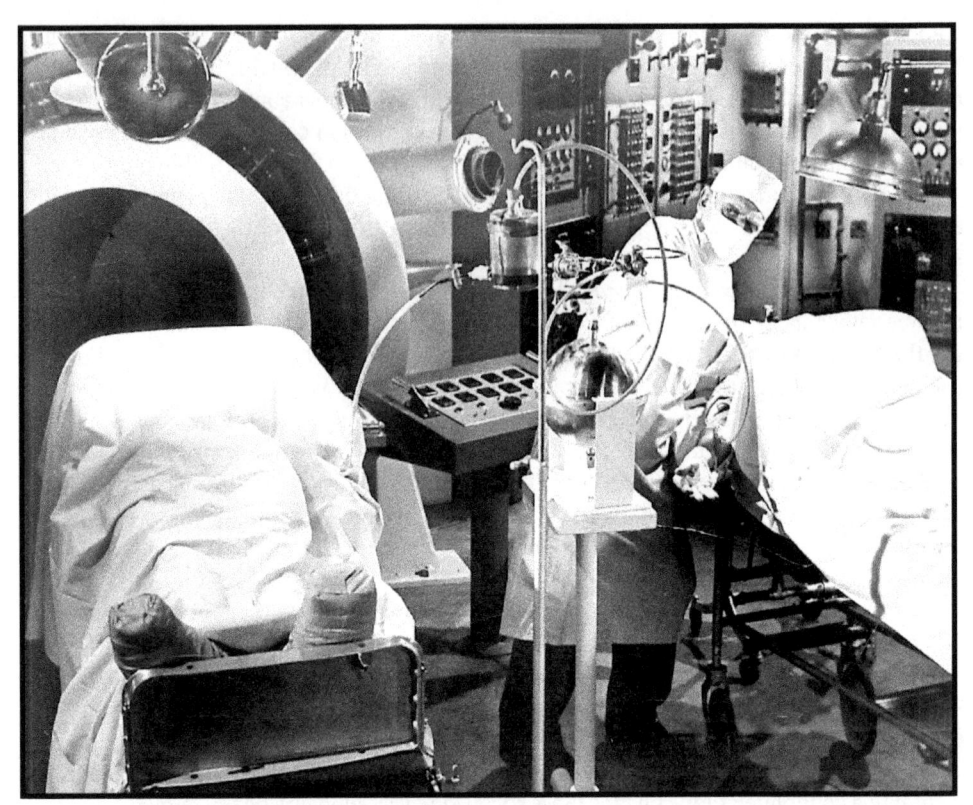

Updating the Frankenstein legend with Boris Karloff (as the doctor) may have sounded like a good idea, but *Frankenstein 1970* falls flat on its Franken-face.

show in exchange for the equipment he needs. When the atomic equipment finally arrives (from the ACME Reactor Company?), the Baron revives his monster. This, unfortunately, proves a great disappointment, for instead of a terrifying patchwork ghoul, the monster is just a large man wrapped from head to toe in white bandages. And on that head rests a ridiculous box-like covering with holes cut out for the eyes. Given this appearance, and the fact that the monster is blind (much of the plot centers around the Baron sending the groping creature out to find a suitable pair of peepers), the monster is anything *but* menacing. ("That 'monster' of Karloff's," laughed Schenck, "that didn't scare you at all.")

The script gives Karloff little to work with and saddles the veteran horror star with pointless clunkers like, "I am now starting up the atomic steam generator," and "All radiation off; zero on geiger modem dial." As one watches, it soon becomes evident that *Frankenstein 1970* was not a stellar moment in Karloff's career. It's embarrassing, even for such a consummate professional as he, to wear silly goggles and apron and comment, "Ah Shuter, yours is not the brain I would have chosen, but at least you are obedient." In another scene, Karloff becomes the butt of an unintentional joke when he clumsily drops the jar containing the monster's intended eyeballs and comically slaps his hand on his thigh in an "oh shoot!" gesture. Occasionally some of the old power and menace shines through, however, such as when Karloff tells the story of the "inquisitive camp commandant" who was found with his tongue cut out ("a beautiful piece of surgery—beautiful"). Still, Karloff gives a horribly overripe performance, one of the worst of his career. "It was theatrical, it was overdone," agreed co-star Charlotte Austin. "I hate to say that, because he was such a gracious man.

But when you're given this kind of dialogue, what can you do with it?... I think he was just doing a job and wanting to go home.... I felt *sorry* for him having to be in a movie like *Frankenstein 1970*—it was degrading." Director Howard Koch realized that Karloff was overdoing it, but was unwilling to rein him in. "I was in awe of him, and we just let him go," admitted Koch. "At that time Boris Karloff had a standing in life, and whatever he did you thought was right. You were afraid to say it was wrong. I was *afraid* to say to him it was too much!"

With one exception, the supporting cast of characters (and actors) prove completely uninteresting. The only intriguing personality is Judy (played by Charlotte Austin), the TV director's feisty secretary and ex-wife. She's still in love with the abrasive director, but spends most of her time fending off an amorous, whiny publicity man. Unfortunately, she's the monster's first victim, and so makes her tragic exit halfway through the film. This, by the way, is the source of another unintentionally humorous moment. When the Baron places her body in his oversized custom disposal unit and starts the machine, it sounds exactly like a toilet flushing! (According to Howard Koch, the original, more realistic "crunching" sound effects were removed at the behest of the censors. "When we showed that to the Code, they said, 'You can't have that sound effect in there, you've got to take it out! Christ, it's the most gruesome thing we ever heard in our lives!'" As it is now, it may very well be the *funniest*!) "Being ground up in the garbage disposal was not fun," added Ms. Austin, "Karloff dropping one eyeball at a time in, and those terrible sound effects! Oh, my God, that was corny!"

Howard Koch directs with a heavy-handed self-consciousness. Apparently Koch's idea of clever innovation is to use the sledgehammer approach to pound his ideas into the viewer's psyche. In one scene the blind monster (still seeking a pair of eyes) approaches his victim: Koch first shows the creature's empty eye holes, then a shot of the victim's eyes, and finally a superimposition of the victim's eyes over the monster's empty eye holes. Subtle. And the impact of the ironic (if not wholly unexpected) twist of revealing that the Baron had created his monster "in his own image" is nullified by the off-handed shot used to present it. Even Koch's boss, producer Aubrey Schenck, admitted the director did a less-than-stellar job: "Well, that wasn't Howard's métier. Howard, he himself didn't like doing these horrible things, with eyes poppin' out and things like that. That wasn't his bag. You know, when you do horror pictures, you have to have someone who *really* believes in this stuff. I don't think we were equipped to do real horror pictures for some reason." Koch himself admitted that, "I don't feel I did such a great job on *Frankenstein 1970*," blaming it on the rushed nine-day shooting schedule. "I didn't have much time to really think." (Compared to the other two Frankensteins, however, Koch had a relatively *leisurely* schedule, since *Teenage Frankenstein* and *Frankenstein's Daughter* were allotted only seven and six days respectively.)

The film's predictable ending also proves disappointing. The monster, whose skull houses the brain of a murdered servant, refuses to harm the heroine as ordered (since she had previously been kind to the servant) and consequently turns on his master. As a result, the Baron kills both the monster and himself by releasing lethal radiation in the form of an unconvincing steam cloud. Quite the anticlimax: The Frankenstein Monster killed by radiation poisoning. In *Frankenstein 1970*, the atomic hysteria of the 1950s reached back to claim even Mary Shelley's timeless creation.

Reviewers were surprisingly mild in their criticism, perhaps out of some respect for King Karloff. *The Motion Picture Exhibitor* predicted, "This horror meller should do okay as part of the program. Its suspense is uneven with some of the horror situations pretty strong and others mild. The story by Aubrey Schenck and Charles A. Moses is confusing at times. The Karloff name, however, should prove an attraction to the box-office. The black-and-white CinemaScope photography is good." *Variety* called it "a competently made production that will do well in its class" and (incredibly) singled out Karloff for praise, stating the actor "does a careful, convincing job with his role, which is competently written." The *Monthly Film Bulletin*, however, proved more astute in its assessment, flatly stating that "the whole inept effort is a slight on the horrific name of Frankenstein." Indeed.

The third point of the post-*Curse* triangle is yet another lackluster variation, though this one boasts not one but *two* monsters. While *Teenage Frankenstein* possesses the most visually impressive (if not altogether convincing) creature in this Frankenstein triumvirate, *Frankenstein's Daughter* excelled in sheer quantity. *Quality*, however—that's another matter.

Dr. Carter Morton (Felix Locher) works in his home laboratory trying to perfect a drug that will "wipe out all destructive cells and organisms that plague man." Carter's assistant, Oliver Frank (Donald Murphy), secretly tests the experimental serum on Carter's teenage niece, Trudy (Sandra Knight). The drug temporarily turns her into an ugly, pasty-faced creature that terrorizes the neighborhood while wearing nightgowns and bathing suits. In the morning, however, Trudy has only a vague recollection and thinks it's all a nightmare. Oliver plans to use the serum in his own secret experiment, for we quickly learn that 'Oliver Frank' is short for Oliver Frank*enstein*, grandson of the famous monster-maker. In a secret room off Carter's lab, Oliver and his assistant Elsu (Oliver's faithful family retainer who poses as the gardener) have constructed a body. "I was only a boy when your grandfather first created life from the dead," Elsu (Wolfe Barzell) tells Oliver, "but I helped your father. Father to son, that's the way it should be." Needing a brain for his creation, Oliver combines business and pleasure when he runs over his reluctant date (Sally Todd) with his car (after she spurns him) and grafts the girl's head onto the prepared body. "A female?" asks Elsu. "That's never been done!" (Obviously Elsu failed to notice, much less *assist* with, *Bride of Frankenstein*.) Oliver counters with the embarrassing 1950s-ism that "The female brain is

Hero John Ashley protects Trudy (Sandra Knight) from the daughter of Frankenstein (Harry Wilson).

conditioned to a *man's* world. Therefore it takes orders." (Of course, Oliver conveniently forgets that this same female brain *refused* to bend to his lascivious will when housed in its original body.) In any case, Elsu finally agrees "She's nicer than the males your father and grandfather made." This "nice" monster still manages to kill several people before Trudy's boyfriend, Johnny (John Ashley), throws a bottle of acid at it in the lab. Though the creature stands only three feet away, Johnny manages to miss his target and hit Oliver standing at the end of the room. The monster ceases its attack on Johnny and moves toward its dying master, only to catch its sleeve on a Bunsen burner. As the creature goes up in flames, the police arrive and the two lovers embrace.

Though there's much to scoff at in this gender-bending cheapie, director Richard Cunha (with a meager budget of $65,000) and cinematographer Meredith Nicholson at least *try* to invest the proceedings with some visual interest, using depth of field, mirror images, and even changing focus within a shot to bring a character into sharp relief at a dramatic moment. The suspicious gardener's introduction, for instance, begins with Trudy resting on the couch reading a magazine when suddenly a sinister shadow passes over the world globe sitting on a table behind her. She looks up, alarmed, and the camera dollies back to reveal the unsavory old man hovering above her.

The first glimpse of the monster is effective as well. The hulking form sits up in shadow and then advances slowly toward the camera. When it steps into a shaft of light, the low-angled shot adds an imposing quality to the shocking sight. Sadly, however, these carefully constructed set-ups are the exception rather than the rule, since Cunha and company could squeeze very little from their just-get-it-done six-day schedule for such time-consuming "extras."

Nicholson's shadowy lighting can't fully disguise the few cramped studio sets and banal exteriors (producer Marc Frederic's own home), and so the picture possesses a cheap, claustrophobic feel. And Cunha can do little with the awful Felix Locher as the elderly scientist, whose whining, oddly-accented delivery becomes so annoying that the viewer breathes a huge sigh of relief upon learning that Carter expired from a heart attack in the hospital and will no longer be gracing us with his painful presence. (Locher, the real-life father of Jon Hall, didn't begin acting until he was 73. Based on his performance here, he obviously should have taken up golf instead.) Then there's the outright non-acting of hero John Ashley, who, despite his preppie shirts and turned-up collar, never seems to look comfortable in front of the camera. His deadpan delivery and immobile countenance are so stiff you could light a match on them. When the two lovers see the monster for the first time, for instance, Sandra Knight gives a healthy scream and looks appropriately horrified while Ashley simply stares blankly, with no emotion crossing his impossibly bland face. "I knew when we were making the film that it didn't seem very frightening," recalled Ashley. "There I was with this table between me and this monster and I'm rocking it back and forth and I couldn't believe that what we were doing was going to somehow be terrifying because it was on the big screen." (Apparently *acting* like it was terrifying was outside his range.) "Maybe the key to my success with exploitation films is that I always liked those movies," opined the actor. "I just enjoyed doing them." From Ashley's wooden demeanor in *Frankenstein's Daughter*, one could never tell.

Though H.E. Barrie's convoluted script sports an occasional gem of dialogue (such as when Elsu offers a rose to Trudy and observes, "I didn't like killing it, but some things are more beautiful in death"), more often the principals have to speak such weak lines as Oliver's "Where are we going to get the brain? I need a brain! I need a brain!"

Arguably the biggest liabilities found in *Frankenstein's Daughter*, however, are two show-stopping, tepid teen tunes by Page Cavanaugh and his Trio—"Special Date" ("Guess I really rate, 'cause I got a special date") and "Daddy Bird" ("I'm hip, daddy bird, let's flip, daddy bird"). These looooong pseudo-rock-and-roll numbers performed at Trudy's time-killing pool-party bring all the bizarre proceedings to a grinding halt and send a picture already teetering on the brink of boredom over the edge into full-blown lethargy.

Fortunately, as Trudy, Sandra Knight at least seems *alive* (and in fact comes off as quite likable), and Donald Murphy gives a hearty performance as the arrogant, brilliant Oliver. He imbues his scornful scientist with a superior air (indeed, his disdain for his pedantic employer seems justified) and a wealth of passion—not only for his work but for his libido as well. Much like Peter Cushing's Baron in *Curse of Frankenstein*, Oliver proves to be one lecherous monster-maker. Oliver not only tries to put the moves on Trudy, but he also nearly rapes Trudy's buxom friend before dispatching her with his car and commandeering her head for his experiment. Apparently Count Zaroff (from *The Most Dangerous Game*) was not far wrong when he observed, "One passion feeds another." Murphy's natural, sometimes intense, delivery even makes lines like "Tonight you'll be alive again, you little vixen," bearable. And he offers the insult, "You nutty old man," with just the right level of bemused contempt to make the laughable line work.

Of course, the most important question to any hapless viewer caught by *Frankenstein's Daughter* is: Is it male or female? To borrow from *I Was a Teenage Frankenstein*, its sister (or is that brother?) production that advertised itself as "Body of a boy! Mind of a monster! Soul of an unearthly thing!," so could *Frankenstein's Daughter* characterize its creation as "Body of a boy! Head of a *girl*! Soul of a *gender-confused* thing!" Much ado has been made over why the creature looks male while the principals refer to it as "she."

This *Daughter* must have been a deep disappointment to her parents.

According to makeup man Harry Thomas, no one provided him with a script and so he was unaware that his monster (played by Harry Wilson, Wallace Beery's long-time stand-in) was female. "I didn't think *he* was Frankenstein's Daughter," griped Thomas. "I thought that Frankenstein's Daughter was Sandra Knight, 'cause I worked on her first." Thomas' confusion only increased as things progressed. "Later, when we were shooting a scene in Dr. Frank's laboratory," recalled Thomas, "they brought Harry Wilson in and asked me to make him up to look as though he had been mutilated. I did just that—the makeup, in itself, represents a man who had been cut up in an accident. Since Dr. Frank had run down a girl [Sally Todd] with his car in a previous scene, I assumed that they were simply going to take a gland out of the man, Harry Wilson, and put it into the body of the woman, Sally Todd. At this point, it seemed obvious that Sally was going to be brought back to life as 'Frankenstein's Daughter.' But I was wrong again, and was flabbergasted when they began shooting a scene with Harry Wilson, Donald Murphy, and the little assistant, who says, 'You have outdone your father—she looks great!, *She*? I thought, oh, God, they're making a mistake." It was no mistake, however, and though Thomas wanted to change the makeup when he finally learned the truth, Cunha couldn't spare the time on this six-day wonder. So Thomas simply slapped some lipstick on Wilson's chops and sent his beefy "daughter" reeling in front of the camera. In any case, the face is so mutilated that it matters little whether it's a male or female countenance under all the stretched cotton, liquid plastic, and spirit gum. As to the body, no one ever says anything to suggest that the *body* is female. In fact, Elsu is genuinely surprised when Oliver brings home a *female* head. So what we have is a male body with a female head and brain. The other monster, however (Trudy under the influence of the disfiguring drug) is definitely all girl—and unafraid to show it as she parades about the neighborhood in form-hugging lingerie and swim-wear.

With tongue firmly in cheek, the monster's mix-and-match androgyny raises *Frankenstein's Daughter* to a level of deep social significance by inadvertently posing the question: Should a person's sex be determined by the brain or the body? If given half the chance, this poor creature might well have demanded that Oliver perform the ultimate sex-change operation and give it a female body to go with its feminine brain, thus becoming the screen's first transsexual monster! The mind boggles.

Though Harry Thomas provides a fairly good road-accident makeup job on the monster's face, Thomas also capped his/her/its head with a pillbox-shaped, wraparound white bandage reminiscent of the turban-style, high-fashion hats worn by middle-aged socialites of the previous decade. (Actually, Thomas blamed this fashion *faux pas* on the film's producer. "Marc Frederic came down to the set," complained Thomas, "and put that bandage around Wilson's head himself. I pleaded with him, 'At least let me put a blonde wig on him so that he resembles a woman.' But he would not give me the time.") In any case, the result makes for an amusing image. And an occasional chuckle is what the viewer must settle for with *Frankenstein's Daughter*, for nothing even remotely frightening ever happens during the whole ludicrous (and overlong) 85 minutes. After the monster's atmospheric introduction, the creature seems more comical than horrific, with its tremulous hands (it seems to suffer from some kind of palsy, for its appendages never stop shaking) held out perpendicular to its lumbering body and its silly M.O. of slow karate chops to the victim's collar-bones. Despite game efforts from Sandra Knight and Donald Murphy, and a half-hearted stab at competence on the technical side, this *Daughter* must have been a deep disappointment to her parents. Perhaps the best that can be said of *Frankenstein's Daughter* is that it's better than its co-feature, the execrable *Missile to the Moon* (another Cunha film which, incredibly, is a remake of the already dreadful *Cat Women of the Moon*, 1953).

Frankenstein's Daughter received the worst reviews of the triad. The long-winded reviewer for the *Monthly Film Bulletin* observed that "Due, possibly, as devotees will surely point out, to Oliver's use of the wrong apparatus, the monsters only frighten facially; indeed, the whole creative process, interrupted by teenage barbecues and jam sessions, is now a most perfunctory matter. The conception throughout is naive and crude, while the almost incredibly weak performance by Felix Locher as an elderly, well-meaning scientist adds an unintentionally humorous note." The more concise *Los Angeles Examiner* simply labeled the film "a dismal clinker." The kindest word came from the *New York Herald-Tribune*: "*Frankenstein's Daughter* is a little better [than *Missile to the Moon*], although much more confusing."

While America answered Britain's *The Curse of Frankenstein* challenge with quantity (three Frankenstein productions released within a one-year period), it didn't come close to its model's quality. Apart from a few guffaws and a plethora of cheesy sets, the terrible trio only offers one mildly interesting monster (in *Teenage Frankenstein*), two passably intense Creators (Whit Bissell in *Teenage Frankenstein* and Donald Murphy in *Frankenstein's Daughter*), and one embarrassing, train-wreck-fascinating turn behind the test tubes by the original Monster himself, Boris Karloff (in *Frankenstein 1970*). Come the close of the 1950s, America's independent filmmakers seemed determined to drag the Frankenstein name through the low-budget mud. Though worse was yet to follow (1966's *Jesse James Meets Frankenstein's Daughter* immediately springs to mind), the late 1950s proved to be the collective nadir of all things Frankenstein.

Frankenstein 1970 was an embarrassing train wreck.

Frankenstein Meets the Spacemonster

by Don G. Smith

The latter half of the 1960s saw a decline in the quality of American horror/science fiction films. The science fiction boom of the 1950s gasped its last about 1962, and the psychodrama sub-genre initiated by Alfred Hitchcock's *Psycho* (1960) had by mid-decade already seen its best examples. Still, no matter how barren the cinematic landscape, producers could always make a buck by having Frankenstein meet something or other. Frankenstein (the Baroness and the Monster) met the Wolf Man in 1943, and in 1948 the Frankenstein Monster met Abbott and Costello. Then in 1965, just seven years after giving us the uninspired *Frankenstein 1970*, Allied Artists trotted the old Frankenstein cow back to the barn for yet another milking. The result was the none-too-subtle title *Frankenstein Meets the Spacemonster*.

In 1965 interest in the space program was still high, and rock-and-roll music was bigger than ever. Since *Frankenstein Meets the Spacemonster* was obviously aimed at an adolescent audience, the combination of space, a rock-and-roll soundtrack, and the Frankenstein Monster was natural.

Derived from *The Mysterians* and, of course, the *Frankenstein* legend, the plot is familiar. Space aliens are interested in abducting Earth women to re-populate their war-ravaged planet. During one of their missions, the aliens mistake an earth-launched spaceship for a deadly rocket and shoot it down. On board the spaceship is Colonel Frank Saunders, an astro robot created by Dr. Adam Steele. When the spaceship is hit and Frank safely ejects to Puerto Rico, alien Princess Marcuzan and her prime minister Nadir send a patrol to destroy the survivor. One member of the space patrol locates Frank on a barren rock and attacks him with a laser gun. Instead of "killing" the astro robot, however, the laser blast burns off half of its face and destroys its electronic control complex. Karen Grant, Adam Steele's assistant, asks, "What if the machine breaks, or what

Derived from *The Mysterians* and the *Frankenstein* legend, space aliens are interested in abducting Earth women to re-populate their war-ravaged planet.

if something goes wrong with his brain?" Heavens, he could become a Frankenstein! And he does. Endowed with the ability to feel pain and an instinct to survive, the hideous Frank goes on a murderous rampage. Meanwhile Princess Marcuzan and Nadir examine Earth women kidnapped by the patrol. Those who pass the perfection test are prepared for shipment back to the alien planet. Those with blemishes, however, become food for Mull (or Mul), a giant caged monster that serves as an inexpensive garbage disposal.

Eventually, Adam and Karen fly to Puerto Rico and locate Frank. Adam sends Karen for help and proceeds to fix Frank. Before she gets far, however, the patrol grabs her and whisks her off to the spaceship. When Karen proves uncooperative, Princess Marcuzan and Nadir put her in a cage next to Mull. Frank, repaired and ready for action, tracks Karen to the spaceship, where he is captured by the patrol. Meanwhile, General Bowers orders a jet strike against the spaceship, which is impervious to conventional weapons. On board the ship, Karen revives the "unconscious" Frank, allowing him to free her and the other captives. One of the spaceship guards frees Mull, and a battle ensues between Frankenstein and the Spacemonster. The monster is winning the struggle 'til Frank grabs a laser gun and blows it away. Then Frank turns the laser gun on the aliens and on the ship itself. As Adam and Karen embrace, they watch the ship explode, marking the end of both Frank and the aliens.

Needless to say, *Frankenstein Meets the Spacemonster* did not open to good reviews. Nor has it garnered much praise since. Both *Leonard Maltin's 1996 Movie and Video Guide* and *Video Hound's Golden Retriever 1996* give the film their lowest possible ratings. A little

Instead of killing the astro robot, the aliens blast off half of its face. Karen Grant (Nancy Marshall) tries to help the Creature.

kinder, Stephen Jones, author of *The Frankenstein Scrapbook*, still awards the film only 1 1/2 lightning bolts on a scale of 4.

All are right. This film is the pits. Yet, as Weldon implies, if you enjoy campy productions, this is for you. So let's sit back, relax, and study the outright silliness of *Frankenstein Meets the Spacemonster*. First of all, the film's pressbook warns viewers not to take the film seriously:

> "Camp," the East Coast's new word to describe the delightfully outrageous, the thing that's called "so way out it's in," the book, work of art, piece of clothing, lamp, or decoration that is just "too much!" has taken over the science film. *Frankenstein Meets the Spacemonster*... is almost pure "camp," and as such should delight audiences of all ages.

Apparently the producers thought that youngsters would "thrill to the evil princess from another planet who space-ships to earth on a mission to capture beautiful girls." While that may be true, the Princess' Freudian dialogue will also elicit a smile from oldsters as well. And don't forget Mull, whose head is a skull with twisted fangs and whose clawed hands are death-dealing weapons. Yes, the kids would like that, and oldsters could find amusement in the monster's generally outrageous appearance while squinting to see it better in all those dimly lit scenes designed to obscure its visibility.

Teenagers are a prime target for this film. According to the pressbook, however, "The exploding popularity of rock-and-roll is being felt throughout the world, not least of all in the

American movie industry. What used to be called the "teen sound" has become the American sound, and moviemakers are discovering more and more that rock-and-roll can be used successfully to back films aimed not only at teenagers." It is true that The Beatles impressed both teenagers and mature audiences with their films *A Hard Day's Night* (1963) and *Help!* (1965), and it is also true that popular spy and action films were successfully using the rock-and-roll beat. So why not infuse *Frankenstein Meets the Spacemonster* with some rock-and-roll?

Of course, rock-and-roll is one thing. But if you really want to grab that teenage audience, throw in a beachful of squirming, gyrating, bikini-clad beauties—and then have someone grab them. American International had been successfully exploiting that angle with such pictures as *Beach Party* (1963), *Muscle Beach Party* (1964), *Bikini Beach* (1964), *Pajama Party* (1964), and *Beach Blanket Bingo* (1965). So, to cash in on the trend, executive producer Iselin included a scene in which the alien patrol abducts several swinging bikini beauties from a pool-side party. Amidst the mediocre rock music, screams fill the air and long lovely legs kick to escape. Now, that's entertainment!

According to the pressbook, "Older audiences will delight in... [Princess Marcuzan's] prime minister, who looks like a pop artist's fantasy. He rubs his hands gleefully at the thought of feeding Earthlings to Mul, and is so thoroughly happy being wicked that one hates to see his fun spoiled." With his obviously false bald head and pointed ears, Nadir (what an appropriate name!) is indeed a sight, and he and the Princess are two of the most ludicrous aliens since *Plan Nine from Outer Space* (1959). One could easily imagine either of them as antagonists in the *Batman* television series, over-acting and having a ball. Still, though Nadir is a bundle of laughs, he does have a chilling chuckle reminiscent of the killer's chuckle in "The Unlocked Window," the most terrifying episode ever produced for *The Alfred Hitchcock Hour*.

If we look at the cast, the only member probably recognizable to today's audience is James Karen, who appeared as the Realtor in Tobe Hooper's *Poltergeist* (1982) and Pathmart television commercials. Unsurprisingly, the other performers remain unknown.

Filmed in black and white (seemingly without synchronized sound), *Frankenstein Meets the Spacemonster* was shot in New York and on location in Puerto Rico. The Puerto Rican setting was probably a bow to cost trimming rather than a desire for an "exotic" setting. Black and white movies still appeared in the mid-1960s, but such American productions were becoming increasingly scarce testaments to low-budget filmmaking. About the same time *Frankenstein Meets the Spacemonster* was before the cameras, Embassy Pictures was shooting a couple of films with even stranger titles: *Billy the Kid versus Dracula* and *Jesse James Meets Frankenstein's Daughter*. At least both of those were in color! Maybe Allied

Unlike Boris Karloff in *Frankenstein* (1931), Colonel Frank Saunders (Robert Reilly), the astro robot turned Frankenstein Monster, is not made of human parts.

Artists hoped to overcome lack of color with a 1950s-style promotional gimmick. Posters for the film featured the following hype: "WARNING! BEWARE THEIR STARE! LOOK! The management will supply you FREE spaceshield eye protectors to prevent your abduction into outer space!!" Interestingly, neither Mull nor the aliens hypnotize people with their eyes, so what good are the special glasses? The pressbook offers the solution. Apparently, those glasses were never made to protect us from abduction into outer space:

> Although *Frankenstein*'s action plot should delight all danger-lovers, an unusual give-away offer makes this program a must for science fiction fans. In recognition of this once-in-a-lifetime double thrill show, all comers will receive free with their tickets a "space shield eye protector." These specifically made glasses are designed to protect the eyes of human beings traveling through outer space. They are effective in warding off the vast variety of cosmic rays and electron particles which could damage human eyes.

Since the book you are holding is called *We Belong Dead*, it is appropriate to spend the remaining space discussing the Frankenstein theme as exploited in *Frankenstein Meets the Spacemonster*. Unlike Boris Karloff in *Frankenstein* (1931), Colonel Frank Saunders, the astro robot turned Frankenstein Monster, is not made of human parts. He is a synthetic man, a mechanical man. Yet, when functioning properly, he is indistinguishable from human beings. Near the film's beginning, Colonel Frank is giving a press conference when suddenly

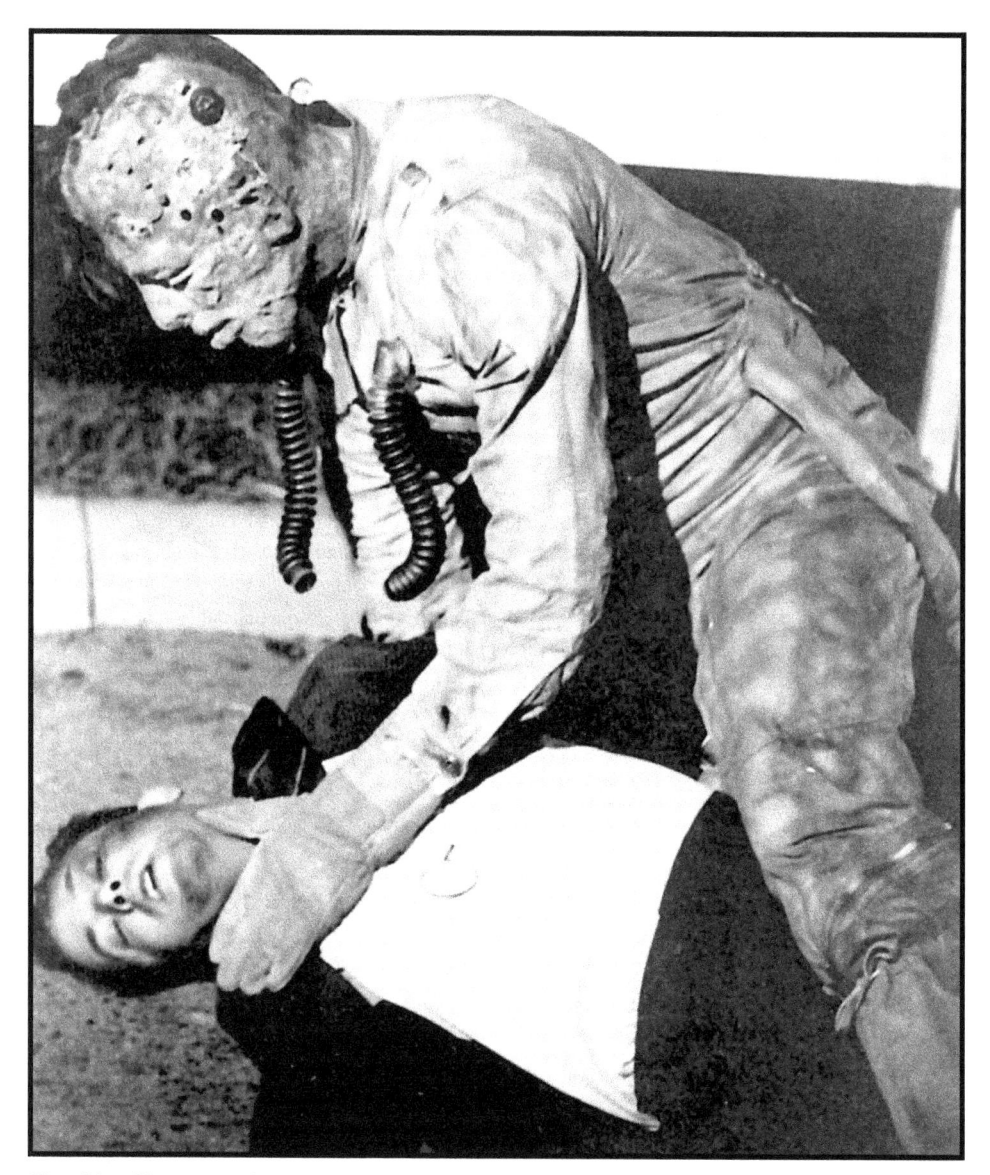

Frank's self-preservation unit apparently registers anything in human form is dangerous. This proves disadvantageous to human beings who stumble upon Frank.

his grin freezes and all functions stop. Adam Steele, who wants the press to accept Frank as human, quickly escorts the robot out of the room, claiming that Frank is really a shy fellow who doesn't want to answer any more questions. After some repairs, Frank is as good as "human" once again. In fact, Frank is so human that Adam chides Karen for not getting it sufficiently straight that Frank is a robot and not a man.

However, one of the main Frankenstein themes—that of man-made machine becoming man-made monster—is the focus theme of *Frankenstein Meets the Spacemonster*. As such, Robert Reilly is fairly effective playing a machine. When an alien blasts him with a laser, burning away half of his face and exposing raw metal, the result is appropriately hideous, though I would disagree with the pressbook's contention that the skills of makeup man John

Alese rival those of Lon Chaney, Sr.! Since Frank feels pain and possesses a built-in instinct for survival, its first act is to kill the alien who shot it. With its control system damaged, Frank's self-preservation unit apparently registers that anything in human form is dangerous. This proves disadvantageous to luckless human beings who accidentally stumble upon Frank. The monster's second victim is an innocent motorist whom Frank strangles. Then Frank comes upon a man chopping wood, takes the man's ax, and mindlessly turns the chopper into "choppee." Though Reilly displays little emotion, his one good eye appropriately registers a hunted gleam. Had the film taken itself a bit more seriously, the screenwriter might have given the audience a chance to sympathize with the robot, as Rod Serling does in his fine *Twilight Zone* episode "The Lonely," starring Jack Warden and Jean Marsh. In that episode, Warden plays a convicted murderer exiled alone to a barren asteroid in outer space. He is given a robot (which looks like a woman) to keep him company. When Warden is pardoned, the ship that arrives to transport him back to Earth does not have room for the robot. By this time Warden has developed a very human relationship with the robot, which for all practical purposes is a tender, caring human being. When Warden protests that she must be rescued too, the audience nods in agreement. Though we know that Marsh is a robot, we still wince in pain when the captain of the transport blasts her face away in order to bring Warden to his senses. The trouble with Frank is that he is never anything more to us than a robot. Consequently, we feel no empathy when he turns into a monster.

The challenge of humanizing Frank should have made the screenwriters of *Frankenstein Meets the Spacemonster* work a bit harder, but it did not.

When Adam Steele repairs Frank, the latter goes on a dangerous mission to destroy the aliens and rescue Karen. Reilly is fine in these scenes as the robot. The final confrontation between Frank and the Spacemonster is mercifully short. Bang, bang, zap, and it's over. Chaney and Lugosi certainly had a more exciting tussle in *Frankenstein Meets the Wolf Man*. Interestingly, as though to evoke the memory of that film, the posters for *Frankenstein Meets the Spacemonster* fill the word "Frankenstein" full of bolts or rivets, much as the word appears on posters for *Frankenstein Meets the Wolf Man*. Be sure, however, that all similarities end there. Closer in quality to the final confrontation in *Frankenstein Meets the Spacemonster* is that of *Dracula vs. Frankenstein* (1971) in which Zandor Vorkov's hammy Dracula dismembers John Bloom's emotionless Frankenstein Monster under conditions so dark that the audience can hardly tell what is going on.

In conclusion, *Frankenstein Meets the Spacemonster* adds nothing of interest to the horror film in general or the Frankenstein sub-genre in particular. Still, while it is certainly a failure as a horror/science fiction film, it does hold interest for some as a camp or cult film. In fact it is receiving increasing attention today as an enjoyable "bad film." As Reilly's Frank decided to destroy himself, Mull, and the aliens by exploding the spaceship, perhaps his robot brain registered the words "We belong dead." If so, undoubtedly and without question, he was right!

Assignment Terror
by David H. Smith

There was a time when commentators used to describe classic Frankenstein movies, like *Frankenstein* (1931) or *The Curse of Frankenstein* (1956), using adjectives like "engrossing" and "awe-inspiring," with performances by creator and created ranging from "thoughtful" to "heart-rending."

No more. Now, a commentary about newer renditions of the Shelley tale, like *The Bride* (1985) or *Mary Shelley's Frankenstein* (1994), is likelier to be about "phallocentric archetypes," the interests of the bourgeois, the "normatively masculine subject," and "homoeroticism." So caught up in their own lofty theories, critics have gotten away from what made the films so popular with audiences in the first place: big, inarticulate monsters with a touch of pathos, scaring the plebeian villagers, carrying off beautiful damsels, and giving their creators just deserts.

One filmmaker never lost sight of the sheer fun inherent with the classic movie monsters of the 1930s and 1940s. His name is Paul Naschy, and his imported, dubbed films as an actor, a screenwriter, and a director have all made him one of the few European B-movie artisans recognized in the United States. Surrealist Luis Bunuel and the irreverent Pedro Almodóvar may be more familiar Spanish directors' names to the U.S. film elitist, but Naschy clearly has his devotees. Enamored of the original Universal film series, Naschy took their milieu of vampires and werewolves and, in one or more of the capacities listed, created a shining array of new tales. The films were, very simply, fun for Naschy, his fellow actors, and the technicians involved; that exhilaration communicated itself past the screen and was felt by audiences the world over.

Much of whatever might have been entertaining about the films originally has, unfortunately, vanished before American eyes. Naschy's most exploitable movies have almost all been imported here, but, whether for theatrical or direct-to-television release, they have all been dubbed so dreadfully that each has become a discordant horror. Selectively xenophobic, American audiences forgive out-of-sync lip

HORROR HISTORY at the beck and call of two mad scientists!

Assignment TERROR!

movements and lumpy voice-overs in Japanese fantastic films dubbed for import, but show little clemency for their European counterparts. In Naschy's films, though the actors still show faint visual signs of depth in their performances, they usually mangle syntax in long discourses or mumble incomprehensibly on the films' English audio tracks.

Paul Naschy captivated European audiences with his takes on the classic movie monsters. Whether playing the role of a werewolf, a mummy, or even Count Dracula, Naschy clearly gives it his all. Some detractors (and there are many) choose to focus more on Naschy's resemblance to comedian John Belushi than on his performances. David Pirie, in *The Vampire Cinema*, dismisses Naschy as "stocky and rather flat as an actor"; similarly, Alan Frank, in *Monsters and Vampires*, describes Naschy as "an actor with serious limitations as a performer." The more astute Barrie Pattison, in *The Seal of Dracula*, declared him "an actor who manages to stay within his limits and keeps a sincerity needed in such unsophisticated material."

Naschy, born Jacinto Molina Alvarez in 1934 Spain, was an architecture student and former weight-lifting champion who became so enamored of cinema he risked being disowned by his own family to become a film extra. His first appearance was in *King of Kings* (1961) for director Nicholas Ray, and from there he went on to minor roles in Spanish and Italian features. For an episode of the American TV series *I Spy* filmed in Spain, Naschy co-starred as a villain alongside guest Boris Karloff.

By 1967, having worked frequently behind the scenes (as a production assistant, location manager, and second unit director) as well as before the camera, Naschy took a gamble and wrote an unsolicited script paying tribute to the Universal horror movies. At the behest of German co-producers, Naschy donned the werewolf getup himself. The release of *La Marca del Hombre Lobo* was a mixed-bag exposure of the man's broadish range shakily establishing him as a force to be watched. It had everything—werewolves, vampires, Satanic rituals, swirling fog, heaving bosoms, splattering blood. And it was unignorable.

But not unneglectable. Though it may have set a number of film elitists on their cerebral ears, it had a hard time making it to the U.S. intact. Independent-International Pictures Corporation, facing a production delay with its own *Blood of Frankenstein* (eventually released far more descriptively as *Dracula vs. Frankenstein* in 1972), slapped the totally incongruous title *Frankenstein's Bloody Terror* on a dubbed version of *La Marca del Hombre Lobo* available from England, and used it to pacify the expectant theater owners with its similar-sounding title.

Fernando Bilbao as the Farancksalan Monster

A stentorian voice-over prologue explained that "the ancient werewolf curse brands the family of monster-makers," and then the movie never mentions Frankenstein again. Audiences felt cheated by the fatuous title change, but rallied at the quality of the movie itself and made it a box office success. The American fourth estate, however, has never forgiven the name alteration, and usually holds the blameless Naschy responsible for it. Nevertheless, overseas, Naschy has played the character in nine sequels.

Assignment Terror (as America would know it), the second of those sequels, came in 1969; though a version of the Frankenstein story to star Naschy as both the doctor and the Monster was promulgated in the 1970s, nothing came of it. This is unfortunately the man's only direct undertaking of the Frankenstein theme on film. Naschy's most acclaimed film, *El Jorobado de la Morgue* [*The Rue Morgue Massacres*] (1972), which earned him a best actor award at the Festival Internacional de Cinema de Fantastic de Sitges (France) that year, would borrow heavily from the idea of life from the dead, but was not a true Frankenstein film. In *El Aullido del Diablo* (1988), Naschy donned the guises of many historical, literary, and screen monsters, including Rasputin, Quasimodo, and Fu Manchu. For a minute's cameo as "Frankie," Naschy wore makeup identical to the Jack Pierce archetype, and respectfully mimicked the original Karloff gait.

Los Monstruos del Terror, the original release title of *Assignment Terror*, was Naschy's ultimate paean to his Universal inspirations, and brought to the screen for the first time in a serious film (as opposed to Mexican comedy and wrestling films) the four classic movie monsters: vampire, werewolf, mummy, and Frankenstein Monster. It is sad the results turned out as shoddy as they did, but inevitable given the production's checkered history.

Jaime Prades, a production executive for Samuel Bronston commissioned a monster script from Naschy, who used it as a golden opportunity to write *Los Monstruos del Terror* as a full-blown homage to the Universal films of the 1930s and 1940s he so enjoyed. Inevitably, Prades ran out of money, and had to sell off rights to companies in West Germany and Italy in order to complete the film. For the first time in one of Naschy's films, casting was completed with a distinct eye toward the foreign market. Naschy's intent to marry the horror and science fiction genres, with the classic monsters wed to an alien invasion, was severely compromised by the budget constrictions, but what did emerge from the nuptials is a fascinating miscegenation.

Earthbound alien leader Odo Warnoff (Michael Rennie) makes contact with his superiors on the planet Ummo. Depicted only as swirling lights, they inform Warnoff that envoys have "incarnated" two recently deceased doctors to act as helpmates in his mission, "exploiting to the full the superstitions prevalent among the Earth creatures." Warnoff and his new compatriots meet at some fairgrounds, where their first objective is on display, and discuss the mission.

Warnoff is contemptuous of the people about him. "This is the world we have to conquer," he says. "Its inhabitants are weak, slaves to their own passions and uncertainties."

"Couldn't we use atom bombs?" asks Maleva (Karin Dor), one of the deceased doctors, a biochemist killed in a car accident.

"Of course," Warnoff boasts. "We could even explode their nuclear arsenal. But we need the planet intact." Their own sun growing colder, the people of Ummo look upon Earth as a perfect spot for mass migration, and have sent Warnoff to either destroy or dominate the human race before the alien colonization.

The three watch Ferzar, a Gypsy fortuneteller, promote his display: the skeletal remains of Janos de Mialhoff, a Transylvanian vampire count, with a stake wedged in its ribs. It is the most overt of Naschy's scene "appropriations," coming from *House of Frankenstein* (1944). Warnoff instructs Maleva to seduce the Gypsy that night, reminding her "the passions and weaknesses from which our race are immune are the very ones to which the Earth creatures are prey."

Maleva returns to the fairgrounds after the sun has set, and submits to the showman's crude lovemaking while her partner Kirian, the war-casualty surgeon, withdraws the stake from the vampire's ribcage. Kirian stabs Ferzar in the back and kidnaps his blonde assistant, whom Warnoff christens Ilona, for good measure. "Beautiful women are like powerful magnets," Warnoff explains. "We shall use them to attract scientists, generals, statesmen! And their secrets."

The next day, Police Inspector Henry Toberman (Craig Hill) confesses to his chief that the case has him baffled, particularly by the "gelatin substance" found on the murder weapon. The theft of the vampire's skeleton bothers Henry too, so, following up on a hunch, he goes to the city library and inquires about a volume written by Professor Ulrich von Farancksalan, an authority on all manner of monsters. The librarian is surprised at his request, in that it is the second that day. After being directed to the archive section, Henry finds the thick tome missing several pages and the caretaker murdered as well. With the same gelatin substance "made of living cells" found on the archivist's body as on Ferzar's, Henry ties the two murders together. Shown through a microscope as bubbling red water, the exact nature of the substance is never really explained. One ghoulish proposition is that Warnoff's reanimated assistants are decaying and leaving putrescent bits of themselves behind.

Henry's research into Farancksalan's *Anthology of the Monsters* leads him to some wild conjecture about the nature of the crimes. The name Farancksalan has long been a mystery to film buffs, and, to date, has been transcribed as phonetically close as the writers hear.

After discoursing on other monsters, among them a living mummy in Egypt, a medieval vampire called *Nosferatu*, and the legendary Hebrew Golem of Prague (the latter two never resurrected due to budget cuts), Henry comes to the story of the man-made Farancksalan Monster. "I wished to create a perfect human being, selecting the best organs from different corpses," Henry reads. "But God punished me for my presumption and fate caused me to insert the brain of a murderer into the human being which I believed to be perfect. Today I shall blow up the castle and bury myself with this terrible monster." Henry also reads about the curse of the werewolf, which makes for a timely segue to Kirian breaking into the tomb

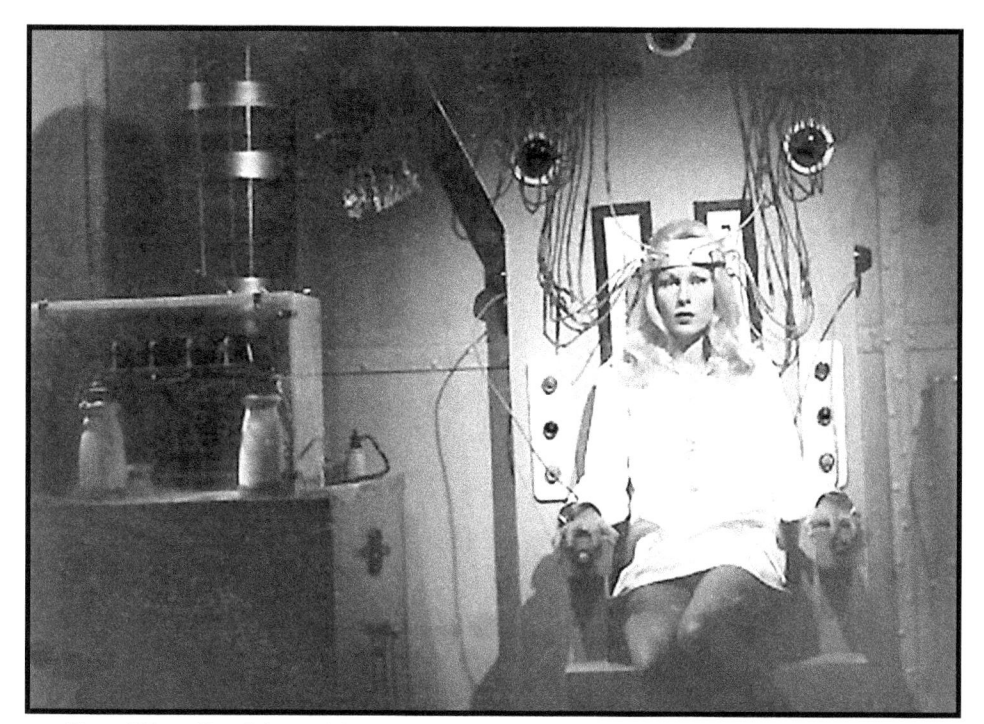

Ilona (Diana Sorel) is punished by Warnoff for failing to keep control of the werewolf.

of Waldemar Daninsky (Paul Naschy) and stealing his body. The nod to the opening scene of *Frankenstein Meets the Wolf Man* (1943) is manifest.

Back at their headquarters at an abandoned monastery, Warnoff and his aides remove the silver bullet from Waldemar's body, reviving him. This sequence, incorporating actual open heart surgery footage, was all that was admired about the movie by Allan Bryce in his retrospective on Paul Naschy films in *The Dark Side*. The alien leader assigns Ilona the task of injecting Waldemar with a serum to suppress his metamorphosis, then details Ummo's invasion plans to Kirian and Maleva: "No human power can withstand the contagion of the vampire. Or the Mummy, a murderer who obeys only the cabals of Egypt. Or the Farancksalan Monster. We shall make thousands of them, and turn them loose on the races of this planet." Maleva confesses strange urges overcame her when she touched Waldemar's body, the same as she felt when she was with the carnival showman. Warnoff cautions her to remain strong

The next night, Waldemar changes into a werewolf and attacks Ilsa (Patty Shepard) as she waits in a car for her date to retrieve her shawl from a restaurant. One of the quickest-thinking of all horror heroines, Ilsa pinches the snarling monster's arm by rolling up the window, then drives away. Frustrated, the werewolf lopes off to find another victim.

Warnoff is angry at this glitch in his master plan, especially at Ilona for failing to keep Waldemar's change in abeyance. He straps her to a chair and, with colored lights flashing, punishes her with ultrasonics. Maleva objects soon after the torture begins, another worrisome sign of dormant human emotions re-emerging.

Henry goes to interview Ilsa about the werewolf's attack, and they recognize each other from their high school days, when she had a crush on him (supposedly he is only three years her senior). Whether this difference in ages is the same in *Los Monstruos del Terror*'s

Assignment Terror **would be the last film appearance of Michael Rennie (center).**

original form is unknown, for the gap between Mr. Hill and Ms. Sheppard is considerably and obviously more than a few birthdays. Ilsa tells Henry of her father's experience as a young man with a werewolf named Waldemar Daninsky. Kismet, anyone?

After determining the exact location of Pakotep, the Mummy's tomb in Egypt, Warnoff sends Kirian and Waldemar to break into it and revive the monster within. Borrowing from Jules Verne's *Journey to the Center of the Earth* and the divination of the correct path to the center of the earth via the shadow of a mountain peak, they find the sarcophagus and resuscitate the gangling, bandaged horror with light reflected by a mirrored ankh.

Henry consults with Ilsa's father, who tells him of his friendship with a man who became a werewolf years before. Continuity in the Waldemar Daninsky films has always been tenuous, and trying to determine whether or not Ilsa's father is supposed to be Waldemar's friend Rudolfo from *La Marca del Hombre Lobo* is futile. One possibility to consider is that Ilsa may be Waldemar's illegitimate daughter, conceived during the two men's rivalry for Hyacinth in that film. The elder man promises to help Henry's investigation any way he can.

Meanwhile, Maleva, tending to Count de Mialhoff, almost falls sway to the vampire's supernatural hypnosis, another indication of resurgent human weakness. Warnoff again warns her and Kirian not to become susceptible to human frailties; even though the bodies they are inhabiting are human, their Ummo brains must be in control. For a *coup de grace*, Warnoff plunges a scalpel into Pakotep's chest. "The Mummy is our ideal," he discourses. "His heart is dried up. It doesn't feel, doesn't live, doesn't beat. He's a corpse who walks and obeys. Tomorrow I shall go to see the other ideal creature, the being created by Faroncksalan. He too has no heart, blood, nor feeling. Only a brain that obeys. His power is electricity, but we shall make him even more powerful with our atomic sources of energy." With the revelation of his imminent departure, Kirian and Maleva exchange meaningful glances

When Count de Mialhoff again makes a move on Maleva, enjoying a quick fondle of her breast in the process, Kirian interrupts and the vampire scampers away. Maleva gratefully embraces her savior, the hormones really jumping now. Simultaneously, Henry tells Ilsa's father that wolf-hairs were found under the fingernails of the victim ravaged the night of Ilsa's attack; the elder man wants to exhume Waldemar's grave to confirm or to allay his suspicion.

Warnoff returns with Waldemar from his offscreen expedition to the ruins of Farancksalan's castle, the dormant Monster (Fernando Bilbao) in tow. The modified name was probably used to prevent potential legal wrangling, a tack similarly employed by the Mexicans in *Santo y Blue Demon contra los Monstruos* (1968) with their mustached "Franquestein" (Manuel Leal) driving the getaway car, but the makeup is blatantly derivative of Universal's trademark Frankenstein Monster image.

The makeup in *Assignment Terror* has always been a bone of contention for Naschy, who felt that credited artist Francisco R. Ferrer was inept, with only the hired assistants showing any proficiency. To a degree, Naschy is justified in his opinion. The Farancksalan Monster makeup is crude and rather unprofessional. It is the worst ever used by Naschy, with brown pancake makeup sufficing for the more familiar yak hairs. However, the vampire and mummy makeup creations are excellent, not only by comparison, but unto themselves. One shot of Warnoff picking at the desiccated flesh near the Mummy's eye is particularly macabre.

Warnoff re-energizes the Farancksalan Monster with what appears to be common electrical power rather than nuclear. To test his control over the creature, Warnoff releases him from the operating table and telepathically instructs him to go and throttle Waldemar in his cell. Maleva demurs again to her leader's tactics, and Warnoff admonishes her scruples as he concludes the test.

Henry and Ilsa's father find a gravekeeper's body when they disinter Waldemar's coffin.

With the full moon approaching, Ilona is instructed to give Waldemar a double dose of the serum necessary to inhibit the change, but instead she injects it into a pillow. For his first dialogue in the movie, Waldemar wonders why, and Ilona professes her love, explaining she is no longer under Warnoff's control. Making their escape, the two are taken aback as Maleva, recognizing their feelings for one another, holds the door for them.

Kirian and Maleva confess their mutual passion. As they embrace, the cat's-paw Farancksalan Monster barges in and strangles Kirian. Distraught, Maleva accuses the impassive Warnoff of surrendering to the latent human jealousies he warned them about so pithily and often. He gives her a session of the ultrasonic punishment for her impertinence.

This lab scene shows the budgetary restraints of *Assignment Terror*.

Another salient reference to *House of Frankenstein* (detractors would say rip-off) comes as Ilsa calls Henry over to her apartment and seduces him. Surrendering to her charms, he refers to her as a "little minx," the same term of affection Carl Hussmann (Peter Coe) had for his manipulative wife Rita (Anne Gwynne).

Waldemar tells Ilona he plans to go see his old friend, Ilsa's father, and tell him what he knows of Warnoff's plans. They realize they have no future together, cursed as he is, and Ilona lugubriously recites the traditional end to a werewolf's suffering (yet again from *House of Frankenstein*), a silver bullet fired by one who loves the man/monster enough to die for him. Thickheaded as well as morbid, the two never think to have a sample of Warnoff's werewolf control serum duplicated for future use. The camera slowly pans around the convenient castle ruins where the pair is hiding out, focusing on broken battlements and flying buttresses as Ilona's forlorn voice trails off.

Again the budgetary constraint rears its ugly head, for Waldemar's meeting with the elder man is mentioned but not shown. Now, armed with some sort of vindication of his theory, Henry goes to confront Warnoff in his monastery lair. Without hesitating, the alien obliges the policeman by confirming his suspicions, even seeking Henry's opinion on "the legends of monsters, vampires, werewolves, (and) the Farancksalan Monster."

Henry coolly replies, "Many fantasies are being transformed into reality by modern science. Transplants of heart and kidney, the cornea, perhaps in the near future even the brain. I have no doubt it'll soon be possible to create a Farancksalan Monster." Imagine his surprise when the genuine article strides in to carry him off to the dungeon. Warnoff also has Count de Mialhoff go and kidnap Ilsa. Ilsa's father convinces the police superintendent to call in the military after Waldemar's visit and his daughter's disappearance.

Waldemar and Ilona sneak back into the monastery and free Henry from his manacles. But then, as it happens, Waldemar changes into his hirsute other self (full moons not being requisite in Naschy's werewolf films) and battles the laggard Mummy, showing uncharacteristic human cunning by setting the bandaged horror on fire with a handy torch.

Warnoff confesses to Maleva he has lost his control over the monsters even as the police and army arrive *en masse* with bullhorns ordering him to surrender. Henry rescues Ilsa and shoves a stake into the vampire, who screams, spins, and collapses into a skein of cobwebs, a scene applauded by Barrie Pattison in *The Seal of Dracula*. It also puts to an end any possibility of the film living up to its advertising in several countries retitled *Dracula vs. Frankenstein* or some variant for British, French, and West German release. The "Dracula" of *Assignment Terror* and the Monster never share so much as a fleeting scene together.

In a reprise of *Frankenstein Meets the Wolf Man*, Waldemar battles the Farancksalan Monster in the laboratory. The werewolf's agility proves more than a match for the slow-moving Monster's brute strength, and the patchwork being is electrocuted by some of the lab equipment; Ilona comes in and, despite being fatally mauled herself in the process, shoots Waldemar, who returns to his human form in her dead embrace.

With the monastery aflame, Warnoff contacts Ummo to apprise his superiors of the situation. "The passion we believed was their weakness is what makes them really strong," he reports, accepting full responsibility for the mission's failure. He pleads that Maleva be spared, but the aliens remind him she was already dead, and make her disappear. In *Keep Watching the Skies!,* author Bill Warren, analyzing *The Black Sleep* (1956), made special note of mad doctor Basil Rathbone's last look of love at his comatose wife (Louanna Gardner) as he resigned himself to his fate at the hands of the monsters he had made. Here, as the smiling Karin Dor fades away, Michael Rennie's momentary shocked expression of remorse is more than a match.

Volatile gases meet and the monastery explodes. Safe and sound, Henry and Ilsa watch the conflagration. Henry moralizes, "While there are men willing to sacrifice themselves for others, nothing will destroy us."

With an eye for international appeal, casting for *Assignment Terror* included names and faces familiar worldwide, even in America. Michael Rennie headlined as Warnoff, which critics chide him for mercilessly. Rennie received his greatest acclaim, but was typecast forever by small minds, as the alien envoy Klaatu in *The Day the Earth Stood Still* (1951); virtually every review of *Assignment Terror* cites that film as an inspiration for Rennie's part, but while it undoubtedly induced his casting, the two share only an extraterrestrial origin as a common denominator. The characters are entirely different in motivation and demeanor.

Assignment Terror was Rennie's last film, though *Subterfuge* (1968), a U.S./British co-production, was actually released later. He died in June 1971.

Nominal heroine Karin Dor was born Kathe Rose Derr in February 1936, and was, by this time, a recognizable face to fans of European horror movies. Her screen immortality was assured, however, by her appearance in the James Bond adventure *You Only Live Twice* (1967) wherein the villainous Blofeld (Donald Pleasence) fed her to his piranha. Unlike most horror heroines who relied on *décolletage* or a fortissimo scream, Ms. Dor paraded through *Assignment Terror* in comparatively modest miniskirts and thick eyebrows, looking more like an austere Joan Crawford than a clichéd "scream queen."

American Craig Hill had emigrated to Europe in the mid-1960s after his film career petered out.

Fernando Bilbao, as the Farancksalan Monster, evinces little impression, and the film fails to exploit his real seven-foot height with expected low camera angles. It is the makeup more than the direction that forces Bilbao to lurch about looking down his nose, making him little more than a somnambulant android at Warnoff's beck and call. A few years later,

The Ultimate in HORROR
DRACULA versus FRANKENSTEIN
Starring Michael Rennie · Karin Dor · Craig Hill

director Jess Franco would hire the somewhat fleshier Bilbao to reprise the Monster role in two features, *Drácula contra el Dr. Frankenstein* [*The Screaming Dead*] and *Les Expériences Érotiques de Frankenstein* [*The Erotic Rites of Frankenstein*], which gave him more to do performance-wise but in decidedly seamier and seedier *mise en scenes*.

Patty Sheppard, the brunette ingenue, would receive greater recognition for the next, unrelated Waldemar Daninsky adventure. *La Noche de Walpurgis* [*The Werewolf vs. the Vampire Woman*] (1970) starred Sheppard as Countess Wandesa Darvula de Nadasdy, inspired by the real Hungarian malefactress Elizabeth Bathory. Fictionalized somewhat, Sheppard plays her as a devil-worshipping sorceress accidentally resurrected by a couple of college coeds, eerily effective in her attacks. Her black organza veils, swirling in ethereal slow motion, make for one of the best depictions of a female vampire ever. It is a shame the imagery was not exploited further in a sequel, which might have made Sheppard the preeminent vampiress in fans' minds, outstripping both Ingrid (*The Vampire Lovers*) Pitt and Barbara (*Dracula—Prince of Darkness*) Shelley.

The principal director (70 percent according to an exhaustive Naschy interview in the double-sized *Videooze* #6/7) of *Assignment Terror* was Hugo Fregonese, an Argentine who helmed a number of Hollywood Westerns and gangster B pictures before going to Europe in the mid-1950s for steadier income. Problems with his own health, coupled with the budgetary production delays, forced Fregonese to abandon the project, and Tulio Demichelli finished the movie as best he could, receiving solo screen credit for it. Though publicity hyped *Assignment Terror*'s epic production time of five months, filming was completed in only six days spread over that time.

At the time of *Assignment Terror*'s production, America was mired in a fruitless war and was torn by race riots. The country was still reeling from the assassinations of Robert Kennedy and Rev. Dr. Martin Luther King, Jr. A foreign film featuring monsters long relegated to late-night TV showings had little chance in American movie houses without a major (read: expensive) marketing push. So, with no interest by the major distributors in a theatrical booking, expedient American International Pictures secured the television rights and released it to the small screen in the mid-1970s with little fanfare. Reviews were not kind.

Far from being deathly serious, Naschy's script and the directors infuse the film with deliberate humor at several turns. European comedy usually does not translate well in

Naschy (shown with son Sergio) portrayed the werewolf in *Assignment Terror*, but he did don the Frankenstein Monster makeup in *The Howl of the Devil* (1987)

America, as witness *Tempi Duri Per I Vampiri* [*Uncle Was A Vampire*] (1959) or *Gebissen Wird Nur Nachts—Happening Der Vampire* [*The Vampire Happening*] (1971), but here several instances pay off. Henry's boss orders him not to arrest any vampires, as he is already anemic; when Henry recounts the legends of the various monsters, the police superintendent loses interest and goes off to mime conducting of the music playing on the stereo. Later, Henry goes to a bar for a glimpse of Warnoff who, already surrendering to those damnable human vices, regularly stops in for an aperitif. The idea of monsters on the loose in the 20th century begins to play tricks with Henry's mind as he waits, imagining one fellow patron with fangs, and seeing his own reflection in the mirror changing into a beetle-browed and shaggy whatzit.

The melding of the Gothic and modern eras has always been a tricky operation in horror films, even by the major producers. *Assignment Terror*, save for Waldemar's intentionally amusing encounter with a car, keeps the monsters amidst the trappings of an earlier era. The stone walls of the monastery and the sterile confines of the lab were all too familiar stomping grounds to these fiends.

In refuting the negative comments written by sanctimonious critics about movies like *Assignment Terror*, one has to applaud the pluck and share the sentiment of Irish writer George Bernard Shaw, who once wrote to a journalist: "Dear Sir, Your profession has, as usual, destroyed your brain."

Assignment Terror, desultory as it is, remains a showcase for Paul Naschy and his admiration for the film monsters of the past, though sadly the Frankenstein-Farancksalan Monster receives short shrift. Derivative? Totally. But the movie's central idea is so goofily intriguing, the enthusiasm by Naschy so synergetic, and the script's uncondescending respect for its forebears so apparent that it would be unfair to dismiss *Assignment Terror* as just another European pastiche of the monsters America knew and loved.

Blackenstein
by David H. Smith

Compiling a retrospective for a book on *Frankenstein* films is a tricky business. Imparting to the readership the quality of the movie is important, and a writer always hopes to bring about a new appreciation for an unsung favorite of his or hers. It's all well and good to tout the performances of Boris Karloff in the archetypal Universal films, or the production values of the Hammer films, or even the good-natured ribbing of a Mel Brooks parody. Readers are usually familiar with these qualities, and, nine times out of ten, usually share the author's opinion.

However, when signing on to analyze a blatantly bad film, one ultimately hopes to find some positive aspect in said film. This is where the difference between being a film skeptic and a film cynic emerges. Skepticism is asking questions, being dubious, being wary, not being gullible. Cynicism is already having the answers—or thinking you do—about a movie or the story behind it.

A movie universally panned tests a writer's ability to differentiate between the two. The movie skeptic says, "I don't think that's true, I'm going to check it out." The movie cynic says: "I know that it's true. It has to be. Like everybody else, I'm going to ridicule it." There is a fine line between them, but it's a line that has to be respected, especially with easy targets like *Blackenstein*.

The floodgates were open in the early 1970s for virtually every film genre. With the decline of the studio system and the majors' hold on the theater chains, the burnished, big-budget product of Hollywood studios now competed for space on movie marquees with the cheapest of exploitation fare. In urban areas, movies targeted exclusively for Black America catered to audiences who usually avoided mainstream opuses. These "blaxploitation" movies were big box office and made scads of money for their white producers.

The civil rights movement had empowered Black voters and helped place Black politicians in power. But in 1972, the emotions of Black Americans were still very raw. There was the bitter disillusionment of the antiwar protesters and the men who fought in Vietnam, and the seething anger that Washington was more interested in leveling hamlets like My Lai than in rebuilding the ghettos of America.

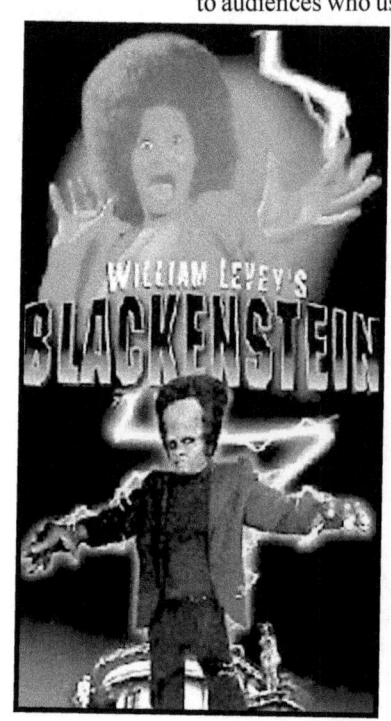

American International Pictures was undergoing a major change at this time. For years it was the largest producer of fantastic cinema for America and the world. The company's co-founder, James H. Nicholson, had just left to become an independent producer after 18 years; he died soon afterward. President and chairman of the board Samuel Z. Arkoff wanted to reassure anxious exhibitors that AIP's commitment to exploitation fare was still first and foremost. With great ballyhoo, he announced that *Blackenstein* would be the company's 100th film (statisticians may argue), and that all the stops would be pulled out to produce a topnotch horror movie. The film would eventually see only extremely limited release by Exclusive International in 1973. It is evident Arkoff's initial reaction to the movie anticipated the critics.

Even before its release, the media were castigating it and others of its ilk. In the March 1974 issue of *Jet*, writer Clarence Brown bemoaned the Black image being slapped onto otherwise white horror films, citing *The Blaxorcist* (a publicity title for 1974's *Abby*) and *Blacula* as examples. He announced forthcoming titles by relying on erroneous ad campaigns for films that never were, e.g., *Black the Ripper* and *Werewolf from Watts*, and proclaimed *Blackenstein* and *Black Frankenstein* (its re-release title) as two new, entirely different features.

Ellen Holly concurred with Brown's assessment in an article about Black horror films in *The New York Times* three months later, saying, "Half the time, the material not only isn't Black, it isn't even original, as white material ready for the boneyard is given a hasty blackwash and sent on one last creaking go-round."

Blackenstein was indeed intended to be a follow-up to AIP's wildly successful and critically acclaimed *Blacula* (1972), a straightforward vampire tale with impressive production values, an intelligent script, and a masterful portrayal of the title character by William Marshall. Though parts of the film have not aged well, particularly the Day-Glo polyester fashions and "jive" vernacular, *Blacula* remains one of the finest horror films of the decade.

Blackenstein is its antithesis.

Product placement and name-dropping were very important in 1970s horror films—they gave the movies a semblance of realism for audiences tired of shabby pasteboard sets and anonymous European locales. While it's doubtful any of the providing manufacturers, chambers of commerce, or services gave *Blackenstein* a ringing endorsement, it's interesting to see them in a *Frankenstein* context. Dr. Winifred Walker (Ivory Stone), an attractive young Black woman, arrives at the Hollywood-Burbank Airport and rents a green Buick Riviera from Hertz. As the movie's blues theme plays and opening credits (in Gothic typeface) roll, she drives to an imposing mansion.

Winifred is admitted by a Black butler, Malcomb (Roosevelt Jackson), whose deep voice immediately labels him more than just a manservant. Winifred asks to see Dr. Stein, whom Malcomb summons from his lab via a horn and a flashing red light. The young woman waits, seated on a stool beside a life-sized statue of the Virgin Mary wearing a halo of red Christmas tree lights.

Dr. Stein (John Hart) and Winifred (Ivory Stone) try to help Eddie, a wounded veteran, in *Blackenstein*.

The Caucasian Dr. Stein (John Hart) remembers Winifred from his teaching days and invites her to join him at dinner. Despite being at opposite ends of an enormous dining room, Winifred and Dr. Stein form a mutual admiration society. She tells him that, even though she now has her Ph. D. in physics, she has never forgotten his tutelage.

"Have you been following my work?" Stein asks her, fishing for compliments.

"Oh, of course, Doctor," Winifred gushes. "I read the results of your winning the Nobel Prize in the medical journals. And I've also read other doctors commenting on your success." She continues by offering to stay on with him as an assistant there in Los Angeles; her fiancé, a wounded Vietnam veteran, is flying in the next day for rehabilitation at the local V.A. hospital. Winifred asks if Dr. Stein could take the time to examine him, but hesitates to disclose the extent of his injuries.

The next day, as they drive to the hospital, Winifred reveals that Eddie Turner, her betrothed, lost his arms and legs after stepping on a land mine. They are directed to the intensive care ward by a supervisor (Karen Lind).

Minutes before their arrival, however, barrel-chested Eddie (Joe DeSue) had asked a harried attendant (Bob Brophy) for some ice cream to cool his dry throat. "Like hell!" the attendant had barked. "This ain't no damn hotel!" He then had launched into a diatribe against Eddie, ridiculing the dismembered soldier for asking for special treatment while he, a 4-F washout, had so much work to do. Only the fortuitous arrival of Winifred and Dr. Stein prevents the taunts from escalating to physical abuse.

Left alone with Eddie, Winifred consoles him and introduces Dr. Stein. Eddie shows reluctance, but she promises they can help. "Eddie, I would like to do anything I can to help," Stein interjects. "Although I can't offer you any positive promises, I have been working in the field of replacing limbs. With your permission, I'd like to see what can be done in your case."

Eddie is still skeptical, but Winifred tries to remain upbeat, telling him that Dr. Stein just "won the Nobel Peace Prize for solving the DNA genetic code."

"Once again I can offer you no promises, other than my good results in the laboratory," Stein says sincerely. "I would like very much to work with you and help you. But you must also want to help yourself. If you do, and are willing to undergo long hours of operating procedure and treatment, I think you'll have quite a surprise."

As the soundtrack echoes those last three words for ominous effect and the theme song swells again, Eddie is transferred by ambulance to Stein's home. Nowadays, with the plunge in the number of war-maimed veterans treated at the agency's 173 hospitals, the V.A. has been turning more of its attention to veterans who are among the nation's drug-addicted or indigent, mentally ill or physically disabled. In hindsight, with films like *Born on the Fourth of July* (1989) and its depiction of a veterans' hospital, Eddie's choice is all the wiser.

Winifred and Dr. Stein inject Eddie with a syringe filled with a liquid that looks suspiciously like urine. "This is going to be your first injection of DNA, Eddie," Winifred chirps, prepping his body for the intended surgery. She departs for rounds with the elder doctor.

First, they visit Eleanor (Andrea King) and inject her with a similar compound. As the 50ish patient lies demurely in bed, Stein explains her condition to Winifred. "Through my experience with the genetic code [of] DNA, I have a formula that's brought her from approximately 90 years of age to what you see before you."

"That's incredible!" Winifred understates.

"But not without a few problems, as Eleanor will tell you," Stein concedes "It's necessary she have an injection every 12 hours to preserve this condition. The DNA formula just isn't taking hold, and we must work on a locking feature." Inept research for a physicist but Stein's methodology is a bit off anyway. The script prepares the audience for a scene that never comes, that of Eleanor rapidly aging. Is it better to be a drug-dependent, bedridden, middle-aged dowager than a vibrant and vigorous senior citizen? we ask ourselves.

Next, they visit Bruno Stragor (Nick Bolin), who has had an amputated lower leg replaced using Stein's miraculous DNA stuff. "This leg was grafted on by laser beam fusion, supplemented by massive injections of my DNA formula. Hardly any scar at all." The doctor then pulls Bruno's bedcover back further, revealing his unscarred leg that has the stripes characteristic of a zebra. "That's the result of an unsolved DNA injection—sort of a part of the primeval theory, a kind of throwback to the jungle," Stein explains, keeping an amazingly straight-face, bungling Charles Darwin and English grammar at the same time. "I'm currently working on the DNA, and I'm hoping to bolster and supplant the DNA, possibly replacing it."

The next scene has Winifred and Dr. Stein anesthetizing Eddie and commencing work. The passage of time in *Blackenstein* is impossible to judge: Virtually every scene is preceded by the same low-angle shot of the doctor's mansion at night, animated fog swirling about, thunder rumbling in the distance. Whether it is later that evening, the next night, or a year later is indeterminate.

Amid the crackling apparatus hauled out of Universal special-effects maven Ken Strickfaden's garage, Winifred and Dr. Stein perform surgery on Eddie. What it is they do exactly can only be determined by stray bits of dialogue later in the film. From some unknown source, they transplant new arms and legs onto Eddie, but it's difficult to tell. Every laboratory scene is shot from overhead, and there are no explanatory close-ups.

"I believe the operation is a success," Stein proclaims.

Winifred, like a teenaged schoolgirl meeting her favorite pop star, enthuses, "This is so great! The whole thing is incredible! Eddie and I are really fortunate that I knew about your work."

Special effects maven Kenneth Strickfaden's garage provided the lab setting for *Blackenstein*.

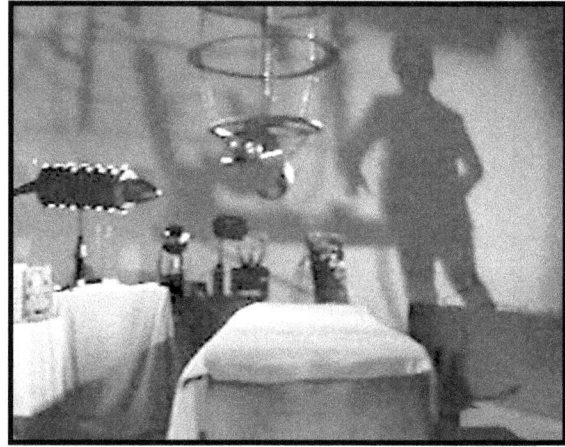

That night (one has to assume), Winifred is awakened when she hears Bruno raving and thrashing about in his room. She arrives to find Malcomb and Dr. Stein binding him in a straitjacket and sedating him. Stein tries to quell her fears. "This is not too unusual, Winifred," he smiles. "It happens occasionally after a shot, but the patient calms down very soon and returns to normal." Foolishly Winifred shrugs it off.

Stein is delighted by Eddie's postoperative recovery. Already his new fingers have sensation, and the doctor reassures Winifred her fiancé's complete recovery is imminent. Later, Malcomb professes his love to Winifred, but she spurns his attentions. Stewing, Malcomb goes to the lab and substitutes Bruno's DNA formulation for Eddie's.

Eddie becomes Blackenstein (Joe DeSue).

With the electrical contraptions sparking and flashing, Winifred and Stein perform follow-up surgery, injecting Eddie with the mislabeled DNA. Sometime afterward, when it is time for his physical therapy, he begs off, telling them he doesn't feel well.

"All our tests show you have total use of your faculties," Stein tells Eddie, then notices conspicuous hair growth on the backs of his patient's hands. Also, Eddie has developed a beetling brow.

Ever the humanitarian, Stein has Eddie moved from his comfortably cozy bedroom upstairs to a convenient dank cell adjoining the lab for closer examination. The doctors study some industrial footage of the bloodstream and try to figure out Eddie's problem.

"Dr. Stein," Winifred says, "the cell matching tests seem all right, so there couldn't have been any error in our selection of the transplant parts."

Stein concurs. "All the blood tests seem all right. No clotting or thickening. Run all the blood tests again." Stein, trying to put out a fire with gasoline, increases Eddie's dosage of the DNA formula.

That night (again we must *assume*), Eddie gets out of his bunk and, already fully dressed down to patent leather shoes, lurches out of the open cell door and into the laboratory. Growling with his mouth closed he sounds more constipated than terrifying. He leaves the house undetected, shuffling along in a pitiful imitation of the cliché Universal *Frankenstein* Monster walk, making his way back to the V.A. hospital

Eddie enters via a conveniently unlocked back door, and finds the attendant who insulted him in a storage closet. With flashbacks to the earlier scene intercut, the two grapple behind a hospital dividing screen, with Eddie eventually pulling the man's arm out of its socket. The soundtrack's signature of Eddie's rage is an amplified heartbeat, played whenever he attacks throughout the movie.

Ambling back to the Stein mansion, Eddie's presence starts a small dog yapping, interrupting the cuddly foreplay of an amorous couple. When the man (Jerry Soucle) goes outside to investigate, again the heartbeat is heard, but the butchery outcome is kept off screen. Hearing her lover's cry, the woman (Liz Renay) goes outside as well. Eddie strangles her, then proceeds to disembowel her. Furthering the distasteful scene, in a sort of harbinger of all those noisome European imitations of *Dawn of the Dead* (1979) that prevailed in the early 1980s, Eddie takes the time to fondle the dead woman's entrails, grunting all the while.

After stopping to clean himself up, Eddie returns to his cell with Winifred and Dr. Stein unaware of his nocturnal jaunt. The next day, Winifred studies those blood tests ordered by her mentor, suspiciously eyeing the vial of chartreuse DNA formula in the meantime. That night, she falls asleep at the work table, and Eddie again clumps out for a stroll.

He goes to a nearby park and hides in the bushes. A car pulls up, and when the driver (Daniel Faure) tries to flatter his date (Beverly Haggerty) in a clumsy seduction, she rolls her eyes and rebuffs him. When he refuses to take her home, she gets out of the car and watches him drive off. Eddie grabs her as she passes by.

The enraged Eddie embarks on a killing spree.

Two policemen stop by Dr. Stein's the next morning, investigating the three murders that have occurred in the vicinity. World-weary Captain Tucker (Don Brodie) and handsome Black Lieutenant Jackson (Jim Cousar)—billed as police lieutenant and police sergeant in the end credits—question Dr. Stein, but the medico, more out of genuine ignorance than slyness, reveals nothing.

There follows a long sequence at a nightclub, where a risqué comedian (Andy "C") and a matronly blues singer (Cardella DeMilo) perform. Having a cigarette in the back alley after his gig, the comic's jaw drops as he sees Eddie's enormous shadow pass. Nearby, Eddie interrupts a man (Robert L. Hurd) about to rape a girl (Marva Farmer). Unfortunately he's more disposed toward handling fresh intestines than meting out justice. Despite the boy's flurry of punches, Eddie tosses him aside, then eviscerates the screaming girl.

Back at the mansion, frustrated Malcomb is about to rape Winifred when Eddie bursts in, raging male hormones evidently an incitement to his attacks. Malcomb manages to shoot him five or six times with a convenient pistol, but the bullets have no effect, and the lecherous butler gets his comeuppance.

Stein leads Winifred out of the room and down the stairs. When Eddie shambles after them, Bruno comes to their defense and, that pesky primeval theory cropping up again, charges at him like a bull. Eleanor cringes close by, both their fates left unresolved.

Down in the lab, Eddie attacks Winifred, but Stein leaps to her rescue. Eddie wrestles the doctor off and tosses him behind the work table, causing an explosion of sparks. For no other reason than to eat up more running time, Eddie leaves just before the police arrive. Tucker calls an ambulance for Stein, hinting at the doctor's survival while Jackson comforts Winifred.

Eddie, his lust for murder or intestines or whatever unsated, grabs a girl (Dale Bach) from a stalled dune buggy and carries her off to a conveniently deserted factory. Where in southern California such diverse landmarks, businesses, and suburbs are located within walking distance of one another is a mystery. The girl manages to slip out of her burly kidnapper's clutches for a time, but, despite her comparative vim and vigor, Eddie manages to overtake her again and presumably kill her as well. If pedantic film historians are perturbed by the inexorable stalking of fleet-footed heroines by mummies and similarly laggard movie monsters, know then that *Blackenstein* would put them in a frenzy.

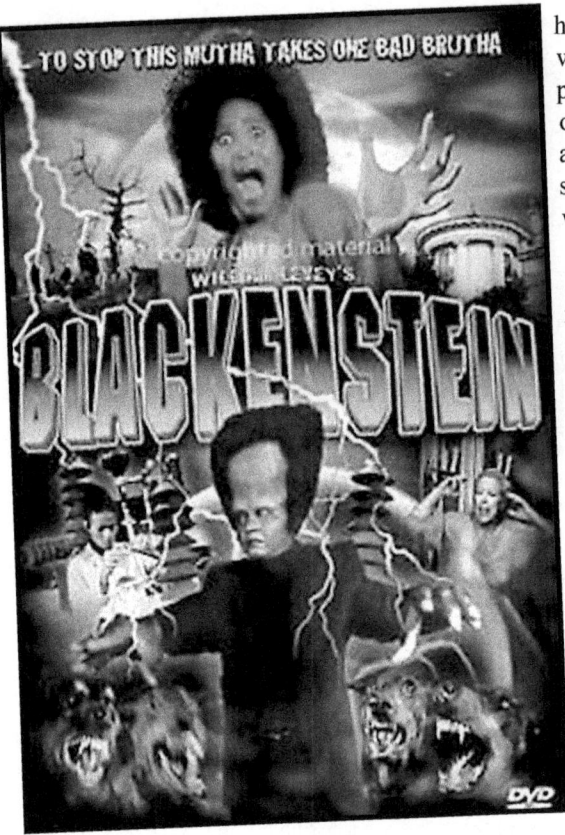

Somehow ascertaining Eddie's locale, the police release their canine corps of Doberman pinschers into the factory, where they take Eddie down without much of a fight. One dog quickly pulls off Eddie's arm, while the others disembowel him. His heartbeat slows to a stop as the camera lingers on his moist intestines. Touché, you hapless Vietnam veteran turned surgically augmented mad killer, you.

Oh, where to start? *Blackenstein* is an embarrassment of riches of bad things, and not just in comparison with other *Frankenstein* or blaxploitation films. The problem is not with the concept, which could quite easily have made an interesting thriller, but that the film is so tawdry and amateurish given the possibilities. Several reviewers hinted they too saw the potential, but came away disappointed.

It's unfortunate that *Blackenstein* and *Blacula* are frequently cited in the same reviews, being polar opposites in almost every respect, but it makes for easy comparison. Michael Weldon, in *The Psychotronic Encyclopedia of Film,* also bemoaned the contrast. "After *Blacula* this was inevitable," he sighed, "but *nobody* could have guessed how bad it would be. It's a totally inept mixture of the worst horror and blaxploitation films."

One of the biggest problems with *Blackenstein*, when relating it to the Mary Shelley mythos, is that it really has no relation to the Frankenstein theme at all. The scientists face no moral dilemma, the dead are not reanimated, and the possibilities of future science are never called into question. New limbs are grafted onto a war veteran, and a brokenhearted butler tries to make him unappealing to his fiancé. That's it. The very name Frankenstein is never even conjured.

It is no wonder, then, the film is so vilified; what is surprising, though, is that audiences as well as an exploitation film mogul shared that sentiment from the beginning. *Blackenstein* was a dud when first released, and it was still a dud a few years later when it was picked up by Prestige Pictures and retitled *Black Frankenstein*. It made the rounds and achieved even greater notoriety. The film frequently played on a double bill with the now famous *Ilsa: She-Wolf of the SS* (1974).

The behind-the-scenes personnel of *Blackenstein* are almost anonymous. Writer-producer Frank R. Saletri was a successful criminal attorney whose Hollywood acting ambitions had been quashed years before, despite an uncanny resemblance to Clark Gable. For *Blackenstein* he enlisted Liz Renay, a blonde showgirl he had dated sporadically for years, to play one of the victims. The exigent and lascivious value of Renay's cameo in *Blackenstein* wearing a low-cut, see-through nightgown was very evident on the big screen, but the effect is virtually lost on Media Home Entertainment's licensed video due to a dark source print and poor resolution.

Concurrent with *Blackenstein*'s premiere, the producers of a nude revue Renay was about to star in convinced her, for publicity purposes, to "streak" across Hollywood and Vine at high noon. Heavy traffic and 5,000 rubberneckers aggravated the harmless stunt, for which she was arrested and charged with indecent exposure. Defended by Saletri, Renay's seven-day trial, a media frenzy in itself, ended with a "not guilty" verdict from the jury, with the bailiff requesting a set of the incriminating photos for the judge to keep.

The one actor of any note in *Blackenstein* was John Hart (Dr. Stein), whose only claim to fame was his donning the black mask and powder-blue duds of the Lone Ranger in the 1950s television series (while Clayton Moore was embroiled in a contract dispute) for 52 of the 221 episodes. A sturdy if vapid leading man, Hart's performance in *Blackenstein* is largely undone by the desultory script. Dr. Stein is the most oblivious of movie mad scientists (and not once is there made a mention of his surname possibly being derived from Frankenstein). Once Eddie starts to metamorphose, Hart virtually disappears from the screen action, leaving Winifred to puzzle over blood tests and to leave crucial doors unlocked.

It isn't even clear whether Hart has been killed at the finale, paving the way, one supposes, for sequels that never came but were nevertheless promulgated for years in the trades and hyped in *Famous Monsters of Filmland*: *The Return of Blackenstein*, *The Fall of the House of Blackenstein*, and *Black Frankenstein Meets the White Werewolf*. The 1974 announcement of the forthcoming *Return of the Ghost of the Bride of the Son in the House of Frankenstein* 198?, again starring Hart and Renay and to be produced by Saletri, must surely be facetious.

Other performances are adequate, most scarcely so. Ivory Stone is earnest, but has little to do, and it's more than a little demeaning when her big scene has her breasts bared when "Malcomb" attacks her. As the lascivious butler, Roosevelt Jackson makes a statement as banal as "Alcohol, doctor," so foreboding that it's a shame he didn't get better opportunities in horror films or, at least, in voice-overs. Joe DeSue, looking (as *Players* magazine described him) like the cartoon ape Magilla Gorilla, is quite dreadful, however. In makeup his waxy features are immobile and incapable of expressing anything—anger, lust, fear, dyspepsia—and even in his early scenes, as the normal double-chinned Eddie, it looks like he can barely remember his few lines, much less display any kind of real emotion in his reunion with Winifred, the one scene that requires it.

The sparse, underlit laboratory of Dr. Stein housed electrical devices contrived by Kenneth Strickfaden, whose contributions to the original Universal *Frankenstein* films set the standard for movie mad scientists' workshops. Strickfaden's contributions were doubtlessly sought to give *Blackenstein* the plausibility of one of those classic films, but the budget was too low for the man to devise anything remarkable, and their function in the film was questionable any-

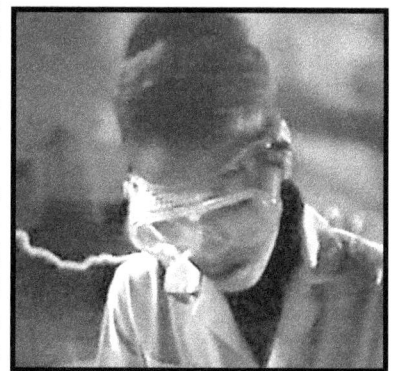

Ivory Stone is earnest but has little to do in the film.

way. One flashing control board is labeled a "memory data register," but its function is never explained. The only scientific work done in the movie is limb transplantation, which scarcely requires pyrotechnics suited to "revive" the dead. Strickfaden's legacy was better served a couple of years later, when Mel Brooks sought his services for *Young Frankenstein* (1974), and a budget was provided and a lab set built to better showcase his brainchildren. Typical of the tenuous respect *Blackenstein* pays to the *Frankenstein* film heritage, Strickfaden's name is misspelled in the credits.

Blackenstein was Connecticut-born William A. Levey's first directorial effort after cutting his teeth in TV and working as a film editor. Save for the incongruously moving *To Be A Rose* (1974), his later films were scarcely better, and, were it not for the novelty of some of today's more famous actors making their debuts in them, Levey would be all but forgotten. Debra Winger made her first appearance in *Slumber Party '57* (1975), Patrick Swayze in *Skatetown USA* (1979), and Jean-Claude Van Damme in *Monaco Fever* (1986). The feckless Levey's efforts were once described in *Variety* as "dirty-old-man direction [that] virtually drools over the screen." Other Levey films with lesser, though no less interesting, casts include *Wham Bam Thank You Space Man* (1975).

To keep enumerating *Blackenstein*'s faults is pointless and eventually tends toward meanspiritedness. As a blaxploitation movie it misses the boat, with Blacks constantly shown servile to a white person in authority. Winifred begs for mentor Stein's help at the V.A. hospital, a Black receptionist (Yvonne Robinson) defers

Two foreign posters for *Blackenstein*

to her white supervisor, the investigating policemen looks for all the world like the cliché Southern plantation owner wielding a riding crop, his kowtowing field hand just off the buckboard.

Scientifically, *Blackenstein* tries to be relevant with the 1970s, a few turgid references to DNA sufficing for acumen. DNA, or deoxyribonucleic acid, contains the genetic codes that distinguish each person from all others and is contained in each human cell, and Dr. Stein's prizewinning work with it does imply the possibility of using DNA to inhibit the rejection problem that comes with transplants, tailoring the body to accede to the new limbs. Unfortunately, when the doctor starts blathering about RNA substitution and primeval throwbacks, theories are tossed out like a baby with the bathwater. Where he and Winifred procure the limbs to graft onto Eddie is passed over and left unexplained.

If there is an unexpected bit to admire, however minor, it's with songstress Cardella DeMilo's bluesy number that plays under the opening credits. This one trivial aspect of *Blackenstein* captures the meaning of Shelley's novel; loss, loneliness, and aloneness.

Some of the lyrics by Ms. DeMilo are especially poignant and apropos to the literary theme: "What have I done? Have I been wrong? Friends I have none, and trouble so long and adding to the misery: I guess I have no one to love me."

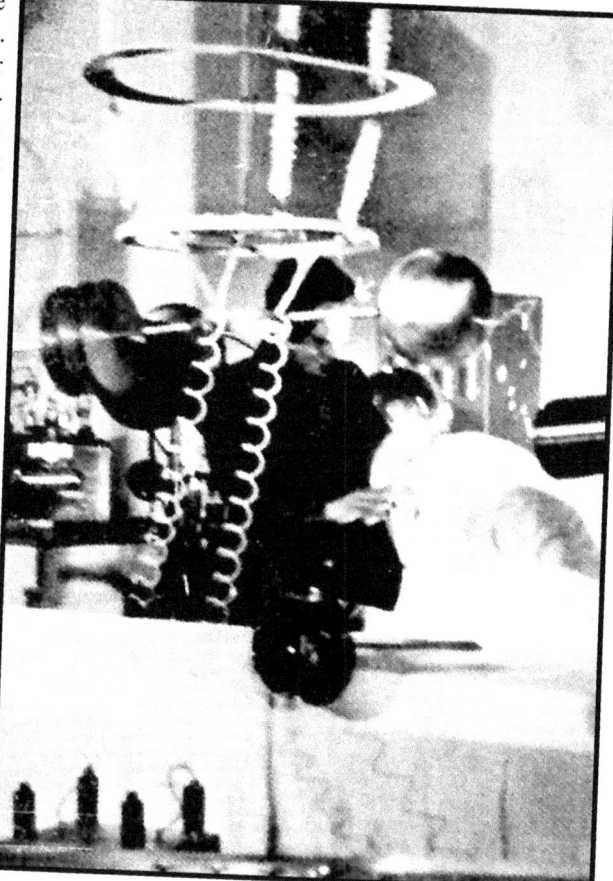

Blackenstein is the most egregious of *Frankenstein* films.

Early on in *Bride of Frankenstein* (1935), the authorities disbelieve housemaid Minnie (Una O'Connor), who claims the Monster still lives. She throws up her hands in frustration and says, "May they all be murdered in their beds!" Frank Saletri was found dead in bed some years later, a .45 caliber gunshot to the head, no struggle or robbery evident. The crime remains unsolved.

American author Ralph Ellison wrote about the depiction of Blacks in the movies, essaying, "In the beginning was not the shadow but the act, and the province of Hollywood is not action, but illusion." Failing even this, *Blackenstein* heralds itself as a bridge between two genres of film, horror and blaxploitation, and can only offend patrons of both.

"What happens when a new work of art is created is something that happens simultaneously to all the works of art which preceded it," wrote T. S. Eliot. The saddest aspect of a poor Frankenstein film is the stigma it gives all those that came before it or will be produced afterward.

There's a place in West Africa called Cape Three Points. It's the one spot on the globe where zero degrees latitude intersects with zero degree longitude. It's also situated exactly at sea level, elevation zero. This place is a perfect metaphor for *Blackenstein*, the most egregious of Frankenstein films, in terms of production and entertainment values.

Lady Frankenstein
by David H. Smith

Have you ever tried lighting junk food on fire? The folks that publish *Earth Island Journal* did, with amazing results. While a Cheez-It flared for just 46 seconds before turning to ash, a single Dorito burned for a full three and a half minutes!

A copy of Nelson Entertainment's videocassette release of *Lady Frankenstein* would no doubt fan the flames for the movie's full running time of 84 minutes. It is the ideal junk food movie, almost impossible to resist, filling but without value, delicious but leaving pangs of guilt after consuming.

Director Mel Welles was an expatriate American whose greatest notoriety came as an actor in Roger Corman's stock company, co-starring in films like *The Undead* (1956), *Attack of the Crab Monsters* (1957), and, most famously, in *The Little Shop of Horrors* (1960).

Welles, working in Italy, had to seek financial backing from Roger Corman and his fledgling New World Pictures back in the States.

With the sets built, stage rented (De Paolis Incir Studios, the oldest in Rome) and scores of people employed in Italy already, it is extremely fortunate for Welles that Corman foresaw the exploitation angle as he did. Corman played it to the hilt when he released it in 1972, with the excellent dubbing work re-christening most of the characters with decidedly middle-American names, like Sarah Wills, John Masters, Seth Atkins, Bill Turner, and Tim Jessup.

"Only the monster she made could satisfy her strange desires," the copy read on the American poster, an angle Welles particularly liked. Though the beehive-wigged blonde depicted on it scarcely resembles sultry brunette star Sara Bay, audiences flocked to see *Lady Frankenstein*.

The period horror film was clearly on the wane by 1972. Normally the province of England's Hammer Films with its Victorian Draculas and Bismarckian Frankensteins, they had lately run out of steam and the studio was even then testing the waters with a modern-day scenario in *Dracula A.D. 1972*. But the beauty of those period pieces was their timelessness, whereby audiences do not "date" the proceedings via fashion or vernacular. As Gene

Kelly put it, "When you work in a period that *was*, you have some distance and a better chance to make a picture last."

Baron Frankenstein (Joseph Cotten) and Dr. Charles Marshall (Paul Muller), his aide, accept the delivery of a corpse from Thomas Lynch (Herbert Fux), the town's resident graverobber. When Frankenstein insists the next delivery be fresher, no more than six hours dead, Lynch raises his price, to which the Baron accedes. He and Charles carry the body into the castle laboratory. Frankenstein admires the patchwork creature they've assembled on the operating table there.

"You know, father, the name Frankenstein still echoes through the halls of the university." Tanya (Sara Bay) embraces her father (Joseph Cotton).

"To succeed in creating life is the ultimate achievement," he tells Charles. "To hesitate, to fear, to doubt now would make everything I've ever done pointless, empty. This is my life."

"But to create life—shouldn't Man leave that to God?" Charles wonders, a bit late in the game.

The Baron smiles. "Here on Earth, Man is God." They bid each other goodnight, preparing for the return of Frankenstein's daughter the next day.

Morning comes, and Tanya (Sara Bay) arrives via coach. Charles greets her and orders the good-looking but imbecilic stableboy Thomas to carry her luggage. Tanya asks Charles if her father is still experimenting with animal transplants, which Charles skirts and changes the subject to the young woman's career at the university.

"I'm like my father," she boasts. "Stubborn. When I want something, I get it. And I did. First in my class. I'm now a licensed surgeon."

The Baron comes in at this opportune moment, offering congratulations. Father and daughter embrace. At dinner that evening, Tanya describes her education: "You know, father, the name Frankenstein still echoes through the halls of the university."

"I'm not surprised," the Baron shrugs. "But I stopped caring about those fools when I left them with their hands clapped over their ears 30 years ago." He goes on to wonder if the family name was a hindrance to her.

"Sometimes," she admits. "Mostly it was my being a woman. The professors have a lot of old-fashioned ideas about a woman's place."

Charles, despite being lame and appreciably older than Tanya, can barely contain his infatuation with Tanya. "I'm sure you will make a fine surgeon," he offers.

Tanya accepts the compliment and proposes she collaborate with them in their experiments. She reveals she has known about them since she was a child. This amuses the Baron, and he acquiesces, "I shall be delighted to discuss it with you. Of course, as doctor to doctor."

"Good," Tanya says. "But I must warn you that my ideas are quite radical. Even more so than yours, Father."

Frankenstein raises an eyebrow. "Really?"

"Of course," she smiles. "I am my father's daughter."

"You are referring to, ah, animal transplants," her father suggests.

Tanya does not bat an eye. "Human," she pronounces.

Lady Frankenstein succeeds admirably in straddling the period and modern film here. Tanya mentions the misogyny of her instructors, but does not dwell on it. She has proven herself to be their equal, perhaps even their superior, in surgery, and even though still a student has been experimenting on a rather radical premise. At the time of *Lady Frankenstein*'s production, it had not been so long since women were supposed to have perfect poise and charm and always wear a skirt in public, never pants. Professional women still wore hats and gloves. In 1972, the women's movement was still newborn. Many women were at the front lines in shattering the dichotomy between work and home, asserting themselves in professions and institutions once closed to them.

Lynch has meantime enlisted some helpers to acquire the fresh corpse. He comes to the castle the next day to demand more money, citing the higher costs that such a special order entails. When the Baron goes to get the money, Tanya comes in. The bumptious Lynch leers at her, his double entendres making her seethe. "My dear sir, you are an obnoxious man," she states. "Extremely vulgar, and I'm certain that whatever you are thinking is merely fantasy on your part. I would say you spend too much time in your fantasies. Be careful: it will soften your brain far quicker than whiskey."

"How can somebody so lovely be such a bitch?" the hooligan wonders.

"It depends on the company I'm with," she counters. When her father reenters, Tanya's mood shifts, becoming demure and fragile. This dual personality, from assertive to docile, shows up in several scenes in the film, changing to suit her or the situation she's in. It can be construed as evidence of Tanya's guile to achieve her ends, or it may, in fact, be mental illness.

Having promised a fresh corpse to the Baron, Lynch waits, along with most of the townspeople, at the gallows two days later for the hanging of Jack Morgan, a notorious criminal. Captain Paul Harris (Mickey Hargitay) parleys with Lynch, trying to goad the graverobber into confessing to some crime or other. Unsuccessful, Harris promises to someday see the man misstep and to cheer when Lynch is sentenced to be executed himself.

Frankenstein and Charles, in the throng as well, are mortified to see Tanya arrive by surrey. She insists, as a doctor, death is nothing new to her and that she should stay, despite their protestations. Eager to curry favor, Charles comes to her defense, and the Baron consents. The condemned man is hanged.

Lynch delivers the body as promised. Frankenstein and Charles pay him off, then go into the lab to begin their work. Tanya comes in via the secret passageway she's used since childhood. "So this is why you no longer use the animals," she realizes. "Human transplants!"

Frankenstein pleads with her to leave, insisting she not become any more involved than she is, should the law intercede. Tanya notes the dead criminal's body prepped for surgery, and tries to examine the patchwork creation nearby. She figures her father and Charles are going to remove the brain and heart, but is hustled out before all her questions are answered. The two men remove the organs.

Later, the Baron describes his experiments to her. "And so for the past 20 years my experiments with animal transplants have been pointed to this week. All the abuses I have endured from my friends, all the accusations against my sanity, and worse, will be thrown into their sanctimonious faces." He looks outside, hoping for an electrical storm to build, "for only lightning will give the creature life. That's why I haven't transplanted the heart and the brain."

Tanya looks surprised, and her father continues, "Oh, I can keep them alive indefinitely in the laboratory. But once I transplant them, they'll survive only a few hours unless activated by lightning."

Clearly enraptured, Tanya prays her father will succeed. "I will," he promises, "and the medical world will be brought to its knees."

"I want that so much, to see you realize your dream," Tanya says. "Something that no one will ever take away from you."

"They won't have to," Frankenstein vows, "I'll give it to them."

Fortuitously, lightning flashes and thunder crashes at that moment. The Baron and Charles leave Tanya and repair to the lab to perform the operations. After the heart is implanted, Charles notices the hypothalamus of the dead man is damaged. Frankenstein insists that, with the necessary storm reaching its peak, there is no time to correct the defect. Charles rightfully contends that portion of the brain is a necessary part of the nervous system, that without its function the creature would be immobile.

When Frankenstein elects to proceed anyway, Charles makes a last-ditch effort to dissuade him. "What about anger and pleasure, two emotions connected to the damaged part of the brain?" he argues erroneously. "Two vital emotions; either one in excess could be devastating."

Despite the argument, Frankenstein decides to continue, and together he and Charles insert the dead man's brain into the shaven head of their creation. They attach the requisite electrical leads, with the Baron proclaiming blasphemously, "Man's will be done."

Lightning strikes, setting the creature's face on fire. They close the skylight and extinguish the smoldering flesh. Charles is horrified at the scarring, but the Baron dismisses it as merely a cosmetic flaw, unimportant in the grand scheme of things. When the elder man cannot detect any vital signs in their creation, he concedes defeat, admitting they should have paused to repair the brain damage. Charles tries to console him, but Frankenstein brushes him off. "Who knows, Charles? Perhaps there are some things Man should leave to God," the Baron says, remarks atypical of most movie mad scientists.

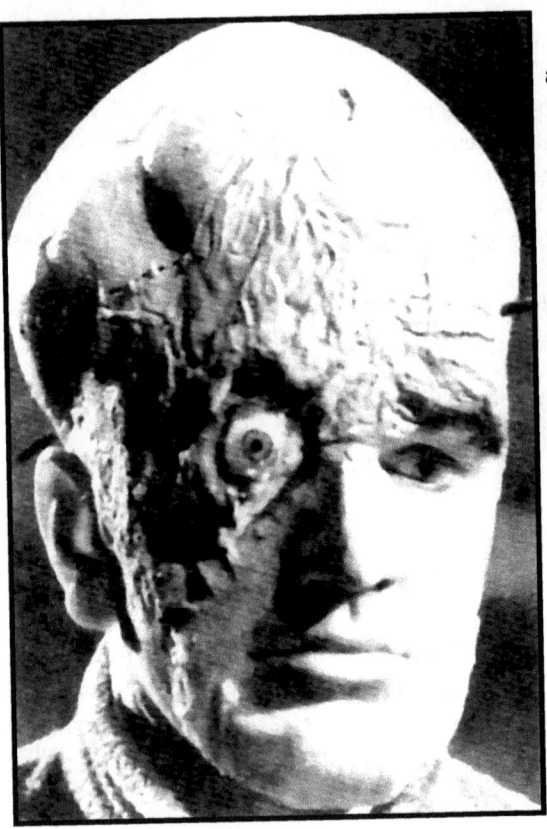

Frankenstein's cool ghoul is decked out in shoulder pads, smock and psychedelic pants.

The creature's hand twitches then, and the Baron finds the heartbeat. He unshackles the newborn thing, ordering it to sit up, then stand. Already decked out in shoulder pads, a smock frock, and psychedelic striped trousers, the Monster silently towers over them, a bloodied eye bulging from its socket amid the lumpy third-degree burn scars.

Frankenstein sends Charles to fetch Tanya, to share their triumph. He urges the Monster to walk toward him. It approaches him, then, as he rechecks the heart rate; it wraps its arms around him and crushes the Baron. The Monster stalks out of the lab into the castle proper, where Charles and Tanya watch it lumber out the front door.

They run to the lab, where Tanya cradles her father's body in her arms. When Charles tries to comfort her, she quickly calms herself and begins to scheme. She tells Charles to inform the police of the murder, but that it was committed by a robber caught in the act. She also tells him to get rid of the hanged man's body in the quicklime tank they have installed for unneeded body parts. Asked what she hopes to gain, Tanya tells Charles, "Time to think of some way to save my father's reputation."

The Monster wanders across the countryside. It comes across a fornicating couple—the swain runs off without a fight, leaving his naked girlfriend to be tossed by the Monster into the rushing stream nearby. Her body is later found by a couple of fishermen.

Summoned to the castle, Harris wanders about the lab, commenting on the oversized operating table and the rows of jars containing pickled viscera. Tanya tries to convince him it was a seven-foot robber who murdered her father, but Harris seems dubious. The police captain tries to find a connection at Lynch's dismal apartment, questioning the graverobber about his drunken associates arrested the night before with money to burn, far too much to be merely Lynch's "collectors" in his loan shark operations.

Back at the castle, Tanya has decided the only way to vindicate her father's memory is to build another creature. Charles protests, telling her Harris will destroy the Monster. Tanya insists no man will be able to, only another creature of like construction.

"You'll be creating another monster," Charles warns.

"Not a monster," Tanya counters. "An executioner. Our creature will kill my father's murderer."

Charles is dismissive. "No, it's impossible," he says. "Even if you found the right brain, your creature, despite the superhuman strength induced by the lightning, would need a physical body strong enough to support it. Where would you find such a man?"

After trying to engage Lynch's services, Tanya is disgusted at the man's proposal to work out his fee in trade rather than cash, so no deal is struck. Charles is outraged at the graverobber's presumption and confesses his longtime love for Tanya. He also admits he never really believed in Frankenstein's dream, staying on only to be near her.

Tanya suggests using the stableboy Thomas' body as a vessel for Charles' brain, creating someone who could make proper love to her and whom she could love back, body and mind. His defenses down, Charles is seduced into the proposition, and the two are married.

Lady Frankenstein with her creation.

The Monster, meanwhile, has been terrorizing the area. It kills a farm couple, but leaves their child in peace. The Monster goes on to murder Lynch in his bed.

Harris feels cheated that it was not he who saw justice served with Lynch's execution. He goes to the castle to question Tanya about Lynch's visit the day before, but she puts him off. As he is about to leave, he asks her, "By the way, you don't believe in monsters, do you?"

"Of course not," Tanya huffs.

"I do," Harris tells her knowingly, insufficient evidence gnawing at him. Later, the Monster kills Lynch's underlings even as they decide to do a bit of body snatching on their own. Harris orders all recent graves must be exhumed.

"What do you expect to find, sir?" a lieutenant wonders.

"Not a damn thing," Harris replies grimly, suspecting the town's graveyard of providing the raw materials for the Baron's handiwork now menacing the populace.

Returning from a shopping excursion, Tanya seduces Thomas by disrobing herself, then undressing the handsome simpleton. She proceeds to mount him, impaling herself, writhing in unabashed naked glory while Charles creeps in and smothers the lummox with a pillow. Tanya climaxes even as Thomas convulses in his last death throe. Given this bit of necrophilia, one has to wonder what Tanya's hands were busy doing under her bustle as Jack Morgan was twitching at the end of the hangman's noose.

Thomas' sister Julie comes to inquire after her brother after a couple of days, but Tanya sends her away, doing little to allay her fears. Tanya then tells Charles the operation will be performed that night.

One of Harris' lieutenants tells him that the villagers suspect Frankenstein to be behind the recent rash of killings, even though the Baron was killed himself. Harris is amazed when that suspicion falls upon the daughter as well, never mind his own notions of the noblewoman's deceit.

Nevertheless, the lieutenant warns his superior that the people are up in arms about the murders, and may take matters into their own hands. "To them the name Frankenstein is six leagues below Satan himself, and they don't care who's wearing it," the junior officer says. Apparently, this ill will has festered for years, but there has been no evidence of it; Frankenstein and Charles attended the hanging without so much as a baleful stare shot their way.

Tanya tries to save her father's reputation in *Lady Frankenstein*.

In the castle laboratory, Tanya hesitates with the brain transplant, but Charles urges her to proceed. The operation completed, Tanya plants a lingering kiss on the lips of the still-dead "Thomas" before she throws the switches to electrically charge his body. Apparently the lightning required before was a bit of theatrical overkill on the Baron's part.

Charles' brain now lives on in Thomas' virile body. Tanya admires her handiwork, testing his coordination and superhuman strength. She even provides him with a wig to cover his shaven pate and promises no one will be able to tell the difference once the stitches are removed.

Captain Harris, alerted by Julie to more of Tanya's machinations, returns to the castle and demands to interrogate Charles. Though Tanya insists her bedridden husband's illness is contagious, Harris bursts into the darkened master bedroom. Tanya apparently took the time to transplant the larynx as well as the heart and brain, for it's Charles' voice that answers Harris' questions from the shadows. Their chicanery is a success, and Harris leaves, but warns them that everyone associated with the Baron is apparently the Monster's intended prey. Harris remains outside the gate to keep watch.

Tanya has a change of heart and wants to leave the Monster to Harris and his men, but "Charles" insists they stay, for only he will be able to defeat the Monster.

The Monster creeps up on Harris and knocks him unconscious, then crashes through the iron gate and enters the castle. The Monster is momentarily nonplussed by Charles' mutilated body, and Tanya incongruously sees this as a method to control the Monster. "Charles" comes to the realization that no matter which of them survives, he or the Monster, Tanya and her father's work will be recognized.

"Charles" and the Monster battle, with the Baron's creation gaining the upper hand, despite having one lopped off by "Charles" and his hatchet. Tanya intervenes by shoving a spike into the Monster's back and through its torso. When the Monster turns to get her, "Charles" buries the hatchet in his scarred head for the deathblow. In a pivotal moment, Tanya calls her triumphant husband "Thomas."

The torch-wielding villagers set the castle ablaze, even as Julie and the recovered Harris search desperately for her brother. They come into the lab and watch as the copulating "Charles" and Tanya undulate on the bloodied floor. "Charles" reaches up and chokes Tanya to death as the flames grow more intense.

Lady Frankenstein ends abruptly there, but the debate over the film's merits (or lack of them) has continued unabated to this day. One of the most polemical aspects of *Lady Frankenstein* is its casting, a cross-section of film genres encompassing mainstream, exploitation, and out-and-out horror. The biggest name (and cast solely for its marquee value, according to Welles in *Fangoria*) was Joseph Cotten. Born in Petersburg, Virginia, the distinguished actor first made a name for himself with his work in the Mercury Theatre with Orson Welles (no relation to Mel). Moving to Hollywood, he became a leading man for directors as distinguished as Alfred Hitchcock and Carol Reed.

Cotten's 1987 autobiography, *Vanity Will Get You Somewhere*, makes no mention of *Lady Frankenstein*; however, he seems to be enjoying himself in the film, shifting from self-assured megalomaniac to diffident worrywart as the script requires. Though Welles claims Cotten worked only a short time on the film, his death scene does not come until the midway point.

In the role of Captain Harris was Mickey Hargitay, a one-time Mr. Universe best known for his tumultuous marriage to 1950s blonde bombshell Jayne Mansfield. The handsome Hungarian bodybuilder had been part of Mae West's revue, where Jayne first met him in May 1956. They married in January 1958, and together had three children and co-starred in some forgettable movies, among them *Gli Amori de Ercole* (*The Loves of Hercules,* AKA *Hercules vs. the Hydra*, 1959) and *Promises, Promises* (1963).

Hargitay's casting in *Lady Frankenstein* came from his relationship with notorious exploitation mogul Dick Randall, the supposed author of the script's basis story. Randall produced *The Wild Wild World of Jayne Mansfield* (1968) with the actress giving a guided tour of sleazy strip joints, big city drag bars, cruise areas, and drug markets she supposedly frequented. When she was killed in an early-morning car crash 25 miles east of New Orleans, Randall tacked on grainy newsreel footage of the accident, and had Hargitay conduct a tour of the couple's 35-room pink mansion. Hargitay and Mansfield's youngest child, daughter Mariska, wet her feet in the horror genre with *Ghoulies* in 1984. Oddly, a film entitled *Jayne Mansfield Meets Frankenstein* was announced in 1965, but never made.

Despite his impressive physique, Hargitay remains modestly clothed throughout *Lady Frankenstein*, perhaps trying for audience acceptance for his acting rather than for his pecs. He's very good in the part of the police captain, dripping sarcasm in his badinage with Lynch and keeping one eyebrow whimsically raised as he takes Tanya's explanations with the biggest grains of salt possible.

As Lynch, character actor Herbert Fux is as delightfully reprehensible as the part necessitates. His name was "obviously a ribald pseudonym," according to Thomas Weisser's masterful *Spaghetti Westerns—the Good the Bad and the Violent*, but it was one he used in good stead in dozens of motion pictures.

But the best performance, inarguably, comes from Sara Bay in the title role. Born Rosalba Neri in 1946, the sultry actress made her film debut in 1957 and, by the time of *Lady Frankenstein*, was a familiar face to U.S. fans of European imports, under both her given name and the *nom de Guerre*. She was in the rambling Biblical epic *Esther and the*

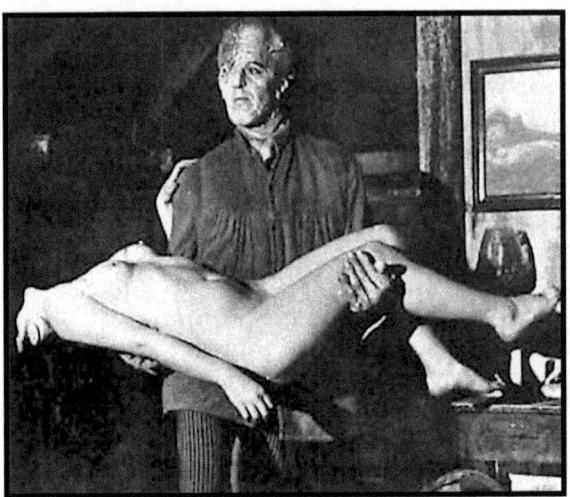

King (1960) with Joan Collins, and sundry Italian films, among them *Hercules vs. Moloch* (1963).

Bay was an exotic, voluptuous brunette with classic Neapolitan features; on the silver screen, she was completely uninhibited sexually and would shed her clothes unashamedly at least once in all of her later films. She was strikingly beautiful, without the reliance on breast implants and collagen shots like the scores of ingenues who doff everything for fleeting fame as one of the centerfolds in the horror film magazines on today's newsstands.

The Monster goes on a rampage terrorizing the village.

And Bay was an excellent actress as well; her performance in *Lady Frankenstein* is unquestionably a *tour de force*. At one moment, she could be the poised scientist scheming to avenge her father's murder, the next a demure coquette working her wiles to achieve that end. Her confrontation with Lynch, rebuffing his advances in no uncertain terms, then abasing herself at the realization of her father's eavesdropping and becoming the dutiful daughter, is remarkable.

Lady Frankenstein is not a well-liked film. The biggest bone of contention is its derivativeness, with the Hammer antecedents still very fresh in filmgoers' memories in 1972.

The greatest amount of meat on that aforementioned bone comes from Bill Warren, now best known in genre circles as the author of the two-volume *Keep Watching The Skies!*, a chronicle of American science fiction films from 1950 to 1962, and as a correspondent for *Famous Monsters of Filmland, Fangoria,* and other film magazines. For *Vampirella* #4 (April 1969), Warren wrote a story entitled "For the Love of Frankenstein" wherein the grand-niece of Dr. Frankenstein, Hedvig Krollek, leads on her deformed collaborator, Eric Hoffstein, so long as he procures the necessary body parts for her creation. She goes so far as to murder Eric and transplant his brain into her creation's skull, smitten with his perfect form. Upon revivification however, "Eric" remembers the degradation he felt and unrequited love he suffered in his other body and kills Hedvig, blowing up the castle and himself.

Understandably indignant, Warren investigated his legal recourse but forewent further proceedings when New World, after first claiming the movie was based on an obscure Slavic short story, retained a nationally famous attorney that intimidated Warren's counsel (working on a contingency basis) enough to drop the case. *Vampirella* publisher James Warren (no relation) reportedly made noises as well—what, if anything, came of that is unknown.

Reminiscing 25 years after the fact, Bill Warren still finds the situation "all very strange." In his opinion his original story was "no great shakes in the first place," so the levying of accusations is moot. Still, Donald C. Willis, listing *Lady Frankenstein* in his fundamental *Horror and Science Fiction Films II*, gives Warren a qualified story credit for the movie.

Most film critics remain oblivious to this bit of suspicious coincidence, and review *Lady Frankenstein* as a cinematic experience in toto. Some recognize that the 1970s versions of *Frankenstein* were as far removed from the original novel and the winsome Universal series as could be. The public's apathy toward graphic violence and acceptance of onscreen sex demanded the *Frankenstein* scenario follow suit. Leslie Halliwell, in *The Dead That Walk*, referred to *Lady Frankenstein* as a "farrago," and likened the plot to D. H. Lawrence's 1928 novel, *Lady Chatterley's Lover*. Fighting a publisher's deadline, author Donald F. Glut had time only to memorialize *Lady Frankenstein* in *The Frankenstein Legend* for its "sexual perversion" in New World's advertising. It was Glut who first informed Warren of the plot similarities, reading from the press kit.

The comparison to Hammer product showed up in several reviews. Editor Phil Hardy censured it to be a "poor imitation of Hammer's *Frankenstein*" in *The Encyclopedia of Horror Movies*, "stressing crudely visceral details and nudity." In his companion volume, *The Encyclopedia of Science Fiction Movies*, Hardy said *Lady Frankenstein* was "a typically Italian sensationalist twist to the *Frankenstein* myth," with Welles directing "with an eye to grotesque detail but with little wit or invention."

By no means is *Lady Frankenstein* a great film, but it is not a bad one. The comparisons to Hammer are fair ones, with the women dashing about in velveteen gowns with Empire waists, the period set decor and the resolute constabulary. Perhaps the movie's lasting testament is that it still stands today as good or better than anything Hammer was producing then, well-made and passionate. It may overstep the boundaries of good taste, but no more so than critics accused Hammer of doing years before. Ultimately, *Lady Frankenstein* does what a *Frankenstein* movie should do in giving the audience an interesting tweak of the familiar, simultaneously reprising and revamping the cliché, and, above all, entertaining its audience.

And lest you think all that burning of junk food serves no good purpose, remember too that forest fires aren't all bad. The seeds of certain trees like the loblolly pine cannot germinate without the extreme heat of conflagration. Reappraised, *Lady Frankenstein* should be given a chance to flourish as well.

The Screaming Dead
and *Erotic Rites of Frankenstein*
by David H. Smith

A performance artist once explained why he clamps clothespins to his nipples during some of his shows. At first the pain is excruciating; but after a while the nerve endings in his nipples grow numb, and his brain unleashes a flow of endorphins; the body's natural painkillers take over. Soon, he's totally high. I bring this up because, for a nostalgist, watching *The Screaming Dead* and its semi-sequel *The Erotic Rites of Frankenstein* is like the first few minutes after clothespins have been applied to the nipples. It is only after the nostalgist's mind-set has been realigned to the director's, and when the viewer's credo of what movies should be and should look like has been similarly attuned, that the pleasure can flow.

In the early 1970s, with the tradition of Universal long gone and the heyday of Hammer fading fast, other filmmakers tried to reinterpret the *Frankenstein* story. For better and (more frequently) for worse, the Monster and the theme of reanimating the dead began to crop up with a kind of regularity. For genre fans the results were welcomed but, like a harsh laxative, those results were sometimes painful. And for most, that simile becomes more a metaphor as Jess Franco's contributions are examined.

Spanish writer and director Jess Franco worked as a film critic and as a pulp fiction writer before he broke into the industry, writing scripts and handling second-unit direction. Working as an assistant to such world-class and globetrotting talent as King Vidor and Orson Welles, he made his solo directorial debut in 1959 and has since made more than 160 films in virtually every genre, from low-brow comedy to fetishist pornography.

Franco's favorite recurring characters include sadistic religious inquisitors, ruthless Wehrmacht commandants, and lesbian prison wardens, all reveling in their basest pleasures in the thinnest of storylines.

Franco's prolificacy has accrued as many admirers as it has detractors, particularly with the advent of videocassettes and the chance for leisurely reappraisals. Franco is a fervid devotee of jazz, and his films, like the music, frequently lose focus (literally and figuratively), wandering off in directions other than what their titles imply, their dialogue reiterates, or their scenes describe. Annoying to most mainstream filmgoers, he indulges his whims for cartoon violence and maddening improvisation. More extreme than any misogynist, and unlike other directors, whose nude scenes obscure cast members' genitalia with bent knees or tousled bedclothes, Franco shows both actors and actresses au naturel with unflattering close-ups. With Franco's films, more than ever, only a few letters and clear enunciation separate prolific and profligate.

This freeform style more often aggravates than ingratiates the viewer, and, with the immense body of work Franco has committed to film, the debate between the two factions will doubtlessly continue to center on why producers indulge his whims and finance his eccentric projects. One wonders until realizing that vulgar results turn a profit, and that audiences spend money to see them while other, worthier films fail at the box office.

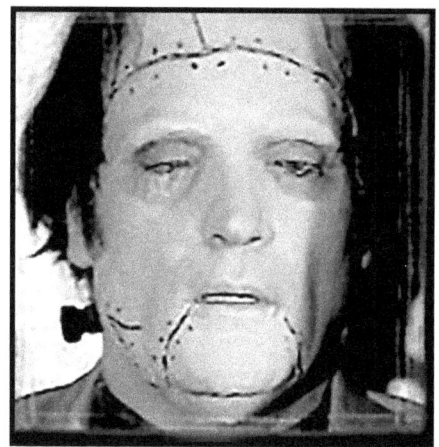

The Monster in *The Screaming Dead* is a blatant copy of the Jack Pierce-designed archetype, with the squared forehead, surgical scarring, and mason's boots.

The Screaming Dead and *The Erotic Rites of Frankenstein*, along with a third, non-Frankenstein film (*La Fille de Dracula*), were made consecutively in 1971-1972. The three, along with a Stoker adaptation, represent Franco's only full-fledged forays into what can be termed the traditional monster film genre. Each embraces the clichés of Universal/Hammer Frankenstein and Dracula films and, at the same time shuns those clichés as well—Franco's idiosyncratic touch is that contradictory. Reassessing his oeuvre in *Fangoria* #90 with Donald Farmer, Franco singled out *The Screaming Dead* with pride, saying, "You know, I think [the film] is one of the best things I ever made, for its presentation of the personalities. I wanted to make a comic strip." His intent, for better and for worse, was realized.

When now-defunct Wizard Video released *The Screaming Dead* in the U.S., it was the first time Americans were given the opportunity to see the film whose title had tantalized many an aficionado since Walt Lee and Donald C. Willis listed it in their respective guidebooks under its original foreign release titles. But Wizard, fearful of potential viewers crying "Foul!" at the movie's unconventional treatment of the familiar, hedged its advertising with, "It's campy fun in the tradition of Hollywood's greatest creature features." Likewise, years before, when Cocinor released the film in France, its poster played on peoples' nostalgia; the copy translated: "If you are not afraid of Dracula nor the monsters of Frankenstein, if you are not impressed by vampires' haunted castles... come all to the Jess Franco film."

The Screaming Dead opens with Dracula, as a bat, fluttering into a room and metamorphosing into human form (Howard Vernon) to attack a young woman (Anne Libert) as she undresses for bed. A thunderstorm outside illuminates the vampire's assault with flashes of lightning in a nifty strobe effect, but the result is diminished by the zoom lens close-up of stage paint simply painted on her neck with no real puncture wound. Dr. Frankenstein's diary is read from, trying to describe some of the bizarre proceedings. His entries record his success at creating a living being from the body of a hanged criminal ("a monster, yes," he concedes) and how he now had devised ''a greater and more daring plan to form an alliance with Count Dracula." Dr. Frankenstein's only concern is the possible interference of the vampire's nemesis, Dr. Jonathan Seward, "whose travels through the mountains of Bohemia had taught him much about vampires and the supernatural."

Even as the diary describes his actions, Seward (Albert Dalbes) is shown journeying to and searching a windblown castle, eventually finding Dracula in his coffin. The doctor gingerly taps a wooden stake into the vampire's chest with a small silver hammer, contradicting the diary entry specifying the need for a silver spike to "render him helpless." The upshot, a real dead bat spread out on the silk interior, the stake laying beside it, is indicative of Franco's techniques.

The diary mentions another enemy—Amira, a Gypsy woman whose motivations are never explained. Frankenstein (Dennis Price) sends Morpho, his mute assistant (Lucas Barboo), to retrieve Dracula's remains. In the interim, he activates the electrical equipment in his lab to revive the Monster (Fernando Bilbao), which seems to materialize out of thin air amidst the crackling apparatus. An economical but good effect shows several wires glowing white-hot, then melting like taffy from the high voltage.

The Monster is a blatant copy of the Jack Pierce-designed archetype, with the squared forehead, surgical scarring, and mason's boots. It's odd that Universal, owning the rights to the trademark image, did not pursue a case of infringement when the movie made it to these shores. The obscurity of *The Screaming Dead*, particularly under such a surreptitious title, worked to its benefit.

Frankenstein sends the Monster out on a mission to procure a source of fresh blood to revive Dracula. At a nightclub, a scantily dressed singer (Josiane Gilbert) performs a vulgar number, *Bah de Boum* to the delight of the mostly male patrons: A bilingual reader of *Video Watchdog* graciously translated the ribald lyrics in one issue's letter column; among them were: "and how he wants to see my pussy/I'm hot—you'll get me!" and the finale, "So, you can see my ass/You'll need to spit/To get yourself in there!" With a flourish of dimpled buttocks, she scampers back to her dressing room, where the Monster bursts from a closet and carries her off. It tussles with a couple of men who leap to her defense, and even shrugs off a pair of bullets fired by an overenthusiastic bouncer.

Back at the lab, Frankenstein inserts a catheter into her neck and drains her blood into a large jar containing a live bat. In an unsavory display, the bat struggles to stay afloat as the plasma pours in, the European branch of the S.P.C.A. evidently not invited to the set that day. With an abrupt jump cut, Dracula suddenly appears, looking none the worse for wear, though where all the blood and the jar itself go is unexplained. Frankenstein directs Morpho to dispose of the girl's body in a convenient personal crematory, but not before the mute pervert fondles and kisses her corpse.

Dennis Price as Dr. Frankenstein and Howard Vernon as Count Dracula in *The Screaming Dead.*

Frankenstein enters the results in his diary with glee: "I had summoned the spirit of the master of vampires, the demon spirit of Count Dracula and now my powers were limitless. Thanks to that victory over the mysterious world of the infinite, I could summon the souls of those I choose—souls I could unite into a great supernatural army of invincible and indestructible shadows. An army of vampires, led by Dracula completely under my control."

In a bit of homage to Dr. Niemann (Boris Karloff) and his dominance of the selfsame vampire (John Carradine) in *House of Frankenstein* (1944), the doctor here elucidates that rather tenuous method of control; "He knew that I could drive a silver spike through his heart while he slept if he did not obey my will, and through him the power of all vampires was mine. They would obey me without question or hesitation. They would work for me to enslave the mortals of the world. This was my dream and nothing stood in the way of realizing it. Nothing could prevent me from bringing all of humanity under my control."

Save perhaps the cartoon adaptation of the Frankenstein story in *Mr. Magoo Man of Mystery* (1964) and the puppetry of *Mad Monster Party?* (1967), here was the first time on film that the scientist Frankenstein was depicted as a delusional potentate intent on world domination. It does substantiate, however, Franco's intent to make a comic strip kind of film, with the mad doctor more akin to Ming the Merciless than to anything envisioned by Mary Shelley. Once content to rock the scientific community back on its heels, this Frankenstein wants to bring all of humanity to its knees. It's a fun cliché, sure; but seen in this context, with only a piecemeal Monster and a sluggardly mute vampire serving as his army, it's utterly preposterous and works to undo whatever negligible realism there might be.

Aware of possible interference by Dracula's destroyer, Frankenstein commands the vampire to kidnap a girl (Mary Francis) under Seward's protection (one source indicates it is his sister, but the relationship isn't clear). Clueless, Seward goes by coach in what must be the most random search ever, and is intercepted by the Monster, which thrashes him unmercifully. It's a nice scene, shot outdoors in a forest in actual sunlight, affording a kind of realism to a screen monster previously allowed outside only amongst papier-mâché boulders and painted backdrops.

Seward is found by the Gypsies and taken back to their camp to recover from his injuries. He is tended by the Gypsy woman Frankenstein's journal mentioned earlier, who recognizes Seward as the man who ended Dracula's evil once before. Amira reveals to him that the vampire has been revived, and that "his spirit is now the prisoner of Dr. Frankenstein. Cruel, ambitious, damned—Frankenstein is the source of terror and death!" She does a bit of fortune telling by way of sifting sand, and argues that only Seward has the courage to confront and destroy the vampire and his master. This is quite an about-face as it was a band of Szgany, or Transylvanian Gypsies, who protected the count and his castle in Stoker's novel. Amira also promises Seward, "On a night when the moon is full and thunder shakes the heavens," the Wolf Man will come to help.

The next night, Dracula and his bride (Britt Nichols) attack Amira, and, proving as incompetent as their manmade compatriot was with Seward, fail to finish her off. Seward finds her and she manages a last bit of forecasting, telling him that this is the night the lycanthrope will arise. "Only [the Wolf Man] can kill Dracula tonight," she gasps. "Only tonight he will sow fear and discord among the demons." Amira dies, but her prophecy does come true: a scabrous, bucktoothed werewolf does appear to invade the other monsters' lair.

Frankenstein, miffed at the vampires' perfidy in acting on their own against old grudges, renounces his alliance with them and stakes them both. "I tried to change you into superior beings, and with no thought of gratitude for what I had done, you betrayed me. You are nothing but putrid carrion and that's what you will remain."

Meanwhile, the Monster and the Wolf Man battle, but the outcome is inconclusive as the patchwork being hurls the tatty werewolf aside and goes back to the lab with his maker. Frankenstein directs his bloodied creation into a silver packing crate, then activates some kind of teleportation device to send him away. He loads the box into his station wagon and drives away to contrive another plot for world domination.

Seward comes in too late to do anything, and the Wolf Man is forgotten, presumably returning to his grave. The bandaged and bewildered Seward, the hero of the film only by default, offers up thanks to God for renewing his strength and for the help of the Gypsy girl in defeating Frankenstein's and Dracula's machinations.

Given *The Screaming Dead*'s obscurity in the U.S. for more than a decade after its release, there is a paucity of critics' opinions, and even then not a consensus. Authors, when they like it, still spend more time apologizing for its inadequacies than promoting its attributes.

The cult of fans growing in support of Franco's work has become more vocal in recent years, with the few favorable words written about the man parsed like holy writ by the congregation of Franco Talmudists. Lucas Balbo, in the reverential *Obsession: The Films of Jess Franco*, describes the film not only as "one of the most misunderstood of Franco's parodies of horror film myth," but also as "a very odd film," with "laughable make-up and special effects."

Few reviewers mention the actors' work, but this is to be expected given the dearth of actual performances, relying as it does on Frankenstein's diary entries.

Seven-foot Fernando Bilbao played the Monster here for the second time in his career. His impressive height had gotten him the role earlier in *Assignment Terror* (1969), another, less perverse throwback to the Universal monster rallies of the mid-1940s, alongside a werewolf, a vampire, and a mummy.

More familiar to American audiences was the actor in the role of Dr. Frankenstein, Dennis Price. Price began to become a fixture in British horror films, turning up in a myriad of parts though never really accruing much of a following. Among these were *The Earth Dies Screaming* (1964), *Horror House* (1969) (in a role intended for Boris Karloff before his death), *Twins of Evil* (1971), *Theatre of Blood* (1973), *Son of Dracula* (1974) (paradoxically as Frankenstein's nemesis Dr. Van Helsing), and several others. The Twyford, England–born actor also stole what little show there was in the perfunctory *The Horror of Frankenstein* (1970); as a shiftless graverobber, it was his clumsiness that damaged the brain intended for the Monster (David Prowse), and, in recompense, the baron (Ralph Bates) pushed him into an acid bath. Plagued by alcoholism, Dennis Price died in 1973.

The dissolutive properties of acid had significance for Price in *The Screaming Dead*'s semi-sequel made later that year. In *The Erotic Rites of Frankenstein*, Price reprises his role of Dr. Frankenstein, as does Albert Dalbes his role as Seward, now more a collaborator than a nemesis. Most of the actors from the first film show up as well, filling other roles and all but ignoring continuity. It's more professional-looking than *The Screaming Dead* and shorter in length (at least in its most common release), but a much busier film.

The movie begins with Frankenstein in his lab, operating with an electric drill on the Monster's (Fernando Bilbao again billed as "Fred Harrisson") brain to facilitate its power of speech. Though the rudiments of Universal makeup are there, the Monster now has silver skin and seems much less a ragamuffin than before. As a matter of fact, posters for the film borrow the Monster's image from a common publicity still of Karloff from *Bride of Frankenstein* (1935), with singed hair and a burnt cheek that Bilbao does not have.

Fred Harrisson [Fernando Bilbao] as the Frankenstein Monster in *The Erotic Rites of Frankenstein*.

Just as he declares the surgery a success to his lackey (Jess Franco himself), Frankenstein is surprised by a couple of intruders. One is a freakish woman (Anne Libert) named Melissa, naked save for some strategically placed feathers. She is the result of "a bird egg impregnated with human semen" by Cagliostro, an arcane wizard living nearby. Amid piercing shrieks and with savage claws, Melissa attacks the doctor while Caronte (Luis Barboo), her cohort, knifes Frankenstein's bewildered assistant.

On to another castle, where Cagliostro (Howard Vernon) is seen on a balcony, watching the crate containing the Monster being unloaded from a wagon in the courtyard below. The real-life Conte Alessandro Cagilostro was an Italian adventurer who traveled all over Europe posing as a physician and alchemist, even finding favor in France at Louis XVI's court, and who was later condemned by the Roman Inquisition as a heretic and a sorcerer. After dismissing a pair of naked concubines, Cagliostro greets the blind Melissa and asks her to use her precognitive powers to foresee his future. She tells him in her singsong voice of "pleasure and death and blood," and of the creature Frankenstein created wholly at his command. "I shall make it more than a dream," Cagliostro vows, then goes to examine the ill-gotten Monster. "Fabulous," Cagliostro beams, admiring the barechested giant. "This is the work of real genius."

Cagliostro puts the Monster under his control, and, to mysticize the proceedings, has Melissa interpret his telepathic commands "through magnetic waves." Through her, he commands the Monster to seek out and kidnap a beautiful young woman to begin the next phase of his plans. This modus operandi seems at first merely a cut rate method of saving Mr. Vernon the necessity of memorizing passages of stilted dialogue; closer examination, however, shows it has a kind of ingenuity. As the film would eventually be dubbed for a number of foreign markets, there would be no need to match the dialogue to the actor's lip movements. Cagliostro simply stands motionless, his eyes bugged to connote his psychic power, while Melissa issues his commands from off-camera.

Meanwhile, Dr. Seward is treating the injured Frankenstein in the latter's lab. Found crawling in the forest nearby by some villagers, with three minor lesions on his cheek to indicate his mortal wounds, Frankenstein reveals his secrets to his tender. "Though we are at odds on some matters," Frankenstein understates, given the previous film, "this time you must help me. The truth is, Seward, that I created a human creature." He tells Seward to save the Monster in the name of science, and that it is his legacy. With a rattling gasp, Frankenstein dies.

At the funeral, Seward meets attractive blonde Dr. Vera Frankenstein (Heather Savon), the late doctor's daughter and sole heir, who is dubbed with a perversely masculine voice. Ignorant of exotic surnames, Seward admits to hearing of Vera's research work, but never suspected she was related to his infamous fellow townsman. When she asks about the circumstances of her father's death, Seward becomes clinical and businesslike. "No vital organs were concerned," he reports. "I would say he hemorrhaged to death." He goes on, "It was apparent he had been mangled and lacerated. He was stripped of flesh." When Vera suggests the possibility of wolves or (nonindigenous to Europe) mountain lions, Seward suggests vultures are more likely. As she leaves, the police inspector (Daniel J. White) investigating the case reacts to her presence by remarking it gave him "gooseflesh just to look at her."

That night, Vera and her assistant Abigail (Doris Thomas) rob Dr. Frankenstein's grave and bring his corpse back to the lab. Abigail is doubtful the body can be revived, but Vera insists she can succeed with reanimating the dead just as her father did. They jolt him and he revives, proud of her effort, his brain "made vital again for a few short seconds with magnetic power." Frankenstein urges her, as he did Seward, to find his creation. She promises to, and to avenge his death on the thieves even as he succumbs again. Seward comes to call, offering his assistance. "Despite our disagreements, I thought highly of your father's work. He was an admirable man of science." Never mind he threw him to the (were)wolves last time around, continuity be damned.

Nighttime again, and the Monster kidnaps a pretty woman in town as she undresses for bed. At Cagliostro's castle, Melissa calls to order a meeting of shuffling zombies (who wear the most economical of decayed makeups or plastic skulls for masks) in the dungeon to announce their master's imminent plan for a super race. These walking dead are the result of Cagliostro's efforts to revive the dead, but are failures compared to Frankenstein's because, "the bodies kept on rotting." With a sword, Caronte lops off the kidnap victim's head ("a clean severance"), and Cagliostro holds it up to admire its beauty.

Vera is at a loss in seeking revenge, so she zaps her father with "a higher decibel" and by increasing "the deep incision ray." More spastic than ever, Frankenstein reveals his murderer, apparently from knowledge gained in the afterlife, to be Cagliostro. He tells her the man is a mad genius, out to destroy humanity, and that "he died many, many centuries ago. His soul is transmuted, and he is constantly reborn as a man."

After Frankenstein dies again, Vera vows to Abigail she will see to it his experiments are vindicated and justice is done. On their way to Cagliostro's hideout, they chance upon the Monster, Caronte, and Melissa, and follow them. When the Monster tries to kidnap an artist's model, Vera intervenes and substitutes herself. Back at his castle, Cagliostro is furious at this turn of events, blaming Caronte for not realizing the Monster's mistake. He has Caronte and Vera stripped naked and tied back to back standing on a platform of upright poisoned stakes. In the movie's most infamous scene, and probably the most discussed in all of Franco's canon, the ebullient Monster flogs the helpless pair with a whip, much to Melissa's and Cagliostro's sadistic joy. Caronte eventually falls, absorbing the wicked death, and Vera is clothed and brought to Cagliostro's private chamber, where she too is placed under his hypnotic control. Melissa tells the subjugated woman scientist of Cagliostro's plan to assemble a woman out of dead bodies as an intended mate for the Monster and as the matriarch of a new master race.

Seward and the police inspector, fretting over Vera's disappearance, play word association games with Abigail, who has been in shock since seeing Melissa earlier. They glean Vera's probable whereabouts, then go to Frankenstein's castle to re-re-revive the late doctor for no particular reason. The fitful victim of his own invention, Frankenstein begs for death, and urges Seward and the policeman not to interfere with Vera's indeterminate plans. Later Frankenstein rises and starts to strangle Seward, but the quick-witted Inspector hurls a jar of sulfuric acid at him. Frankenstein's head and hands come off, and he finally falls dead for good.

Meantime, Cagliostro has assembled a female, and bids Vera to bring her to life with the deep incision ray. The creation takes her first breath as Melissa invokes mysterious gods to look kindly on their efforts. Pleased, Cagliostro gives his bird-woman helpmate a victim from his dungeon for her to devour. Cagliostro then reenergizes the Monster, like his Universal predecessors. Seward sneaks in and tells the Monster to rebel against these people, the murderers of Dr. Frankenstein, its true master. Seward hides before he can convince the Monster further, as Vera comes in and leads the giant out to an assembly of chanting zombies. Melissa announces that once she was intended to be Cagliostro's offspring, but a flaw left her blind and unworthy. Now, after using Vera Frankenstein's help with the manmade woman, Cagliostro hopes to create "a new being, never before seen by men of science. She is a synthesis of all women, each part of her is divine." Evidently, those concubines ended up serving their master in a new way.

Melissa proclaims, "Their procreation is perfection! They are fabulous creatures!" as the Monster comes in to mount its naked bride. Seward bursts in and reiterates his claim, this time freeing the Monster from Cagliostro's spell. Frankenstein's creature becomes enraged, tearing through Melissa and the spindly zombies, trying to reach the evil wizard. The Monster starts to strangle Vera, but Seward shoots it dead. Cagliostro escapes, his laughter echoing in the night. "His laughter is a mad and jubilant one," Vera remarks, "meaning he has not been vanquished. In nine months' time, Cagliostro is again going to be reborn." It paves the way for a sequel that never was.

Never licensed for official release in the U.S. in any format, *The Erotic Rites of Frankenstein* has a great more notoriety than its predecessor, due no doubt to its more suggestive title, its unabashed full-frontal nudity, and offbeat storyline. In some markets, there was an entire subplot involving Gypsies again, padding the length by almost 20 minutes, and one cast listing has a mention of longtime Franco paramour Lina Romay making her screen debut as the Monster's girlfriend. Alternate export versions include one with all the nudity deleted and the actors wearing blue underwear in pivotal scenes. Oddly, Ms. Romay appeared only in the tamest version; in other Franco films, the man's probing camerawork would prove more invasive of her nether region than any OB-GYN's exam.

William Burns in *European Trash Cinema* #12 defended the Spaniard's style of filmmaking, and found *The Erotic Rites of Frankenstein* "surreal, idiosyncratic, one more example of Franco's startlingly individualistic view of cinema. With this work, he effectively shuts the door on the Universal/Hammer measuring stick for horror films."

Compared to his god-awful, slack-jawed, mute Dracula of *The Screaming Dead*, Vernon is the best thing about *The Erotic Rites of Frankenstein*. While his goatee does change from scene to scene (much as Dalbes' hair color does), his intense, literally eye-popping performance makes up for a lot of the film's many flaws. The blind, shrieking, flesh-eating, clairvoyant, feathered and flightless character of Melissa, while enjoying a fair amount of critical praise in some kinder reviews, serves only to show just how far off the beaten path Franco was willing to go with his monsters.

Appreciation of these, or any, films by Jess Franco is difficult to acquire. But if whole cults can spring up in America to celebrate a director's ineptitude (Ed Wood), eccentricity (Tim Burton), paranoia (Oliver Stone), outrageousness (John Waters), bravura (John Woo), egotism (Spike Lee), or plain weird inscrutability (David Lynch), then surely a retinue of Franco converts will someday appear on these shores.

Likening Jess Franco's Frankenstein films to the man's love of jazz, there are some elements of the beat, or rhythmic intensity (innate pervertedness of the villains and their henchmen), stressing of weak beats of the measure (ineffectuality of Seward, the so-called hero), riffs or repetition of short rhythmic phrases (the ad nauseam zoom lens close-up); vocal inflections like glissandos (unwanted quirks in Melissa's and Vera's voices); and minute flattening of some scale degrees (dubious taste with necrophilia and necromancy).

"What is a filmmaker?" author Margaret Atwood asked in a TV documentary about *Frankenstein*. "A filmmaker is someone that creates artificial life." To some, Jess Franco is a bit of a Frankenstein, creating monster after monster with his catchpenny films.

The Rocky Horror Picture Show

by Susan Svehla

> "I've been making a man
> with blond hair and a tan
> and he's good for relieving
> my tension.
> So come up to the lab
> and see what's on the slab...
> In just seven days,
> I can make me a man!"

In 1975 Twentieth Century-Fox put a new spin on the Frankenstein story with the release of *The Rocky Horror Picture Show*. The familiar father/son relationship was tossed out the castle door. Dr. Frank-N-Furter (Tim Curry), in traditional mad scientist mode, did create his monster. But this monster was no hulking, green-tinted horror. He was Rocky (Peter Hinwood) a hunk of beefcake who not only rings the chimes of Frank-N-Furter but also sweet and innocent Janet Weiss (Susan Sarandon).

There are so many clever scenes in *Rocky Horror*, it's difficult to select a favorite, but after numerous viewings one of the funniest is the scene of Rocky's birth, where Frank-N-

Dr. Frank-N-Furter, in the best Universal tradition, creates a man with the assistance of Magenta (Patricia Quinn) and Columbia (Little Nell).

Furter, so excited by his new love-toy, squeals in delight as he chases the confused Rocky around the lab. Tim Curry has never been funnier.

The Rocky Horror Picture Show began as a musical in a London workshop production in 1973. The play would run in London for seven years. Creator Richard O'Brien's love of old horror movies is apparent throughout the film. O'Brien, who plays Riff Raff in the film, wrote the play, music, and lyrics, as well as co-writing the screenplay for the film with director Jim Sharman.

Rocky Horror began achieving cult status in 1976 following its 1975 release when it began playing college campuses and midnight shows. In the 1990s the film celebrated its 25th anniversary and saw release on videotape and laser disc and later DVD.

Today crowds still stand in line for midnight viewings of this cult classic. It was even the focus of an episode of the television series, *Cold Case.* That show featured an appearance by Barry Bostwick (*Rocky*'s Brad) as a religious serial killer.

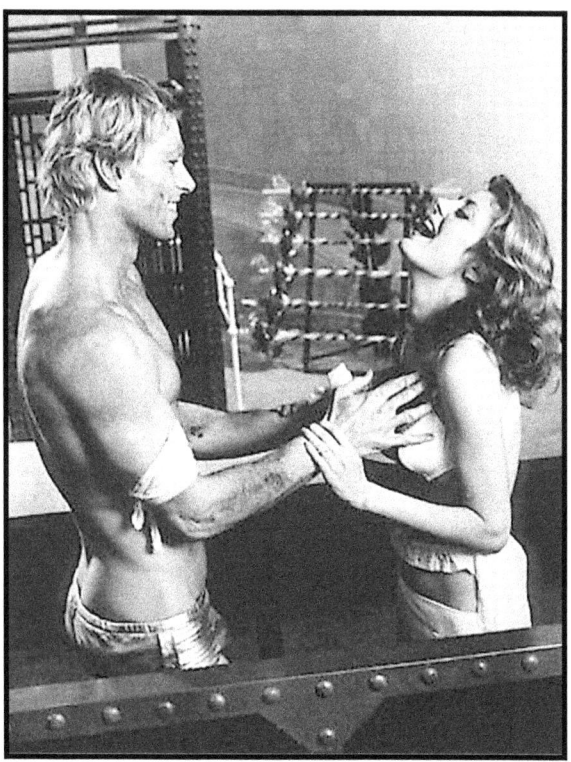

Rocky (Peter Hinwood) and Janet (Susan Sarandon) share a touchy-feeley moment in *Rocky Horror*.

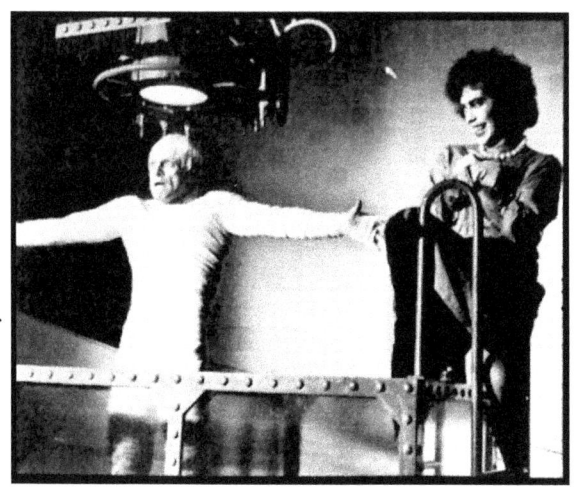

Tales of Frankenstein
In the late 1950s Hammer Film Productions submitted a half-hour U.S. pilot for an intended *Frankenstein* series to star Anton Diffring as Baron Frankenstein. In the pilot, Don Megowan played a very Universal-ized Frankenstein Monster, but the pilot never sold.

Frankenstein Invades American Homes

For decades Frankenstein's Monster had haunted American theaters.

It was only logical that he would eventually invade and conquer American television as well.

Frankenstein offers everything that U.S. TV wanted—the veneer of a literary, time-tested classic blended with a pop culture horror story of a gruesome, murderous monster. But actually, television didn't come searching for *Frankenstein* as quickly as you might think. In the early 1950s an episode of *Tales of Tomorrow* featured Lon Chaney, Jr. as the Frankenstein Monster in a live TV version that Chaney, Jr. mistakenly thought was the final dress rehearsal; thus, he was careful not to smash any of the furniture that he was to destroy in the live broadcast.

In the late 1950s Hammer Film Productions submitted a half-hour U.S. pilot for an intended *Frankenstein* series to star Anton Diffring as Baron Frankenstein. In the pilot, Don Megowan played a very Universal-ized Frankenstein Monster, but the pilot never sold.

But it wasn't until the epic four-hour (TV time, including commercials) *Frankenstein: The True Story* arrived on American television in 1973 that the perfect synthesis between novel and TV emerged. The Universal-produced adaptation featured an all-star cast with expensive production values. But what it featured most was an attempt (more as promotional gimmick than reality) to return to the Mary Shelley novel as the source of the screenplay. This quest to produce Mary Shelley's vision on film became an obsession which has never been quite fulfilled despite *Frankenstein: The Ture Story* and *Mary Shelley's Frankenstein*, which was directed by Kenneth Branagh.

Months before the Branagh version hit movie theaters, a TNT-produced version of *Frankenstein* appeared on American television. It starred Randy Quaid as the Frankenstein Monster and remained a version very close to the original source novel.

Truth be told, American television has often provided the most artistically satisfying versions of the Frankenstein mythos.

Dennis Fischer offers an analysis of made-for-TV movie *Frankenstein: The True Story*. Fischer is a longtime contributor to *Midnight Marquee, Cinefantastique*, and other periodicals. He is the author of a book *Horror Film Directors* and another on *Science Fiction Film Directors*. Fischer continues to teach high school English in California, is married, and is father to two children.

Arthur Joseph Lundquist used to be an eccentric, "freaky" student at Andover High School until he came into contact with English teacher Mr. Svehla and his school-sponsored Film Club. Soon Lundquist was hooked on film, becoming a frequent contributor to *Midnight Marquee* and appearing in low-budget films such as *Pledge Night* (where he played the psycho killer) and portraying the starring role of Dr. Robert Clarke (a sly tribute) in Ted Bohus' *The Regenerated Man*. Lundquist lives in New York and appears in local theater productions.

Frankenstein: The True Story
by Dennis Fischer

Despite Columbia's recent efforts to make big-budget, lavish new film versions of the classic monsters (*Bram Stoker's Dracula; Mary Shelley's Frankenstein; Wolf*), the most epic version of the Frankenstein myth remains *Frankenstein: The True Story*, originally a two-part NBC miniseries produced by Universal and filmed at England's famous Pinewood Studios.

What sets *Frankenstein: The True Story* apart was that it was one of the first adaptations since the Whale version that set out to be a prestige production all the way. The year 1973 was a very significant one for the horror genre as the box office returns of *The Exorcist* suddenly made the formerly disreputable genre into a potentially highly lucrative field for those with the potential and talent to plug into the audience's appetite for such fantastic fare.

While the many talented actors who appeared in the production all praised the script, which was initially entitled *Dr. Frankenstein* and began production on March 15, 1973, it falls short of being Mary Shelley's version of the story. Of course, Shelley's work, *Frankenstein, or The Modern Prometheus*, was a work of fiction and far from a "true story" itself, but the subtitle suggested that viewers would finally see Shelley's work onscreen rather than yet another variation on the play adaptation that had been the basis for the earliest films on the subject.

Though the various movie versions remain popular, fewer people are reading Mary Shelley's famous novel these days, and it is a pity. I admit I wasn't too receptive to its pleasures myself when I was a teenager. It seemed far too verbose and lacked the thrills of Bram Stoker's *Dracula*. In fact, it seemed far too sophisticated a book to have come from the pen of a teenaged girl.

Little did I know then how right I was. After some research, I came across the little-reported fact that *Frankenstein,* as we know it, was extensively rewritten by Shelley's more famous husband, the poet Percy, who deserves, but does not get, collaborative credit. Percy assuaged Shelley's creative anxiety by embroidering her plot with his fancy prose, allowing her to meet her father's and his expectations that she would one day publish something of merit.

(Ironically, it is Percy's poetic influence and his inflating the language of Mary Shelley's novel that makes it difficult reading for the modern reader. Someday, an enterprising publisher should release an edition that presents the book the way Mary actually wrote it, as a first draft text does exist. A small example of Percy's editorial influence is that Mary referred to Frankenstein's laboratory as his workshop—it was college-educated Percy who substituted the more technical terms such as laboratory and who provided background as to what authors Frankenstein might have researched.)

Researching Mary Shelley's life does provide some interesting clues as to how to read the novel. From her earliest years, Mary Shelley was expected to contribute to the world of letters. She read voluminously and described her childhood as being spent in "waking dreams" of literature, hoping she would prove herself "worthy of [her] parentage, and enroll [herself] on the page of fame."

The death of her mother haunted Mary, who enjoyed escaping into the world of literature by reading books on her mother's grave. She also had rendezvous with her lover Shelley there, finding it a fine and private place (and disproving Marvel's contention that none do there embrace). Her romance with Shelley caused her to be estranged from her father, and it is not insignificant that all the major and most of the minor characters in the novel *Frankenstein* are orphans.

Because giving birth was a dangerous procedure for women in the late 19th century, it is not surprising to notice that the novel is suffused with birth anxiety. Most women married early, and lacking birth control, were constantly plagued by fears of pregnancy, childbirth, and infant and personal mortality. From the age of 17 to 21, Mary was almost continuously pregnant, "confined," or nursing.

Frankenstein in the novel describes the production of the monster in suggestive terms. He labors in a "workshop of filthy creation" where he undergoes "incredible labours," is "emaciated with confinement," and "nervous to a painful degree," etc. He ultimately produces and fears his creation, abandoning it to a cruel, prejudiced world. His "offspring" in turn murders his bride, causing Frankenstein to pursue him to their mutual destruction.

The monster itself is Frankenstein's doppelgänger, increasingly taking on aspects of his creator throughout the novel. One aspect that most filmed adaptations have ignored is that the monster is also clearly meant to represent an embodiment of Frankenstein's subconscious, and he sets forth to murder only when Frankenstein is asleep (shades of the Id monster in *Forbidden Planet*). The only version that really suggests anything like this is the David Wickes cable version from 1993.

Victor makes the connection when he says that the monster is "my own spirit let loose from the grave and forced to destroy all that was dear to me." The monster may kill those whom Frankenstein loves, but on a deeper level, he really kills those whom Victor wants him to kill—those who stand between him and his parents and/or success: a charming brother, a happier friend, and his intended bride who is merged with his mother in a shocking dream.

Curiously, Mary Shelley had just given birth to a young son, William, when she wrote the novel after having had a miscarriage (a girl whom she had dreamed of bringing back to life). That the monster's first victim is Victor's younger brother, a young boy named William, provokes an association that is inescapable, and in fact, Mary's William died only a short time later. Only one of her three sons by Shelley survived into manhood, and it is obvious that Mary felt tremendous guilt, which her characters all seem to share. (It's also worth noting that several of the characters in the book feel this guilt and all blame themselves for William's death including Justine, Elizabeth, the Monster, and Frankenstein himself.)

When Christopher Isherwood and Don Bachardy were assigned to do an adaptation of Shelley's novel, they decided to return to the original source for some of their story, incorporating material that had been left out of previous versions, but there is also no question that they were inspired by those previous adaptations as well. In fact, their screenplay actually begins with a framing story à la *Bride of Frankenstein*, which introduces us to Mary Shelley, Percy Shelley, Lord Byron, and Dr. Polidori, who then reappear as characters in Mary's story. However, this idea was subsequently dropped from the final production.

The man who assigned them to the task was Hunt Stromberg, Jr., son of the famous film producer Hunt Stromberg, who produced many of Greta Garbo's films and who had won an Academy Award for *The Great Ziegfeld*.

In 1972, Stromberg came up with the idea of producing a version of *Frankenstein* that was closer to the original novel and had the idea approved by Universal's president of television, Sid Sheinberg. He then approached Isherwood, best known for his "I Am a Camera" stories, which became the basis for the play *Sally Bowles* and the fine Bob Fosse film *Cabaret*. It was also decided to film in England to take advantage of such historic locations as Cliveden, the former home of Lord and Lady Astor, as well as nearby sites at Hedgerley, Hambledon, Denham, and Bray.

Stromberg selected Jack Smight to direct after seeing and liking many of his films, which included *The Illustrated Man, Harper* with Paul Newman, and the pilot for *Banacek*.

For his cameraman, Stromberg selected Arthur Ibbetson, known for his work on *Anne of a Thousand Days, Willie Wonka and the Chocolate Factory*, and *Where Eagles Dare*. He wanted and got the same makeup man who did such brilliant work on *Kind Hearts and Coronets*, Harry Frampton. His production designer, Wilfred Shingleton, won an Academy Award for his work on David Lean's *Great Expectations* and had also worked on *The African Queen, Beat the Devil*, Polanski's *Macbeth*, and *The Innocents*.

With an excellent crew assembled, Stromberg was also able to acquire an especially fine cast. James Mason accepted the role of the villainous Dr. Polidori, explaining in studio publicity material, "When I was offered the part I was fascinated because I was so struck by the quality of the script. Since I have played one or two sympathetic parts recently, I no longer fear the typecasting syndrome." For the plum part of Dr. Victor Frankenstein, Stromberg went with Leonard Whiting, fresh from his success in Zefferelli's version of *Romeo and Juliet*. That the Creature be played by Michael Sarrazin was the suggestion of George Santoro, a Universal executive. Smight suggested Nicola Pagett from the British TV series *Upstairs, Downstairs* for Elizabeth, Frankenstein's paramour.

David McCallum was initially reluctant to play the key role of Dr. Henry Clerval, noting in studio press releases, "Somebody telephoned and said they were doing *Frankenstein*, and I laughed heartily and said, 'Not again!' I had no intention of coming over to England, but when I read Christopher Isherwood's script I changed my mind. In fact, I jumped at the part. It's a wonderful script."

Even minor supporting roles were filled with top talent. Ralph Richardson appears notably as Lacey, the blind man who befriends the Creature. John Gielgud appears even more briefly as a police inspector investigating the incident at the ball. Jane Seymour, who was shortly to become the queen of the telemovie, shone in a dual role as Agatha, the Cockney farm girl, and as Dr. Polidori's Prima, the soulless socialite.

Agnes Moorehead, doomed to be remembered best for her ongoing role in the insipid *Bewitched* TV series rather than her wonderful work for Welles or her inspired radio acting, appears as Mrs. Blair, Victor Frankenstein's kindly landlady. Tom Baker seems to be reprising his role of Rasputin in *Nicholas and Alexandra* in his cameo as the sea captain.

Respected actress Margaret Leighton amuses in her role as a foreign lady who first meets the Creature at the opera and then later appears at the Fanshawe ball in a Little Bo Peep outfit in the mistaken belief that it was to be a costume ball. Her real-life husband, Michael Wilding, played Elizabeth's father, while James Mason's real-life wife, Australian actress Clarissa Kaye, essayed the role of Elizabeth's mother.

The original television broadcast began with James Mason in modern dress giving a short speech about Mary Shelley before running the opening credits, but this was dropped from subsequent broadcasts. Instead, the story begins abruptly with Victor proclaiming his love for Elizabeth and then seeing his brother William drown. (The script makes it clear that William got himself entangled in some weeds, but this detail was omitted from the final production.) Victor tries to save him, but it's too late.

William's death is the motivation behind Victor's striving to conquer death. Frustrated with the empty words of the clergyman at William's funeral, he tells his fiancée, "Any fool with a sword or a gun can give death. Why can't we give life?"

"But we can!" returns Elizabeth. "One day, if God blesses us, when we are man and wife—"

"So can a pair of animals. Life out of life—that's no miracle. Why can't I raise life out of death? Out of my brother's corpse?"

"That's how Satan tempted our Lord."

"If Satan could teach me how to make William live again, I'd gladly become his pupil."

As with many other versions of the myth, Frankenstein affirms his willingness to go against the natural order to achieve his ends. He is not after god-like power for himself, which is more the ambition of Dr. Polidori, who wants to be the master manipulator behind the scenes, nor does he seek fame and fortune as Dr. Henry Clerval does. In this version of the tale, both Frankenstein and his creation are basically decent, but because they are considered transgressors against the natural order, they become pawns in the hands of fate. Victor's greatest failing is his inability to meet the needs of his creation.

The greatest scene of horror in the film occurs early on when Victor decides to return to his studies at the hospital rather than marry Elizabeth and settle down into a practice now that he has his doctorate. En route, he assists a man run over by a carriage to the hospital and then assists the surgeon, Dr. Henry Clerval, with the amputation of the man's arm. The reality of practicing medicine without anesthetic other than strong drink is made very real and very grim, making one thankful for the blessings of modern medicine. Clerval takes pride in his ability as a "sawbones," and following a fit, inadvertently reveals that he is carrying away the amputated arm in his bag for an experiment. Henry informs Victor that, "The professors here are cowards—afraid to venture beyond what their obsolete books have taught them," and mentions mysteriously something about "power over nature, power over death...."

In Shelley's novel, Frankenstein seeks knowledge from the ancient alchemists who were subsequently ignored, but in the miniseries Frankenstein and Clerval are more forward thinking. Rather than repeat the cliché about lightning reanimating dead tissue, Isherwood and Bachardy have their monster makers use solar energy to bring to life their creation, which sets it off from the Hammer resurrections as well (where the reanimating agents varied from laboratory-generated electricity to chemicals to atomic power).

Just as Shelley sprinkled her novel with quotes from Coleridge's "Rime of the Ancient Mariner," a source of inspiration for her, Isherwood and Bachardy make the most of various Biblical references. Clerval equates life being brought forth from the lifeless with transub-

Michael Sarrazin is the Creature in *Frankenstein: The True Story*

stantiation—the doctrine that the wine of the Eucharist becomes blood and the bread of the Eucharist becomes living flesh.

To allow Victor to credit his belief, Clerval shows Frankenstein how he can reanimate a dead beetle using electricity and that he has kept the amputated arm alive for several weeks. As with Shelley's novel, Henry proclaims himself a modern Prometheus, bringing not fire but power from the sun, the solar energy that gives life to the Earth and from which he proposes to create a living, breathing man—a new Adam. However, he needs Frankenstein's help as his poor health does not allow him to complete the work needed on his own. Frankenstein, ready to be an explorer rather than a follower of established truths, readily agrees.

The now-neglected Elizabeth seeks her errant fiancé, and Victor reveals to her his and Clerval's plans, much to Clerval's displeasure. Victor invites her back to see a reanimated butterfly, but Elizabeth's disgust with the implications causes her to smash it with a Bible, a symbol of holy vengeance perhaps? "It's unholy," she declares.

Just as Elizabeth leaves, realizing that Clerval's dreams have supplanted hers in Victor's head, Mrs. Blair arrives to announce that seven men were killed in a quarry accident. The young doctors rush off to see what they can salvage, practicing graverobbing before the night is through to acquire the parts needed for their creation. Henry ironically complains that they don't have a suitable brain, only to suffer a heart attack and die after Victor leaves. Clerval's tragic flaw was his vanity. The irony here is that while he was concerned about brains, of which he had plenty, he dies because of his heart, with which he proves underly endowed.

Victor returns the next day, missing Clerval's note that the process that reanimated the amputated arm is reversing itself because Henry failed to complete it before his demise.

Len Whiting and James Mason

Assuming that Clerval would wish it, he transplants Henry's brain into their Creature, who will later name himself "Legion," after hearing the Biblical passage, "My name is Legion, for I am many." (Whether this is meant to imply an awareness on the part of the Creature of the details of his own creation remains unclear, though its aptness makes for a suitable bit of dramatic irony.)

Isherwood and Bachardy's script abounds with little literary ironies, such as the clergyman's funeral oration for Henry including the words, "For the trumpet shall sound, and the dead shall be raised incorruptible and we shall be changed. For this corruptible must put on incorruption, and this mortal put on immortality. Oh, death, where is thy sting? Oh, grave, where is thy victory?" Henry's brain is now in an "incorruptible, immortal" body, capable of enduring massive damage (a plunge from a cliff, point-blank gunshots) and still surviving.

Additionally, Dr. Polidori, an old associate of Clerval, arrives at the funeral saying, "I fear this beautiful weather can't last much longer. We must make the most of the sunshine, mustn't we?" indicating his knowledge of what Frankenstein and Clerval have been up to.

Unlike Frankenstein's hideous creation in the book, the Creature is initially quite attractive. Rather than fleeing from his offspring as he does in the book, *True Story*'s Frankenstein develops a rapport with the Creature and tries to teach it about language and life. The Creature proves particularly enchanted with operatic music, which he dubs "Figaro." However, despite having Henry's brain and being able to pick up words such as "beautiful" and "rest" quite quickly, the Creature never becomes the fully articulate Creation of Shelley's original work, and only in the presence of Dr. Polidori does Clerval's old personality and perspicacity come out. Sarrazin's Creature remains yet another largely mimed performance rather than the loquacious Miltonic New Adam of the original.

The Creature is portrayed as innocent as a young child, akin to an infant and initially sleeping 10 hours a day. Frankenstein is delighted by its ability for mimicry and its attempts to please. He is extremely pleased when a foreign lady mistakes the Creature for his lost brother William, but his pleasure turns to anger and frustration when he realizes that the Creature has started to degenerate. The Creature cannot fathom the source of Frankenstein's displeasure and pushes insistently for another evening at the opera, dressing itself up in evening clothes complete with opera cloak.

When Frankenstein leaves it locked up in his room, the curious and concerned Mrs. Blair comes to investigate. The Creature leaps forth at her looking like a demented Hyde and pleads for "Figaro," which proves enough of a shock that it eventually kills her. The result is unfortunate but not intentional. Frankenstein roughly intercepts the Creature on its way to the opera and sends it home where it comes to realize that its features are changing and that its "father" has in some way spurned it, which drives it to attempt suicide, first by stabbing itself with some jagged glass, and then by throwing itself off a cliff. (Victor is relieved at the idea that he does not have to take responsibility for the Creature's supposed destruction. Throughout he is portrayed as an errant parent who fails to help his creation.)

Of course, part two makes clear that the Creature survives and encounters Lacey, the kindly blind man, who lives with two peasants, Agatha and Felix. Lacey invites the stranger in, offering him warm clothes and entertaining him by playing the fiddle, but the Creature does a quick fade when Agatha and Felix arrive. The young lovers become determined to get a look at Lacey's visitor and sneak back unexpectedly one day, surprising the Creature and causing him to throw Felix hard enough against the wall that his head is split open. Agatha runs in terror and winds up being run over by a coach.

Despite these deaths, the Creature cannot be considered responsible. He remains innocent and pitiable. He takes Agatha's crushed body to back to his birthplace and encounters Dr. Polidori, who being a mesmerist, hypnotizes him and discovers that Henry's brain dwells within the Creature. (Polidori believes that the shock of solar energy was the source of the Creature's degeneration and that Clerval had stolen some of his secrets.)

Polidori takes the Creature back to his Creator, who is celebrating his wedding with Elizabeth. Polidori insists that Frankenstein assist him in a further experiment, explaining that he has lost the use of his hands by taking stupid risks with chemicals. Polidori extorts Frankenstein by threatening to expose his connection to the Creature to the wedding guests. The simple Creature is delighted at seeing Victor again but quickly realizes that Victor does not share his sentiments. Fearing exposure, Frankenstein reluctantly agrees, even though it means abandoning Elizabeth on their wedding night. Polidori has created a new body and has Frankenstein attach Agatha's head, though the resulting creation, Polidori's "Eve," which he names Prima for being the first of her kind, evinces none of the peasant girl's personality.

The creation sequence for Prima is one of the epic's most attractive scenes with Polidori's Chinese servants scurrying about, a nude recumbent female figure lying in a chemical womb, and multi-hued chemicals mixing and coalescing as the steadily deteriorating Creature waits hopefully for this likeness of his beautiful Agatha to be restored to him.

When the Frankensteins finally return from their honeymoon, they find that Dr. Polidori has insinuated himself into the Fanshawe family household with Prima being introduced as his ward. Prima is a perfect mimic and Polidori proves a more thorough teacher than Victor, so that she has mastered manners and speech and even recites romantic poetry (Lord Byron's "She Walks in Beauty," to be precise).

However, Polidori neglects to provide Prima with any scruples. She makes a pass at Victor and later cruelly attempts to strangle a cat without any sign of anger or compunction. There is clearly meant to be something cat-like in her demeanor, especially as she licks up the purple drops that bleed from her where the cat had scratched her. She always wears a close-fitting neck ribbon, in imitation of the fairy tale about the woman whose head came off after her husband untied her neck ribbon.

Indeed, in one of the most memorable moments from the film, the Creature abruptly pulls her head from its body after his unwelcome appearance at her coming-out ball, which Polidori hoped to use to ensnare a rich suitor that would allow Prima to enter society, before embarking on affairs with men of state whom he would be able to manipulate through her. If, as Wordsworth stated, "the child is the father to the man," then Prima proves as unscrupulous as her "guardian."

The Creature's rage is explained by Polidori's attempt to immerse him in an acid bath before leaving for London with Prima. Frankenstein's conscience gets the better of him, causing him to warn the Creature at the last moment, which results in the death of one of Polidori's servants and the entire laboratory going up in flames.

In the final part of the story, we get a different perspective of the now fed-up Elizabeth. She pleads with the police that both Polidori and Frankenstein were delusional, but while her husband should be let go, she makes up a story about how Polidori is a wanted man on the Continent. Once on shipboard bound for America, Elizabeth discovers first that Polidori managed to make passage, and then that the Creature has stowed aboard as well. Satisfying herself that Polidori intends to continue his association with her husband, she allows Polidori admittance to his room without telling him that the Creature is inside waiting for him, hoping that these banes of Frankenstein's existence will succeed in destroying each other.

All ends disastrously as Polidori is destroyed by lightning, the crew abandon ship, the Creature sets course for the North Pole, Elizabeth is killed by him, and finally Frankenstein and his creation are buried under an avalanche of ice. (Though not as close as the Branagh version, *Frankenstein: The True Story* does retain the Arctic ending of the book.) The script ends with a suggestion that the Creature survives, but this was wisely not retained in the final film which suggests that both figures finally achieve the peace they seek in the bittersweet finale.

In reassessing the epic after all these years, I find that it does fall short of being the best version of the Shelley myth, but it still ranks as one of the finest. The direction by Jack Smight is competent and occasionally better than that. Smight's attempts at directing adaptations of Roger Zelazny's *Damnation Alley* and Ray Bradbury's *The Illustrated Man* were both disastrous, but given a good script as he has here, he can be quite fine. Filming outdoors and at Pinewood offered greater scope than the Hammer Frankenstein films could achieve at Bray, but in the creation scenes and in Phillip Martel's music supervision, there are clear echoes of Hammer's influence. Whether he was responsible for the few departures from the published script is uncertain, but those departures are all for the benefit of the project (e.g., the scene where Mrs. Blair is frightened to death is more touching than as originally written, and the scene of the Creature trying to commit suicide is more spectacular and interesting because he hurls himself off a cliff rather than drowning himself in a river as was originally written).

The cinematography by Arthur Ibbetson is frequently dark and moody, though not especially artistic, but it is nonetheless effective for the project. Elsa Fennell's costuming is quite good, capturing the proper period feel, and the set designs by Fred Carter have a lavish look, though the inclusion of a nude statue at an early Victorian coming-out party was a mistake as it is not in keeping with the morés of the period.

Leonard Whiting makes for a sympathetic Frankenstein, not as crazed as Colin Clive's nor as fascinating as Peter Cushing's, but nonetheless an eager explorer of knowledge who has failed to find solace in faith and who ultimately seems more sinned against than sinning. Michael Sarrazin will never make anybody forget Karloff, but his semi-articulate interpretation of the Creature as an eager innocent is touching and one of the better ones committed to celluloid. He gives the Creature an inner sweetness and allows for greater personality than most interpretations have.

James Mason was a master at conveying suave menace, and his Dr. Polidori proves no exception. Polidori has no corresponding character in the Shelley novel, proving more akin to Ernest Thesiger's Dr. Pretorius in *Bride of Frankenstein*, but he does pump up the conflict quotient in the miniseries' second half and is suggestive of a truly evil and deceptive personality. He never does anything overtly menacing, but we perceive the threat in his cultured tones much as we did in Mason's sinister antique dealer in *Salem's Lot*. The only aspect of his performance that doesn't work well is his character's presumed fear of lightning (which is supposed to explain why his character attempts a different form of resurrection), as well as the cornball device of his getting killed by lightning as if God struck him dead for his sins.

Given the shortness of screen time, Ralph Richardson isn't able to make much of Lacey, his performance recalling more his blinded character from *The Four Feathers* than it does O.P. Heggie's magnificent blind man in the Universal films. Jane Seymour succeeds in making Agatha and Prima distinctly different personalities, and David McCallum expertly depicts the arrogant, driven man of science, the Byronic monster-maker more typical of other Frankenstein films. Lastly, Nicola Pagett is an ultimately unsympathetic and forgettable Elizabeth, making it perhaps understandable why Victor would prefer to lose himself in his work rather than her attentions.

Overall, the film is not frightening or really horrific, nor was it intended to be. Instead, it offers up interesting characters who are aptly played by a talented cast and are confronted with conundrums of existence. We have the themes of the prejudice of man favoring beauty over ugliness, of the power of faith versus the power of science, of what actions are to be considered good and what actions are evil. Although the film was later trimmed down to 123 minutes and released theatrically in Europe, I prefer the full, uncut version with all its metaphysical melodrama in place.

Despite its title it cannot be considered the "true story." Nonetheless, the film remains a respectful and entertaining adaptation that led me back to rereading Mary Shelley's original work. In its own way, it powerfully portrays the drama of man uncovering new vistas and thereby encountering new problems, new ethical dilemmas, and new responsibilities.

Frankenstein TNT, 1993
by Arthur Joseph Lundquist

By 1993, somebody was going to film a faithful adaptation of *Frankenstein*. The aging of the moviegoing population had made Merchant-Ivory–style costume pictures big box office. At the same time, the Hollywood studios had become ingenious at selling big-budget remakes of movies or television shows that baby boomers and generation X-ers remembered loving as children. So a modern remake of a 19th-century public domain novel with the name recognition of *Frankenstein* was going to happen. And Kenneth Branagh was there to make it so. Thus it came as no surprise in early 1993 to find full-page advertisements in *Variety* celebrating the end of principal shooting of *Frankenstein*, with the slogan "The REAL Story Is The Most Horrifying Of All." Kenneth Branagh's name, however, was nowhere to be seen.

For as George Pal and Norman Jewison learned, when that historical moment is right, a Kurt Neumann or a Roger Corman is going to get his *Rocketship XM* or *Death Race 2000* into the theaters cheaper and faster. And once in a while, these harder working little brothers do it better.

Even their press releases echoed. In *Fangoria*, director/writer David Wickes, who had previously remade *Jack the Ripper* (1988) and *Jekyll and Hyde* (1990) for television, announced "Nobody's ever done the novel. It was written in 1818 and is a serious work of literature—all about cloning and genetic engineering, very topical. We've seen the Hammer versions; we've seen Peter Cushing in a lab with lightning flashing; we've seen Boris Karloff with a bolt through his neck.... So since nobody's ever really done it, I decided it was time to do so." Neither Wickes nor any of his crew, however, ever boasted that their film would be "more than just another horror film."

Randy Quaid in the TNT production of *Frankenstein*

The telefilm premiered on TNT to some truly nasty reviews. The

New York Post's Michele Greppi summed up the general consensus. "TNT's *Frankenstein* leeches most of the life out of one of the most enduring horror/monster tales ever told." Many reviews compared it unfavorably to the Branagh film without even having seen the film.

Well, the final film has its missteps, but it manages to miss a few that tripped up even Branagh. *Frankenstein* begins with a few stock shots of the frozen Arctic wastes, and immediately cuts to the chase. A surprisingly well-armed group of polar explorers encounter two dog sleds in a life-and-death chase across the snow, mercilessly driving their dogs with whips. One sled capsizes, and fearing for the downed man's life, the explorers drive off his pursuer with rifle fire. Going to the downed sled, its bearded driver (Patrick Bergin) introduces himself and out-pauses Branagh himself: "I'm (pause) Doctor (pause) Victor (pause) Frankenstein."

This *Frankenstein* begins and ends at the Arctic.

The opening credits roll as the explorers carry Victor Frankenstein back to a nameless tall ship trapped in the ice. We hear composer John Cameron's exciting main theme music, a chorale that sounds reminiscent of Carl Orff's "Carmina Burana," which had been used in many films like *Excalibur* to evoke savage times. (Cameron provided similar service for Wickes in *Jack the Ripper* and *Jekyll and Hyde*.)

Dr. Frankenstein warns the nameless Captain "...he'll be back.... He's not a man. He could tear this ship to pieces with his hands... You're in terrible danger. He'll wait until dawn. And then he'll attack. He'll send the wolves in first. And then he'll kill everyone on board without a thought... Is your crew armed? They must be armed. They must be ready."

On deck, we get a sample of the nameless ship's desperate position, as the Bosun (Michael Gothard) fights sloth from one sailor (played by a little person, for no particular reason, but it's a nice individual touch) and near-mutiny among the men personified by a nasty-looking sailor named Zorkin (Marcus Eyre). Though mostly nameless, the sailors are actually very well differentiated, at least compared with Branagh's faceless crewmen.

By sheer coincidence there follows a shot that is an almost exact duplicate of one in Branagh's film. We see a hulking figure watching the distant ship from his campfire. Branagh showed us only its hand, while here we see the whole figure. Yet, seeing the entire figure doesn't necessarily tell us any more than the hand (I wonder if someone had not learned a lesson from W. Lee Wilder's 1954 film *The Snow Creature*).

The arctic scenes were filmed on very impressive Shepperton Studio sets. Like every set in this film they are not as beautifully stylized as the equivalent settings in Branagh's film, but for a TV movie they do the job. The snow flakes may look a little more like soapflakes, but on the whole only the lack of breath clouding from the actors' mouths spoils the illusion of Arctic cold.

Frankenstein explains, "I'm a scientist. From Ingolstadt... Last year I made a discovery, and I wish with all my soul that I had not... Something so dangerous that it could destroy every living thing on board this ship."

With that we flash back a year (and the film moves to beautiful locations in Poland) to the university at Ingolstadt where the students are as close to open rebellion as the Arctic sailors. An awards ceremony honors Doctor (not a student) Frankenstein for his "work on the human body." This work is, however, valued less than "the religious work of Professor Cloyburg..." This slight causes a riot among the students, who carry Frankenstein out on their shoulders, while Cameron's main theme music plays triumphantly.

Frankenstein berates his students "...it is your job to build a future for science. To take what I have given you and to use it, not to cause a riot. Now go back inside, and take up your books." He says this between coughs, and we notice carts taking away cholera dead.

The intriguing idea of Frankenstein being assisted by dozens of ardent student followers is, alas, abandoned along with the academic setting for the rest of the film. Instead we follow the solitary Frankenstein to a house of the sick, where his attempts to use science to combat cholera are frustrated by the superstitions of the local monsignor.

Into this house (where a white "x" is being painted on the door) comes a well-dressed gentleman (Lambert Wilson).

> **Frankenstein**: (Looking up.) Clerval.
> **Clerval**: Your father sent me. He wants me to take you home... He thinks your life's in danger. So does Elizabeth.

This movie does not waste time in establishing relationships and moral themes.

> **Frankenstein**:... cholera can be cured with a simple saline solution. And one day I'll prove it to the world. These people are not just dying of disease, they are dying of ignorance.

But something else is preying upon Frankenstein, and not just his coughs.

> **Frankenstein**: Clerval, remember those days when we spoke of ambition, when we swore to reach the heights? Me with my science and you with your art?

This Clerval, you see, is a poet. A stand-in, obviously, for Lord Byron. This device seemed a lot fresher in *Frankenstein: The True Story* (Cushing's Frankenstein was himself the Byronic hero in the Hammer versions). We never see Clerval write or recite any of his poetry, so for all the difference it makes to the story, Wickes may as well not have bothered.

Frankenstein takes Clerval to his charmingly simple garret of a laboratory. "Come and meet my friends," he offers. We see a snake with a cat's head. A rabbit with porcupine quills. We never see or hear anything about these mutant animals again, though one would think that they alone would be enough to make anyone's reputation in the world of 19th-century science.

He shows Clerval a glass tank filled with fluid. "Every living creature is composed of elements, Clerval," explains Frankenstein. "And there they all are. All the elements of life." Beside the tank is an electromagnet. By placing his arm in the magnetic field, an electromagnetic field in the tank causes a transparent arm to appear in the fluid, which then ickily begins to fill with blood. It's sort of like broadcasting analog sound.

This is a unique creation method, harkening back all the way to Edison's 1910 adaptation. Wickes was quoted in *Fangoria*: "Mary Shelley was very careful not to describe how he was made. She has Frankenstein talk about how 'I used all my skill and all my art to create him'—there's no suggestion that he was stitched together from bodies found in graves."

Well, maybe. While Mary Shelley never comes out and says "I grafted my Monster together from dead bodies," she does write, "Who shall conceive the horrors of my secret toil as I dabbled among the unhallowed damps of the grave... I collected bones from charnel-houses and disturbed, with profane fingers, the tremendous secrets of the human frame... The dissecting room and the slaughter-house furnished many of my materials..." And certainly in her introduction to the novel she out and out writes, "Perhaps a corpse would be reanimated; galvanism had given token of such things: perhaps the component parts of a creature might be manufactured, brought together and endued with vital warmth." Ah, delicious words, these.

However, in 1993 a movie about reanimating the dead may be fun, but it is not that holy grail of modern popular art, relevant. Wickes: "I had to give a 1993 audience something a bit more acceptable, so what we have done is invent what I hope is very credible early 19th-century technology for producing a cloned human being."

Frankenstein explains in this film's variation of The Mad Scientist Speech:

> "What if I could make a living man, Clerval. Stronger than you or I. Bigger. More intelligent. Perfect in every way. A new kind of man. Immune to all diseases. More powerful than any man on Earth. Would that be a trick, too, or would it be the greatest gift this world has ever known?"

Just how Frankenstein hopes to improve his carbon copies is not mentioned. Time will tell if this method actually does manage to tap contemporary concerns about cloning. Seeking to fit these concepts into today's zeitgeist, Bergin was quoted in *Premiere*: "Because of the ways Frankenstein tries to re-create himself, the most obvious comparison, media-wise, would be to somebody like Michael Jackson."

Frankenstein and Clerval argue.
    Clerval: Blasphemy.
    Frankenstein: Oh my poor dear poet.

Clerval carries the burden of voicing the conservative religious side, though we never learn just what his religion is supposed to be.

Their argument is brought to a halt by another bout of Victor's coughing. Taking advantage of the pause in conversation, Frankenstein sends Clerval away. Frankenstein opens another tank, revealing to us a full-grown man in the fluid lying naked and in a fetal position. Frankenstein gives his creation a charge of electricity from some voltaic cells, and with a chorus of the main theme music, the being within the tank comes bursting through its glass walls. This film may not have the artistry of Branagh's, but boy does the story move along.

Frankenstein's creation is referred to in the end credits as "The Monster," which in this day and age is surprisingly refreshing. Just about every Frankenstein film since the 1940s has referred to its creation as "The Creature" and thought itself very original.

This "Monster" is not that bad looking. Since it wasn't assembled from the dead, there is no stitching across its muscular arms and legs. Most of its deformity consists of some scarring on its cheeks and a few protruding veins on the forehead and neck. Michele Greppi's review in *The New York Post* described it as "...Freddie Krueger at Muscle Beach ..."

Fangoria quoted makeup creator Mark Coulier, "The inspiration was the idea of a man forming in a tank of liquid and the experiment being turned off before it is completed. We went for a look where the tendons and the muscles hadn't completely formed on part of his head and took it from there. We tried to keep some idea of what people expect the Monster to be—a horrific creature. But he has to create sympathy too, so you can't get too gruesome. Hopefully, we've kept him relatively human." Reading comments like these, I'm glad nobody told Karloff and Jack Pierce back in 1931 that their monster couldn't be gruesome.

Said Randy Quaid (the Monster), also in *Fangoria*: "I've never been a big horror fan. But I am now, because I really appreciate what goes into them, pulling off the effects and the makeup. It's not easy to really act in these; it takes a special knack to pull off the character." Damn right, Randy.

Quaid is not the obvious choice for this role. As Terry Kelleher wrote in her *New York Newsday* review, "Although no one can doubt Quaid has the size for his role, he also has a sort of natural goofiness (recall his stint on *Saturday Night Live*) that needed to be suppressed for this performance to work."

As the Monster stumbles to its feet, a bout of sickness renders Frankenstein incapable of preventing it from walking out into the streets. Where the newborn Monster's brain got all this knowledge about standing and walking is not addressed.

Morning finds the Monster in a sculptor's outdoor studio, where it clothes itself in a tarpaulin (how the newborn Monster's brain learned to tie knots is not et cetera, et cetera). Then the film gets down to the business of making us feel sorry for him. We see the innocent Monster contrast itself with the physical perfection of the sculptures on display. In fact, he doesn't look that much worse than many of the homeless I share

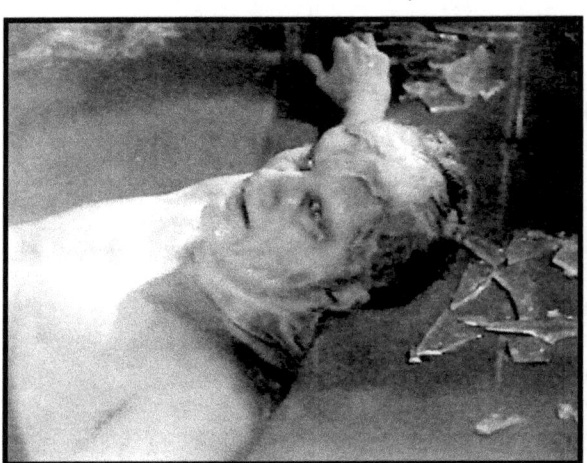

Frankenstein gives his creation (Randy Quaid) a charge of electricity, and the being within the tank comes bursting through its glass walls.

subways with. Then two menial workers enter.

Finding believable excuses for the Monster's first encounters with humanity to be both brutal and guilt-free has always been one of the biggest stumbling blocks in writing Frankenstein movies. The first hostile move must never come from the Monster. The Monster must only fight back in self defense. It must then be hounded mercilessly by the local populace. Never make the Monster too nasty.

While magistrates on horseback chase the Monster out of town to the tune of the opening theme music, Clerval nurses Frankenstein through cholera. From his sickbed, Frankenstein somehow experiences the Monster's exertion and pain. It falls down a deep ravine (the stunt dummy is not bad, but suffers in comparison to the beautiful fall in *Frankenstein: The True Story*) and is left for dead.

Morning finds the Monster in a sculptor's outdoor studio, where it clothes itself in a tarpaulin.

Frankenstein takes full responsibility, "Like a child with no one to guide him. No one to help," he narrates, "...the guilt was mine. All mine. If only I'd been able to teach him, to prepare him, I might have saved so many lives..."

Well, perhaps. In order to keep its main character sympathetic, this film is a little more no-fault than that. It's not Frankenstein's fault that he succumbed to cholera as his creation was achieving consciousness. It's not the Monster's fault that it wandered off into the streets. Tragic misunderstandings accumulate for most of the film. Most of what goes wrong is not inevitable, it's just dumb luck. If there's any moral, it's "Never clone alone."

Then the film returns briefly to the framing sequence in the Arctic. While the Monster burns its sled to survive the night, Frankenstein continues his explanation: "We are one, Captain, he and I. I made him, like I made the hand, from me. We are two parts of a single man."

It has been a cliché of crime movies for years to have the detective and his quarry be variations of the same person. The script here drops the idea in our laps and does little to explore it. Beyond their psychic connection, this Frankenstein and his Monster are alike in no other way. But then, I'm sure that in real life most homicide detectives are nothing like the murderers they seek.

Returning to his story, Frankenstein says, "He was unformed, you see, unfinished." This sounds to my ear like a deliberate echo of Shakespeare's description of Richard III: "Deformed, unfinished, sent before my time into this breathing world, scarce half made up..."

Looking quite the noble savage in his tarpaulin, the Monster wanders blindly across the countryside, unconsciously following his creator's carriage to the Frankenstein family estate. There the introductions come fast and furious. We meet Elizabeth (Fiona Gillies), playing the harpsichord for Victor's father (Ronald Leigh Hunt) and Justine (Jacinta Mulcahy), a family friend and social equal who is in love with Clerval. We meet Victor's brother

PATRICK BERGIN   RANDY QUAID

THE LEGEND
HAS BEEN TOLD
FOR GENERATIONS...
THE REAL STORY
IS THE MOST
HORRIFYING OF ALL.

FRANKENSTEIN

William (Timothy Stark) spurring his horse as the headstrong young man he is (with his own variation of the main theme music).

The film barely pauses from the introductions before rushing into a montage of Elizabeth nursing Victor, their romantic walks together, etc. Perhaps realizing that we've barely met the girl, the screenplay throws in a quick speech to flesh out her character and establish she is no mere fainting love interest: "Victor, who nurses the sick in Ingolstadt? ...I'd like to help them like I helped you. Do you think they'd let me? ...why can't I be trained like the nuns?" Victor proposes.

In this central section, the film skips back and forth between generally interesting scenes with the Monster and generally uninteresting ones with the Frankenstein family.

Among the most uninteresting are any scene involving Clerval and Justine. Their characters are about as blank as they are in Mary Shelley's novel. Wickes, like Branagh, deserves praise for putting Justine into the script, though he gets even less from her character than Branagh. Lambert Wilson and Jacinta Mulcahy are pretty in their costumes, but neither they nor the script fill in many of the blanks.

In an incident from the book, the Monster (its features visibly decaying) rescues a young girl (Amanda Quaid) from drowning and receives in thanks a bullet to the chest. Miles away, Victor feels the gunshot and finds a bruise above his heart. As the wounded Monster is washed down some rapids, Victor experiences the Monster's pain. Like most movie atheists, the scientist wimps out when the heat is on and cries out to divine providence for help.

Providence answers in the form of the traditional blind hermit, named, as in the book, De Lacey (John Mills), though without any other family. He takes the dying Monster home and, gaining its trust, cuts the bullet from its heart. Monster and creator both heal and begin to enjoy their respective families.

Over another romantic montage (the Wickes equivalent of Branagh's polka dancing), Victor narrates, "That was our golden time, both his and mine, a summer full of laughter. Elizabeth and I had pledged our love. And his world? His world was filled with laughter." Enjoying more leisure time than it gets in just about any other Frankenstein movie, the Monster helps De Lacey at chores and somewhere in there begins to talk. De Lacey sews it a suit of animal furs. This is an improvement over the tarp it'd been walking around in, eliminating the minor distraction of how underdeveloped Randy Quaid's chest and arms are. The furs, and its growing beard, give this Monster a unique look, at once monstrous and humane. It also reminds me of Dave and Max Fleischer's Old Man of the Mountain.

Once it starts to talk, however, all these elements come together and the Monster starts to develop into a really interesting character, with a sad grandeur all its own. To avoid any problem with his American accent, the script gives Quaid only two or three words to say at any time. This technique, which made an acceptable performer out of nonactor Rondo Hatton, works quite beautifully with consummate actor Randy Quaid. Quaid may not have the ideal physique, but his deep, brief line readings give him the most sadly beautiful Monster voice since Karloff. *Newsday*'s Terry Kelleher felt that Quaid "...achieves real poignancy in several scenes, particularly the Monster's parting from his blind benefactor De Lacey..."

With autumn comes a pair of bounty hunters, who believe the Monster to be an escaped prisoner with a price on its head. Showing great but not unreasonable physical strength, the Monster chases them away without doing any permanent damage.

At the Frankenstein home, Victor sees clouds gathering. Elizabeth tells him, "This has been the perfect summer, hasn't it?" People should know better than to say things like that in a horror movie.

Branagh's $55 million budget had been able to recreate every season and climate on the soundstages of Shepperton. The budget of even a generous TV movie prevents Wickes from painting the midsummer Polish forests in the melancholy colors of autumn, but his crew do the best they can, finding a beautifully barren grove of trees for the parting of De Lacey and the Monster, while John Cameron provides a suitably bittersweet theme. Fearing the return of the bounty hunters, De Lacey sadly sends the Monster, looking primevally impressive in his animal skins, out into the world.

> **Lacey**: It's a long way from home, isn't it?
> **Monster**: Home?
>
> **Lacey**: Yeah. Where you live. In your own country.
> **Monster**: No home, Lacey. No home.

They do have a nice chemistry together. John Mills, with movie experience since 1932, is a great sounding board for Randy Quaid. He brings to De Lacey the same feeling of an old man facing a corrupted world that he brought to the *Quatermass* conclusion back in 1979.

Wickes' script places the Frankenstein family home within a short distance of Ingolstadt, which makes it a lot easier to swallow the ease with which the Monster covers the territory without attracting too much notice.

Now, up to this point, the Monster has been developing into a sympathetic, entirely unmonstrous character. There is no inevitable tragedy in the offing. If he could somehow find his way to the eminently responsible Frankenstein, he might still find his place in the world. Which might be an interesting plot direction. Some day. The Monster is certainly nothing like the fiend that Frankenstein had described in the Arctic. As a matter of fact, so far he has the lowest body count of any Frankenstein Monster in movie history.

Arriving near Frankenstein's home, the Monster is attracted to Justine. He breaks into her home that night and attempts to woo her with a flower while a thunderstorm rages. Understandably, Justine panics. She runs out into the storm, and in the confusion that follows, William is thrown from his horse and dies (making William an advanced adolescent rather than a boy makes this murder a lot less like child molestation than it reads in the book). The incident unhinges Justine's mind.

There being no competent witnesses, the blame falls on William's horse, which is immediately shot by Father. The unbalanced Justine becomes another victim of ignorance, receiving inadequate counseling from the local priest, who rants that she is possessed.

At William's interment, there is a haunting shot of Frankenstein staring down at William's grave while the Monster approaches from the distance behind him. Frankenstein senses his creation's presence, but the Monster runs away.

John Mills as the blind hermit De Lacey is a great sounding board for Randy Quaid.

Realizing what must have happened, Victor does what few Frankensteins have ever done before. He tells his family everything. They seem to believe him.

Deciding "I made him, I must destroy him," Frankenstein arms himself and searches for the Monster. The film's main theme music plays as he searches, and the mental contact between hunted and hunter becomes more acute. Frankenstein seems to recollect seeing places that only the Monster had seen before. (The script turns their psychic connection off and on at random whenever it becomes convenient for the plot.)

The film slows down considerably as Frankenstein runs into De Lacey at a pub. Touching Frankenstein's face, De Lacey seems to sense the connection with his friend. Their faces are in no way alike. Frankenstein follows De Lacey home and spends time cruelly terrifying the old man to no good purpose.

Film critic Michele Grippi described the film's pacing this way: "It moves like a glacier when writer-director-producer David Wickes... needs to fill time cheaply. But it moves like quicksilver when confronted with nuts and bolts aspects that neither his budget nor his imagination are equipped to deal with." The film is about to display the latter approach.

At last Victor spots the Monster and the two run off on a chase across the beautiful mountain forests of Poland, the main theme playing away around them.

The Monster traps and disarms Frankenstein at a crevasse, and the two have their big scene together. The Monster says:

> "You come to kill me. Now you will give... You made me. And you give me nothing. You made me. And you teach me nothing. ...Men come for me with horses. Hunt me with guns. ...You have everything. I see you. In your houses. In your gardens. You have everything. And I have nothing. You made me like this. Now you will give... A woman. A woman, like you have a woman, you will give me a woman... Tall and strong. Like me. To love me. As I am. As a woman loves you. And I will go. Away from this place. Away from your horses and your guns. Away from all of you. You will see me no more. But first, you will give me a woman..."

Watching this scene, my heart really goes out to Randy Quaid. The comments I made about the lack of campfire light in the equivalent scene in *Mary Shelley's Frankenstein* seem like the smallest quibble compared with the lack of support Quaid is given here. For a full three minutes Quaid reads this speech. Without benefit of camera angles or dramatic lighting or background music or even a single close-up. That would be a compliment if said of a Jim Jarmusch film, but not here, as the Monster stands in the midday sunlight, shouting away in a medium shot interrupted by a couple of cuts here and there. All of the subtle feeling Quaid had been nurturing in his Monster are gone. Rightly or wrongly, it looks like the crew had run out of time and just slapped the scene together.

The Monster's speech reads as if it had been written in the wake of the L.A. riots, as another thuddingly literal grasp at relevance. Indeed, Randy Quaid confirms in a quote from *Premiere*, "When the Monster confronts the doctor and asks 'Where's my place? You have everything and I have nothing'—I think those words echo for most of the population."

The Monster runs off, leaving behind the threat "You will see me on your wedding night," (the one line from the novel filmmakers want to keep).

Victor returns and immediately explains his decision to create a mate for his Monster. Elizabeth argues against it, but when she realizes the depth of the link between Frankenstein and the Monster, she demands that she be the model for the she-monster. At first Frankenstein refuses.

> **Frankenstein**: Elizabeth, you're my whole life.
> **Elizabeth**: So the creature you make from me will be his. The perfect match. Isn't that what he wants?

Up until now, the relationship between Elizabeth and Victor has seemed rather shallow and perfunctory. Now it begins to come alive. In these two scenes, Elizabeth and Victor establish the relationship and connection that has eluded them in this film so far, that eluded Branagh and Bonham Carter in their entire movie. By working together, their relationship comes together.

The creation of the she-monster is treated as a major set piece, and since we never actually witnessed the creation of the Monster, there's never the feeling that we've seen it all before.

Frankenstein prepares for Elizabeth a table surrounded with magnets. She lies upon it dressed in a pretty white nightgown. She experiences discomfort as soon as the magnets are switched on. In the tank, a transparent fetus appears that begins to fill with blood. Her pain increases as the fetus grows. The main theme chorale soars. Fiona Gilles does a good job of conveying Elizabeth's agony. I'd love to know what her emotion memory was. The full-grown she-monster becomes flesh-colored. Elizabeth starts to scream.

Frankenstein can bear her pain no more, and shuts off the machine. The unfinished she-monster expires. Through a skylight above the tank, the Monster watches as his bride breaks up into bloody chunks. This is the closest any film has come to the way Victor destroys his she-monster in the novel. (Some day I hope to actually see that scene in a movie.)

Beholding the crumbling of his hopes (and his bride), the Monster breaks through the skylight and goes berserk. Tearing at some electrified wires, he receives a nasty shock and crumples to the floor, apparently dead. Rather than make sure with the nearest scalpel, Frankenstein accepts appearances and carries Elizabeth away.

They arrive at home to discover that Justine has OD'd on laudanum. Clerval angrily blames Frankenstein for her death.

The film speeds up again, leaping ahead a month to Victor and Elizabeth's wedding, along with the inevitable group dance.

Things seem to be going well. Victor and Elizabeth dance happily. Clerval arrives and is reconciled with the Frankensteins. Father boasts that he is about to go on vacation. Alas, this is the equivalent of saying, "I am about to die in agony."

As the guests leave, Frankenstein senses the Monster's nearness and sends a servant for troops. Delayed in arming himself, Victor runs upstairs to find Father dead in a pool of blood and Clerval impaled to a wall (which, unfortunately, sort of resembles a Monty Python gag). Victor reaches the bedroom in time to see the Monster kill Elizabeth (though we don't).

Running to the deserted courtyard where only hours before they had danced, Frankenstein cries vengeance: "Can you hear me? Can you hear me? I swear by the God who made me, I will destroy you. I will follow you to the ends of the Earth, and I won't rest until you are dead. You hear me? Dead. Dead. Dead."

This is the first movie adaptation of the vow Mary Shelley's Victor makes at his loved ones' graves. Mary's speech is very beautiful "... I call on you, spirits of the dead, and on you, wandering ministers of vengeance, to aid and conduct me in my work..."

The troops arrive and promptly accuse Frankenstein of all the murders. Frankenstein runs off, a fugitive, and thus begins his pursuit of the Monster.

With this, we return to the Arctic, where, closing his story, Frankenstein gives the Captain a copy of his diary and notes.

The Captain sends a group of sailors to kill the Monster, led by the brutal Zorkin, who has the beautiful line "I fought Napoleon, Captain. He won't see the sunrise." Dawn, however, finds their bodies being eaten by sled dogs.

The ice cap chooses this propitious moment to (gently) break up. Before they can sail away, however, Frankenstein finds himself trapped in the Captain's cabin for his final confrontation with the vengeful Monster.

> **Monster**: Now you will pay. Here. In this place.
> **Frankenstein**: What are you going to do, kill me? Why here? Why kill me here? You had your chance a hundred times before this. Why lead me here? Why?
> **Monster**: To make you feel pain. Like me. Fear. And pain. Like me.
> **Frankenstein**: To make me feel your pain? You did all this to make me feel your pain? There was no need. I felt it from the start. Your pain is

mine. It's my pain, not yours. Perhaps you haven't understood. You kill me, you will die. We're one. But you know it. Can you feel it? We (pause) are (pause) one.

(As you can see by my quotes, there are a lot of repetitions in the dialogue. I can't tell if this is due to the script, or to giving loose rein to Meisner-trained actors.)

Now, the Monster's need to make his creator feel his pain has always been one of the subtexts of Frankenstein movies. Just about every classic horror story has subtexts like these that touch something vital in generation after generation of audiences. *Dracula* with the repression of sexuality. *The Wolf Man* with the onset of puberty. When the Phantom of the Opera says, "There is no escape for you, my dear," one of the things he is also saying is "I'm lonely." And we can sympathize with that. The problem with so many adaptations today is that they take those unspoken texts and bring them up to the surface. Today's Phantoms usually start out saying "I'm lonely," but it doesn't necessarily touch us. Giving the Monster the vocabulary of a contemporary talk show, it even sounds silly.

The Monster begins to weep, "Please help me." Frankenstein repeats a couple of times, "I will. I will help us both." He leaps against the Monster, driving both of them through a window out into the freezing Arctic waters, where they die in each other's arms.

Without wasting time, the Captain sets sail for home, bringing Frankenstein's journal back to the world. The credits roll, with a final rousing rendition of John Cameron's main theme.

I kind of like the ending. Usually all of Frankenstein's notes are lost to the world. Here there is a chance that, in spite of all the mistakes, the world will learn the truth.

David Wickes' *Frankenstein* will always exist in the shadow of Kenneth Branagh's *Mary Shelley's Frankenstein*. So, the question we all want to know: Which one is better? Neither one of them is the definitive *Frankenstein*. Branagh's film certainly looks better. Branagh and his crew could afford to fill each frame with interesting details that may or may not advance the plot. Comparing costume, makeup, special effects, music... the phrase "less ambitious, less elaborate, sometimes more interesting," would pretty much sum up just about any aspect of Wickes' film.

So which one is closer to the novel? Uh, the Branagh film, certainly, except for the last 20 minutes. But Wickes keeps a few touches from the novel that Branagh doesn't. By not sticking so close to the novel's plot, Wickes' script is able to explore some of the more interesting tangents that the story comes across, fleshing out the framing scenes, for example. And sometimes, in spite of a limited budget and schedule, the direction, script, and performance mesh to work their unpredictable magic, and the movie comes to life. I hope future filmmakers will learn its lessons.

In an incident from the book, the Monster (its features visibly decaying) rescues a young girl (Amanda Quaid) from drowning.

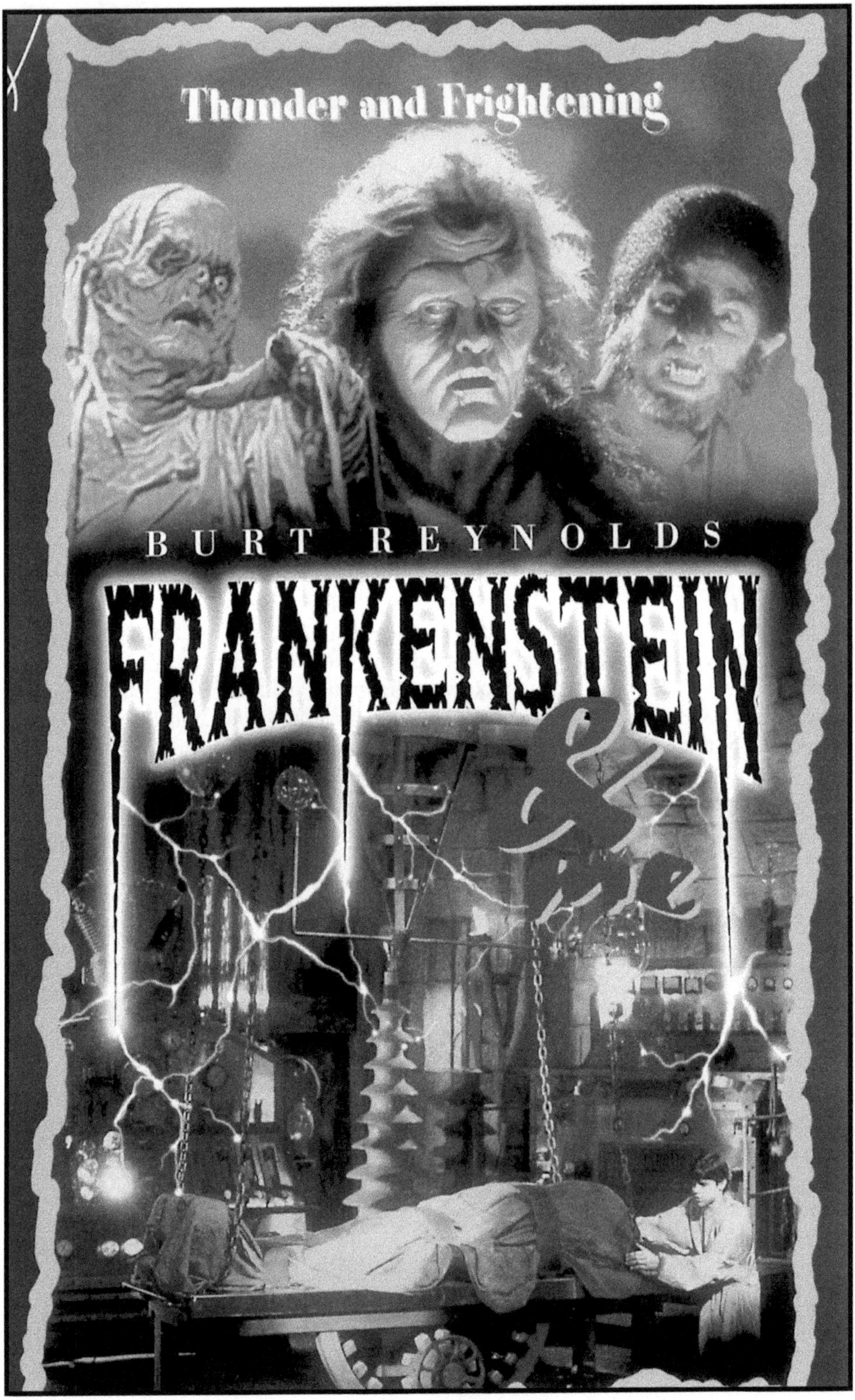
Thunder and Frightening
BURT REYNOLDS
FRANKENSTEIN
& me

The Modern Prometheus

Almost 100 years since the Edison *Frankenstein*!

Nearly 75 years since Universal's 1931 *Frankenstein*.

Yet, well into the 2000s, the legend of Frankenstein continues to thrill movie and television audiences across the world.

During the last 30 years several movies have been made attempting to depict that "haunted summer" in 1816 when Mary Shelley was inspired to write *Frankenstein*. Other movies attempted to spoof both the novel and all those legions of movies produced in its wake: *Young Frankenstein* and *Frankenweenie* immediately coming to mind. The highly anticipated yet box-office fizzle of *Mary Shelley's Frankenstein*, starring no less a talent than Robert De Niro as the Frankenstein Monster, attempted to reinvent the literary classic for a new generation, but this movie had precious little new to offer.

It is often the lower-budget efforts that provide unexpected diamonds in a field of big-budget Hollywood rhinestones. One of these efforts to take note of is the Robert Tinnell–directed *Frankenstein and Me*, which uses the icon image of Frankenstein's Monster and mythos of the Frankenstein legend as the starting point to weave a sympathetic ode to horror movie lovers everywhere. These variations seem to be most successful, showcasing creative young filmmakers cutting new paths into the Frankenstein terrain instead of simply reinventing the original wheel by returning to Mary Shelley's novel.

Robert Alan Crick delivers in-depth looks at two of the finer spoofs of the Frankenstein mythos: *Young Frankenstein* and *Frankenweenie*. Crick, also a high school English teacher in Kentucky, is a longtime contributor to *Midnight Marquee* and authored *The Big Screen Comedies of Mel Brooks*.

Arthur Lundquist and Bryan Senn also contribute chapters on the modern Prometheus.

One thing is certain, as long as visionary filmmakers flourish, inspiring variations will continue to be produced based upon Mary Shelley's inspirational novel and Universal Pictures' cinema classics. Just as the novel itself attests, Frankenstein, both the scientist and the Monster, will never die; future generations await the twitching fingers rising from the laboratory table allowing all to cry in unison, "It's Alive!"

Start the Operation Without Me:
Monsters, Madmen, and Maturity in Mel Brooks'
Young Frankenstein
by Robert Alan Crick

Young Frankenstein may well represent Mel Brooks at his very best, perhaps arguably his most artistically satisfying film.

In *Young Frankenstein*, virtually all the vital elements crucial to good comedy work together in unison—the near-perfect casting, a top-quality script, the crispness of the editing, a sublimely atmospheric John Morris score, some extraordinary directorial choices from Brooks—to create the single most endearing blend of humor and horror since the similarly themed genre send-up *Abbott and Costello Meet Frankenstein* from 1948. Even better, while *Young Frankenstein* is as bright and funny as one might expect from the man who brought us Maxwell Smart's shoe phone and a spaced-out stage actor named L.S.D, it is at the same time as tender and touching as the original Mary Shelley novel and Universal film series that inspired it. Man's boundless arrogance, his unquenchable thirst for achievement, his stubborn determination to cheat death, his insatiable urge for procreation, his tireless quest for Godlike power—all the themes that have kept Shelley's tale told and retold a thousand different ways since she first authored *Frankenstein* in 1818 have been maintained by Brooks in his 1974 film, and, even while turned on their ear for the sake of slapstick humor and sly parody, these themes' overall integrity have been lovingly, even exquisitely maintained. *Young Frankenstein* displays, in other words, all the brazen, side-splitting outrageousness for which Brooks' comedy has won fame through the years, yet paradoxically, it also remains one of the most reverent and respectful productions of Brooks' illustrious career. Just as he would make fun of Hitchcock's style and themes in *High Anxiety* while simultaneously revealing a heartfelt admiration for his awesome talents and technique, so did Brooks in *Young Frankenstein* at once playfully tease and pay loving tribute to both Shelley's original concept and the classic Universal film series spawned by it in the 1930s and 1940s. In short, Mel Brooks was a tremendous *Frankenstein* fan, and it showed.

In scripting their comic take on Shelley and Universal, for example, Brooks and co-writer Gene Wilder were obviously well aware that the studio's original film series, which was, after all, about a creature stitched together from the remains of stolen corpses, bore a clear preoccupation with body parts. Indeed, every *Frankenstein* picture Universal produced showcased some character's obsession with either creating life out of others' anatomy or "fine-tuning" the human body in order to improve it: the creation of a Monster from stolen corpses in director James Whale's original *Frankenstein* (1931), and then a mate for it in Whale's *Bride of Frankenstein* (1935); a Frankenstein heir's attempt to cure his father's original creature of its violent impulses to restore the family honor in Rowland V. Lee's *Son of Frankenstein* (1939); the effort of another well-meaning Frankenstein son to replace the Monster's brain with that of a dead scientist in Erle C. Kenton's *Ghost of Frankenstein* (1942), only to be tricked into inserting that of the villainous, misshapen Ygor instead; attempts to cure a self-loathing werewolf of his curse and to restore the Monster's strength rather than destroy it in Roy William Neill's *Frankenstein Meets the Wolf Man* (1943); the same werewolf's dream of a new brain and a lonely hunchback's wish for a new body, courtesy of a deranged scientist who seeks only to exploit them both (and Frankenstein's

Peter Boyle as the Frankenstein Monster

Monster) in his quest for power and revenge in Kenton's *House of Frankenstein* (1944); the Wolf Man's eventual (though evidently temporary) cure, and plans to heal a sweet but hunchbacked nurse in Kenton's *House of Dracula* (1945); and Count Dracula's attempt to re-energize the Monster and replace its brain with that of a dim-witted, easy-to-manipulate baggage handler in Charles T. Barton's *Abbott and Costello Meet Frankenstein*.

Quite logically, then, as many critics have noted (Maurice Yacowar makes a particular point of it in his intriguing study *Method in Madness: The Comic Art of Mel Brooks*), *Young*

In *Young Frankenstein*, virtually all the vital elements crucial to good comedy work together in unison. Gene Wilder as Dr. Frankenstein and his Monster (Peter Boyle).

Frankenstein uses this theme of body parts and human improvement to its best advantage. Again and again in the film, Brooks and Wilder draw both humor and pathos from not only the title scientist's efforts to create a Monster from the deceased and mold it into the sort of being he desires, but also from specific aspects of the human anatomy, and from its frequent inability to serve our needs as we wish. Brains, eyes, tongues, hands—throughout the movie, these and other anatomical elements fail to function as their masters (or others) wish, and beneath the comedy provided by such failures often lies faint traces of tragedy, as if the story of the human condition is that of man's inability to master even his own body, let alone his own destiny.

Just as Gene Wilder's "young" Frankenstein of the title spends much of the film denying his own ancestry ("That's Fronk-en-steen") yet in the end falls prey to precisely the same egotistical ravings that destroyed his grandfather ("Destiny! Destiny! No escaping that for me!"), by the same token he is surrounded by others whose bodies rather than spirits refuse to conform to their longings: the police inspector whose Dr. Strangelove-like wooden arm cannot be controlled, and who wears a ridiculous monocle atop the patch covering his blind eye; the painfully skinny, bulging-eyed hunchback who seems ignorant of his infirmity ("What hump?") yet elsewhere is clearly aware of his inability to conceal it ("Call it... a hunch!"); the warm-hearted blind man whose offers of soup, liquor, and cigars intend kindness but create only mayhem; the man-made Monster whose inarticulate tongue and massive frame brand him a fiend even when he seeks only friendship. Lesser screenwriters might have dismissed the notion of finding meaning in the failure of soul and body to work together in harmony (why bother adding depth and exploring character when sight gags, pratfalls, and bellylaughs will likely be enough?), but Brooks and Wilder mine its vast potential for character development—and uproarious humor—at every turn. Naturally, the result is a Frankenstein spoof far richer in tone and texture even than the admittedly hilarious (and deservedly beloved) *Abbott and Costello Meet Frankenstein.* Not content merely to make their audiences laugh (though succeed in this aim they most assuredly did), Brooks and Wilder also saw in their send-up of Shelley and Universal an opportunity to offer food for thought—wisdom as well as wisecracks, humanity as well as humor.

But it is not only in its witty use of the conflict between body and will that *Young Frankenstein* achieves a depth of feeling rare among horror comedies, though certainly the screenwriters' attention to the idea makes for a nice touch. Self-improvement is another key theme, with Brooks and Wilder telling the story of not one but two childlike, underdeveloped figures—both the Monster and the scientist who creates him—struggling against their own dark impulses to emerge as nobler, gentler human beings. Frankenstein's lumbering, growling Monster may be both physically and psychologically primitive, after all, but in *Young Frankenstein* his smug, self-absorbed creator is hardly the personification of self-control, warmth, and tenderness himself. Surely it is not by accident that Brooks and Wilder supply scenes in which both creature and creator are summoned by violin music ("It's in your blood," housekeeper Frau Blucher tells Frederick. "It's in the blood of all Frankensteins!"), for, physical dissimilarities notwithstanding, these two characters are almost certainly far more alike than they are different, and indeed they end up even more alike than ever in the film's final scene.

Young Frankenstein pursues this notion as well, and it seems that with the Frankenstein myth Brooks found a near-perfect framework upon which to hang his comic treatment of the impaired development theme. Perhaps Shelley would have been startled to see her tale, concerned with no lesser issue than man's struggle to usurp God's dominance as life-creator and to defeat all-conquering death, used by a wisecracking movie comic to tackle a theme explored in his previous works by way of tap-dancing Hitlers and therapists tortured by falls from high chairs. But then one of the secrets to the longevity of Shelley's novel has always been its curious ability to reshape itself to suit the spirit of each new age. The notion of the creator whose reckless arrogance and unbridled will brings his own self-destruction transcends time and technology, after all, whether the man-made Monster run amuck takes the form of atom bomb, robot, computer, or epidemic—so why shouldn't it hold up in parody form as well?

In a way, *Frankenstein* is but a 19th-century version of classic tragedy, its origins going back to Shakespeare, Sophocles, and the very roots of ancient myth: Man desires that which he should not, pursues it mindless of the consequences, and pays for his obsession in ways he should have foreseen. In *Young Frankenstein*, of course, the title character's egotism and obsessiveness is all part of the fun, used to make Gene Wilder the most lovably kooky Dr. Frankenstein Wilder and Brooks could imagine. Yet they also serve to help explore such everyday domestic issues as love, maturity, nurturing, and compassion along the way, for Brooks' fascination with the grown-up who has not yet reached true adulthood finds perhaps its best expression yet in *Young Frankenstein*, which comically yet tenderly explores this theme of the child-man not only through its amusingly immature title character—Wilder's Dr. Frederick Frankenstein, the creature's boyish, frizzy-haired creator—but also the oversized offspring to which he "gives birth." After all, what is Shelley's tale if not the saga of a literal child-man, an artificial being given life by a father figure who ultimately displays all the child-rearing wisdom of a mere boy himself?

It is only after Frederick and Inga (Teri Garr) bring the creature to life that he discovers, to his horror, that his Monster possesses the brain of a violent lunatic.

    In a sense, Shelley's *Frankenstein* relates a tale of an immature parent, a self-centered, irresponsible creator quite clever enough to create artificial life yet utterly unable—or unwilling—to offer the love, dedication, and selfless nurturing his offspring needs. From this perspective, Dr. Victor Frankenstein occupies the role of the failed father, the parent who brings life into the world only to casually cut it loose once it proves more than he bargained for. Like so many modern fathers, physically able to procreate but terrified by (or repulsed by) the awesome responsibility true parenthood entails, Frankenstein "buckles from the pressure" once his reproductive drive delivers him the child he was never truly prepared for. In *Young Frankenstein*, Brooks gives the whole "immature parent" theme a zany new spin, for while young Dr. Frederick Frankenstein begins the film an uppity, cold-hearted lecturer who cruelly mistreats his test subjects, ruthlessly defends himself against the snide inquiries of a snotty student, and arrogantly rejects his own ancestry, then emerges as a manipulative, childish "father" given to sulking, exploitation, and delusions of grandeur, by the movie's end he has evolved into a caring, self-sacrificing parent and savior to the misjudged "nice boy" he has given life, thus making *Young Frankenstein* one of the few versions of the *Frankenstein* saga to conclude with scientist and subject utterly devoted to each other—buddies, even—instead of vengeful, distrustful, or afraid. For once, there is no hand-to-hand combat atop burning windmills, no exploding castles, no fiery infernos destroying creature, creator, or both. No, at the conclusion of *Young Frankenstein*, one is left with the title scientist enjoying his honeymoon, having found true love not with his original fiancée but with a woman to whom he is far better suited, and with his Monster, once a wild,

At the Transylvania depot, Frankenstein meets his new assistant, bug-eyed, hunchbacked Igor (Marty Feldman)—pronounced "Eye-gore."

foul-tempered beast, now pajama-clad, bespectacled, and perusing *The Wall Street Journal*, a calm, quiet family man wed to a passionate, electric-haired beauty who, for now at least, just couldn't be happier. It's a highly amusing wrap-up—and, after years of Frankenstein tales whose idea of a happy ending is to have the obsessed, dark-hearted scientist who has caused all the problems to escape unharmed while his Monster is engulfed by flood or fire; it's also quite a refreshing change.

Ironically, the intricate tapestry that is Mel Brooks' *Young Frankenstein* boasts a relatively straightforward plot, often following the storylines of the original Universal entries virtually point by point—proof positive that the line between outrageous comedy and serious drama is a very fine one indeed. Put simply, the plot of *Young Frankenstein* is as follows: Brilliant young scientist Dr. Frederick Frankenstein (Gene Wilder, splendidly moving from

Kenneth Mars is so colorful as Kemp—that today it's almost impossible to watch key moments from Atwill's generally dignified original without laughing.

calm and collected to near-maniacal as effortlessly here as in Bud Yorkin's 1969 genre spoof *Start the Revolution Without Me)*, conceited, logic-minded grandson of original Monstermaker Dr. Victor Frankenstein (in Whale's original, the given name of Shelley's original Dr. Frankenstein is altered to "Henry"), learns he has inherited his grandfather's castle in Transylvania. Though maintaining that his late ancestor was a misguided lunatic whose experiments he has no interest whatsoever in continuing (indeed, so embarrassed is he by his grandfather's pseudo-scientific endeavors that he insists his surname be pronounced "Fronk-en-steen"), Frederick says goodbye to his uptight, never-a-hair-out-of-place fiancée Elizabeth (Madeline Kahn) and departs for Transylvania to claim his birthright. At the Transylvania depot, he meets his two new assistants, bug-eyed, hunchbacked Igor (Marty Feldman)—pronounced "Eye-gore," he insists, after hearing Frederick's odd pronunciation of his own name—and Inga (Teri Garr), while at Castle Frankenstein he encounters grim, stern-faced old housekeeper Frau Blucher (Cloris Leachman, in a sort of trial run of the Mrs. Danvers send-up she would take even further as a *Rebecca* homage in Brooks' *High Anxiety* three years later), who flirts with Freddy only minutes after meeting him.

Drawn to a secret library by mysterious violin music on his fitful first night at the castle, Frederick discovers his ancestor's lab records and becomes obsessed with duplicating his grandfather's experiments despite all his earlier claims of disinterest. With Igor's help, he steals an enormous corpse from a newly dug grave, prepares it for surgery, and sends Igor out for the brain of a deceased genius and humanitarian. Accidentally destroying this brain, however, Igor substitutes another to cover his mistake, but it is only after Frederick, Igor, and Inga bring the creature (Peter Boyle, as the most endearing Frankenstein Monster since Boris Karloff's) to life by harnessing the energy of an electrical storm that Frederick discovers, to his horror, that his Monster possesses the brain of a violent lunatic.

While Frederick is distracted by the probing inquiries of one-armed, one-eyed policeman Inspector Kemp (Kenneth Mars)—emissary of nervous villagers who fear Frederick may set loose some monstrous horror upon them as his grandfather did—a well-meaning Frau Blucher releases the Monster from its bonds. Returning with Igor and Inga, Frederick learns Frau Blucher was the unseen violinist, that she was deeply in love with his grandfather, and that she has tricked him into continuing her lover's experiments. Though Frau Blucher's violin music seems to touch its very soul, in a sudden accident, the Monster becomes outraged and frightened, and flees into the night, leaving Frederick guilt-stricken about the huge, undisciplined brute he has unleashed.

Lonely and unloved, the Monster enjoys brief acceptance with a little girl, then another fleetingly happy moment at the shack of a blind hermit, but eventually a disguised Frederick lures it into a trap with the music of a violin, and he, Igor, and Inga sedate it and return it to the castle. Here Frederick tenderly—though also a bit selfishly—vows to help his tragic creation by teaching it style and grace, and soon the Monster (in a scene more than a little reminiscent of Universal's 1933 hit *King Kong*) is unveiled before the scientific community at a public exhibition, where it performs both simple pet tricks and an extraordinary song-and-dance number alongside Frederick in top hat and tails. During the presentation, however, another accident once more sends the Monster into a fit of outraged panic, and Kemp's police overpower the creature and imprison it in chains.

Anguished by guilt over his creation's fate, Frederick conveniently disregards his engagement to Elizabeth and begins a relationship with Inga, one his intended's arrival brings to a quick halt. The Monster, meanwhile, tormented by one of Kemp's officers, breaks free and returns to the castle, where it becomes smitten by Frederick's prim and proper fiancée and kidnaps her. In the forest, the usually aloof Elizabeth discards her inhibitions and succumbs to the Monster's primitive masculinity, but it is soon drawn back to the castle by the allure of Frederick's violin. Determined to cure his creation of his mute, violent nature, Frederick nobly sacrifices part of his own great intellect to the Monster in a dangerous brain operation, but seconds before the procedure is complete, Kemp and an angry mob storm the lab. Just as an unconscious Frederick is about to be hauled away to an uncertain fate, however, the Monster—now articulate, charming, and docile—demands they leave his creator alone. Defending Frederick in a moving, passionate speech, he soon changes the minds of the villagers, who now welcome the reformed creature (and thus, Frederick) to their community. A short time later, Frederick and Inga are married, as are the now extremely domestic, largely passionless creature and a remarkably liberated Elizabeth, and now Frederick—having exchanged some of the Monster's primal passion for some of his wisdom, charm, and sophistication—finds himself enthralled by the violin and more wildly romantic than ever.

And that is essentially it—the entire plot of *Young Frankenstein*, reduced to its most basic elements. On the surface, little about the description seems to merit special attention, to offer any clue to the movie's genius, for many of the plot points detailed above are little more than slightly modified versions of storylines filmed and re-filmed dozens of times before in earlier versions of *Frankenstein* at Universal and elsewhere. At its heart, then, Brooks' and Wilder's script is essentially paint by numbers *Frankenstein*—just another reworked version of every other *Frankenstein* script ever filmed.

Yet in a good comedy—or a good drama, for that matter—execution is everything, and the real strength of *Young Frankenstein* lies in both the amazing way it tips its hat to the time-honored Universal classics and the outrageous irreverence with which it slyly twists the admired and familiar into new outlandish shapes. Indeed, Brooks and Wilder took great pains to keep the movie firmly entrenched in horror movie traditions, drawing inspiration from classic films as diverse as *Son of Frankenstein* and *King Kong*, while at the same time cleverly re-inventing them by way of zany musical numbers, outrageous slapstick, nonsense wordplay, and daffy allusions to everything from Groucho Marx to Irving Berlin. In short, *Young Frankenstein* delights us so because it brilliantly squeezes in just about everything we'd ever expect to see in a *Frankenstein* film—sometimes virtually duplicating specific scenes—and, in so doing, just about everything we'd never expect to see in one too.

In the Brooks version, however, each of these elements from the original has been turned inside-out for laughs as well as pathos. Wilder's Frederick, for example, may bring to mind Colin Clive, but only Wilder and Brooks would display the man's cold, scientific arrogance by having him knee a frail old man in the groin to demonstrate stimulus-response (and mumble an unconcerned "Give him an extra dollar" to an assistant as the poor old gent, writhing in pain, is wheeled out on a gurney!); accidentally stab his own leg with a scalpel—yet proudly pretend he hasn't hurt himself—in a fit of philosophical bombast to drive home a point; break down like a two-year-old after a perceived failure, with a childish physical assault upon his Monster's presumably lifeless form (after which he must be dragged off amid pathetic cries of "I do not want to live!"); pout like a baby at breakfast later by slapping his fingers atop his meal after Inga observes that he hasn't touched his food ("There! Now I've touched it! Happy?"); or patronizingly pop a doggy treat into his offspring's mouth as if his creation were some obedient trained pooch. Clive's Dr. Frankenstein was a pompous windbag all right, but until *Young Frankenstein* this trait had never been played for broad humor the way it is here.

As for the scientist's fiancée, it took Wilder and Brooks to turn Elizabeth into a hilariously uptight, emotionally repressed neatnik who early on recoils even from a kiss blown from a distance for fear it may disturb her hair, dress, or makeup, then becomes a passionate tigress enraptured, not by Frederick after all, but the powerful, take-charge Monster who kidnaps and dominates her; to convert the lab equipment into a locale for zany sight gags involving both Frederick's physical attraction to Inga and a lab assistant who one second is flying kites on the roof and the next is miraculously seen downstairs (Clive's Dr. Frankenstein calls up to his assistant through a door in the roof in much the same way); and to equip the castle with a secret room featuring rows of human heads (giving Igor, his own head positioned in line, the chance to sing a few words of "I Ain't Got Nobody"). They also introduced a grim yet schoolgirlish housekeeper who carries an unlit candelabrum as if it's blazing helpfully away ("Stay close to the candles. The stairs can be treacherous"); and add horses in the courtyard who rear up and whinny in dismay at the mere mention of her name.

Similarly, the theft of a criminal brain by a sneaky Fritz (Dwight Frye) in Whale's earlier film is wittily reworked in *Young Frankenstein*, wherein the classroom-lab of the original has become a local "brain depository" complete with a convenient drop box and a sign reading, "AFTER 5:00 P.M. SLIP BRAINS THROUGH SLOT IN DOOR" and a warning label on the brain a frightened Igor—like Fritz before him—takes home after dropping the genius brain in a moment of fright: "DO NOT USE THIS BRAIN! ABNORMAL." Fritz' persecution of the chained Monster by tormenting him with fire turns up too, though here

The Monster is unveiled at a public exhibition, where it performs an extraordinary song-and-dance number alongside Frederick in top hat and tails.

it is a policeman exercising the cruelty (and in a prison cell, as in *Bride of Frankenstein*) rather than the sweet-tempered Igor. The child floating flowers by a lake here becomes a little girl (Anne Beesley) dropping petals down a well, and asking the creature, "What shall we throw in now?," to which her new friend gives Brooks' camera a knowing glance before settling on accidentally catapulting her safely into her bed by sitting too heavily upon his end of a seesaw.

The grave-robbing scene gets a comic twist too, as Frederick and Igor find their work hindered by rain at Igor's mere comment that things could be worse because, after all, it "could be raining," after which their attempt to wheel the body home is sabotaged when their cart picks up too much speed and spills the corpse onto the cobblestones. Even better is Frederick's effort to disguise his crime by pretending one of the cadaver's huge hands is his own, using a hidden Igor to manipulate it into shaking hands and saluting in the presence of a good-humored constable ("Need a hand?" the man offers. "No, thanks," says Frederick casually. "Have one!").

The angry mob from *Frankenstein* appears too, though Whale never envisioned their using the local police chief as a human battering ram (nor their being unable to decipher his thick German accent), and, while the Monster's overall appearance is basically the same as in the original, surely Whale would have been just as surprised seeing Jack Pierce's legendary neck bolt makeup replaced by a convenient zipper!

The now extremely domestic, largely passionless Monster and a remarkably liberated Elizabeth (Madeline Kahn) are happily wed,

Returning too is the Monster's assault upon its creator only to be subdued by a hypodermic. Frederick, being strangled, flails about wildly in a madcap game of Charades for a dimwitted Igor and Inga: "Give him a sedative!" The Monser's fear of fire appears too as the old blind hermit (Gene Hackman), introduces him to tobacco and lights the poor creature's thumb instead of a cigar. The Monster is also confined to a lonely castle cell as in the original, but here Frederick, seconds after issuing strict orders to Igor, Inga, and Frau Blucher not to open the door once he's inside, no matter how desperately he begs, crumbles in the Monster's presence once inside and screams for release ("Mommy!"). The Monster's frightening confrontation with Frankenstein's bride-to-be likewise returns, yet again with oddball results as Elizabeth, kidnapped by him as in *Bride of Frankenstein*, ends up preferring her brutish, manly captor to her own fiancé. Then too, Elizabeth's ill-timed visit to the castle, also originating in *Frankenstein*, is used here for a bit of farce involving the fact that, just before her arrival, Frederick has essentially dumped his intended for lab assistant Inga.

Whale's *Bride of Frankenstein* likewise inspired some of *Young Frankenstein*'s best scenes, for not only is it in Universal's second entry that Frankenstein's fiancée, terrorized by the Monster in the first film, actually is held prisoner by it, but it is also here that Elizabeth's liberating lightning-streaked hairdo, donned after her abduction, first appears on Elsa Lanchester as the Monster's ghoulish "bride." *Bride of Frankenstein* likewise gives us the original scene in which the creature briefly finds nourishment, lodging, and compassion with a lonely, blind hermit, as well as the creature's love of the violin, a fondness exploited for both comedy and tenderness in the Brooks and Wilders script. It is also *Bride of Frankenstein* that first features kite-flying as a means of attracting lightning, used in Brooks' film for one quick gag allowing Igor to move from castle roof to lab below in practically the wink of an eye, and in which the Monster is first chained and imprisoned by townspeople only to break free (a similar scene, by the way, appears in *Ghost of Frankenstein* two films later).

On the other hand, in Gene Wilder's overall appearance—clean-shaven in his previous two Brooks efforts, Wilder here sports a dapper mustache not unlike that worn by Basil Rathbone—he chiefly revives memories of Rathbone's erratic Dr. Wolf von Frankenstein in Universal's third entry, *Son of Frankenstein*. In fact, the comedy's similarity to *Son of Frankenstein* becomes especially evident in three key scenes: Frederick's journey to Transylvania to claim his inheritance, a journey illustrated by two almost identical train trips, the latter ending not with the conductor's eerie call of "Frankenstein!" as in Lee's film but Frederick's through-the-window musical inquiry, "Pardon me, boy. Is this the Transylvania station?" (followed by the lad's helpful response, "Yah, yah! Track Twenty-nine! Oh! Can I give you a shine?"); his furious, hostile dart game against the visiting Inspector Kemp (broadly lampooning Rathbone's dizzyingly over-the-top performance in *Son of Frankenstein*, in which the new Dr. Frankenstein hurls darts and sarcasm with the same bitter energy); and the film's happy conclusion, in which the hero's bravery finally redeems him in the eyes of the townspeople who before viewed him only with suspicion and dread.

Other scenes invite comparison to Lee's film as well, however (even the title is closest of any in the series to Brooks'), notably a breakfast table scene not entirely unlike the one in *Son of Frankenstein*, the presence of a small metal chest left behind by the original Dr. Frankenstein containing information about his legacy, and some distant shots emphasizing the sparseness and size of the castle decor. It may not seem entirely ludicrous either to note that in *Son of Frankenstein*, Wolf's so-cute-he's-infuriating little boy has a wild, frizzy head of hair not at all unlike Gene Wilder's. There's also the matter of all the secret passages at Castle Frankenstein in the Lee film (in one of Brooks' best slapstick moments, poor Frederick gets the wind knocked out of him when he tries to block the path of a swiveling secret door), not to mention the fact that the new, "young" Frankenstein in each movie insists he has no interest in monster-making but ultimately becomes so obsessed by his ancestor's work that he too becomes involved.

Additionally, the suspicious nature of the townspeople, convinced only evil can come of a new Dr. Frankenstein's arrival, also appears in *Son of Frankenstein* (though mob violence appears in all other Universal entries as well), as do the oversized castle door rings used for a zany Brooks double entendre as Igor pounds one to gain entrance. Also, while Marty Feldman's Igor performs essentially the same function as Dwight Frye's Fritz in the original *Frankenstein*, his use of a hornlike instrument and his name (even if oddly pronounced) providing clear references to Bela Lugosi's sinister, broken-necked Ygor in both *Son of Frankenstein* and *Ghost of Frankenstein*.

Likewise, the suspicious Inspector Kemp's *Son of Frankenstein* counterpart is Lionel Atwill's wooden-armed Inspector Krogh, both of whom have an artificial limb pulled from its socket by the Monster at one point, though in Brooks' film the event is the accidental result of a well-meaning handshake (Kemp's reaction: "To the lumberyard!"). To his credit, in fact, Kenneth Mars is so colorful as Kemp with all his *Dr. Strangelove*-like shtick with the arm—it makes odd wind-up noises as it snaps into place, and is used for everything from a handy spot to imbed projectiles during dart games (Krogh uses it for the same purpose) to convenient wood for lighting his cigar—that today it's almost impossible to watch key

Clearly, *Young Frankenstein* remains one of the best comedies of the 1970s, and is easily one of the best genre parodies of all time.

moments from Atwill's generally dignified original without laughing. No wonder Brooks had reason to hope that the sight of a dancing, singing, hippie Adolf Hitler in *The Producers* might prevent anyone from seriously embracing Nazi politics ever again. With *Young Frankenstein*, he really did turn a not-half-bad performance by one of horror cinema's better actors into something now drawing uncontrollable giggles.

Clearly, *Young Frankenstein* remains one of the best comedies of the 1970s, and is easily one of the best genre parodies of all time. Sumptuously photographed in black-and-white, just like the classic Universal originals (and even using lab equipment first used in *Frankenstein* back in 1931), *Young Frankenstein* gave Mel Brooks perhaps his best chance since *The Twelve Chairs*—the film whose theme song "Hope for the Best, Expect the Worst" has pretty much described the attitude of many critics towards Brooks' films since his *Young Frankenstein* days—at producing what his detractors have called genuine "art"; it was his finest opportunity yet to say something meaningful about the human condition even while leaving us shaking with laughter with his unique brand of quirky, off-the-wall humor.

Thankfully, it was an opportunity Brooks and Wilder (whose tremendous impact on the film both before and behind the cameras should not be underemphasized) wholeheartedly embraced, leaving behind a film that not only amuses and entertains, but also compares quite favorably to Universal series which had given Shelley's novel so much renewed interest. At once wicked parody and appreciative homage, *Young Frankenstein* still works extraordinarily well as both comedy and character study, brilliantly alternating between the mirth-laden and meaningful in a fraction of a second, and often providing both elements in a single instant. On this occasion, at least, Brooks' lyrics—and critics—got it wrong; we hoped for the best, and that's exactly what we got.

Frankenweenie
by Robert Alan Crick

The often macabre but always masterful Tim Burton has come such a long way since directing his little-seen black-and-white film *Frankenweenie* for Walt Disney Studios in 1984 that one feels almost foolish studying it at length. Offering a detailed critique of an obscure 27-minute live-action project about a small boy who uses makeshift lab equipment to bring back to life the family dog after the playful little beast is struck down by a car seems as pointless as undertaking an analysis of—well, Burton's other barely publicized short film for Disney, 1982's stop-motion animation Vincent Price tribute called *Vincent*.

One need not dismiss *Frankenweenie* quite so casually, however, for this delightfully engaging take-off on the 1931 James Whale–directed movie version of Mary Shelley's 1818 horror tale *Frankenstein* shares much of the offbeat whimsy of Burton's more mature works, even surpassing some of those later efforts for pure high-spirited fun. Imaginative, good-hearted, and laced from start to finish with sparkling doses of satirical wit, *Frankenweenie* is easily one of the most amusing live-action shorts since the days of Mack Sennett and Hal Roach—and one of the most endearing tales of loneliness and social isolation director Burton has put to film.

Although its title—and the name of its main character, pre-teen Prometheus little Victor Frankenstein—suggests Burton's film was directly inspired by Shelley's original cautionary tale of the ego-driven scientist who arrogantly dares to create life, in truth *Frankenweenie* draws far more of its imagery from James Whale's classic 1931 film version (and Whale's arguably superior sequel *Bride of Frankenstein*) than its 19th-century literary forebear. The brainchild of Burton and screenwriter Lenny Ripps (who worked from Burton's initial idea), *Frankenweenie* is both an admiring tribute to Whale's film and an affectionately topsy-turvy parody of it. At once deferential homage and madcap send-up, *Frankenweenie* delivers what is essentially the 1931 Boris Karloff vehicle compressed, updated, and playfully turned inside-out—Universal's *Frankenstein* as seen through a child's eyes, in which obsessed scientist becomes heartsick schoolboy, brutish monster becomes overeager housepet, and vengeful European villagers become shortsighted suburbanites in housecoats and putter pants.

Frankenweenie is, in fact, with its "Happy Halloween" banner visible in Victor's science classroom, one of Burton's earliest Halloween stories, predating other projects somehow revolving around the ghostly holiday. One should not be surprised that, having tossed an appreciative nod to original *Nosferatu* silent film star Max Schreck by way of the similarly named Christopher Walken character in *Batman Returns,* Burton would enjoy similar

Sparky is the beloved pet of young Victor Frankenstein in *Frankenweenie*.

Victor (Barret Oliver) and Sparky share a tender moment.

wordplay in *Frankenweenie*, in which a boy scientist is named Victor Frankenstein and his happy-go-lucky bull terrier is named—what else?—Sparky. What better name, in a children's comedy, for a beast brought back from the dead, like some canine Karloff, through the awesome power of an electrical storm?

Indeed, *Frankenweenie* is perhaps most fascinating not so much because of its contribution to American filmmaking (a single episode of, for example, Steven Spielberg's *Animaniacs* cartoon TV series, complete with in-jokes about classic cinema, tongue-in-cheek wordplay, parody, social satire, and oddball visual tricks, is arguably every bit as offbeat, creative, and fun), but rather for what it says about Burton's own quirky sense of humor and his near-obsessive preoccupation with the surreal and the strange. One can learn a great deal about a filmmaker from the sort of projects to which he is attracted or, even better, creates for himself on his own—that Brian De Palma is a fan of Hitchcock and Eisenstein, for instance, or that George Lucas admires fairy tales and ancient myth, or that Frank Capra enjoys rooting for the underdog, the common man—and from Tim Burton projects, even one as seemingly insignificant as the little-seen, seldom-heard-of *Frankenweenie*, one discovers far more about Burton himself than even some of his more prestigious, two-hour creations reveal. In fact, were *Frankenweenie* rereleased today on the big screen to accompany the latest full-length Burton film and promoted to the unknowing as an all-new Burton featurette, it is likely not one viewer would suspect the movie was created in the early 1980s, well before Burton's oddball storytelling style became well known. Furthermore, some elements of *Frankenweenie* today seem so downright prophetic—inadvertently forecasting upcoming Burton projects, hinting at themes soon to become permanent fixtures in the Burton lore—that it is entirely possible to forget it was made well before such hits as *Edward Scissorhands* and *Batman*

Returns and to imagine that Burton is slipping in after-the-fact allusions to those productions, just as if the insertions are actually knowing, tongue-in-cheek references to earlier movies.

Consider, for instance, the film's opening scene, in which 10-year-old Victor Frankenstein (Barret Oliver) proudly presents his faithful dog Sparky in *Monsters from Long Ago*, an ultra-low-budget black-and-white horror film, to his parents and friends in the Frankenstein living room. Forget for the moment that young Victor, exuberantly creating home movies featuring papier-mâché volcanoes, cardboard palm trees, toy pterodactyls, caveman dolls, and his own beloved pet dressed as a stegosaurus, may very well represent a sort of idealized version of Burton himself, who, like so many future filmmakers, as a boy likewise composed many an 8 mm creation devoted to the offbeat and strange. No, what most surprises one now, so many years later, is that a full decade after *Frankenweenie* Burton would base an entire film, *Ed Wood*, on a real-life director whose own low-budget black-and-white horror films, despite their big-screen pretensions, frequently looked only slightly better than those little Victor cooks up in his own backyard. At the time of *Frankenweenie*, the very idea of devoting a whole movie to an obscure "bargain basement" filmmaker notorious for cheesy-looking effects work was virtually unthinkable, yet, in some bizarre way, the first subtle hints of what would eventually become *Ed Wood* turn up right here, in *Frankenweenie*'s opening scenes.

Already present too is Burton's habit of poking fun at eccentric, gossip-minded suburbanites, whom the director would satirize most famously just a few years later in *Edward Scissorhands*, portraying them as jaded, idiosyncratic buffoons desperate for something fresh and offbeat to spice up their drab, sterile lives, yet, as exhilarated by jealousy and suspicion as by the unexpected and new, just as eager to censure and condemn.

The countless similarities to the situation in *Frankenweenie*, of course, require little explanation, for in many ways the Disney short seems almost a "trial run" for what would eventually emerge as *Edward Scissorhands*. Slightly stuffy Mr. Chambers (Joseph Maher), bedecked in checkered trousers and white belt; muu-muu-clad, fright-wigged Mrs. Epstein (Roz Braverman); suspicious, gossip-spewing Mrs. Curtis (Helen Boll); even, to a degree, Mr. Chambers' blonde-haired, pretty but shallow, leotard-wearing offspring Ann (Domino)—in a sense, each of these character types, in altered form, would turn up again in *Edward Scissorhands*, still prying into their neighbors' affairs, still imagining the worst about the weird-looking new occupant from next door, still forming an angry mob determined to hunt down the well-meaning, tormented figure for whom they once professed affection. Indeed, the ending of *Frankenweenie*, a hilariously topsy-turvy reworking of the climax of the original James Whale *Frankenstein* substituting enraged European villagers wielding clubs and torches with California lawnmower-and-hedge clipper types bearing flashlights, crutches, canes, baseball bats, and croquet mallets, seems doubly entertaining today in light of its foreshadowing of the finale of *Edward Scissorhands*. Add to this the fact that, like Sparky, Edward too is something of a misunderstood "man-made monster," the garish, patchwork product of an eccentric but loving scientist's secretive experimentation, and one quickly realizes the *Frankenstein* references in *Frankenweenie* are anything but a passing fancy; on the contrary, Burton's big-screen interest in the classic horror movie "mad scientist" type had really just begun.

Of course, the most obvious link between *Frankenweenie* and Burton's other films—beyond the fact that his movies, with their calypso-dancing ghosts, bug-eyed, gum-chewing spacemen, and waddling armies of death-bearing penguins, almost always seem downright weird—is its touching examination of the social misfit, the peculiar, isolated figure who,

Victor is obviously a misfit whose best friend is Sparky.

however much he may try to appear "normal" in public or even imagine himself so, remains forever the outsider, the "square peg" trying hopelessly to wedge himself into society's "round hole." Burton populates his films with an unprecedented variety of pariahs and derelicts, he creates for himself a human zoo of the unhappy and the friendless, the freakish and the off-the-wall. In *Frankenweenie,* young Victor himself is obviously a misfit of a sort (any little boy so determined to bring his pet dog's corpse back from the dead that he turns his parents' attic into a mad scientist's mini-lab, and decks himself out in surgical tunic and protective gloves like some pre-teen Colin Clive would have to be), but the character who really fits this role is of course not Victor himself but Sparky, beloved housepet one day, sewn-up, electrode-fitted Jack Pierce monstrosity the next. Like the sympathetic but murderous Karloff monster from Whale's films, Sparky means well, unwittingly traumatizing schoolgirls and neighborhood busybodies despite the fact that, throughout his harmless investigations behind windowshades and inside darkened toolsheds, his tail keeps wagging in cheerful canine merriment the whole time. Whether lumbering about on two legs or clumsily blundering about on four, it seems, a monster is a monster, and sooner or later the mob mentality is bound and determined to want him dead.

Quite naturally, of course, the appearance of this motif in *Frankenweenie* is hardly unexpected, since virtually every adaptation of Shelley's story ever done, Whale's included, has explored the original's idea of the man-made creation whose terrifying ugliness inspires only hatred and dread. What does surprise, however, is how again and again since *Frankenweenie* Burton has returned to this same theme, albeit in wildly different forms.

Likewise, in *Edward Scissorhands*, Johnny Depp's Edward is at once deadly and delightful.

Of course, *Frankenweenie*'s theme of death is likewise a constant motif in Tim Burton films, especially in the *Batman* series (and the original *Batman* in particular), in which comic book creator Bob Kane's costumed vigilante has devoted both his lifetime and his fortune to the defeat of villainy and corruption after having seen his parents murdered before his horrified eyes as a child—a moment not unlike the shock young Victor receives as he witnesses his pet's untimely death in *Frankenweenie*. Like the orphaned Bruce Wayne, a child whose traumatic experience so haunts him that the passion to prevent similar violence becomes the one driving force behind his entire life, so is the once-happy Victor plunged into despair after his devastating loss—so

Victor decks himself out in surgical tunic and protective gloves like some pre-teen Colin Clive to bring his beloved pet back to life.

much so that he too cannot rest until he can take action, can make right again what has gone so terribly, inexplicably wrong. Like Bruce Wayne, Victor too becomes obsessed, waging a battle beyond logic, fighting against not crime but death itself, and, like Batman, emerging victorious despite the near-insanity of the fixation that pushes him on.

Death in Burton films need not necessarily turn shell-shocked schoolboys into bat-garbed crime sentries or lab-coated scientists.

Its typically Burtonesque preoccupation with death aside, *Frankenweenie* includes several other elements foreshadowing later Burton projects as well. The cute little drawing of Sparky that a grieving Victor sketches in his notebook during science class, for instance, bears some resemblance to the featured pooch in Burton's short-lived TV show *The Family Dog*, begun as a 1986 animated segment of Steven Spielberg's *Amazing Stories*. The film also seems to have a strange preoccupation with cats, as comical-looking felines or near-feline creatures—most of them oddly reminiscent of the Felix the Cat–inspired Max Shreck corporate logo from *Batman Returns*—appear on pet cemetery tombstones, cookie jars (the one in the Frankenstein's kitchen is evidently meant to resemble a "happy-face" clock, but with its whiskerlike clockhands atop its button nose, it strongly recalls a similar cat clock in *Batman Returns*), wall-hangings, and Felix-like clown-cat miniature golf course displays, not to mention the fact that neighbor Mr. Chambers himself has a real-life fluffy white cat of his own next door. In addition, Victor's makeshift lab equipment in *Frankenweenie*, a zany improvisation assembled from plundered hair dryers, swingsets, and electric toasters, provides Burton the perfect training for filming Pee-wee's madcap gadget-loaded house in *Pee-wee's Big Adventure* the very next year.

Of course, to his most severe critics, the word "perfect" may seem a tad strong with which to label even the most low-key aspects of Burton's films, and indeed, despite its many strengths, it is true that *Frankenweenie* shares many of the same faults common to Tim Burton movies, most notably the director's frequent failure to work out some fairly significant logic flaws in his scripts before filming begins. *Frankenweenie*, unfortunately, abounds with such lapses, leaving the viewer constantly asking himself questions—"Since Victor seems bright but not a true genius, how can he learn so quickly about science and electricity?"; "Don't Victor's parents ever go up to the attic to see what's going on up there?"; "Shouldn't Victor's mother notice the appliances missing from her kitchen?"; "Wouldn't

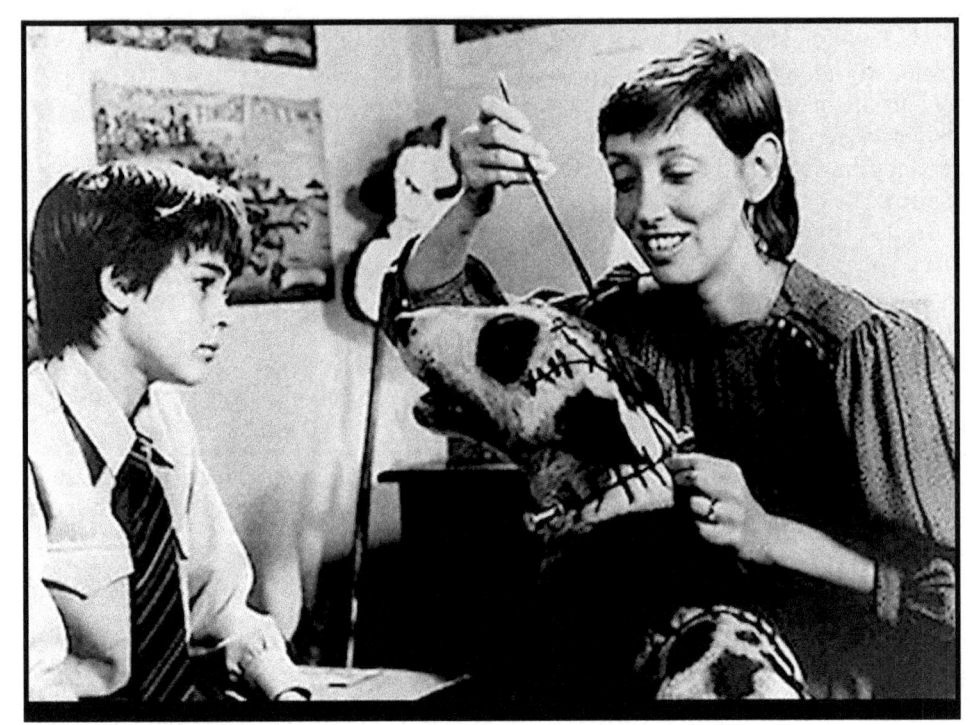

Mom (Shelley Duvall) helps Victor repair the reanimated Sparky.

the neighbors at some point ask the Frankensteins what they're doing with a swingset on their roof?"—when he really should simply be sitting back and enjoying the show.

Actually, considering its mere 27-minute running time, *Frankenweenie* includes an unusually high number of such scripting slip-ups, even for a Burton film, though for once, since *Frankenweenie* is at heart a children's film, even a fairy tale of sorts, the demanded willing suspension of disbelief functions far better here than in several of Burton's more "grown-up" projects. At times, in fact—as in the scene in which, as the Frankensteins' well-intentioned "Meet Sparky" hors d'oeuvres party disintegrates into a chaotic "Kill Sparky" lynch mob, their guests inexplicably seem to produce baseball bats and croquet mallets from out of nowhere—the utter absurdity of the breakdown of common sense creates moments of inspired lunacy, like something from a particularly off-the-wall Warner Bros. cartoon.

Additionally, at other times the sheer sweetness of the tale's heartwarming "boy and his dog" story elements manages to almost completely override such logic concerns, especially in its notion of an artistic but otherwise relatively average little boy's performing what in real life would be a Nobel Prize–worthy feat of earthshaking scientific and theological significance using nothing more elaborate than common household equipment and a stack of checked-out library books. It isn't money, power, or prestige that compels Victor to attempt the impossible, after all; it is the pure, big-hearted love of a child for his pet that brings Sparky back to life.

The potential for double meaning in Burton's title actually suggests an interesting point about the film—namely, that *Frankenweenie*'s illogic at times may sometimes even work a bit to its advantage, at least for parody's sake. One of the great appealing oddities of Universal's *Frankenstein* series, after all, has always been its peculiar refusal to establish a clear-cut sense of time and place, its strange mixture of the old and new, the familiar and foreign. The Universal series frequently seems set in Germany, for example (Shelley's original novel is set in Switzerland), yet so many characters speak with such decidedly non-German accents that the viewer is often not quite sure *where* he is. Horse-drawn wagons and carriages are common, leaving one to imagine that perhaps the tale is set only a few years later than the original novel, but we also see relatively modern passenger trains and, startlingly, even an occasional 20th-century motorcar—not to mention all manner of "cutting-edge" science and medical equipment far beyond anything even Shelley could have envisioned. Some characters dress very much like old-world European peasants (German? Swiss? Dutch?), quaint, old-fashioned butter churn-and-shepherd's hook types from the pre-industrialized 19th century, while others inexplicably wear the same sort of necktie-and-trousers attire sported in boardrooms and business offices by the very up-to-date Hollywood movie executives who made the films. Given the original series' precedent for indiscriminately juxtaposing elements from conflicting eras and cultures, then, perhaps we can forgive *Frankenweenie* for showcasing 1950s-looking vehicles alongside sleek new cars of the 1980s; for featuring weird, knoblike European hills just down the block from a flat-as-a-pancake California suburb; for dressing a pre-teen girl in a very 1980s leotard while sending Victor to school and play in tidy dress shoes, trousers, and button-down shirts like some 1950s TV high schooler from *The Many Loves of Dobie Gillis*; and for any number of other such stylistic inconsistencies. If a parody of the Universal series is what Burton was after, showcasing time-and-space-defying incongruities like these, Burton has succeeded.

Victor manages to create a fairy tale dream lab in his attic.

What ultimately makes *Frankenweenie* so entertaining, however, is its enchanting ability to turn the classic Universal *Frankenstein* series on its ear, with the transformation of the classic torch-wielding villagers scene into a zany mob of flashlight-bearing, golf club-toting Sparky-haters just one of the film's many examples. In Burton's hands, the legendary creation sequence from Whale's *Frankenstein* becomes an exhilarating spoof in which Sparky's playfully wagging tail recalls the triumphant "It's Alive!" scene from Whale, etched forever in memory for the monster's fingers' chilling movement as they alert its creator of success, and the once high-tech machinery from Whale's Castle Frankenstein has been replaced by an ingenious array of makeshift lab equipment comprising modern-day household appliances and childhood playthings—just the sort of lab a resourceful, determined little boy might dream up. (The same may be said, by the way, of the "new" Sparky's bold, exaggerated stitches, which really do look like the sort of clumsy needle-and-thread work a grade school-age boy might do.) Dr. Henry Frankenstein's ascending surgical platform, used to hoist his monster through his castle skylight to take in the life-giving energy of a violent electrical storm, now becomes a clever rooftop swingset, with Sparky's lifeless body resting between a pair of canvas swings, and, recalling the *Bride of Frankenstein*, Victor releases kites into the storm, one of them appropriately bat-shaped—a fitting choice for a Halloween story, and a nice reminder of Universal's 1931 Tod Browning version of Bram Stoker's vampire novel *Dracula*, released the same year as Whale's *Frankenstein*.

Victor and Sparky accidently are trapped in the burning miniature golf course windmill.

Indeed, the whole "resurrection" sequence is loaded with amusing sight gags spotlighting Victor's one-of-a-kind approach to science in the suburbs, with the child making use of, among other items, an upright vacuum cleaner; a static-filled TV; a blender; a fish tank (its bubbles turn the blades of a tiny plastic windmill, neatly foreshadowing the blazing windmill climax to come); an upturned bicycle whose hand-cranked wheels emit electrical sparks; a wall clock, its hands racing furiously, the numbers lighting up with each spin; a garbage can lid absorbing electricity between a pair of table lamps; a trio of plastic backyard Christmas reindeer, wildly rocking and lighting up in sequence; an eerily luminous, smoking toaster; and even a strangely glowing helmet-style hairdryer. Thanks to Disney's top-notch effects team, little Victor's attic is the crackling, spark-spewing 1931 *Frankenstein* set turned topsy-turvy—mad scientist's lab as cartoonist Rube Goldberg might have envisioned it, had Goldberg sketched the scene as a 10-year-old boy.

But other legendary sequences from Whale receive stellar treatment in Burton's parody as well. The strangely off-kilter, weirdly expressionistic world Whale created (especially in his more highly stylized *Bride of Frankenstein*) is spectacularly alluded to in *Frankenweenie's* pet cemetery—tombstones planted at odd angles, the hills unnaturally rounded, the sky a surreal, cloudy-gray backdrop. The very notion of transplanting the traditional *Frankenstein* graveyard scene to a pet cemetery instantly draws smiles. The entire graveyard sequence, its arrival heralded by superbly bombastic *Frankenstein*-type music from Michael Convertino and David Newman, seems to be winking at the viewer with its exquisitely satirical array of visual jokes. Where else does one encounter tombstones shaped like fire hydrants, or doghouses, or goldfish bowls (dedicated amusingly enough to "Bubbles"), or find monuments adorned with or shaped like dead kittens or dead squirrels (this one is named—what else?—"Earl"), or carved out long and skinny in tribute to dead snakes (labeled "Edward" or otherwise)? The only gag missing, it seems, is a stone for James the Whale (evidently no one thought of that one), but the tribute is endearing just the same—reverential to the classic Universal horror films it parodies, yet fiendishly satirical and fun at the same time.

The same can be said of Burton's reworking of the famous "burning windmill" scene from the 1931 *Frankenstein*, with the original confrontation between Dr. Henry Frankenstein and his vengeful monster providing another exceptionally well-delivered send-up, this time with little Victor, his outraged neighbors just behind him, pursuing Sparky to an abandoned miniature golf course, where—though by accident this time—this latest Frankenstein "monster" (and his owner) is nearly burned alive in a small-scale windmill instantly recalling the one in Whale's film. Once again, the viewer already familiar with the 1931 film can barely suppress his enjoyment at being let in on the joke this way, especially since the windmill's interior so closely resembles the one in *Frankenstein*, and it is hard not to relish the irony of the moment in which a surprised Victor tumbles out of sight as a trapdoor gives way, since

Karloff's Monster survives the inescapable blaze (at the start of *Bride of Frankenstein*) by falling into the millpond below in much the same way. The allusion, like so many in *Frankenweenie* (not the least of which is its last-minute *Bride of Frankenstein* reference in which Sparky finds true love with a cute black poodle with a streaked Elsa Lanchester hairdo), is a particularly nice touch—and great fun.

Add to all of this some thoroughly entertaining acting from a top-notch cast (particularly Shelley Duvall and Daniel Stern as Victor's oblivious but well-meaning parents and, as pint-sized monster-maker Victor himself, 1980s child star Barret Oliver, utterly convincing in every scene) and some unusually inventive camerawork from director Burton (colorful dog's-eye-view shots to capture Sparky's perspective; a powerful zoom-in on Victor's horrified face as he sees Sparky struck dead; a look at Victor's baseball as it rolls casually to a curb, bounces off ever-so-slightly, and stops dead, just like the helpless little dog killed chasing it into the street; symbolic "rain"—really only water from Mom's garden hose—streaming down glass as Victor, still in funeral attire, gazes mournfully from a living room window), and the viewer has one of the most inventive, infinitely enjoyable short subjects ever made. Indeed, even compared to most full-length cinematic fare, *Frankenweenie* holds up remarkably well, and its main idea—a child's innocent, unconditional devotion to a friend whose appearance and manner unsettles the bigoted and fearful—is, combining the best traditions of both "boy and his dog" yarns and tales of undying love, timeless. *Frankenweenie*'s themes are so universal, so uncannily in touch with the heartsick, faith-keeping little child in each of us that, when Sparky scurries into the path of an oncoming car, we share his young master's horror and pain, for we too have loved pets and lost them, and when Victor impossibly achieves the dog's return through some magnificent miracle of faith and science, we too remember how it felt in childhood to wish, and hope, and pray that somehow all might magically be made right again. Small wonder then, that, even after being eclipsed in both fame and acclaim by so many bigger, bolder Tim Burton releases, *Frankenweenie* remains one of the director's most sensitive, satisfying creations—one that, thanks to home video, Burton fans denied their chance to see it in 1984 can still discover even now. Like Sparky himself, it seems, *Frankenweenie* now has its big chance at life after death.

Top: Sparky and the Bride of Sparky
Below: Victor's journals

Hollywood Tries to Reanimate Universal
The Bride and Van Helsing
by Gary J. Svehla and Susan Svehla

The Bride (1985) is the perfect case that the whole can be *less* than the sum of the individual components. The film starts out spectacularly with a 10-minute reprise of Universal's creation sequence from *Bride of Frankenstein* complete with a similar two-story watchtower laboratory, Dwight Frye look-alike who prepares the electrical apparatus up above, and the elevation of a gauze-wrapped corpse who is brought to electrical life. The sequence even ends as the watchtower explodes. Brilliant! Then *The Bride* becomes two different films awkwardly joined via herky-jerky editing. The first movie, starring Sting and Jennifer Beals, is utterly worthless featuring uninspired performances and unintentionally hilarious dialogue.

The second movie, starring Clancy Brown as the Monster who befriends Rinaldo, a little person, is closer in tone to *Of Mice and Men* than it is to *Bride of Frankenstein*—but it is exceptional. Clancy Brown turns in a Lennyesque performance that is totally different from Karloff's performances as the Monster. Not that Brown is better, but his sections of the movie are dynamically acted and emotionally involve the viewer. If *The Bride* developed this one aspect of the movie's two stories, it would have been thoroughly wonderful. But unfortunately, we are constantly interrupted by Sting and Jennifer Beals (whose best sequence is her nude descent from the Gothic stairs—of course "performed" by a body double!) trying to ignite a spark that never quite catches!

Clancy Brown as the Frankenstein Monster and David Rappaport as Rinaldo in *The Bride*

The New York Times' Stephen Holt was not overly impressed by *The Bride*'s avante garde take on the classic Frankenstein legend:

> *The Bride*, a very loose, freewheeling remake of *The Bride of Frankenstein*, never makes up its mind whether it is a horror movie spoof or an earnest exploration of the genre's myths.

In its earliest sequences, the film...is a gothic farce full of comic book thunder and lightning and machinery gone haywire. Minutes later, it aspires to the icy historical detachment of films like *Barry Lyndon*. In others scenes, it becomes a sentimental fairy tale spouting inspirational cliches out of a Sylvester Stallone movie. But even in its lighter moments, the film, which was directed by Franc Roddam, proceeds at a funereal pace.

"Follow your heart, it's the key to everything—follow your dream!" advises the midget Rinaldo (David Rappaport) to Viktor (Clancy Brown), the dimwitted lug who has fled the castle of his creator, Baron Frankenstein (Sting), during a roof-raising inferno. The story of Rinaldo and Viktor's blossoming friendship after these two outcasts have teamed up for mutual protection provides the movie with its most coherent sequences. Mr. Rappaport's Rinaldo is a canny little wheeler-dealer with an appealing streak of tenderness. And his nefariously plotted death in a circus accident provides the movie with its only touching moment.

Lloyd Fonvielle's screenplay is structured as an allegory relating the Frankenstein myth to *Pygmalion* and *Beauty and the Beast*, but the connections seem painfully forced and heavy-handed. As Frankenstein, Sting is a glowering supercilious fiend spouting philosophical gibberish. When he announces to his best friend that "the new woman" he has created will be "as free and as bold as we are—a woman equal to ourselves," he sounds like a Nazi racial propagandist expressing decidedly warped feminist sympathies.

If Jennifer Beals, as Frankenstein's "new woman," exuded any spirit, the story of her education and her eventual rebellion against her creator might have generated some amusing psychological humor. Eva is supposed to become an accomplished equestrian and a cutting social wit. But in her riding scenes, Miss Beals communicates only fearful discomfort, and when she wows the local gentry with *bon mots* about Shakespeare, she speaks in an uncomprehending near-monotone. Her Eva isn't a spitfire but a Barbie doll whose only visible sign of passion is a slight widening of the eyes. Miss Beals's performance sinks this already muddled mess of a movie like a stone.

Boxoffice Online Reviews, in a review of the DVD release of *The Bride* is a little kinder:

> One of the most anachronistic films of the 1980s, *The Bride* has all but faded into obscurity, savaged by critics, ignored by audiences and disowned by *Frankenstein* aficionados for its unorthodox approach to the legendary *Bride of Frankenstein* tale. Fifteen years after the fact, however, *The Bride* begins to look like a film considerably ahead of its time —a clear product of the '80s' more overtly glamorous film stylings that nonetheless manages to translate those stylings into something deeper. This is by no means on a par with the original *The Bride of Frankenstein* which remains one of the cinema's great untouchables. But it does carve a niche of its own, and Sting and Beals are undeniably compelling. Clancy Brown's take on the monster and the late David Rappaport's turn as the dwarf who befriends the monster are likewise meritorious.

Director Franc Roddam contributes an audio commentary that's dry and informative in a kind of typically English way, but also very emphatic about his efforts to do the famous tale differently than it had been done before.

Was *The Bride* doomed by comparison to the classic Universal films as well as Hammer Films? Or were audiences not taken in by a film obiously geared to MTV audiences, the golden goose demographic of the film industry? Unfortunately, *The Bride* was one of the first Hollywood attemps at the horror classics that chose to rely on over-the-top special effects and young beautiful actors rather than intelligent plots and actors with depth and character.

Universal's Van Helsing would indulge in CGI excess to the extreme. As the song says, "everything old is new again." A new decade—a new vampire film, which will soon arrive to haunt our nightmares. Universal will always be known as the home of the classic movie monsters. Will they add a new chapter to their fiendishly glorious history with their new monster rally offering, *Van Helsing*?

Hugh Jackman's Van Helsing is in a different league than the lunatic Van Helsing Anthony Hopkins portrayed in *Bram Stoker's Dracula*, becoming closer in concept to Hammer's *Captain Kronos—Vampire Hunter*. Jackman's Van Helsing is a lean, mean evil-fighting machine who has become the world's most famous monster hunter. He works for a group dedicated to ridding the world of demons. Jackman's foray into scary cinema includes the tormented Wolverine in *X-Men* and *X2*. Lovely Kate Beckinsale, as Anna Valerious, is Van Helsing's worthy compatriot in his battle against the malevolent monsters. Princess Anna of Transylvania is sought out by Van Helsing because she is the last living member of an ancient family that is committed to the destruction of Dracula. She reluctantly joins forces with Van Helsing to accomplish this goal. Beckinsale's genre film appearances include *Underworld*, where she portrayed the seductive Selene, a vampire huntress out to exterminate lycans (werewolves). Richard Roxburgh joins the ranks of horror greats when he assumes the cape of Count Dracula. Roxburgh's credits are vast and varied but he will be remembered as the decadent and jealous Duke in *Moulin Rouge!* Newcomer Will Kemp portrays the Wolf Man (Universal is using the two word description, as they did in the original film starring Lon Chaney, Jr.). This Wolf Man, as in the Chaney versions, is tortured by the curse that has tragically befallen him. Kemp, is Velkan, the

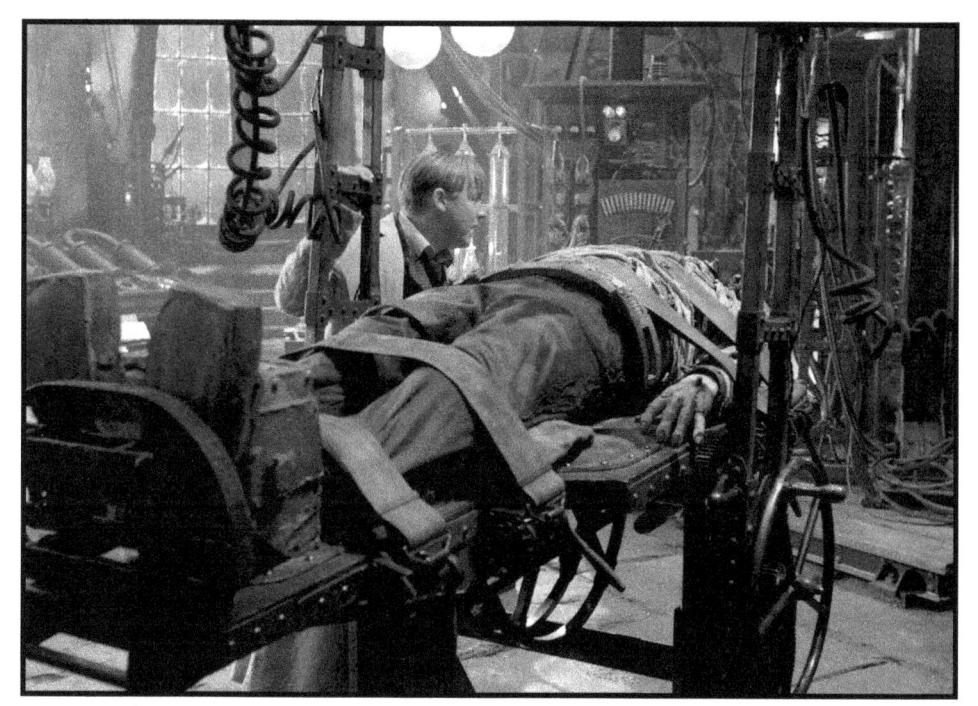

Frankenstein and his Monster become pawns of Dracula in *Van Helsing*.

brother of Anna, who falls victim to the curse when his and Anna's plan to catch a werewolf goes horribly wrong. Kevin J. O'Connor happily slithers into the classic Igor role (not Ygor as in *Son* and *Ghost of Frankenstein*) as the assistant to Frankenstein who is doomed when Dracula seeks to gain control of the Monster. O'Connor told us he endured four hours of makeup a day for his transformation into the Dwight Frye-inspired role. Horror film fan O'Connor appeared in *The Mummy, Deep Rising, Gods and Monsters* and *Peggy Sue Got Married*. Sommers on Horror.com said of O'Connor's role, "He's the only one who I knew was a done deal. He's the only one I write for."

Van Helsing director Stephen Sommers approaches the movie monsters as troubled humans, although admittedly their plights are not your average everyday problems. He managed to drive a stake into the heart of Universal's classics by realizing audiences related to the misunderstood monsters rather than the upper class that created/destroyed them.

Sommers opens the Van Helsing in the classic black-and-white horror motif, including the Monster creation and the burning windmill.

In an interesting bit of promotional gimmickry, *Van Helsing: The London Assignment* will debut May 11, 2004. This is a 30-minute animated prequel project "unveiling the extraordinary beginning of the Van Helsing adventure..." Hugh Jackman provides the voice of Van Helsing. The DVD will contain bonus features including interviews and information on the special effects.

Universal's promotional materials for the film include this description: Deep in the mountains of Carpathia lies the mysterious and mythic land of Transylvania—a world where evil is ever-present, where danger rises as the sun sets and where the monsters that inhabit man's deepest nightmares take form. Innovative filmmaker Stephen Sommers—who so imaginatively re-envisioned Universal's classic Mummy character in the worldwide blockbusters *The Mummy* and *The Mummy Returns*—now widens his cinematic scope and multiplies his

The creation scene in *Van Helsing*—the Monster was portrayed by Shuler Hensley.

creative inspiration by breathing new life into the most time-honored pantheon of classic Universal monsters and setting them in a stunning new world of fantastical reality. Sommers' all-encompassing vision for a world as tangible, real and visceral as any caught in the stranglehold of inescapable evil blends the recognizable and the unimaginable into a vivid, epic backdrop for his tale of ultimate evil set against a lone force of good: Van Helsing.

Audiences will be drawn into a visionary, supernatural but seemingly all-too-real world of Sommers' singular creation—set in 19th Century London, Rome, Paris and Transylvania—where mankind is in constant danger from incarnate evil in a multitude of forms: monsters that outlive generations, defying repeated attacks from the doomed brave souls that challenge them in their never-ending war upon the human race. In Sommers' hands, Dracula, Frankenstein's Monster, the Wolf Man and others are effectively reborn as dynamic heirs to the traditions handed down by the filmmakers of the classic Universal monster pictures. Honoring their legacy while propelling them into the next generation of cinema, Sommers turns what was once classic into cutting edge.

Into this world, brought to life and played out on massive sets and sweeping locations, Sommers brings Van Helsing (Hugh Jackman), the legendary monster hunter born in the pages of Bram Stoker's *Dracula*. In his ongoing battle to rid the world of its fiendish creatures, Van Helsing, on order of a secret society, travels to Transylvania to bring down the lethally seductive, enigmatically powerful Count Dracula (Richard Roxburgh) and joins forces with the fearless Anna Valerious (Kate Beckinsale), out to rid her family of a generations-old curse by defeating the vampire. Also populating Sommers' dense canvas are:

Tony Award winner Shuler Hensley as Dr. Frankenstein's misunderstood Monster; Will Kemp, who is a former Matthew Bourne company leading dancer, is Anna's stalwart brother who transforms under the full moon into the Wolf Man; Kevin J. O'Connor as Dr. Frankenstein's loyal yet treacherous assistant, Igor; David Wenham as Carl, a friar entrusted with ensuring Van Helsing's safe return; and Elena Anaya, Silvia Colloca and Josie Maran as Dracula's three bloodthirsty brides who will stop at nothing to help their master in his plan to subvert human civilization and rule over a world of havoc, fear and darkness.

Simply stated, will the Gothic Expressionistic world of early sound cinema, the cinematic vision and monster mythology created by directors James Whale, Rowland V. Lee, Erle C. Kenton and William Roy Neill translate into the fast-paced action agenda of modern horror cinema? Will the classic horror fan base be ready to accept CGI- enhanced monsters that rely more on effects and makeup than human performances? Will younger audiences still care about the creaky classics—Frankenstein's Monster, the Wolf Man, Count Dracula—when Freddy Krueger, Jason and Leatherface have become their classic monster reference point? And most curious of all, will the actors who play the monsters in *Van Helsing* create subtle human performances or simply be stunt men in makeup? As far as Richard Roxburgh goes, his portrayal of the villainous Duke in *Moulin Rouge!* suggests he is a fabulous choice to play Count Dracula. However, I am not so confident with the actors who portray Frankenstein's Monster and the Wolf Man. Will these classic Universal monsters seem old-hat for the current generation, or will the steroid-driven and beefed up modern conceptualizations seem too *outré* for the baby boomer generation? One thing is certain, the cinematography of Allen Daviau (*E.T., The Color Purple, Congo*) and the production design of Allan Cameron (*Starship Troopers, Shanghai Knights, The Mummy, Tomorrow Never Dies*) elicit both the feel of Dracula's castle from 1931 as well as the watchtower laboratory set from the original Universal Frankenstein. In color and widescreen, these and other set pieces resemble a blending of the best of Hammer and Universal but emphasize an overwhelming Universal flavor. Basically, the look of *Van Helsing* is superb, but now the ultimate test—can the script and performances live up to the cinematography and production/set design? In a project almost doomed to inferior comparison from the get-go, Stephen Sommers' *Van Helsing* might be audacious enough to pleasantly surprise the boomers and razzle-dazzle younger audiences. The thought of resurrecting a monster rally, a Universal monster rally no less, might seem blasphemous to some, nirvana to others, but the time is certainly ripe to revisit those classic monsters that first invaded movie theaters over 70 years ago. Indeed, everything old is new again!

Peter Travers' review in Rolling Stone says:

> Here's a shrieking bore of a horror flick that's meant to sex up an anemic genre by casting X-Men hunk Hugh Jackman as Van Helsing, the vampire hunter from Bram Stoker's Dracula. Stephen Sommers, the manic director of both Mummy movies, has no faith in the story. Desperate to keep goosing the audience, he throws in Frankenstein, the Wolf Man and three of Dracula's bloodsucking brides. I'm surprised he didn't give Van Helsing a shot at Osama bin Laden. More, more, more adds up to less, less, less.

Unfortunately, Travers was more on the money than Roger Ebert who rather liked the film. Don't get us wrong, the movie is a quirky thrill ride filled with visual eye candy, perfect vacation fodder, but for serious Universal fans, well let's just say there are some angry villagers out there with torches at the ready.

Gothic
by Arthur Joseph Lundquist

In her introduction to *Frankenstein*, Mary Wollstonecraft Shelley tells us, "In the summer of 1816 we visited Switzerland and became the neighbors of Lord Byron. At first we spent our pleasant hours on the lake or wandering on its shores; and Lord Byron, who was writing the third canto of *Childe Harold*, was the only one among us who put his thoughts upon paper. These, as he brought them successively to us, clothed in all the light and harmony of poetry, seemed to stamp as divine the glories of heaven and earth, whose influences we partook with him."

That may be well and good, but what *really* happened that summer at the Villa Diodati that gave birth to *Frankenstein* and Dr. Polidori's *The Vampyre*?

Speculation was rife even before that summer was over. "Rumour had it," writes Emily W. Sunstein in *Mary Shelley: Romance and Reality*, "...that Byron, the incestuous lover of his sister; [Percy] Shelley; Mary Godwin [Shelley]; and her 'sister' [Claire Clairmont] had formed a League of Incest in which [William] Godwin's daughters slept with both men. Canny Dejean [who ran the trendy Hotel D'Angleterre] rented telescopes to his guests, who took Diodati's tablecloths drying on the balcony for the girls' petticoats."

In the tradition of those inquiring observers and their somewhat selective interpretation of what they saw comes what Ken Russell called his "black comedy," *Gothic*.

Gothic started life when a first-time spec script by advertising executive Stephen Volk found its way to Al Clark, head of production of England-based Virgin Films. As *Sight and Sound* quoted Clark: "It was worlds removed from the scripts one predominantly gets sent in this country, with their literary ambiance and dependence on a sort of linguistic authenticity. I felt it offered a perfect springboard to a director; the question was whom to approach. Then I saw *Crimes of Passion*."

Now, I don't know about you, but I remember my first exposure to Ken Russell. When I saw *Women in Love* (1969) back in the early 1970s at Washington D.C.'s late lamented Circle Theatre, Russell's vibrant, impassioned presentation of D.H. Lawrence's novel made every historic film I had ever seen seemed choked in cobwebs.

Today, when you see actresses in Jane Austen adaptations scampering around in the heat of passion while the camera whirls about them, you're seeing the influence of Ken Russell. When *A Room With A View* stops its plot so that Julian Sands can swim naked in a forest pond, you're hearing an echo of *Women in Love*'s nude wrestling scene. That film (and to a great degree, that scene) made Julian Sands a star. In a profile for *The New York Times,* Sands expressed respect for both Russell and *View*'s director James Ivory, concluding, "James Ivory is like an Indian miniaturist, and Ken Russell is a graffiti artist."

Presented with *Gothic*, as Al Clark told *Sight and Sound*, this graffiti artist, "responded keenly to the script, and they immediately agreed it was the basis for a horror film, not a bio-pic."

A more conventional filmmaker might have begun his horror film on a sober note and slowly eased our way into madness and the supernatural. Not Ken Russell. As he explained the following year to *Film Comment*, "My films are not bio-pics or social tracts. They're about the union of the Spirit and flesh, body and soul."

Gothic begins by giving each of its characters a vivid, visual introduction before anyone has a line of dialogue. We see Mary Godwin (Natasha Richardson), sitting with her shawl pulled tight about her, aboard the little boat that Percy Bysshe Shelley (Julian Sands) rows across the Swiss Lake Leman to Lord Byron's summer home, her stepsister Claire Clairmont (Myriam Cyr) draped ecstatically over the bow like a ship's figurehead. No sooner do they touch shore than a pair of teenage groupies attack Shelley, who runs euphorically to Byron's estate crying "Sanctuary! Sanctuary!" with Claire chasing after him while Mary carries all the luggage. We discover Lord Byron (Gabriel Byrne) at the top of a staircase, before a huge portrait of himself, looking down at his uninvited guests. He obviously has designs on everyone in the group. Byron's physician and biographer, Dr. Polidori (Timothy Spall), is revealed to us at the top of a stairway, standing with a hugely teated goat.

Not all the visuals are character oriented. The film is just as enamored of such striking sights as a fish drowning or Claire dropping a mouthful of spaghetti.

When the dialogue kicks in, it is every bit as vivid as the visuals. Take for example, this scene that introduces everyone and their attendant obsessions:

> **Byron**: Tolerance is a virtue, my dear Shiloh. Alas, I have no virtues.
> **Mary**: I trust there are some left in this house.
> **Polidori**: (To Mary) Miss Godwin, I ...
> **Byron**: (Correcting him) Mrs. Shelley.
> **Shelley**: Well, by nature if not by name.
> **Claire**: (Singing to Byron) "For to let the world know that I died for love."
> **Shelley**: (Savoring his drink) A robust little opiate.
> **Polidori**: Opiate? Laudanum in liquid form.
> **Butler**: My lord, dinner awaits your pleasure.
> **Byron**: (Indicating Claire) She also awaits my pleasure.
> **Claire**: (Gleefully) What's for first course?
> **Byron**: Your lips.
> **Claire**: Second course?
> **Byron**: Your body.
> **Claire**: (Laughs) Dessert?
> **Byron**: Your soul.

The sheer density of information packed in this little exchange is amazing: Byron's romantic posing, Mary's reticence, Mary and Percy's marital status, Claire's wooing of Byron,

Mary Godwin (Natasha Richardson) aboard the boat that Percy Bysshe Shelley (Julian Sands) rows to Lord Byron's summer home. Claire Clairmont (Myriam Cyr) is draped ecstatically over the bow.

Percy's casual drug use, the drug of choice at the Byron residence, Byron's casual use of Claire, Claire's eager acquiescence. (Historical note: "Shiloh" was Byron's pet name for Shelley, after "the Shiloh," the second Christ who was supposed to be born to religious fanatic Johanna Southcott, who claimed herself to be the New Savior.)

The creation of *Frankenstein* and *The Vampyre* is never far away from Stephen Volk's dialogue. Shelley: "Do you hear the lightning? ...It sounded like the end of the world." Or Byron: "Of course, I eat merely to live. Imagination is my sustenance, for such time as life offers more pleasure than death."

The Villa Diodati, usually played by stately Wrotham Park in Hertfordshire, is made to look like a carnival funhouse, often with music to match. Production designer Christopher Hobbs, who had done such good duty by Ken Russell before in *The Devils, Savage Messiah, Tommy,* and *Valentino*, fills its hallways with suits of armor draped with pythons, statues wearing veils, and pornographic automatons which Mike Southon photographs at all sorts of odd angles using distorting, disorienting lenses. By contrast, Dr. Polidori's room, stocked with jars of leeches, is a stark, shall we say bloodless, chamber. Hobbs gets a lot of value out of a relatively low $3 million budget.

Under Russell's direction, the performances, with one exception, are similarly over the top. *Women's Wear Daily* quoted Gabriel Byrne on Russell: "His way of working becomes the only way. If you go with the flow it all goes easy, but if you try to resist, he'll feed you to the baboons." Thus Byrne's Lord Byron hobbles about on his club foot, toying with everyone's darkest secrets, using Claire and Polidori without conscience, switching sexual obsessions at will. Julian Sands' Percy Bysshe Shelley runs around shouting like an overdosing crack fiend. Myriam Cyr's Claire, who in real life may simply have been jealous of Mary and wanted to possess a poet of her own, is here a feral nymphomaniac obsessed with bearing Byron's child. Timothy Spall, as Polidori, poses elegantly as the man who would one day write *The Vampyre*, always the gentleman even when his homosexuality, which the film treats as a devouring unholy appetite, threatens to consume him.

It is the Russell way to thus embody the artistic impulse via recognizable sexual and neurotic drives. In *Song of Summer* and *Savage Messiah* this makes the artist accessible. Other times it reduces *The Music Lovers* to "The Story of Tchaikovsky, A Homosexual Married to a Nymphomaniac" and *The Rime of the Ancient Mariner* to "The Story of Samuel Taylor Coleridge, Poet and Drug Addict."

Julian Sands defended this approach often in the press. He told *The New York Times*, "I think these portraits are rooted in reality. If people think otherwise, it's because of the late Victorian whitewash of them. They were subversive, anarchic hedonists pursuing a particular line of amorality." *Women's Wear Daily* quoted him, "The Victorians created this image of Shelley and Byron as quill-pushing, ethereal, middle-distance poofters, but in their time they were seen as renegades, the David Bowie and Mick Jagger of their day." Of course, Russell treated the pre-Raphaelites the same way in *Dante's Inferno*.

Mary Shelley herself might have responded to the film's speculation as she did at the time to the suggestion that she write a tell-all book. As Emily Sustein quotes her, "Years ago, 'When a man died the worms ate him.' —Now a new set of worms feed on... the world's love of tittle tattle..."

All too soon we come to what might have been the heart of the film. In a single scene it attempts to encapsulate Mary Shelley's account of the conception of *Frankenstein*:

> **Shelley**: Science was a fascination I shared with Mary's father. And he and I studied the work of Cornelius Agrippa. Smells and fumes filled my rooms and the hum of the galvanometer.
> **Byron**: The sky is your galvanometer tonight.
> **Shelley**: I surrounded myself with the instruments of life, beckoning the spark of creation.
> **Byron**: Ah, Shelley, the modern Prometheus.
> **Shelley**: But perhaps something alive can be created.
> **Polidori**: (Winding a piano-playing automaton) Galvanism has given token of such things—although I am not really qualified to comment on such scientific—
> **Mary**: What is your field, Doctor?
> **Polidori**: I think of myself as a general physician. However, the processes of the mind interest me more than the body. (He cannot resist groping for Shelley's pectorals.)
> **Shelley**: I've transcribed my dreams since.
> **Byron**: Opium dream?
> **Shelley**: All dreams.
> **Byron**: Nightmares?
> **Shelley**: It is an age of dreams and nightmares.
> **Byron**: Yes, and we are merely the children of the age. We have all we need of blood. *The Castle of Otranto. Vathek. The Monk....* (Brandishing a book) I picked this up from a bookseller in Geneva. *Phantasmagoriana*.
> **Mary**: Ghost stories!

They begin reading ghost stories, and some snatches of the ones Mary Shelley mentioned in her introduction are dramatized for us. For a few moments it seems that this weekend with

What the film really has in mind is to be a historical "black comedy." Timothy Spall as Polidori joins Sands and Richardson.

Byron is a framing device for an anthology of short ghost stories, including *Frankenstein* and *The Vampyre*. Some day I'd like to see that film.

> **Claire**: Why don't we invent our own ghost stories?
> **Polidori**: A competition?
> **Claire**: Yes! the five of us.
> **Polidori**: (To Byron) What about a dark English nobleman who draws men in to him and drinks their blood and discards them empty?
> **Byron**: Oh, yes, or an obscene Italian doctor raised by the Benedictines who turns to sin and buggery.

Thus the script sets in motion the gears that would create *Frankenstein*.

When Ken Russell has something to say, he usually says it with simplicity and feeling (*Song of Summer*, *Savage Messiah*, the first half of *The Music Lovers*). When he doesn't, or has already said it once, he ups the noise quotient and batters you to death with lurid imagery (*Tommy*, *Lisztomania*, the second half of *The Music Lovers*). *Gothic*, having shot its artistic wad, is about to leap wholeheartedly into the second condition.

Byron and company decide to hold a seance and raise the dead.

So this is what the film really has in mind: not a dramatization of the weekend that produced *Frankenstein*, but a historical "black comedy" ghost story featuring the poets you had to read in high school. The idea's not bad (Roger Corman made a second career out of it with Poe), and much could be easily forgiven if the results were more fun, but Russell's approach makes *Gothic* difficult to love, when it's not difficult to merely enjoy. And unless you bring to the film a working knowledge of the lives of Romantic poets, *Gothic* can be pretty difficult to follow.

After the seance, the film slows down considerably while we wait for the ghosts, and in the meantime tries to keep us interested by dwelling upon the seamier secrets of the Romantic poets.

Byron calls for his servant (note the name), Justine, who disrobes ritualistically upon entering and puts on a mask while Byron fondles her body and cries the name of his sister, "Augusta."

One scene between Julian Sands and Natasha Richardson dramatizes a domestic problem of the Shelley household: The shadow of death and desperation would arouse Percy's need for sexual and emotional intimacy, while diminishing Mary's. With all the deaths in store for their loved ones, it would have a tragically alienating affect on their union.

In a nice quiet moment, the camera sits still, Timothy Spall brings his performance way down, and Natasha Richardson delivers a lovely (and historically accurate) speech:

> My husband—Shelley, is too full of his own tragedies to bear mine. We were wonderfully happy once. We would meet at my mother's grave. He would write love poems. We would kiss, pledge eternal love. Last year, in March, we had a child. It was born prematurely and died. In my idle moments I dream that my little baby came back to life again. That it'd only been cold and we rubbed it before the fire and that it lived. My fear, Doctor, is that I'd give anything to bring that child back to life again.

Of course, Mary had another child living at this time, but you will look in vain for it in any of the films about the summer of 1816.

Much of the film's imagery comes from well-known paintings. Most notably, Henri Fuseli's painting *The Nightmare*, which was used as the official poster of the film. In another scene, Byron kisses Shelley's neck, looking like Edvard Munch's *The Kiss*, which wishful-thinking historians, including those at New York's Metropolitan Museum of Art, typically mislabeled *Vampire*. Later, Mary finds Shelley submerged in a bathtub, looking like Jacques Louis Davis' *Assassination of Marat*. Unlike other filmmakers who borrow compositions from classic paintings, Russell clearly wants you to remember the original.

Thomas Dolby's enjoyable musical score eases the way for us, going from carnival music one moment to a pop *Rite of Spring* the next to a genuinely touching love theme for those privileged moments when the movie slows down.

Then the ghosts start to come.

Ghost stories are tricky things. If you leave the ghosts completely to the imagination, as in *The Haunting*, you run the risk of the audience nodding off after an hour or so when they realize that they're never actually going to see anything. Or in films like *Poltergeist* you can give your ghosts unlimited powers to do anything they set their minds to. But unless the ghosts obey rigidly defined limits or rules that we can follow, the sheer arbitrariness can make an audience nod off just as easily.

The ghosts in *Gothic* do indeed follow a set of rules. As Shelley helpfully explains to us, "We've given life to a creature, a creation, a jigsaw of all our worst fears in flesh and blood." This is a very interesting idea, and Stephen Volk's script does a fair job of relating those fears to the historical facts. However, these demons are being brought to life for us via another mind, the mind of Ken Russell.

Byron (Gabriel Byrne) and company decide to hold a seance and raise the dead.

Take for example, Polidori's fear of the wrath of God. At one point we see Polidori cowering and murmuring the words, "Part leech. Part penis. Part grave." Now, during production of *Gothic* there were numerous sightings in the press of a stage prop that Marybeth Kerrigan described in *Women's Wear Daily*, as "...a seven-foot-high phallus, sprouting a dead baby's skull and leeches." Alas, the seven-foot phallus does not survive the final cut (I can't imagine why), but a fair approximation of it can probably be gained by a re-examination of Roger Daltrey's eight-foot erection in *Lisztomania*.

So everybody runs around the house, yelling out their lines, Polidori drinks a jarful of leeches, we see women with eyes on their breasts or crawling naked carrying rats in their mouths, and other supernatural manifestations that seem more arbitrary than they actually are. As Jim Faber in *Video Review* noted, however, "Amazingly, even with all these theatrics, there is almost no drama."

When Byron decides they must exorcise the demon they have created, Volk's script valiantly works to relate this to the themes of *Frankenstein*:

> **Byron**: It must die.
> **Mary**: It's your creature.
> **Byron**: It's a monster.
> **Mary**: It didn't ask to be born. And what if it goes wrong? What if we can't get rid of the horror? What if we create more monsters?

Alas, Volk learns, as Paddy Chayefsky did in *Altered States* (1980) before him, that even well-written dialogue doesn't necessarily make much sense if it is shouted.

The final exorcism doesn't make a whole helluva lot of sense, but after a lot of stuff happens, Mary finds herself in a room of doors. Through each door Mary sees visions of the future. The death of her and Claire's children. Polidori's suicide. Byron's death in a sickbed. Shelley's drowning and cremation, though not the fabled plucking out of his heart (and who said Ken Russell lacked restraint?). If you weren't aware of the historical frame before you enter the theater, however, Russell's parade of dead babies and leech-covered poets can leave a by-this-time shell-shocked audience staring at the screen numbly, as so often happens in the films of Terry Gilliam, the heir to Russell's noisy side.

The narrative reason for this scene is that the ghosts are tempting Mary to commit suicide in an attempt to change the future. Alas, Russell's approach robs Mary's life-or-death choice of any emotional impact.

But just when you were looking forward to the film's ending with relief, in its final scene *Gothic* achieves that strange tenderness that pops up in even the most overwrought Ken Russell film. Maybe it's just relief that Russell is not kicking you in the balls anymore. Or maybe it is the

Byrne's Lord Byron, comforting Shelley, toys with everyone's darkest secrets.

result of some kind of personal exorcism that all of Russell's pyrotechnics were intended to accomplish in the first place. Mary comes out into the morning sun, contemplating the futures she has seen for her friends, to find them young and whole and happy. She talks of the ghost story she will write. "My story is the story of creation, of a creature who's wracked with pain and sorrow and hunger for revenge. Who haunts his mad creator and his family and his friends—to the grave." Richardson's reading of that line is quite moving, and would have been more so if only the rest of the film had been about its genesis.

The film dissolves into the present day, with tour groups on the grounds of Villa Diodati being lectured on the ends of the people with whom we have shared this night, and its one survivor.

There is a final shot of a dead baby floating in the river. It is just right, resembling the Pierce/Karloff Frankenstein Monster not enough to get laughs, but just enough to evoke our memory of Mary Shelley's greatest child.

On April 15, 1987, *Variety* noted "*Gothic* (Vestron) opened April 10 to six unfavorable reviews ...and three inconclusive..." Perhaps the most positive was Joel Weinberg in *The New York Native*: "It makes you want to go out and ingest massive quantities of drugs..."

More typical was Vincent Canby in *The New York Times*: "With one exception, the actors are little more than adequate, possibly because it's not easy to give a serious performance in these fun-house circumstances, speaking lines that are most effective when they can't be clearly understood. When they are understood, they are alarmingly inconsequential." Canby's one exception is Natasha Richardson whom he likens to, "a flesh-and-blood wraith."

Richardson gives an affecting performance, but my admiration for it is tempered by the fact that no other actor in the cast is given half her chance. Russell usually allows Richardson the luxury of simply listening and reacting to her fellow actors. I wonder if Canby

Ken Russell directs Gabriel Byrne on the set of *Gothic*.

would have found her quite so wraithlike had Russell directed her as he had everyone else, to be "on" all the time, feverishly wrestling with guilt and lust and madness. As it is, she told *The New York Times*, "I myself was sort of shattered by the end. It became difficult to turn off and turn on. We'd get to the umpteenth take and I just couldn't stop crying between takes."

A classic Universal pose

I actually have more fondness for Timothy Spall's Polidori. Unlike Richardson, he has to put in the most over-the-top performance in the film, but takes Russell's direction and runs with it, managing to embody Polidori with real style, often looking like a Dwight Frye for the 1980s. *Halliwell's Filmgoers and Video Viewers Companion* classifies Spall as "British character actor, often in grotesque roles." Grotesque character actors rarely get the chance to do more (look at Dwight Frye), so it was especially gratifying to see Spall's touching, understated performance as a loving brother in Mike Leigh's *Secrets and Lies* (1996).

Most of my sympathy, however, goes to Myriam Cyr. She got a lot of bad press for some reported on-set problems. Mainly, her reluctance to do a scene wearing nothing but creamed spinach. Well, if you don't want to get dirty, don't work with Ken Russell. And if you do, don't wear your own clothes.

Haunted Summer
by Arthur Joseph Lundquist

In contrast to the fever dream of *Gothic* stands *Haunted Summer*, Ivan Passer's cool and contemplative meditation on that summer with Byron. Whereas *Gothic* is a black-comedy/horror film, *Haunted Summer*, in spite of a few supernatural touches, is closer to that recent sub-genre of romantic costume drama, tales of beautifully dressed Brits on Italian vacations. Like the 1996 Robert E. Howard biopic *The Whole Wide World*, this is that rare public service, a dating film to which horror fans can take their non-fan dates.

As its opening credits unfold before details of misty landscape paintings by J.M.W. Turner and intriguing music by Christopher Young, it is obvious that we will not be traveling in *Gothic* territory. Often the film's hazy photography of lakes and mountains will take inspiration from Turner, a visual style actually closer to Mary Shelley's richly romantic style of writing than the expressionist cinematography filmmakers usually lean toward when they adapt her novel.

Lewis John Carlino's script takes its luxurious time introducing us to Mary Godwin (Alice Krige), Percy Bysshe Shelley (Eric Stolz), and Claire Clairmont (Laura Dern) as, filled with the indestructible confidence of youth, they ride by coach over some stunning Alpine mountainscapes. In one scene we see Percy skinny-dipping in a mountain stream while screaming "Alive! I am alive!" This incident is based on an entry in Claire Clairmont's diary of that summer. As Miss Clairmont told it, however, Shelley demanded that the coach driver stop by a mountain stream and appealed to everyone to get out and get naked, but the coach driver, fearing Shelley was serious, refused to even slow down. This is typical of how *Haunted Summer* handles the historic record. (Totally gratuitous note: While Julian Sands discreetly kept his back turned to the camera for his nude scene in *Gothic*, Eric Stolz bravely puts his manhood on the line.)

Claire (Laura Dern), Mary (Alice Krige) and Byron (Philip Anglim) spend a haunted summer together.

The script does a nice job of painting some of the details of

Shelley family life. For example, we are shown Mary lying in bed, reading aloud a political tract while Percy indulges in laudanum. Claire enters, terrified from a nightmare. Mary calms her and the three go to sleep in each other's arms. The real Claire Clairmont was prone to such moments of hysteria, which Percy Shelley would occasionally provoke for the enjoyment of seeing Mary calm her down.

Haunted Summer leaves the strong impression that Claire and Mary occasionally shared Percy, which, while in line with the views they expressed in print, is historically open to question. It presents the trio's relationship in a fairly idealized form (probably the way Shelley had wished it to be), little hinting at the petty annoyances and jealousies that would ultimately drive them apart. At the fashionable Hotel D'Angleterre (filmed at the Italian Villa Melzi) Claire introduces us to the other principals of our drama, Lord Byron (Philip Aglim) and his personal physician, Dr. John Polidori (Alex Winter). "Are you ill, my lord?" asks Claire. Byron replies: "The world is ill, missy. I am well." Claire's pursuit of Byron is apparently the secret purpose of this trip.

At a luxurious hotel we see Mary and Percy playing hide and seek, Byron smoking a hookah and singing with Claire, the entire group dressing elegantly and eating sumptuous meals in flower-filled dining rooms. In a heavenly sequence the quintet listen to distant music while boating on Lake Leman. Production designer Stephen Grimes, who was responsible for such visual feasts as *Lawrence of Arabia* and *Out of Africa*, finds sumptuous settings for the action in and around Italy's Lake Como. If you can't afford to go on vacation yourself, there are worse films to rent than *Haunted Summer*.

Unlike *Gothic*, in *Haunted Summer* we are shown Mary, Percy, and even Polidori constantly dipping feather quills and scribbling their thoughts onto paper. So it must have been in life, though I think these social animals of the pre-telephone age would have carried almost permanent ink stains on their beautiful fingers. That is the kind of realistic detail that Ken Russell at his finest always managed to find.

If you ever sit down and read *Frankenstein*, you'll find Mary Shelley's writing style so peppered with references to art and poetry and mythology that it becomes intriguing to imagine what conversation was like at the Godwin and Shelley households. *Haunted Summer* actually makes a pretty good stab at it, though without most of the classical references.

> **Shelley**: No, no, no. Evil is absolutely excluded from the system of the universe. And it only exists in man when he violates its laws of harmony and love.
> **Byron**: Bollocks. There is evil in the universe. Evil, apart from man.
> **Shelley**: I disagree completely.
> **Byron**: Evil is a terrible, manipulating force. Look around you, Shelley; all is war, attack, defense, surrender, conquer. Good against evil, the Devil against God.
> **Shelley**: God? Ha ha, Albie, you are a slave to the vilest and most vulgar prejudices. And in addition you are as mad as the winds.
> **Byron**: True, but my title adds considerable weight to my opinions.
> **Shelley**: God and the Devil are only projections of human tendencies. Man can determine his existence, change his world.

It is fun to recognize direct quotations from Shelley and Byron sprinkled by Carlino into the dialogue. According to a press release, Carlino typed into his word processor "everything these five characters wrote in the diaries or letters that were in any way pertinent...

As a result, I could fetch up real dialogue on any subject they were discussing." As dialogue, however, it sometimes sounds a little clunky flowing off the tongue.

A problem with both *Gothic* and *Haunted Summer* is that since both stories take place on luxurious estates, surrounded by all the privilege inherited money can buy, we never see the Shelleys and the Byrons in the context of the social world against which they were rebelling. Without that very real, very cruel reality breathing down their necks, these poets come across like pampered elitists on holiday. Or as Jami Bernard put it in *The New York Post*, "They make poets as a class look about as useful to society as the idle rich." Ultimately they would have to go back to the world and pay the price for their flouting of convention. After Shelley's death and the loss of his financial security, Mary would pay dearly for her youth the rest of her life.

The infamous Villa Diodati as it appears today.

In particular, Eric Stolz's Percy talks a good revolution, but spends more of *Haunted Summer* blowing bubbles and getting high than actually doing anything. Stolz has the pretty face down pat, but the poetry Shelley supposedly writes seems to come out of nowhere. The script doesn't help him all that much. We see so little of what Shelley was capable of creating that in the end he looks little different from any dozen campus poets with photogenic joint in hand. It was Ivan Passer's decision to people his cast with Americans, probably for some of that uninhibited New World energy we allegedly carry. Stolz' English accent is not bad, but lines like, "Excuse me, these are topics that lie close on my soul," would be difficult to make sound natural in one's primary dialect. Not working in his primary language, Czech-born Passer may not have noticed.

Laura Dern's Claire has a little less of an accent problem. But she also has less to do. Indeed, after announcing her pregnancy, she doesn't get to do much of anything but quietly suffer while looking pretty. According to press releases, Passer hired Dern based on her poetic innocent in *Blue Velvet* (1986). This innocent seems to genuinely love Byron, which, given how outspokenly hostile the poet is to emotional attachments, makes her a little stupider than the film intends. The film gives no hint as to why Byron should give her any more of his time than he does any other Byron groupie.

Alex Winter is just right as Polidori: less innocent than Claire, less in love with than financially, emotionally, and artistically dependent on Byron. He tolerates the humiliations as the price of being close to greatness. Winter will probably make a good Salieri in *Amadeus* one day.

The plot is slow in developing. As critic Michael Wilmington said of Ivan Passer, "He's a director who rarely forces his material on you; it blooms slowly, urged on by a quietly lyrical, realist style."

It is through the talk of art and politics that we slowly (very slowly) come to sense the actual story of this film. We begin to notice its patterns in the way Byron's conversation includes and agrees with Percy. And slowly excludes Claire. The way he prods at Polidori's insecurities, giving him only the bare minimum to keep him near, while making "Poly" (or "Poly-dolly") pay in constant petty humiliations. In the way he probes Shelley for points of weakness. Surprisingly, though Mary is the quiet one, the one who gives the least of herself, the story belongs to her. Byron senses the depths of feeling beneath her silences and probes for them, sometimes with flattery and sometimes with insults. "We needn't have brought the ice, Polly. Mary could have chilled the wine," he says at one point. Many acquaintances found the real Mary Godwin cold, until they got to know her better.

Up to this point, the film has so little invoked the supernatural (this book *is* about horror movies, after all), that you may wonder if it is going to avoid it altogether. Yet, surprisingly enough, *Haunted Summer*'s three male leads were all chosen because of their performances as monsters. Philip Anglim had starred (without makeup) in Bernard Pomerance's play *The Elephant Man* from its original off-Broadway production through the 1979 Broadway run and a television presentation on "ABC Theater of the Month." Eric Stolz' career was made with his similarly deformed protagonist of *Mask* (1985). Passer was inspired to cast Alex Winter as the author of *The Vampyre* based on his blood-sucking performance in *The Lost Boys*.

We get our first hint of the supernatural as Byron shows off a painting to his guests.

> **Byron**: Ladies, Shelley, I would like your opinion of my recent acquisition...
> **Shelley**: It's Fuseli's work.
> **Byron**: Yes. It's called *The Nightmare*.
> **Polidori**: The creature on the woman is called an incubus. Said to cause dreams of terror by sitting on the sleeper's chest and breathing in her face.
> **Mary**: And the horse?
> **Polidori**: The specter of the night mare, upon which the incubus rides to his victims on his visitations of horror.
> **Claire**: Ghastly.
> **Byron**: It's unfortunate, Polly, that your perceptions always seem to deal with that which is puerile and superficial. It's common knowledge that the origin of the painting comes from the unhappy passion Fuseli had for a woman he desperately sought to possess. If you used your eyes as they were meant to be used, you would see that the creature's weight is not centered on her chest, but closer to the lady's more erogenous anatomy. And it is not that he has been breathing in her face, but rather taking her breath away. Her expression, even in sleep, is obviously post-coital. And

Lord Byron (Philip Anglim, right) awaits opium from Dr. Polidori as Mary (Alice Krige) looks on and Percy (Eric Stoltz) blows bubbles.

>just look at the creature's expression. See how he dares anyone to take what is his by right of ravishment. What you are witnessing is a rape in return for unrequited love.
>**Shelley**: (Blissed out on laudanum.) I find it—accurate.

Thus we begin to sense the real story of *Haunted Summer*, Byron's desire to possess Mary. The bizarre is merely the reflection of hidden sexual obsession. (Historical note: Fuseli was one of Mary's mother's great loves. But if anyone possessed unrequited love in that liaison, it was Mary Wollstonecraft. Now, if someone were to dramatize the painting in that light, *there'd* be a movie.)

Having made a tentative connection with Shelley, Byron attempts to pull him away from Mary. In another of the film's passes at the supernatural, Byron takes his guests down to the ancient dungeons of Chillon Castle. This scene is treated as a major set piece, yet Ivan Passer directs it very simply, with a minimum of atmospherics. In this place, dripping with evil karma, Byron has Shelley take opium, then look into Mary's eyes to see the face of evil within us all. Since Percy is also taking laudanum, it comes as no surprise that he does, and faints screaming. What we see is Mary's face lightly made up and slightly photographically distorted. I'd actually expected Shelley to see Mary's evil in the form of the famous vision of a woman with eyes on her breasts, but that kind of directness is alien to Passer's film (and, of course, Ken Russell had already been there). This film has no interest in the supernatural for its own sake. All its demons are private demons, its monsters, human monsters. The film has no interest in them beyond how they directly apply to human beings in the light of day.

Claire Clairmont (Laura Dern) pursues the object of her affections, Lord Bryon.

When Claire reveals that she is pregnant by Byron, it produces the following tirade:

> **Byron**: See, I believe one day scientists will move beyond the natural boundaries of human knowledge and instruct us how to propagate life without coupling. We'll fornicate only for pleasure and man will create himself in laboratories with the aid of electricity and chemicals.
> **Mary**: Without women?
> **Byron**: Eminently possible. Think of the advantages, Mary, to displace God, create ourselves, and live forever. What an Eden!

That night, Mary dreams of a monstrous figure that comes to her bedside with the face of Byron and Fuseli's incubus. The moment is over quickly. This is, of course, the dream that was the moment *Frankenstein* was conceived. The dream as shown here is nothing like the one Mary described in her introduction to the book, but it is in line with the psychological tug of war that *Haunted Summer* is truly interested in.

That is as close as *Haunted Summer* will come to the historic events that came to create *Frankenstein*. There will be no further discussion of the artificial creation of life. No reading of ghost stories, no challenge for everyone to write his or her own.

Haunted Summer is not disinterested in the origin of *Frankenstein*. It simply goes about it in a very subtle, rather restrictive way. Byron is the monster. Mary will write her novel about him. End of story.

According to a press release, Lewis Carlino intended that his script, "would focus on the nature of evil, as viewed by Byron and Shelley... Byron saw evil as existing apart from men, a force unto itself, while Shelley saw it as a creation of man and his institutions." Well, the final film becomes less about the nature of evil than about the tentative love story between Mary and Byron.

Having established the monster beneath Byron's stylish clothes, Mary will spend the rest of the film searching for the frightened, pain-racked humanity beneath the monster. Her quiet looks of judgment at Byron's treatment of Polidori cause Byron to give her ample *Frankenstein* material: "I don't ask you to excuse me, but I would like you to try to imagine, strange as it may seem to you, that this heart was once, a very long time ago, affectionate by nature." Or later: "Don't you think, Mary, that wherever physical deformity exists, it can be always traced to the face. However handsome you can be. Very odd that because one has a defective foot, one can never have a perfect face. Very odd."

Surprisingly, coming from the stage star of *The Elephant Man*, Anglim's club foot is less of a handicap than Gabriel Byrne's was in *Gothic*. It is hard to imagine anyone seeing him as unattractive.

Alice Krige has Mary down pat, from the quiet, thoughtful exterior to those moments when a look from Percy causes her to toss aside all qualms and abandon herself to a beautiful smile. You can easily imagine her leaving her whole world behind to live with him. It's harder to imagine her as the Borg queen in *Star Trek: First Contact* (1996).

Mary proposes an experiment. They return to the dungeons of Chillon Castle, where both Byron and Mary take the opium pipe. (Don't try this at home.) She says, "You've caused Shelley to look at what you call the evil behind the mask of ourselves. Now you and I will look." From out of the shadows comes a vaguely batlike creature, with the eyes of Fuseli's incubus. It goes to Byron and kisses him. Byron tries to stand firm, but finally runs from it hysterically.

Of course, the batlike creature was Polidori in costume. This is the only hint in the film that Polidori would write *The Vampyre*.

Byron, recovering in bed the next morning, acknowledges his demon to Mary. "It was more than the terror. It was the monster's great longing, sadness. And I knew. It was me." Then and only then does Mary give of herself. She and Byron make love. *Haunted Summer* is now over. The rest of the film is all good-byes. We see Shelley and Byron beside the lake, standing aloof from each other, but in a strange way they seem to have wordlessly shared something.

Claire and Byron part fairly amiably. The film gives few hints of how much Byron and Claire would come to loathe one another in the future.

The film ends with a long, lingering shot of a Turneresque landscape. Over it Shelley reads some lines of verse. Then a few titles explain the fates of Byron and company. It notes "a year after the summer of 1816, Mary published the story of the monster, Frankenstein." Of course, as we all know, Frankenstein was the creator, not the monster. But this film can be excused for its tunnel vision, since it is about the pain of its monster, Byron, to the exclusion of just about any other aspect of the story.

A final credit in the film reassures us, "This film is a dramatization of certain events in the lives of the characters depicted in this photoplay. The main

Alice Krige (left) has Mary down pat, from thoughtful exterior to moments when a look from Percy causes her to abandon herself to a beautiful smile.

events and incidents in this film actually occurred." Of course, depending on how you define the word "main," that disclaimer would have covered *Gothic*.

Anne Edwards' novel *Haunted Summer* came to the attention of Lewis John Carlino, the Academy Award–nominated (for 1977's *I Never Promised You a Rose Garden*) screenwriter whose credits go all the way back to the Frankenheimer-directed *Seconds* (1966). According to a press release, after obtaining the rights to the novel with his producer Martin Poll, Carlino's resulting script interested veteran director John Huston, and a package was made with Menahem Golan and Yoram Globus' Cannon Group.

Haunted Summer is a product of that brief, shining moment when Golan and Globus used the cash from economically made commercial films like *Enter the Ninja* and *Delta Force* to make a bid for artistic respectability.

Originally *Haunted Summer* was supposed to hit the screens at the same time as *Gothic*, but John Huston's failing heath caused delays, and his eventual death nearly scuttled the project. Pre-production was so far along, however, that Ivan Passer was brought in. Passer immediately fired Huston's all-British cast (ouch) and chose to replace them with Americans. The sole hold-over was South African–born Alice Krige, best known then as the opera singer in *Chariots of Fire*. All of the Americans were virtually unknown at the time of filming, though many were on the cusp of international stardom (Eric Stolz was awaiting release of *Some Kind of Wonderful* and Alex Winter of *Bill and Ted's Excellent Adventure*).

Alas, Cannon's days were numbered almost as *Haunted Summer* completed filming, as the ambitious studio fell into a morass of debt from which it would never recover. Unable to afford a risky release, Cannon gave *Haunted Summer* almost no play in the United States: a fruitless engagement in Los Angeles in December 1988 to qualify for Oscars, with a few other cities to maximize its asking price on video.

Lord Byron threatens to kill Polidori (Alex Winter) when he discovers him stealing his personal journals. He is restrained by Shelley and Mary.

Passer's laid-back style found some acceptance with the California press. Michael Wilmington in the *Los Angeles Times* felt "Carlino has given us exactly what [Ken] Russell's scenarist, Steven Volk, didn't: a sense of Shelley and Byron as poets, of Mary and Polidori as novelists, a real delight in the kind of language they used and their own relish in using it."

Outlook's Jerry Roberts obviously saw the film in just the right spirit. "Framed by Guiseppe Rotunno's beautiful cinematography, the film washes around you like a lazy sunlit Sunday boat ride in the park. Lie back and close your eyes to half-mast. Have a champagne split."

The reviews in New York were vicious. Caryn James in *The New York Times* summed it up: "...it cannot have been easy to turn material so rich with imagination and drama into such a tepid, excruciatingly slow film... Ken Russell's *Gothic* covered the same story and scarcely touched down in reality. But it conveyed the dark imaginings and appetites that made these people and this historical moment endlessly fascinating... But while [*Haunted Summer*] offers some shimmering landscapes and lurid, Fuseli-inspired nightmares, it has nothing of Turner's ghostly beauty and no hint of the Romantics' genius."

For all the recreational drug use, Lewis John Carlino has written a sweet, sober screenplay which Ivan Passer has directed in a simple, sober style. And maybe that's a little too much sobriety. In my more wistful moments, I wonder what the amply lubricated John Huston had in mind for Carlino's script (Byron's treatment of Polidori echoes Huston's treatment of Ray Bradbury), or how Passer might have handled Stephen Volk's more ambitious thematic potpourri in *Gothic*.

Roger Corman's Frankenstein Unbound
by Arthur Joseph Lundquist

In the 1980s Universal Pictures was audience-testing different word combinations as prospective film titles. A surprising number of people expressed an interest in seeing any film entitled *Roger Corman's Frankenstein*. Universal head of production Tom Mount, who along with half of Hollywood had begun his career working for Corman, was intrigued. Corman was contacted, and while the director had no interest in the Frankenstein theme at that time, Mount continued wooing Corman, even after leaving Universal to form The Mount Company and becoming involved with Tri-Star.

In 1986 *Cinefantastique* reported that Corman had settled upon the idea of filming the Frankenstein story in "...an almost surrealistic future. I didn't want to do Frankenstein as a contemporary picture—I felt the elements in it work best in an abstract world; and since it had been [placed] in the past so many times, that left no option but the future.... I came up with an idea based on DNA. I wanted to make it in relationship to what we know of the frontiers of science today, and one of the areas getting the most attention in research is what is crudely referred to as gene-splicing. I felt that out of that might come an entirely new Frankenstein Monster, something that had never been done before because nobody had the concept."

Concept in hand, Corman hired Wes Craven to write, and a few drafts later Corman had a script that he hoped to advertise with the catch-phrase: "In the absence of God, it becomes necessary for man to invent God."

Somewhere along the line someone showed Corman the 1973 Brian W. Aldiss novel *Frankenstein Unbound*. A new first draft script by Corman was given to F.X. Feeny, a former film critic, whose dialogue was further revised by *Robocop* scribe Ed Neumeir. By this time the financial reigns had passed to Twentieth Century-Fox, who anted up most of the biggest production budget Corman had ever seen. As

Cinefantastique quoted the king of economic movie making: "It's theoretically $9 million, but more than half of that went to what we call 'above-the-line' costs. Less than half was available for the actual production." Production commenced in Italy around Lake Como and at last in November 1990 came the clumsily titled "Twentieth Century-Fox release of a Mount Co. production": *Roger Corman's Frankenstein Unbound*.

Twentieth Century-Fox gave Roger Corman's contribution to the Frankenstein canon a limited play in a dozen or so cities and quickly went to video. The critics mostly treated the entire exercise as a joke, but overall even the most hostile reviews were leavened with the kind of affection reserved for an old, guiltily loved director.

Whether you were first introduced to him with *Not of the Earth* (1957) on TV or *The Masque of the Red Death* (1964) at your local drive-in or *The St. Valentine's Day Massacre* (1967) at a first-run theater, I think all of us were anxious to see a new Roger Corman film. Corman stopped directing in 1971 at a moment when everyone who could "talk to youth" (i.e., get high school kids into a theater) appeared to have a finger on the new tide that was taking over America. His protégés already beginning to take over Hollywood, Corman himself seemed to have outgrown pop-culture ephemera like *The Wasp Woman* and *The Haunted Palace* (1963), and was on the verge with *The Wild Angels* (1966), *The Trip* (1967), and *Gas-s-s* (1970) of presenting an artistic vision to divided America. Jumping ahead 20 years, a lot of us were curious about what the old guru had to say. Or at least what the creator of *Teenage Caveman* (1958), *The Undead* (1956), and *Attack of the Crab Monsters* (1957) would do with a decent budget.

The awkwardly titled *Roger Corman's Frankenstein Unbound* begins with close-up images of chemicals moving around, a high-tech version of the swirling paints behind the credits of Corman's Poe films. In a nod to the audience test that started it all, the film's title appears for a few seconds as *Roger Corman's Frankenstein* before it is joined by the word *Unbound*. Corman productions have always had intriguing opening credits. Be it the (almost) animated drawings of *Attack of the Crab Monsters*, the classical sculptures of *Atlas*, or the weird paintings of *Queen of Blood* (1966), Corman always managed to hand a camera and no money to some young filmmaker who would put his heart and soul into these nascent music videos. Sometimes, as in *The Last Woman on Earth*, they evoke everything the subsequent film does not.

The film proper begins promisingly with the sight of a man walking over a barren, snow-covered landscape. A voiceover tells us, "After the first atomic bomb, Einstein said 'If I had known where this would lead, I'd have been a watchmaker.' So, here I am, either at the end of a world, or the beginning of one."

Raul Julia as Frankenstein and John Hurt as Dr. Joseph Buchannan

We flashback to "New Los Angeles, 2031" and meet scientist Dr. Joseph Buchanan (John Hurt) of "the Hawking Institute." Though Feeny's script stays fairly faithful to the novel's plot and much of its dialogue, Aldiss' protagonist was a minor politician, not a scientist. Said Corman, "That to me was the key to giving a different dimension to the film."

We see Buchanan demonstrating a new weapon, "...a particle beam that simply makes the enemy disappear." Someone points out that it also causes "freak weather, people disappearing, and these time slips..." "All right, so we have a side effect to contend with," replies Buchanan. But once alone he looks at a charged cloud hanging over New Los Angeles and sighs, "I wanted to create a weapon that wouldn't destroy the world, and look what I did."

Going home, Buchanan summons one of the most interesting characters of the film, his talking, self-driving car. It has a female voice and all the personality of the *Lost in Space* robot. They drive past some interesting matte paintings depicting futuristic Los Angeles. This film has more special effects than Roger Corman commissioned in the first 10 years of his career.

Via radio news broadcasts we catch glimpses of 2031, a fairly typical *Robocop* dystopia with mentions of the lost ozone layer, the end of the tropical rain forests, etc. It sounds hip, but we don't actually see any signs of environmental devastation (it can be done without harming the plot; see 1989's *Robojox*). No one even wears a hat.

After some disposable business from the novel about some kids burying their old bike, Buchanan and his car are swept into one of those charged clouds, and are deposited in the mountains someplace where the car can detect no radio, television, or satellite broadcasts.

Hiding his car in a convenient barn, Buchanan walks to the nearest town, passing several ominously disemboweled sheep. Buchanan has pretty much realized that he has traveled back in time because everyone is wearing 19th-century peasant dress. Actually, he has landed in Movieland, where everybody speaks English. Taking a note from the Coneheads, Buchanan explains away his own clothing and speech by saying, "I am from America."

He goes to an inn for lunch, and immediately finds himself sitting next to a Dr. Frankenstein (Raul Julia). "I've heard of your work," says Buchanan. Either Frankenstein is an accepted historical figure in the world of *Roger Corman's Frankenstein Unbound*, or Buchanan is taking Mary Shelley's book *very* seriously.

When Dr. Frankenstein leaves, Buchanan turns Nancy Drew and stows away on the back of Frankenstein's coach. Why? Doesn't the lost time traveler have problems of his own? That night Buchanan witnesses a meeting between Frankenstein and some huge, unseen figure who demands, "Give me what I want."

A fall knocks Buchanan unconscious so he can have a vision absolutely pregnant with significance. Buchanan walks through a misty interior full of disfigured people. "Who is responsible for this?" asks Buchanan. He is answered, "Who do you think?"

The next morning, Buchanan makes his way back to his car. Having figured out that he is in Switzerland in 1818, he asks his car to compute a way home. To kill the 96 hours till then, Buchanan drives to Geneva (he has no trouble from onlookers or pre-industrial age roads, nor does the car ever get spattered with mud or dung) to pursue the Frankenstein story.

Buchanan buys a suit of contemporary clothing and fortuitously catches sight of Frankenstein, attended by his fiancée Elizabeth (Catherine Rabett). Buchanan follows them to the trial of Justine Moritz (Catherine Corman), wrongfully accused of witchcraft and the murder of Frankenstein's brother William. The court and jury seem convinced that the young lady broke the boy's neck and wrenched an arm from his body, ignoring scads of evidence of a giant sheep-killing monster stalking the hills.

Lord Byron (Jason Patric), Percy Shelley (Michael Hutchence) and Mary Shelley (Bridget Fonda) meet the actual Frankenstein in this version of the film.

Sitting in the gallery is also Mary Godwin, the soon to be Mary Shelley (Bridget Fonda), collecting material for a book. Gary Gibbins, writing for *The Village Voice*, had a strong reaction to this device. "I've never read Aldiss, so for all I know he may be a better writer than teenage Mary. Still, there's something detestable in the conceit that finds one writer insisting that the imaginings of a predecessor, whose work he is appropriating, were nothing more than faithful journalism."

Actually, the book is a little more complicated than that. Aldiss' Mary is writing her novel independently of the Frankenstein story, which is occurring at the same time. Either Mary is receiving a premonition of the story or, in the manner of *The Lathe of Heaven*, her creative act is affecting the weakened structure of reality. There is some question as to whether the story is actually happening at all.

Back in the movie version, Buchanan introduces himself to Mary and they watch as Justine is judged guilty. They also observe Frankenstein receive the verdict without emotion.

Following Frankenstein yet again, Buchanan is grabbed by that hulking figure, the Frankenstein Monster (his title credit reads "Introducing Nick Brimble"). For all the added budget and technological advances at Corman's disposal, makeup designer Nick Dudman's Monster is not all that more convincing than Paul Blaisdell's mutant for Corman's *The Day the World Ended* all the way back in 1956. The nameless Monster has a high forehead, prominent neck muscles, and protruding cheek bones (the monster in Aldiss' book is actually beautiful). The main innovation in Dudman's design is a pair of metal plates on the left and right sides of the forehead that seem to serve the same purpose as the much-abused bolts in Boris Karloff's neck. Each of his hands has a second thumb, but you'll miss them if you're

John Hurt as Buchanan carries scenes with a warm conviction, bringing with him his patented sense of fallible, conflicted humanity.

not looking for them. On the Monster's eyes are a pair of contact lenses that are painted to look as if the eyes themselves had been stitched and sewn up. They don't look like they've actually been sewn up, they look like they've been painted that way. The makeup overall would look great at a Halloween party, but it never for a moment looks believable.

Fortunately, Corman does not subscribe to the school of filmmaking that says the most effective monster is the one you see the least. Since the 1950s, Corman always gives us ample opportunity to gaze at and study our beloved monsters, only resorting to angles and quick cutting when the monster design is truly pathetic (*It Conquered the World* [1956], *Carnosaur* [1993]).

Brimble gives his refreshingly traditional Monster a lumbering walk, moving his arms in unison with his legs, rather than in opposition. Brimble gives the impression that his Monster is constantly annoyed at how flimsy human beings turn out to be.

Buchanan listens as creator and creation talk. The Monster confesses to William's strangulation, though he has trouble grasping the concept of murder and the fact that Frankenstein didn't create everyone else he has met. The script tries to give the Monster an ongoing quest for the creator of all things, which it hopes to parallel with Buchanan's own quest as a scientist. The Monster demands that Frankenstein create him a mate.

Frankenstein drives away the monster with gunfire. The two scientists then argue.

> **Frankenstein**: I wanted to give man the power to create life, to free him from a cruel and fictitious god. What man ever achieved that?
> **Buchanan**: Scientists have made far greater monsters than yours, Victor... What about Justine? Who will free her from the mob? You cannot let her pay for your sins.

Frankenstein: What sins? I am a scientist, I cannot sin. She must die. The truth is too unbearable.

According to Feeny, "My idea was to make him [Buchanan] the inventor of a device that is itself monstrous... When he meets Frankenstein, it's like a buddy film between two mad scientists. That helps enhance the theme of moral responsibility. Having someone who resembles him in his own eyes makes that dramatic." Maybe, but there are a few stumbling blocks along the way. Buchanan is all for responsibility from the get-go. Frankenstein doesn't show him anything he doesn't already know. The Victor Frankenstein in Mary Shelley's book is being eaten away with remorse by this time. Feeny's script will make much of that guilt as the motivation of this movie's climax. However, when Raul Julia's Frankenstein says he feels no guilt, I believe him. This disparity will have a strong impact on that climax.

Nick Brimble as the Monster gives the impression that the Monster is constantly annoyed at how flimsy human beings turn out to be.

Showing Frankenstein his car and a few future marvels, Buchanan hopes to convince his predecessor to write a letter clearing Justine. Frankenstein is suitably impressed, saying, "We are brothers, Doctor." Buchanan does not like the sound of that.

Meanwhile, the Monster traps a couple of children to ask them, "Who made you? Did Victor make you?" A passing gatekeeper provokes the Monster by blowing a whistle until the Monster has no choice but to rip out the gatekeeper's heart and show it to him.

Buchanan runs Frankenstein's letter to Elizabeth to no avail. When the letter turns out not to clear Justine, Buchanan goes to the Villa Diodati to visit Mary Godwin. Along the way he bumps into Lord Byron (Jason Patric) and Percy Bysshe Shelley (Michael Hutchence, lead vocalist for the Australian band INXS, who died under mysterious circumstances in November 1997). The script doesn't give Byron and Shelley much to do and, well... the actors don't do very much with it, except stand about languorously, looking every inch the "quill-pushing, ethereal, middle-distance poofters" that Julian Sands warns us about in the chapter on *Gothic*. They all seem to be focusing a lot of energy on their accents. They should. Terry Kelleher in *Newsday* described Fonda's accent as "...nouveau no man's land." The film unambiguously presents Mary as the mistress to both poets. On the whole this entire interlude is a waste of Buchanan's time. And ours.

Meanwhile, Buchanan notices more charged clouds in the sky.

Buchanan returns to Geneva, just in time for the hanging of Justine. He tries to intervene, which only causes the cleaned, shaved, and well-dressed mob to throw him into Lake Geneva.

Whether they depict peasants at market or gentry outside the courthouse, all the crowd scenes are indifferently directed. There is never much feeling of actual life going on as the extras wander back and forth, not doing much in particular, as washed and pressed and spontaneous as performers in a theme park.

The film gives Byron and Shelley little to do, but Mary appears to be sleeping with everyone.

After a quick dream sequence in which an evil double of Buchanan seems to cut a good Buchanan apart with a laser beam (in movies, dreamers are always meeting their doubles, though I don't recall it happening in any dream of mine), he awakens to find Mary has fished him out of the lake.

Buchanan summons his car. Mary exhibits only mild surprise as she is approached by a self-propelled, talking machine. As they drive, Mary expresses none of the Futurist exhilaration of someone experiencing speed for the first time. She's quite comfortable in the speeding vehicle, tossing off phrases like "Stop the car" with the ease of a... well, like a 20th-century actress. The car does, however, raise her estimation of Buchanan. Soon Mary is saying, "I've never even imagined anyone like you before." I guess we've all dreamed of a new car having that effect. Bridget Fonda isn't stiff, she seems kind of numb, like she's afraid her accent will slip if she betrays emotion. Maybe she's trying to express the coolness that people of her time had perceived in Mary Shelley. Or maybe not.

Buchanan tells her, "I know of your book because I've read it... And you'll finish it, and you'll publish it, and you'll add a new word to every language on earth—Frankenstein."

Well, if all Mary is doing is writing down what's been actually happening in Geneva, then the Frankenstein case is in the public record and Mary's not adding anything.

After traveling a great distance without attracting a whole helluva lot of attention, the pair have a conversation that is probably the heart of the film:

> **Buchanan**: I wanted to do the world a favor. But like Victor Frankenstein I've created a monster.
> **Mary**: Then it's true, Dr. Frankenstein has created a man.
> **Buchanan**: I'm afraid it is.

Mary: It is an abomination in the eyes of God. You don't believe in God.
Buchanan: I don't know
Mary: I see. Science is your religion.
Buchanan: I never thought of it like that.
Mary: I've tried to imagine what a man of science must live with. I think he lives with madness.
Buchanan: Madness.
Mary: The madness of possibility. I'm sorry if I've said something to upset you.
Buchanan: Upset me? Mary, you amaze me. You live in the 19th century and yet you understand the future infinitely better than I do.

This movie really makes me want to raise my hand and ask, uh, is the Monster "an abomination in the eyes of God" because it kills, because it is ugly, or because it is man-made? If the latter, does that make Buchanan's car an abomination in the eyes of God? If the former, is the amoral Frankenstein an abomination too? If the Monster were pretty, would God's eyes still abominate it?

Cinefantastique quoted Corman as saying "I don't want to push it or pound it home or even discuss it at any great length, but there is a slight religious overtone to the picture. If we can create life, then to a certain extent we are challenging God." Well, "slight" is in the eye of the beholder, and Corman covers his butt by qualifying his statement with "to a certain extent," but without even going into the question of whether Frankenstein is creating life or simply reviving it, any intelligent human act challenges God. You are no more challenging God by restarting a heart or cloning a sheep than by lighting a fire or building a house or... making a movie.

Frankenstein and his doomed Elizabeth (Catherine Rabett.

After their talk, Mary invites Buchanan to have some sex ("Percy and Byron preach free love. I practice it"). I guess we've all dreamed of a philosophical discussion having that effect. Due to the R rating, all we see is some pillow talk, during which Mary theorizes, "I think you're here to stop Dr. Frankenstein." Perhaps Mary feels that she lives in a universe where God intervenes in the lives of individuals at vital moments. Or perhaps she's been watching *Quantum Leap*.

John Hurt carries these scenes with a warm conviction, bringing with him his patented sense of fallible, conflicted humanity. He has been in enough genre films (*The Ghoul, Alien, The Elephant Man, 1984*, etc.) that 30 years ago he might have become a horror movie star like Peter Cushing and Vincent Price. In the 1980s, however, the very concept of "horror movie star" seemed to vanish, and even people with prominent genre credits appear to have little trouble moving between genres.

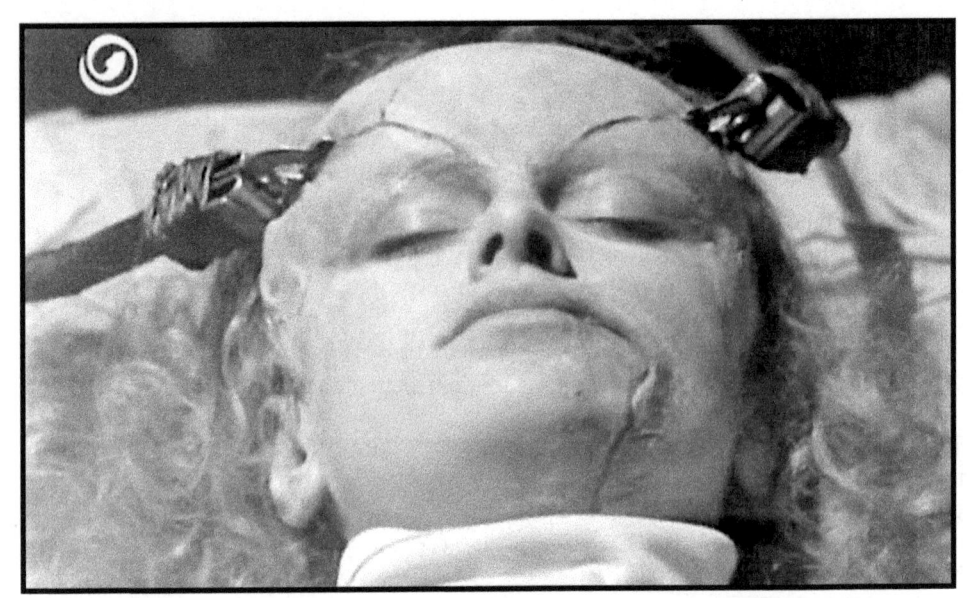

The She-Creature was sewn together out of Elizabeth's body but is still one foxy Monster.

No matter how ludicrous the plot, the film retains dignity from a musical score by Carl Davis. I'm most familiar with him for scoring the wonderful British documentary series about American silent films, *Hollywood*, as well as contributing scores to a series of silents like *The Crowd*. He's a pretty classy guy to find writing music for a monster movie. At FANEX in 1994, James Bernard, the man who scored all of Hammer Films' classic Frankenstein movies, spoke movingly about how little professional respect he got in the 1960s. Times have changed, however, when Davis, like Hurt, finds no indignity in a genre that would have typecast a career 30 years ago.

Buchanan sets off to find the mad scientist. Mary doesn't go with him. She doesn't send Byron or Shelley to help. She doesn't do anything. After Mary and Buchanan have sex, the screenplay rather thoughtlessly discards her for the rest of the film.

The fact of the matter is, Mary Godwin could be cut entirely and it wouldn't affect the film's plot in the slightest. All the themes would still be there, people just wouldn't be talking about them.

Buchanan discovers that Frankenstein has already decided to create a She-Creature to head off the Monster's threat to kill Elizabeth, though Frankenstein has never expressed much affection for the woman. Meanwhile, we see the Monster chase down Elizabeth and break open her sternum. The scientists arrive in time to discover her body. Frankenstein has a short speech that hints that his mind has become unhinged, but Raul Julia doesn't play him all that differently from any other part of the film.

A mob arrives, and jumping to conclusions, gets ready to lynch Buchanan. The Monster lumbers in and fights them off with incredible strength. To keep his feats of strength from looking too phony, Corman photographs every punch and stunt fall and ripped-out arm and decapitation from a moving camera in the briefest possible close-up. This is an old Corman tactic: If you can't make it convincing, make it quick and the audience won't have time to see the corners you've cut.

Losing consciousness, Buchanan has another quick dream that gives Mary one last chance to say, "An abomination in the eyes of God." The basic moral of all the dream se-

Both Brimble and Hurt equate themselves well in *Frankenstein Unbound*.

quences seems to be that any scientific advance can be misused, so all scientific advances are evil and all scientists equally guilty.

Buchanan wakes up to find Frankenstein has commandeered his car, wanting to use its electrical system to power the creation of the She-Creature. Frankenstein demands Buchanan's help even though "...it could take me a few days to analyze this machine on my own." Oh sure, all he has to do is bridge 200 years of high technology.

They need a power source, so, taking a page from *Back to the Future*, the Monster connects the car's electrical system to a lightning rod atop the tower where the She-Creature is to be created. Buchanan plays along, surreptitiously directing his car to create a "laser-generated implosion" which will send them elsewhere in space and time. Hurt brings a nice concern and urgency to Buchanan as the scientist commands his car to "Load laser implosion program!"

Like a pesky child, the Monster keeps bugging Buchanan with questions like, "Victor did not make you, did he? ...Who made you? ...Who is 'God, maybe'?" Brimble is at his best in this scene, an unsettling combination of innocence and angry resolve. He shares the screen well with Hurt, when it must have been difficult to even hear his fellow actor through all those prosthetics. Brimble is not bad overall, but I can't help feeling that he had more to offer than this film had time to bring out. It might have been nice to have seen his performance evolve over a series, like Dick Durock's Swamp Thing.

We don't get a good look at Frankenstein's laboratory, which is another Corman tactic: If it don't look good, make it look dark and let the audience's imagination fill in the details.

Frankenstein turns out to have sewn the She-Creature together out of Elizabeth's body. Frankenstein explains, "It is Elizabeth I cannot live without, and she will have new life." Buchanan observes, "The pain and guilt have driven you insane." Well, we'll have to take his word for it, because Raul Julia doesn't seem too concerned. Julia probably should not be playing a mad scientist. His acting style is somehow too understated to give life to delicious

The She-Creature/Elizabeth (Catherine Rabett) recognizes Victor, figures out what has happened, and promptly commits suicide.

lines like "There, now, it begins. Pull the first lever." Julia does, however, get the best line in the entire movie, "A soul? That's a crutch for weaker men than you and I, Buchanan."

As the She-Creature coughs herself to life, Buchanan's car triggers the time vortex. Before the charged cloud consumes them, Buchanan tells Frankenstein with an understated yet comic-book grandeur, "Meet my monster."

Buchanan, Frankenstein, the Monster, and the She-Creature find themselves and the tower transported to a sound stage that represents a frozen wasteland in what everyone assumes is the far future, but at first glance could be any part of Greenland in the past couple of millennia. I guess the car is still back in Switzerland.

The Monster is not too concerned about their location, because the She-Creature lives. Except for the bald cap and the plates on her skull, her face is bare of special makeup. She-Monsters are always foxier than their male counterparts. She recognizes Victor, figures out what has happened, and promptly commits suicide (overall, the Frankenstein parts of this movie make a pretty close blueprint for Kenneth Branagh's *Mary Shelley's Frankenstein*).

In vengeance, or just to clear up loose ends, the Monster breaks the still-nonchalant Frankenstein's spine and wanders off into the snows. Dying, Frankenstein gasps to Buchanan, "Kill him," referring, I suppose from process of elimination, to the Monster. Given the endless desert of snow around them, why bother?

Buchanan sets off after the Monster, and the film is back where it started. Buchanan tells us in a voiceover: "The rupture of space and time is spreading in a chain reaction. Who knows what exists in this frozen tomorrow? Apart from him, the only signs of life in this remote place are remnants of a future civilization." We have to pretty much take his word for all this, since we don't actually see any chain reaction or futuristic remnants. The voiceover may have been added in post-production to cue the audience in on what is happening, the way Corman put Jack Nicholson and Dick Miller against a blank wall to explain the incomprehensible plot of *The Terror* (1963).

Buchanan starts clapping his hands, which causes lights to flash on. More hand clapping causes the lights to focus themselves on the Monster, killing him.

Buchanan finds an open manhole cover leading underground to a psychedelic light show that is probably the abstract future world that Corman wanted to bring to life in Wes Craven's abandoned script. Buchanan discovers a room full of glass tubes and flashing colored lights that sometimes seem to change when the scientist claps his hands together. A mechanical voice says "Welcome, Dr. Buchanan." How does it know his name? It doesn't look anything like the lab he left in 2031. Is this some highly evolved descendent of the car he left in Switzerland? Does the room read minds or does it just know everything? These questions are less intriguing than annoying.

Then the Monster shows up and starts smashing equipment. His dialogue has suddenly improved, because he gets great lines like, "This world you made is better than Victor's. It is barren as I am barren. Lonely as I am alone." He helpfully tells us, "This is the brain of the great city beyond. The last refuge of mankind." How did he figure that out?

The Monster and Buchanan battle. There is lots of fast cutting and moving camerawork. Back in the 1950s, in the days of heavy cameras, Corman's commitment to keeping the camera in motion made his films more interesting to look at than most B movies. Today, when anybody can rent a steadycam, it makes them more confusing.

> **Monster**: What am I that you must destroy me?
> **Buchanan**: An abomination in the eyes of God.
> **Monster**: What are you?
> **Buchanan**: I am Frankenstein.

This line was probably a climax of one of the drafts of the film. Perhaps it still would be if Buchanan's pursuit of the Monster was the moment he finally accepted responsibility. But

Buchanan was never a Frankenstein blindly searching for knowledge or an Edward Teller eager for the next generation of superweapon. His disintegrator is an eminently responsible alternative to nuclear weapons. On the whole, the script feels like it was combined from several drafts and lost something from each one. So in the final film, Frankenstein seems to be a title for all scientists, regardless of field, since some results of scientific research inevitably are destructive.

Buchanan cripples the Monster's left arm with a pistol shot and stabs a metal pipe into its belly. This does not slow down the Monster, who rips off his useless arm and uses it as a club. Nice touch. If you were a young horror fan back in the 1950s and 1960s, you may still be haunted by the alien implants of *Night of the Blood Beast* (1958) or the blood-drinking scenes in *Attack of the Giant Leeches* (1959) and *Beast from Haunted Cave* (1959). Back then, Corman productions tended to give more imaginatively gruesome moments than most films at any budget level were willing to try. Since then Corman's descendants have far surpassed him. In *Roger Corman's Frankenstein Unbound* the gore effects are not excessive, but they tend to be pretty imaginative, when we can see them.

Buchanan stabs a metal pipe into the belly of the Monster at the finale of Frankenstein Unbound.

For no particular reason, Buchanan starts clapping his hands, which causes some of the lights to flash on. More hand clapping causes a number of the lights to focus themselves on the Monster. They sort of seem to be killing him. Then the Monster sort of seems to fall down dead.

A door opens and Buchanan steps out into the open. He sees a matte painting that looks like an abandoned oil refinery and starts walking toward it. I guess this is supposed to be the city the Monster had been talking about, but is it inhabited? Is it ruins? Is it an abomination in the eyes of God? As he walks, Buchanan hears what may or may not be the Monster's voice saying, "You think you have killed me, but I am with you forever. I am—unbound." What, did the Monster take over the computer? Or is this voice in Buchanan's imagination? The movie just sort of ends here, on a semi-positive note, without answering any of these questions, but it's an old Corman trick: If you can't make it intelligible, make it vague and let the audience fill in the blanks themselves.

Corman explained it to *Cinefantastique* his own way: "I'm a believer that you can't say everything in a film, that the audience should contribute. You can imply certain things, and the audience solves the equation. The film becomes more meaningful for the audience if it participates in the process." Well, maybe, but like anyone who has worked with Corman more than once, if I have to participate that much, I want to get paid.

Mary Shelley's Frankenstein
by Arthur Joseph Lundquist

Back in the early 1970s, the major studios had given up on horror, and every release from AIP or Hammer seemed cheaper and less imaginative than the one before. I remember wondering why horror films had to be trash. Why were they never made by artists the world respected? I mean, was it too much to hope that someday, someone with the renown of Laurence Olivier could bring respect to the genre?

In 1994, it finally happened. Hot on the heels of the financial success of 1992s *Bram Stoker's Dracula*, it was announced that Kenneth Branagh, one of the world's most respected dramatic artists, whose *Henry V* (1989) was the most exciting Shakespeare film adaptation since Zeffirelli's 1968 *Romeo and Juliet*, was going to put his creativity to work interpreting Mary Wollstonecraft Shelley's *Frankenstein*.

The drama built with every press release. Branagh announced, "The film has an epic sweep to it because it's about building a creature that's larger than life, set in a countryside that's larger than life (the Alps), and it takes two people on a passionate, romantic, and ultimately tragic journey in which all of the emotions are larger than life."

Francis Ford Coppola, Hollywood's hottest gun for hire, was producing. He would assemble a team of craftsmen and a budget of more than $50 million to bring the story to life. Helena Bonham Carter, delightful in *A Room With A View* (1985), would play Elizabeth.

Robert De Niro was to play the Monster! Press releases proclaimed that he'd accepted the role "... because I knew that Ken was going to make more than just another horror film, that he was going to give it a deeper meaning." The press were denied access to photos of the Monster's makeup, shrouding De Niro's Monster in mystery.

As it premiered in time for Halloween of 1994, Liz Smith wrote for *Newsday*, "Branagh and his crew have given the story scientific heft, historical and epic significance (man's fate, etc.) and have tried to be as faithful as possible to Mary Shelley's original, great novel. (One liberty has been taken toward the end, but Branagh likes to think Mary Shelley would have thought of it herself had she been writing for the screen.)"

When I finally got to see it, I guarded against excessive expectations. Accept it for what it is. Don't hold it up against James Whale's classic or *The True Story*. Don't analyze it, just enjoy it.

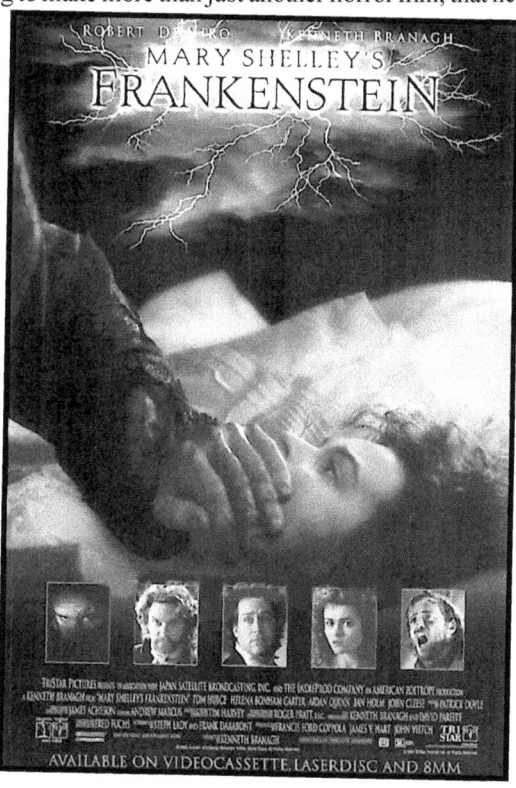

As the film begins, the screen goes dark and the voice of Mary Shelley calls out to us, "I busied myself to think of a story which would speak to the mysterious fears of our nature and awaken thrilling horror... one to make the reader afraid to look around, to curdle the blood and quicken the beating heart."

Titles begin to roll announcing (unless otherwise noted, all quotes and production comments come from the published screenplay): "The dawn of the 19th century. A world on the brink of revolutionary change. The lust for knowledge had never been greater. Among the pioneers: Captain Robert Walton, an explorer, obsessed with reaching the North Pole. ...[H]is voyage would uncover a story to strike terror in the hearts of all who venture into the unknown..."

Two thoughts immediately leapt to mind: (1) You should never announce how full of horror and terror your story is unless you're able to deliver. (2) As *Dune* teaches us, when a movie starts out explaining itself with multiple introductions and title cards, that movie is probably in trouble.

Kenneth Branagh tackles the oft filmed *Frankenstein*.

The movie begins, sort of. On a stormy night a ship is tossed about on tremendous waves. It's not much like Shelley's book, but like the opening of *The Tempest*, with Indiana Jones–style noise and faceless sailors being thrown about as the ship rams an iceberg.

Daylight finds the ship *Alexander Nevsky* photogenically trapped in the ice. We meet our first and only crewman, Grigori, who informs the captain (and us) that the crew is on the brink of mutiny, and appeals for them to turn back. Captain Walton (Aidan Quinn) coldly replies, "We'll chop our way to the North Pole if we have to." Had the movie started with this scene, we wouldn't have missed a thing.

The crew is startled by the sound of an inhuman howl in the distance. Out of the haze steps a man, dragging a sled that seems to have the bodies of dogs hung above it. "I haven't time to talk," says the stranger, "Bring your men and your weapons, and follow me." This interesting plot direction is instantly derailed by Captain Walton shouting, "Stay where you are. I give the orders here."

Another distant howl panics the *Nevsky* sled dogs, who break loose and dash across the ice toward its unseen source. The stranger, revealing to us the matinee idol face of Kenneth Branagh, says, "Leave them, they're already dead," while in the distance we hear the dogs crying in pain.

From "Another Part of the Ice Floe" (a charmingly Shakespearean stage direction) we see the hand of an unseen figure who is watching over the distant hulk of the *Nevsky*.

During questioning, the stranger learns of Captain Walton's obsession with reaching the North Pole. (Changed, for some reason, from the book's search for the secret of the North Magnetic Pole.) He responds ominously, "Do you share my madness? ...My name is Victor" (a long pause) "Frankenstein."

We flash back to "Geneva, 1773" where we find seven-year-old Victor Frankenstein (Rory Jennings Linnane) dancing with his mother to a polka played on a harpsichord by their servant, Mrs. Moritz (Celia Imrie), whose four-year-old daughter Justine (Christine Cuttall) watches. This will not be the last dance in the movie.

The Frankenstein home is full of bright colors and open space. As production designer Tim Harvey explained in a press release, "We wanted to get away from the idea of the sinister Frankenstein castle and create for the first time a warm and happy home for Victor to grow up in."

Into this happy home comes six-year-old Elizabeth (Hannah Taylor-Gordon), who has lost her parents to scarlet fever. As Victor's mother explains, "She's coming to live with us. You must think of her as your own sister. You must look after her. And be kind to her. Always." The children join hands, a gesture of union that will be a recurring motif for them, sometimes looking a bit like the Sistine Chapel painting of the hand of God giving life to Adam.

We jump ahead 10 years to find Victor (now played by Branagh) at work in his study. He plays with a single candle flame, which lights the scene in the manner of interior paintings of the period. His very pregnant mother comes in to say sweet and lovable things like "life shouldn't be all study. There's such fun to be had." Unfortunately, when subsidiary characters are sweet and lovable early in a modern film, we're probably soon going to see them die in agony.

Until then, Victor's mother is adequately depicted by Cherie Lunghi who, in 1986, played the girlfriend of both Robert De Niro and Aidan Quinn in *The Mission*. Nine years later, she's lucky to be playing the hero's mother.

First, however, Victor and Elizabeth (Helena Bonham Carter) dance the polka for us while Justine wistfully plays for them on the harpsichord. There will be no Gothic organs in this film. Victor offers to dance with Justine, and his mother goes into labor. In 1994 there is nothing to restrain filmmakers from showing just how bloody and painful childbirth could be, and Branagh does not shrink from the challenge.

Victor's doctor father (Ian Holm) is powerless to save his wife as she gives unanesthetized cesarean birth to Victor's younger brother Willie. As his mother dies, Victor sees a tree blasted apart by a lightning bolt.

The lightning bolt comes from the book, but Mary Shelley had Victor's mother die while nursing Elizabeth through scarlet fever. The screenwriters probably thought they were being more faithful to the spirit of Mary Shelley, who lost her own mother at birth. In a weird symmetry, Elizabeth's mother, who in the book died in childbirth, in this adaptation dies of scarlet fever.

Jumping ahead another three years, we find Victor prone to saying things like, "No one need ever die," while playing with mechanical energy, bioelectricity (electric eels), and lightning. He also finds time to run around majestic mountain peaks and, of course, to dance the polka. There is more dancing in this film than in most Jane Austen adaptations. The 17-year-old Justine is in of all these scenes, though she has little more to do than stand about on the sidelines and express concern for Willie.

Hot on the heels of *Bram Stoker's Dracula*, it was announced that Kenneth Branagh was going to direct Mary Wollstonecraft Shelley's *Frankenstein*.

Frankenstein's young manhood is photographed with the kind of whirling camerawork that is probably the legacy of Ken Russell. It is often used in British costume films to convey the vitality of the characters and avoid that lethargy we all remember from the days *Masterpiece Theatre* presentations were shot with heavy videotape cameras. By the end of the movie, every time Victor and Elizabeth share a scene, the camera circles them around and around. Anthony Lane in the *New Yorker* uncharitably noted, "Branagh the director treats every human figure as if it were already dead and could somehow be goaded back to life with one whip of his tracking shot."

At a huge grand ballroom dance to celebrate Victor's departure for medical school, everyone dances the polka and his father (Ian Holm is very good here) emotionally presents Victor with a book, long ago selected by his mother. "In it she has written, 'This is the journal of Victor Frankenstein.' The rest of its leaves are blank, waiting to be filled with the deeds of a noble life."

Victor and Elizabeth leave the ball to pledge themselves to each other and exchange kisses which the script specifies must be "lustful and steamy." Notes to the script hint that the filmmakers were trying to duplicate the passionate romance between Mary and Percy Shelley, whether or not it was in the book Mary wrote. The climax of the film will depend on us caring about this relationship. The filmmakers try hard but are handicapped by the fact that Kenneth Branagh and Helena Bonham Carter have no onscreen chemistry.

Victor arrives in "Ingolstadt 1793" to begin his studies, with the town gates thrown open to admit the students. Victor finds a spectacularly spacious loft apartment and meets Henry Clerval (Tom Hulce), fellow med student, not the childhood friend of the book. This is a good change, because it gives Victor somebody to confide his feelings to while away

Victor is impatiently studying at an institution whose motto is "Knowledge is power only through God."

from home. He also expresses them in letters home, which Elizabeth reads with Helena Bonham Carter's patented slow burn.

Victor is impatiently studying at an institution whose motto is "Knowledge is power only through God." He argues with his professors, "We don't know where life ends or death begins. Hair continues to grow after what we choose to call death. So do fingernails...," which sounds suspiciously reminiscent of Tom Stoppard's musing in *Rosencrantz and Gildenstern Are Dead*—"Another curious scientific phenomenon is the fact that the fingernails grow after death, as does the beard." Victor announces his intention to synthesize modern science with the "more philosophical approaches" of Corneilius Agrippa, Albertus Magnus, and Paracelsus.

He finds a more willing teacher in Dr. Waldman. Henry Clerval hints that Dr. Waldman has a history of "illegal experiments," which isn't in the book, though it did happen in *Frankenstein: The True Story*, whose medical school scenes are echoed here (including a reanimated arm).

John Cleese is adequate as Dr. Waldman, though he seems intent on squelching any drop of humor from his performance, leaving Tom Hulce to provide the much-needed comic relief.

I think the casting of John Cleese as Dr. Waldman is a beautiful bit of dramatic payback from Kenneth Branagh. I don't remember a single drama student in England in the late 1970s who didn't study re-runs of *Monty Python* and *Fawlty Towers*, feeling we were learning new insights in comedy at the feet of an unorthodox master.

Alas, unorthodox professors don't last long in horror movies, so it's not long before Dr. Waldman, inoculating feral beggars to head off a smallpox epidemic, is stabbed to death by a peg-legged beggar played by Robert De Niro, who is promptly hanged for the crime. From the gallows he cries "...you doctors are killers....Evil, you're evil.... God will punish you!" The film offers nothing to disagree with this world view.

Grief gives Victor the motivation to finally attempt reanimating the dead. It's taken us a third of the movie to get here, and it may be instructive to note that James Whale's *Frankenstein* started at this point.

Victor uses Waldman's notes, which show that Waldman had actually reanimated a corpse himself (we hear no more about it). Victor paces, mumbling about "raw materials" which the cholera epidemic amply provides.

Back at the Frankenstein Mansion (it is never referred to as Castle Frankenstein), Elizabeth, worried by Victor's lack of letters and the rumors of cholera, is told by Justine, "If he were mine, I would have left already. But he isn't mine, he's yours. And you must go to him." Elizabeth is surprised by the intensity of Justine's feelings, and we may be excused if we are as well, since Justine has had almost no dialogue in the film so far.

Mary Shelley's Elizabeth stays at home, for it was neither simple nor respectable for a single woman of even the 19th century to travel across the continent unescorted. But as Branagh helpfully explained in a press release, "It was important to me to have a very strong woman's role in a film of this size and not just a token love interest. All too often the women are just peripheral, and I wanted Elizabeth and Victor to be two equal partners, utterly entwined from the beginning. These two people were absolutely meant to be together."
Back in Ingolstadt, Victor assembles his "raw materials": Waldman's brain, the feral beggar's body, a fresh leg from a college athlete named Schiller, and gallons of amniotic fluid obtained with the assistance of Ingolstadt's midwives.

The film finally builds some steam as Victor gears up for what the filmmakers clearly intend to be the mother of all creation scenes. As Branagh gleefully observed: "The lack of specific information that Shelley provides about the creation process leaves filmmakers free to imagine it all sorts of ways." Branagh's reanimation process mixes galvanism with Chinese acupuncture with Leonardo DaVinci's sketches of the human body in a laudable and totally original attempt to make Frankenstein's science appear historically and scientifically believable.

The momentum is interrupted as Henry and Elizabeth appeal to Victor to leave the cholera-quarantined city. When Victor refuses, Bonham Carter becomes the first Elizabeth in history to ask her Frankenstein "Well, let me help you." As costume designer James Acheson helpfully explains "...she is in a very vivid, blood-red riding habit. It's as if the life blood has been drained out of Victor at this point, and she is symbolically bringing her blood and her life force into his world." Victor inexplicably rejects both, and a lot of film is spent agonizing over this betrayal of his promise to include Elizabeth in all aspects of his life.

Henry and Elizabeth leave. "Freed of the demands of a precious, unconvincing love story," wrote Janet Maslin in *The New York Times*, "the film here achieves some of the terrifying exhilaration with which *Frankenstein* is usually associated." The feverishly driven Victor loses his shirt so we can admire his chest (Branagh's exercise regimen received almost as much press as his direction). To prepare us dramatically for its resurrection, the pre-animate body is shown with its arms symbolically spread sideways. The script explicitly demands, "The Creature lies on a pile of crates, draped like Christ in Michelangelo's *Pieta*."

Religious symbolism isn't the only kind we get. The Creature is sealed in a copper tank filled with amniotic fluid. From the ceiling is suspended what appears to be a huge sack of parachute material. When I first saw the sack I remember thinking, "What the hell is that

Grief gives Victor the motivation to finally attempt reanimating the dead.

supposed to be?" It is shown to be full of electric eels and I still couldn't see the sense of it. Only when a friend pointed out the way the sack was attached to the copper tank, by a long glass tube through which the electric eels slide down into the tank and hurl themselves against the animate, did it become painfully apparent that the entire reanimation process was supposed to look like sexual intercourse. The sack is actually a giant scrotum. The art department even painted in veins. How ever did they resist the temptation to give it hair?

That still does not answer the question: Why? Are we supposed to be aroused? Is sexual symbolism supposed to give the creation scene a dramatic weight that Kenneth Strickfaden could not provide? Are we not supposed to notice? Or is it just a joke? Whose idea was this, anyway?

Branagh himself wanted to express "... the frustration men feel at being unable to have children on their own, and alongside that goes revulsion at the birthing process." At any rate, there is lots of smoke, zapping electricity, roller coaster camerawork, things banging into other things, and Victor lying on top of the birth tank while grasping a phallic lever and chanting "Live! Live! Live!" like a high school cheerleader.

In one seldom-used detail from the novel, Victor realizes the Creature is coming to life when he sees its eyelids flutter.

After the obligatory, "Oh-I-guess-the-Monster-didn't-come-to-life-after-all" scene, the Creature bursts out of his birth tank, barfing up a geyser of fluid from his lungs.

Branagh told *The New York Post* that "I had an image in my mind of this creature being born naked and cooked in amniotic fluid and wrestling in an almost biblical way, like the wrestling scene in *Women in Love*. I wanted to put them closer together, two primal beings."

After the obligatory, "Oh-I-guess-the-Monster-didn't-come-to-life-after-all" scene, the Creature bursts out of his birth tank.

Well, I don't recall noting many biblical or sexual overtones as Victor and the uncoordinated Creature slosh about in the inch-thick puddle of amniotic fluid. I mostly hoped nobody was living below Victor's loft.

While Victor hoists the Creature aloft on some chains (for more Christ imagery), a falling weight conks the Creature on the head, apparently killing it. Then, as in the book, Victor goes to bed.

Shelley had Victor awaken to find the Creature parting his bed curtains. The movie consciously decides not to show this, but doesn't come up with anything else provocative except a quick shot of the Creature lumbering about. How could anyone see this and not compare it to the first good look we got of Boris Karloff in 1931? Could anyone forget how, amidst total silence, the camera slowly cut closer and closer to Karloff's eyes, as we studied his grotesque features? In the Branagh version, a loud crash of music announces a single medium shot of De Niro, which cuts away before we get a good look. It is as if the film trusts neither the actor, the makeup, nor the audience's attention span. From that first look, which the script describes as "Naked. Beseeching," the Creature looks frightened and misunderstood, as if the filmmakers couldn't wait to make you feel sorry for him.

Victor, however, is incredibly grossed out and flees.

Having gotten the knack of walking, the new Adam quickly realizes he is naked, and puts on Victor's huge overcoat. He will wear this increasingly shabby garment for the rest of the film.

Victor comes running home carrying an ax (Branagh could not have intended this image to get as many laughs as it does) to discover the Creature has departed.

Perhaps, had Victor stayed and nurtured the Creature, it might have gained some of Victor's refinement. Instead, it learns behavior from the inhabitants of the garbage-strewn streets of Ingolstadt. (For production designer Tim Harvey "...a very strong graphic statement with large expanses of grim, decaying stone wall..." Costume designer James Acheson: "...really Hogarthian in its filthiness...") Mistaking the Creature for the living embodiment

The Creature (Robert De Niro) yearns for the more tender comforts of life.

of cholera, a lynch mob immediately starts beating him with sticks.

Valentine Cunningham speculated in the *London Observer* "...*Mary Shelley's Frankenstein* was butting in first with cautions about where such modern prometheanism might lead—the creativity of Victor, of course, but also the Creature's doings conceived as an allegory of the unleashing of the killing passions of the mob." The Creature learns fast, fighting the mob off with incredible strength.

Robert De Niro does not sport the muscles he had in either *Raging Bull* (1980) or *Cape Fear* (1991). The filmmakers do not try to make him appear any larger than he is. Branagh: "...the idea of his being a giant has been seen too many times. It can also suggest the wrong sorts of comic possibilities, ...which might be distracting. Mel Brooks' *Young Frankenstein* was such a brilliant parody that we wanted—without losing all humor in the film—to stay far away from 'size gags.'" (Oh, suddenly he's worried about extraneous sexual details!) Unfortunately, when this little guy tosses townsfolk around like rag dolls, it doesn't look real.

The Creature escapes town on a cartload of plague victims. Victor awakens to find himself recovering from pneumonia, nursed by Henry and Elizabeth. Denied this family safety net, the Creature wanders the forests of Europe alone, finally finding refuge in a pig sty.

Fortunately, this pig sty is attached to a cottage housing Felix (Mark Hadfield) and Marie (Joanna Roth), their two children Maggie (Sasha Manau) and Thomas (Joseph England), and a blind grandfather (Richard Briers).

Safe in his new home, the Creature discovers Victor's journal in his coat pocket. Not being able to speak, let alone read or understand the significance of writing, the fact that he keeps it is one of the harder plot twists to swallow, even if it comes directly from Mary Shelley.

Through a hole in his pig sty wall, the Creature peers in at family life. From observation, he learns to speak and write and play a recorder, a process the film expends not the slightest effort to make believable, unlike the Herculean effort Mary Shelley expends in the novel.

The scenes between the Creature and the blind grandfather (Richard Briers) suggest the interludes could have made an entire film.

The cold, impoverished life of the family is nicely rendered in the style of British pastoral painting and in a few, broad strokes, like the vapor blowing from their lips (making these scenes feel colder than the prologue in the Arctic).

The Creature yearns for the more tender comforts of life. He sets about helping the family, known to them only as "the Good Spirit of the Forest," by harvesting their fields and killing their cruel landlord.

Always just out of sight, the Creature smiles at his unknowing charges like a benevolent gnome. It is here that the film approaches Branagh's goal (as quoted in *The New York Times*) of being, "less a horror film than a larger-than-life Gothic fairy tale." De Niro comes closest to fusing the grotesque and the whimsical in a nice moment when he ponders the meaning of friendship while absent-mindedly picking stitches out of his face.

The sequence culminates in a sweet, all-too-brief dialogue between the Creature and the blind Grandfather that suggests this interlude could have made an entire film. Alas, this film has other objectives, so all too soon the new Adam is cast out of paradise.

Rejected by the family he loved, the Creature discovers his origin from Victor's journal and his thoughts turn to vengeance.

We are treated to an awesome shot of the Creature walking like death personified over the snow-covered Alps, momentarily achieving Branagh's desired epic sweep.

Reaching Geneva before Victor, the Creature meets and promptly kills young Willie. We don't see this abduction and murder, which would effectively kill all sympathy for the Creature. He then leaves an incriminating locket with Justine. Not waiting for the drawn-out court trial and coerced confession in the book, a mob lynches her.

Branagh should be applauded as one of the first filmmakers to explore in-depth Mary Shelley's character of Justine. Alas, Justine does not turn out to be the unexpected delight that Texan Quincy P. Morris was in *Bram Stoker's Dracula*. Her character just doesn't seem to connect to anything. Branagh and company work hard to fill in the gaps Mary Shelley

The filmmakers try hard but are handicapped by the fact that Kenneth Branagh and Helena Bonham Carter as Elizabeth have no onscreen chemistry.

left in her characterization, peppering the script with moments showing the hostility of her mother, her concern for Willie. In the shooting script there are even some lines suggesting more of a relationship between her and Victor, but they don't survive the final cut. Trevyn McDowell does a lot with very little. Her attraction to Victor is so obvious that I can't help but wonder how the film would have fared had she played Elizabeth. As it is, Justine adds little to the story except running time.

At this point, the Creature suddenly becomes supernatural. He appears to Victor in a flash of lightning, demanding they meet at "the sea of ice," then vanishes.

According to the script, without a word of explanation, "Victor rides off, leaving Elizabeth stung to the marrow."

Moving back into Indiana Jones territory, Victor climbs the sheer walls of a nearby glacier, showing more stamina than Shelley's Victor ever did. The Creature leaps through the air upon Victor, his coattails flying like Superman's cape, tossing Victor down the roller coaster shoots of an ice cave.

Coming to rest deep within the glacier, Victor and the Creature sit beside a fire and share the most important scene in the movie. It is here that we get to see the Creature as a thinking, intelligent being, to hear things from his point of view, and maybe accept him as less of a monster (the strategy of a similar scene in Scorsese's *Cape Fear*).

> **Creature**: Yes, I speak. And read. And think—and know the ways of Man....Do you think I am evil? Do you think the dying cries of your brother were music to my ears? ...You gave me these emotions, but you didn't tell me how to use them. Now two people are dead. Because of us.

There is something I want. A friend....A companion. A female....I have love in me the likes of which you can scarcely imagine. And rages the like of which you would not believe. If I cannot satisfy the one, I will indulge the other.

Branagh did not make things easy for De Niro. As the director was quoted in a press release, "He had to be two things—he had to be hideous, but he also had to be tremendously sympathetic because of his terrible plight." That would seem to be a description of Boris Karloff's performance. De Niro did indeed watch his predecessor's films, but concluded "...they had nothing to do with what I saw in our script. Our whole approach is completely different. It is based on the novel, and it's more psychological."

And what was that different approach? Again quoting Branagh, "I wanted a wise, articulate, intelligent and multifaceted Creature who could be angry yet have a sense of humor, however darkly ironic." Wise? The Creature's supposed to be wise? "The Creature's rage is the product of clearly articulated confusions about where he's come from and what he's made of... like an ordinary man. But one without a name or an identity."

De Niro had his work cut out for him. Some aspects of his Creature are reminiscent of his supernatural redneck in *Cape Fear*. But his style does not necessarily mesh with Branagh's (the way Denzel Washington's does in 1993's *Much Ado About Nothing*). He's not a stage actor. Some of his nicest bits are subtle, tiny touches (like his intonation of the word "beautiful" to the blind grandfather) which tend to get lost among Branagh's overheated ensemble. Also, that very understated realism lacks the comic book grandeur you routinely got from old-school actors like Lugosi. At least Branagh's camera tends to sit still when De Niro is onscreen.

Critics were, to say the least, divided on the results. Janet Maslin in *The New York Times* was kind. Anthony Lane for *The New Yorker* noted that while "De Niro shows us the pathos under the menace, which is easy, Karloff shows another knot of danger, deep within the pathos. There is always more trouble to come. The fight went out of De Niro some time ago, however, and it sure hasn't come back here."

He's not really helped by Daniel Parker's makeup design, which consists (logically) mostly of skin stretched between stitchings. The full body suit in the birthing scene makes a nice sculpture, but the face is not particularly interesting. More than one critic likened it to a baseball. Even the less sophisticated makeups in most Hammer Frankensteins were more fun to look at.

Director of photography Roger Pratt lights the conversation in the ice cave by a blue glow filtering through the ice. I suppose it would have been too conventional to light it by the book's flickering light of a camp fire, "around which," as Mark Twain wrote, "the most impossible reminiscences sound plausible..."

However, throughout this film there is a conscious effort to avoid anything that looks or sounds like conventional horror movie expressionism. Instead, it takes its look from 18th and 19th-century genre painting, so much so that scene after scene began to remind me of a walk through London's Tate Gallery. A conscious decision was also made to avoid the detailed period authenticity of *The Age of Innocence*, perhaps a bad call since Scorsese's 1993 film is probably the best remake of *Night of the Living Dead* that we will ever see.

Victor returns from the mountain top and begins to assemble a she-creature. At this point the film begins to deviate ominously from the book. Tired of waiting for Victor to explain what has been happening, Elizabeth prepares to leave him. The film cuts back and forth between these two plots as if they were of equal importance. Victor abandons his she-

Mary Shelley's Frankenstein **opened to tepid box office and reviews that went from mild to downright nasty.**

creature and Elizabeth proposes to him. The lovers are wed in a hasty ceremony in front of Victor's father's sickbed, which is more pleasure than Mary Shelley allows the old man in her entire book. Veteran actor Ian Holm (who, *The New York Times* informs me, is currently in London playing the world's first nude *King Lear*) brings the scene a touching wistfulness.

Alas, there is a price for pleasure. For brevity's sake, the elder Frankenstein, who dies of grief in the book, is quickly killed by the Creature as the couple embark on their honeymoon.

The newlyweds, unable to reach the last ferry out of town, spend their first night together in hastily rented lodgings. They attempt to consummate their union in an extended sequence that goes on like an overlong Victoria's Secret video, with none of the awkwardness one might have expected of two 18th-century virgins.

All this is brought to a halt when we hear the Creature playing music on his recorder. Victor dashes from the room. It seems that only her virginity was keeping Elizabeth alive this long, for Victor has barely slammed the door before the Creature has clapped his hand over Elizabeth's mouth saying, "Don't bother to scream" (which perhaps the studio had hoped to use as an advertising slogan).

In spite of having relied on plot twists out of every horror film since 1980, the production still clings to the idea that Elizabeth is not a conventional horror movie heroine. So Helena Bonham Carter is not allowed to scream or panic or even get particularly emotional when she discovers the hideous Creature lying on top of her on her wedding night.

The Creature does not throttle Elizabeth, he plucks out her heart and shows it to Victor in full Indiana Jones fashion.

At this point, *Mary Shelley's Frankenstein* abandons the book altogether and becomes really symbolic. Victor decides to bring Elizabeth back to life. Branagh: "The romantic idea of souls being together forever—and in the wake of this scientific knowledge, literally together forever—is something that appeals strongly to his visionary instincts." Victor carries the body of Elizabeth home and upstairs to his laboratory, wrapped in a long, red cloth that drapes symbolically behind them like a bloody bridal train (the scene also resembles Rhett carrying Scarlett upstairs for some husbandly rape).

Victor dashes Elizabeth through an encapsulated repeat of the first creation scene (with the same music), scavenging Justine's body for spare parts, plus some new twists like Victor cutting off Elizabeth's head with a meat cleaver. I'm sure Branagh didn't originally intend this to be comic relief.

Victor brings Elizabeth back to life, though this time we don't get a good look at the electric eels, probably to keep us from wondering who's been taking care of them all this time.

The creation scene ends, but we've seen all this before. However, as Victor stands before his reanimate bride (whose stitched features are kind of cute in a punk way), we all must wonder "What is supposed to happen now?"

Well, the first thing they do is dance to the tune of that damned polka, which explains why we had to sit through all those dance scenes.

The Creature enters, and the two men each claim the she-creature as their own. The disoriented she-creature seems to find them both attractive. When the Creature tries to polka with her, however, Victor flies into a rage. Obviously inspired by the ending of *Bram Stoker's Dracula*, the film decides Victor has violated Elizabeth's freedom of choice by bringing her back to life without her consent. Elizabeth asserts her sexual independence by grabbing a lamp and setting herself on fire. She goes up so fast that Victor must have been using kerosene instead of amniotic fluid. The house explodes into flames wherever Elizabeth goes. (This must be symbolic of something or other, but I didn't buy it in *Barton Fink* and I don't buy it here.) The script says that "Elizabeth hurtles shrieking toward the camera, still trying to claw the dead flesh away, pulling off giant flaming pieces of herself..." This is not in the final film.

Somehow, Victor escapes the inferno. We don't see Henry Clerval again, so I guess he must have died. (Actually, in the script he survives, but a final scene with Victor was cut.)

With this, we return to the framing story on the *Alexander Nevsky* and Victor's narrative to Captain Walton. Ending the story, Victor dies.

Captain Walton goes out to argue with his men, and as in the book, that old inhuman howl calls him back, to find the Creature crying over Victor's body.

Walton: Who are you?
Creature: He never gave me a name.
Walton: Why do you weep?
Creature: He was my father.

This is actually a nice distillation of several pages of dialogue in the book. It is also a very appropriate ending for the movie, which is now effectively over. All that remains is for the Creature to spring from the cabin window, onto the ice floes, and be "borne away by the waves and lost in darkness and distance."

But the movie, like the Creature, refuses to die. The crew members load Victor onto a pile of wood and pour kerosene or whale oil or something on top. Also on the pyre is Victor's journal. The Captain Walton in the book would never have allowed that, but this film finds little value in the pursuit of knowledge. The crew treats the Creature with surprising deference while he stands close by, the designated mourner. This is not unlike giving Mark Chapman a place of honor at John Lennon's funeral. Captain Walton reads from a Bible appropriate verses like "For in much wisdom is much grief: and he that increaseth knowledge, increaseth sorrow," which I hope is not the moral Branagh wanted inner-city kids to take away with them. Meanwhile, the audience shifts in their seats, feeling for their coats.

I remember wondering why, why are they wasting this much time on burning Victor's body? Then it became obvious, of course, they're trying to evoke the cremation of Percy Bysshe Shelley. (The staging is even inspired by Fournier's famous painting of the event.) I wondered how they'd resist the temptation to have the Creature pluck out Victor's heart.

This film was made, however, in the 1990s. TriStar had too much money at stake to risk ending on such a quiet note, so the film squeezed in one more roller coaster ride. As Captain Walton approaches the pyre with a torch, the ice cap breaks up. Actually, it does not so much break up as explode. Once more anonymous crewmen are tossed about as they flee back to the *Alexander Nevsky*.

The Creature grabs the torch and swims for Victor's pyre, as Captain Walton appeals, "Come with us." The idea of sailing back to England with an indestructible Charlie Manson–level murderer would be off-putting to some, but fortunately the Creature declines, saying, "I am done with man."

Climbing onto the pyre, the Creature holds the torch high above him, posing momentarily to look like Prometheus, then brings it down, embracing Victor as the flames consume them both.

The movie, however, is STILL not over. Back on the *Nevsky*, the crewmen appeal one more time, "Where to now, Captain?" and Aidan Quinn replies, "Home." As if we're supposed to care. I suppose the idea made some kind of sense at one of those screenplay-writing workshops. The film ends with the *Alexander Nevsky*, looking like the Flying Dutchman, sailing home.

Mary Shelley's Frankenstein opened to tepid box office and reviews that went from mild to downright nasty (*The New York Native*: "...Kenneth Branagh's ponderous, irritatingly masturbatory valentine to the actor Kenneth Branagh.") After four months of release, *Variety* reported the worldwide box office of Branagh's $55 million feature to be $33.5 million.

Of course, this entire article is Monday morning quarterbacking. Branagh's decisions on how to adapt Shelley's novel come with a lot of thought. They're quite logical. I can't find fault with the film in Branagh's head. Only the one on the screen.

Branagh, screenwriter Steph Lady, and Darabont work very hard to make the story adhere to contemporary themes of parental support and scientific responsibility. But I don't need anybody spelling out how relevant the myth of Frankenstein is. Just give us a story that lives, and then people like me will spend hours explaining how it reflects the spirit of the age.

There is no misstep in this film that could not be forgiven if only the movie were more fun. But the film seems so bent on explaining its seriousness of purpose that we can never just sit back and enjoy it.

Well, why isn't it fun? How could Branagh, who showed such a wonderful sense of just what scenes to cut and keep from *Henry V*, who made a popular dating movie out of *Much Ado About Nothing*, who shot *Hamlet* (1996) uncut and still made every scene entertaining, how could he show such a tin ear to the myth of Frankenstein? The answer, I think, is that Branagh cares about Shakespeare. His films show a true love and appreciation for what makes the Bard's plays work. To this player, *Mary Shelley's Frankenstein* is more of an academic exercise than the complete *Hamlet*. In it we experience a great love of period detail (in a Richard Lester sort of way) and the compositions of classic paintings, but no feeling for horror or science fiction, just as the ghost scenes in Branagh's *Hamlet* were the most unimaginatively stage-bound of that very imaginative film. (*Macbeth* is probably the last Shakespeare play he should consider adapting.) It's a lack of love, not of money or talent. Indeed, I venture to say that if Laurence Olivier himself had attempted an adaptation back in his heyday, the results would have been much the same.

I am ashamed to admit that I never cracked Mary Shelley's novel until it was time to write for this book. I'm glad for the kick in the pants. It's not as easy a read as *Dracula*, and has a classical elegance that is off-putting if you're expecting the Gothic creepiness of Edgar Allan Poe. The characters are fairly alike, and you only get to differentiate them through action. The pre-MTV Shelley is in no hurry to get the plot moving, but if you take it at her pace, and let her novel weave its spell, it can be quite awesome. (I'd also like to put in a plug for the vision of universal death in Shelley's *The Last Man*, if you can get through a slow first half that is longer than the entire length of *Frankenstein*.)

In writing for this book, it became interesting to notice that every film claiming to be a faithful adaptation of Mary Shelley's novel ends with the Monster and its creator embracing in death. This is not what happens in the book. Well, we might easily neglect the plot devices of a 19-year-old first-time novelist, were it not for the fact that all three of Mary's best known works of the fantastic end on the selfsame note. The orphaned Frankenstein Monster, the deathless hero of her short story *The Mortal Immortal*, and the sole survivor of a plague that has obliterated the human race in *The Last Man*, all live in a world alone, without friends or loved ones. And they all face a savage and unknown wilderness offering a tiny hope of salvation and most likely death. But they, like Mary Wollstonecraft Godwin Shelley herself and her closest friends and loved ones awaiting her in the grave, do not embrace death. They do not ask for our sympathy as they step forth into that wilderness, to be "borne away by the waves and lost in darkness and distance."

Frankenstein and Me
by Bryan Senn

For those of us who grew up with monsters, *Frankenstein and Me* is not only a poignant trip down memory lane, but a validation of secret childhood wonder—feelings that monsters do exist and, if one believes strongly enough, anything is possible. The story, set in 1970, centers around a relatively poor but happy family living in a small community in the California desert (the film carried the shooting title of *Mojave Frankenstein*). The father, a likable, soft-spoken trucker (sensitively played by Burt Reynolds), is a dreamer, a man who loves to spend his time tinkering with impractical gadgets in the garage and indulging his two young sons in their love of monsters. The mother, however, disdains her husband and sons' penchant for imagination and cannot see past the more "practical" day-to-day drudgery of making ends meet. Tragedy soon strikes, however, for, in one of the film's most powerful moments, the father succumbs to a heart attack. It is a truly lump-in-the-throat scene, sensitively handled by director Robert Tinnell and his actors to evoke the awful pain and loneliness of this tragic moment.

After this, the story focuses on the two boys, particularly Earl (Jamieson Boulanger), who feels most keenly the loss of his father—his one validating adult. Temporarily abandoning his rich fantasy life (centering around monster movie scenarios), Earl visits a cheap traveling carnival which claims to have the "real" Frankenstein Monster—an imposing but lifeless figure. When the Monster falls off the back of a departing carnival truck, Earl gets it into his head to try to revive the creature. With reluctant help from his skeptical friends, he builds a primitive lightning-rod apparatus (based on a design his father had doodled out for him before he died) in an old abandoned mining building. Everything comes to a head during the climactic storm, and the characters, in this milieu of trying to create life, learn something about life itself.

Tinnell's charming story wonderfully captures both the enthusiasm and loneliness often felt by monster lovers over the course of their childhood. It also deals thoughtfully with the pain of loss, making the boy's admittedly irrational actions a desperate tribute to his father, who always regretted that he didn't follow his dream. (Dad's dream was to make it big in Hollywood, but he lacked the conviction to stick it out. In

Burt Reynolds, shown with Jamieson Bouhanger and Ricky Mabe, sets aside his macho persona to deliver a subtle, touching performance.

one of the film's most heartwarming moments, we see that as a present for their beloved father, the two boys have built a makeshift HOLLYWOOD sign up on the rocks behind their house.) To screenwriters David Sherman and Richard Goudreau's credit, *Frankenstein and Me* remains poignant without becoming cloying, and the script beautifully captures that sense of wonder so strong in childhood that makes such things as Frankenstein's Monster almost magically real.

Technically, Robert Tinnell and his crew (filming exteriors on the very edge of the Mojave desert in Victorville, California while shooting the interiors in Montreal, Canada) have put their heart and soul into this production, creating beautiful, finely detailed sets (belying the film's relatively low $2 million-plus budget) which stand as loving homages to such films as *Frankenstein, The Wolf Man, Brides of Dracula*, and *Night of the Living Dead*. In these memorable settings, Earl plays out his rich, movie-influenced fantasy life. (Production designer Michael Marsolais transformed an old train warehouse into uncanny replicas of scenes from these seminal horror classics. Especially impressive is the windmill set from *Brides of Dracula*, which is so detailed that, as Tinnell laughingly related, Marsolais even placed fake pigeon droppings on the windowsill!)

The film sports some wonderfully evocative camerawork (courtesy of director of photography Roxanne di Santo), utilizing shots both subtle and blatant to enhance a mood or punctuate a point. Thankfully, Tinnell sidesteps the dreaded "Young Directors Syndrome" (characterized by over-reliance on flashy film school technique) and swoops his camera only when appropriate. (Sadly, even "Old Directors" like Woody Allen and Martin Scorsese succumb occasionally, as evidenced by Allen's pointlessly circling camera in *Shadows and Fog* and Scorsese's wildly inappropriate aquatic ballet at the climax of *Cape Fear*.)

Burt Reynolds sets aside his macho persona and sometimes broad, tongue-in-cheek acting style to deliver a subtle, touching performance (arguably his best since *Deliverance* and before *Boogie Nights*), bringing the sad scenario to painful life by emphasizing the

Clever, touching, and entertaining, *Frankenstein and Me* is tailor-made for every monster-lover whose heart has remained true to his or her childhood dreams.

quiet affection and deep bond between himself and his dreaming son. The child actors do an admirable job as well. The only fly in the acting ointment is Myriam Cyr (best known for starring in Ken Russell's *Gothic*) playing Earl's mother. Her reactions—moving from an almost bitter contempt for "dreamers" (which definitely includes all monster-lovers) to a tearful wild-eyed, chest-swelling pride when she finally recognizes the wonder of that beautiful quality in her son—are a tad too sharp and jarring.

"It's what I've always wanted to do...," declares Burt Reynolds' character, "paint my dreams across the silver screen." With *Frankenstein and Me*, writer/director Robert Tinnell has courageously put himself on the line to show his love and respect for the genre films of his youth and perhaps expose the roots of his own dream. In so doing, the dreamer has *lived* the dream. Bravo, Bob.

According to the film's publicity, "Robert Tinnell was able to share his enthusiasm for old movie monsters with [his child stars], who weren't necessarily familiar with Boris Karloff, Bela Lugosi, and the other greats of that era." Though one should generally take such press releases with a grain of salt, the director himself related that his young thespians

The kids have gathered all this junk in an attempt to mimic the images they've seen in films.

would eagerly gather in Tinnell's hotel room to watch the old classics. *Frankenstein and Me* wonderfully reflects this affectionate enthusiasm.

Leaving no homage unpaid, Fan-turned-filmmaker Tinnell even casts that guru of fandom, Forrest J Ackerman, in the cameo role of a priest (a rather amusing part for "Father Forry"—who is a steadfast secular humanist!).

Though *Frankenstein and Me* made its debut on the Disney Channel, don't be fooled into thinking it's just another "children's film." As Tinnell puts it, this is not so much a kid's move as a *fan*'s movie. Clever, touching, and entertaining, *Frankenstein and Me* is tailor-made for every monster-lover whose heart has remained true to his or her childhood dreams.

Frankenstein and Me
by Robert Tinnell

Whenever I'm asked what kind of film I'd like to make I have a stock answer. I don't want to do a film about Frankenstein or King Arthur or Dracula where I am simply adapting the original stories. What I am interested in is using these icons as starting points. Rather than doing a film about King Arthur himself, I did *Kids of the Round Table* where I worked within the echoes of Arthurian myth. In *Frankenstein and Me* I approached the film the same way. Stop and look at the tremendous presence this story and these images (as well as Dracula's) have on society. They are truly iconic figures, like everything from the cross to a bottle of Coca Cola. That fascinates me. It's one of the reasons I wanted the kids to build the Hollywood sign in *Frankenstein and Me*. That sign is another icon burned into the popular subconscious. I'm not certain there's a point I particularly want to make when I work this way, but I do know exploring this iconography leads to stories and backgrounds that challenge and excite me.

During the production I could hardly wait to get to the point when we could start shooting the fantasy scenes. As a kid I dreamt of walking around those dream worlds created by James Whale and Terence Fisher and company. I particularly enjoyed walking up the steps to the tower lab we used for the Frankenstein sequence. The kid in me would always pause dramatically at the door and almost hear the wolves howling in the night. It was so cathartic, working with all that imagery. Once completed, I felt I'd lost a ton of weight. Carrying around all those pictures in your head for years and then finally being able to let them go was fantastic. It's freed me to allow other ideas to bubble to the surface.

I suppose that goes to the heart of my fascination with monsters. These images were so present in my imagination that I had no choice but to attempt an exorcism. I still enjoy watching the scenes in the mine where Earl attempts to revive the monster. The kids have gathered all this junk in an attempt to mimic the images they've seen in films. Earl wants to send up kites because they did it in the movies. Who cares if it's impossible? Just get the set dressing right so I can enter the imagery. Besides, it doesn't really matter if the monster

"It's Alive!" Jamieson Boulanger does his best Colin Clive impression.

Stop and look at the tremendous presence this story and these images (as well as Dracula's) have on society.

comes back to life or not because just making the attempt is so much fun. It's that old thing when Christmas morning is never as rewarding as the hours spent dreaming over the Sears catalog. I hate to borrow from pop music, but like the song says, "Life's a journey, not a destination." Getting there is half the fun.

One could also go on and on about the parallels between the Frankenstein story and Earl's troubles in *Frankenstein and Me*, but I think they are fairly obvious. Earl has just lost his father and if he can bring the monster back to life, then who knows? Could Dad be next? And if that's impossible, at least he would have an adult male in his life. Also there's Earl's bond with Victor Frankenstein: both are intelligent loners, rebels, dreamers. It's apparent how much Earl identifies with Victor; he even mimics Colin Clive's manner of speaking. (Earl also mimics Peter Cushing's Van Helsing, another loner, an intellectual here who is unafraid to take charge.) What would Earl be like as an adult? Maybe he's a movie director.

While I have my share of disappointments (starting with changing the title from *Mojave Frankenstein* to *Frankenstein and Me*) regarding the film, I must say that I'm so grateful it exists. When I'm dead and buried someday my daughter and son can look at this film and retain a piece of me as well as a very real part of my childhood. It recreates a time when one ran for the new issue of *TV Guide* to scan every page in a desperate search for that film long read about but never seen. No VCRs, no cable. No overexposed sequels where makeup effects people take the place of the real stars. A world where you wish Boris Karloff would move in next door or that you lived in the black-and-white world of the Universal backlot. Of course, those far away innocent times were also peopled by the thought police ("you read too much kid. You queer?") Those types are eternal.

Kids who have no idea who Boris or Bela are or even what a set of rabbit ears look like nevertheless respond to *Frankenstein and Me*. I think (I hope) the reason is that for all its faults, there are moments when *Frankenstein and Me* really captures what it's like to be a kid. To hurt, to love, to lose, to be challenged, and to reach for one's dreams. I'm proud of that.

Footnotes and Credits

Frankenstein
CREDITS: Producer: Carl Laemmle, Jr.; Director: James Whale; Screenplay based on the Play by Peggy Webling based on the Novel by Mary Shelley: Garrett Fort, Francis Edwards Faragoh, and Robert Florey (uncredited); Based on the Composition by John L. Balderston; Film Editor: Clarence Kolster; Director of Photography: Arthur Edeson; Art Director: Charles D. Hall; Set Designer: Herman Rosse; Makeup: Jack P. Pierce; Special Electrical Effects: Kenneth Strickfaden, Frank Graves, Raymond Lindsay; Music: David Broekman; Running Time: 71 minutes; Released November 21, 1931, by Universal Pictures

CAST: Colin Clive (Henry Frankenstein); Mae Clarke (Elizabeth); John Boles (Victor Moritz); Boris Karloff (The Monster); Edward Van Sloan (Dr. Waldman); Frederick Kerr (Baron Frankenstein); Dwight Frye (Fritz); Marilyn Harris (Little Maria); Lionel Belmore (Herr Vogel, the Burgomaster); Michael Mark (Ludwig)

Bride of Frankenstein
CREDITS: Producer: Carl Laemmle, Jr.; Director: James Whale; Screenplay: William Hurlbut, from an adaptation by William Hurlbut and John L. Balderston; Director of Photography: John J. Mescall; Music: Franz Waxman; Musical Director: Mischa Bakaleinikoff; Film Editor: Ted Kent; Art Director: Charles D. Hall; Special Photographic Effects: John P. Fulton, David Horsley; Electrical Effects: Kenneth Strickfaden; Makeup: Jack P. Pierce; Running Time: 75 minutes; Released May 6, 1935, by Universal Pictures

CAST: Boris Karloff (The Monster); Colin Clive (Henry Frankenstein); Valerie Hobston (Elizabeth Frankenstein); Ernest Thesiger (Dr. Pretorius); Elsa Lanchester (Mary Shelley/The Monster's Mate); Una O'Connor (Minnie); E. E. Clive (The Burgomaster); O. P. Heggie (The Hermit); Gavin Gordon (Lord Byron); Douglas Walton (Percy Bysshe Shelley); Dwight Frye (Karl); Reginald Barlow (Hans); Mary Gordon (Hans' Wife); Anne Darling (Shepherdess); Ted Billings (Ludwig)

Son of Frankenstein
CREDITS: A Rowland V. Lee Production; Producer, Director: Rowland V. Lee; Original Screenplay: Willis C. Cooper; Director of Photography: George Robinson; Film Editor: Ted Kent; Art Director: Jack Otterson; Musical Score: Frank Skinner; Musical Director: Charles Previn; Musical Arranger: Hans J. Salter; Special Photographic Effects: John P. Fulton; Set Decorator: Russell A. Gausman; Costumes: Vera West; Makeup: Jack P. Pierce; Running Time: 94 minutes; Released January 13, 1939, by Universal Pictures

CAST: Basil Rathbone (Baron Wolf von Frankenstein); Boris Karloff (The Monster); Bela Lugosi (Ygor); Lionel Atwill (Inspector Krogh); Josephine Hutchinson (Baroness Elsa von Frankenstein); Donnie Dunagan (Peter von Frankenstein); Edgar Norton (Benson); Lionel Belmore (Emil Lang); Lawrence Grant (The Burgomaster)

Frankenstein's Children
Acknowledgments: Many thanks to Laura for computer lessons and editing. Also, to George Stover who provided a necessary tape, and to Jeff Hillegass who supplied some needed credits.

Frankenstein—Or, "My Heart Belongs to Daddy"
[1]In 1976, when I wrote the first version of this essay, which won Wayne State University's Tompkins Award for Creative Writing, graduate division, this revelation seemed liked pretty startling news. It has

since become a commonplace of much *Frankenstein* criticism—which both reinforces my argument and, alas, makes it appear less original.

[2] See Don G. Smith's chapter on *Frankenstein* in *Boris Karloff* (Baltimore: Midnight Marquee Press, 1996), pp. 8-19, for a discussion of the Monster as child.

[3] To prove his point, Waldman adds that Henry inserted an abnormal brain into his pride and joy's skull. This troubles Frankenstein, who has a parent's fear of passing on bad traits to his offspring, but he attempts to shrug it off as inconsequential.

And it is inconsequential. Robert Florey, one of *Frankenstein*'s scenarists and its originally scheduled director, added this good brain/bad brain business. Perhaps, had Florey controlled the production, he would have made some dramatic point out of this unnecessary complication, but the brains mix-up is just a MacGuffin—horror-film schtick, 1931 movie gore—which provides inattentive audiences with a facile, false explanation for the creature's violent actions. The Monster's antisocial behavior is not determined by "heredity" but by environment: It never exhibits any real criminal tendencies but simply responds to outside stimuli and only kills out of ignorance or self-defense/preservation. (See Don G. Smith, pp. 11-13.)

[4] For years, Waldman's actual jabbing of the Monster with the hypodermic was missing from prints of *Frankenstein*. The MCA video version finally restored this injection shot—thank goodness, because otherwise, it was never clear why the creature eventually succumbed to a sedative that didn't seem to have been administered.

[5] See R.H.W. Dillard's "Even a Man Who Is Pure in Heart," in W.R. Robinson's anthology, *Man and the Movies* (Baton Rouge, LA: Louisiana State University Press, 1967), pp. 64-70.

[6] Gregory William Mank, in *It's Alive: The Classic Cinema Saga of Frankenstein* (New York: A.S. Barnes & Company, Inc., 1981), p. 22, quotes Colin Clive's "major attraction to the story" from a *New York Times* interview, "Clive of *Frankenstein*" (15 November 1931):

> I think *Frankenstein* has an intense dramatic quality that continues throughout the play and culminates when I, in the title role, am killed by the Monster that I have created. This is a rather unusual ending for a talking picture, as the producers generally prefer that the play end happily with the hero and heroine clasped in each other's arms.

Mank adds, "Little did Clive realize when he said this that a happy Hollywood ending, very similar to what he scoffingly described, would be tacked on at the last minute!"

[7] See "Frankenstein's Hidden Skeleton: the Psycho-Politics of Oppression," *Science Fiction Studies*, 10, no. 2 (July, 1983), pp. 125-136.

[8] Don G. Smith, for one, thinks so. See Smith, p. 16.

[9] The restored footage of the little girl being drowned was removed after it shocked preview audiences' sensibilities. Leo Meehan's response was apparently typical: "I won't forgive Junior Laemmle [the film's producer] or James Whale for permitting the Monster to drown a little girl before my very eyes" (*Frankenstein* review, *Motion Picture Herald*, 14 November 1931; quoted by Mank [p. 35] and others).

But deleting the drowning actually defeats the sensitive censors' purposes. Fritz Lang, in *M* (1931), purposely refrained from depicting any of his psychopathic child-murderer's killings onscreen because he knew that nothing he could have shown would be half as horrible as what viewers would imagine. Similarly, *Frankenstein*, as it was cut, allowed viewers so inclined to imagine that something *worse* than an accidental drowning occurs here—that the Monster sexually molests the little girl. (Apply the false conclusion that can be drawn from this deleted sequence to the Monster and Elizabeth's bedroom encounter, which the filmmakers *intentionally* keep offscreen.) The restored scene clarifies the Monster's motivation and shows that it's not sexually interested in a fellow child—only in its father's mate.

[10] Don Glut, *The Frankenstein Legend* (Metuchen, NJ: The Scarecrow Press, Inc., 1973), p. 53.

[11] Rhona Berenstein finds certain homosocial truths revealed in *The Rocky Horror Picture Show* (1975). See her *Attack of the Leading Ladies* (New York: Columbia University Press, 1996), p. 122.

[12] Kenneth Mars' police Inspector Kemp in *Young Frankenstein* is not as funny as he might have been because his mannerisms too closely mimic Lionel Atwill's Inspector Krogh's in *Son of Frankenstein*

without going beyond them. His tricks with his wooden arm, including using it as a dart holder, are just like Atwill's tricks with his wooden arm in *Son*. Mars' shenanigans aren't amusing because we've already seen Atwill perform them. Atwill made these antics part of his total characterization, whereas Mars plays Kemp as a caricature of Krogh—all he has are the mannerisms, not the character—so his role is unsuccessful.

The only difference between Kemp and Krogh is Kemp's overly thick German accent, an attribute he'd be better off without. It's good for only one joke in the film, when the villagers make Kemp repeat some statement because even *they* can't understand him. For the rest of the film, Kemp's unintelligible accent is merely irritating, and one wishes Mars' speeches were subtitled or that he spoke with the more comprehensible accent he used in *The Producers* (1968).

[13] "Monster Mash," in *Time*'s "Cinema" section, 30 December 1974, p. 2.

[14] One might argue that, far from making any thematic point, this repetitive device is a practical necessity. How else could the Monster be reintroduced from film to film if a scientist didn't find and revive him? Well, many movie Monsters (e.g., Godzilla) just show up, hale and hearty, when each new picture begins, go through their paces, and then disappear 'til next time. They don't need a scientist to recharge them. (The Monster has done just this in several series of comic-book adventures.)

The cinema versions of *Frankenstein* always take a more particular approach to the story, always dealing with the central theme of birth without women, and therefore a male scientist is indispensable to their plots. The Hammer *Frankenstein* series makes this issue abundantly clear, for there the continuing character is not the Monster—or even *a* monster—but Dr. Frankenstein (Peter Cushing) himself, always striving to give artificial life.

[15] Her reaction is necessary for the scene to achieve its comic intent; if she didn't enjoy the rape, it would be a downright brutal attack, out of keeping with the humor of the story. Still, one cannot help but deplore Wilder and Brooks' reliance upon this familiar device of female capitulation because it's an insidious form of male chauvinism perpetrated by the movies and designed to show that, no matter how women pretend to protest or struggle, they really love "it."

I Was a Teenage Frankenstein
CREDITS: Director: Herbert L. Strock; Producer: Herman Cohen; Original Story & Screenplay: Kenneth Langtry (Aben Kandel & Herman Cohen); Director of Photography: Lothrop Worth, A.S.C.; Production Manager: Austen Jewell; Music Composed & Conducted by: Paul Dunlap; Art Director: Leslie Thomas; Set Decorator: Tom Oliphant; Makeup: Philip Scheer; Editorial Supervisor: Jerry Young; Music Editor: George Brand; Sound Effects Editor: Kay Rose; Sound: Al Overton; Assistant Director: Austen Jewell; Script Supervisor: Mary Gibsone; Property Master: James R. Harris; Wardrobe: Einar Bourman; Production Secretary: Barbara Lee Strite. American International Pictures, 1957; 72 minutes.

CAST: Whit Bissell (Professor Frankenstein); Phyllis Coates (Margaret); Robert Burton (Dr. Karlton); Gary Conway (Teenage Monster); George Lynn (Sergeant Burns); John Cliff (Sergeant McAfee); Marshall Bradford (Dr. Randolph); Claudia Bryar (Arlene's Mother); Angela Blake (Beautiful Girl); Russ Whiteman (Dr. Elwood); Charles Seel (Jeweler); Paul Keast (Man at Crash)

Frankenstein 1970
CREDITS: Director: Howard W. Koch; Producer: Aubrey Schenck; Screenplay: Richard Landau, George Worthing Yates; Story: Aubrey Schenck and Charles A. Moses; Director of Photography: Carl E. Guthrie; Editor: John A. Bushelman; Production Design: Jack T. Collis; Music: Paul Dunlap; Makeup: Gordon Bau; Allied Artists; 1958; 83 minutes

CAST: Boris Karloff (Baron Victor von Frankenstein); Tom Duggan (Mike Shaw); Jana Lund (Carolyn Hayes); Donald Barry (Douglas Row); Charlotte Austin (Judy Stevens); Irwin Berke (Inspector Raab); Rudolph Anders (Wilhelm Gottfried); John Dennis (Morgan Haley); Norbert Schiller (Shuter); Mike Lane (Hans)

Frankenstein's Daughter
CREDITS: Director: Richard Cunha; Producer: Marc Frederic; Screenplay: H.E. Barrie; Director of Photography: Meredith Nicholson; Camera Operator: Robert Wyckoff; Editor: Everett Dodd; Music: Nicholas Carras; Songs "Daddy Bird" & "Special Date" by Page Cavanaugh & Jack Smalley; Art Direction: Sham Unlimited; Set Decorations: Harry Reif; Production Manager: Ralph Brooke; Sound Mixer: Robert Post; Special Effects: Ira Anderson; Makeup: Harry Thomas; Sound Effects Editor: Harold E. Wooley; Script Supervisor: Diana Loomis; Costumes: Marge Corso; Assistant Director: Leonard J. Shapiro; Property Master: Walter Bradfoot; Chief Electrician: Frank Leonetti; Key Grip: Grant Tucker; Astor Pictures Corp., 1958; 85 minutes.

CAST: John Ashley (Johnny Bruder); Sandra Knight (Trudy Morton); Donald Murphy (Oliver Frank, aka Frankenstein); Sally Todd (Suzie Lawlor); Harold Lloyd, Jr. (Don); Felix Locher (Carter Morton); Wolfe Barzell (Elsu); John Zaremba (Lt. Boyle); Robert Dix (Det. Dillon); Harry Wilson (Monster); Voltaire Perkins (Mr. Rockwell); Charlotte Portnoy (Woman); Bill Koontz (Warehouseman); George Barrows (Warehouseman); Page Cavanaugh and his Trio (Themselves)

Frankenstein Meets the Space Monster
CREDITS: Executive Producer: Alan V. Iselin; Producer: Robert McCarty; Director: Robert Gaffney; Original story: George Garret; Photography: Saul Midwall; Editor: Lawrence C. Keating; Makeup: John D. Alese; Running time: 78 minutes; 1965

CAST: Jim [James] Karen (Dr. Adam Steele); David Kerman (General Bowers); Nancy Marshall (Karen Grant); Marilyn Hanold (Princess Marcuzan); Lou Cutell (Nadir); Robert Reilly (Colonel Frank Saunders and Frankenstein Monster)

Assignment Terror
CREDITS: Screenplay: Jacinto Molina Alvarez; Director of Photography: Godofredo Pacheco; Editor: Emilio Rodriguez; Music: Franco Salina; Production Manager: Ramon Plana; Supervisor: Luis M. Caceres; Production Assistant: Jalme DiOrs; Cameramen: Ricardo Andreu and Fernando Espiga; Set Decorator: Adolfo Cofino; Consultant: La Casa del Medico (Madrid); Makeup: Francisco R. Ferrer; Assistant Editor: Angela Grau; Special Effects: Antonio Molina; Administrator: Jose F. Labrador; Co-ordinator: Jose M Ricarte; Laboratories: Fotofilm Madeld-Barcelona; Totalvision and Eastman Color; Associate Producer: Victor Tarruella Lacour; Producer: Jaime Prades; Directors: Tulio Demichelli and (uncredited) Hugo Fregonese; English Version: Peter Riethof; a co-production of Producciones Jaime Prades S., Eichberg Film GrnbH and International Jaguar Cinematografica; Released in the U.S. by American International Television; 1969; Running Time: 87 minutes; Originally titled *Los Monstruos del Terror* in Spain. Frequently advertised but never released as *El Hombre Que Vino del Ummo* released to British theaters and on U.S. truncated video as *Dracula vs. Frankenstein*, released in France as *Dracula contre Frankenstein*, released in West Germany as *Dracula jagt Frankenstein*, released to U.S. television as *Assignment Terror*, released in Mexico as *Operacion Terror*

CAST: Michael Rennie (Dr. Odo Warnoff); Karin Dor (Maleva); Craig Hill (Inspector Henry Toberman); Patty Sheppard (Ilsa); Angel del Pozo (Count Janos Demialhoff); Paul Naschi [sic] (Waldemar Daninsky); Manuel de Blas; Fernando Bilbao (Farancksalan Monster); Peter Damon; Diana Sorel; Ferdinand Murolo; Luciano Tacconi; Gene Reyes; Eli Gessler

Blackenstein
CREDITS: Executive Producer: Ted Tetrick; Written and Produced by Frank R. Saletri; Director: William A. Levey; Director of Photography: Robert Caramico; Music: Cardella DeMilo and Lou Frohman; Production Manager: F.A. Miller; Assistant Director: Paul Heslin; Second Assistant Director: Don Goldman; Assistant to the Producer: Don Brodie; Film Editor: Bill Levey; Assistant Editor: M. Idergand; Assistant Cameraman: Bob Isenberg; Production Sound: Dick Damon; Script Supervisor: Judy Redland; Boom Man: Ray Hill; Property Master: Bud Costello; Gaffer: Larry Lepoint; Key

Grip: Carl Tunberg; Best Boy: Frank Smith; Electrician: Stu Spohn; Makeup Created by Gordon Freed; Prosthetic Creation by Bill Munns; Makeup Staff: Jerry Soucie; Wardrobe Mistress: Sharon Lally; Special Electronic Effects: Ken Strickfaden and Frank R Saletri; Production Assistant: Edward Interrera; Production Secretary: Christine Triff; Stunt Advisor: Joe Ponto; Post-Production: The Jamz; Music & Sound Effects: Walco Productions; Sound Re-recording: Ryder Sound Service; Titles and Optical Effects: Cinefx; Color by Deluxe; Copyright 1972 by Frank R. Saletri; Released by Exclusive International; Re-released by Prestige Pictures Releasing Corp; Running Time: 87 minutes; Re-release title: *Black Frankenstein*

CAST: John Hart (Dr. Stein); Ivory Stone (Dr. Winifred Walker); Joe DeSue (Eddie Turner); Roosevelt Jackson (Malcomb); Andrea King (Eleanor); Nick Bolin (Bruno Stragor); Karen Lind (Hospital Supervisor—Mrs. Wayne); Yvonne Robinson (Hospital Receptionist); Bob Brophy (Hospital Attendant); Liz Renay and Jerry Soucie (Couple in Bed); Beverly Haggerty and Daniel Faure (Couple in Car); Andy "C" (Nightclub Comedian); Cardella DeMilo (Nightclub Singer); Marva Farmer and Robert L. Hurd (Couple in Alley); Jim Cousar (Police Sergeant Jackson); Don Brodie (Police Lieutenant); Dale Bach (Girl in Dune Buggy); Stunt Men: Jay Goldner and Robert L. Hurd

Lady Frankenstein
CREDITS: Original Story: Dick Randall; Story and Screenplay: Edward Di Lorenzo; Art Director: Francis Mellon; Costumes: Maurice Nichols; Assistant Directors: Joseph Pollin and Anthony Bishop; Continuity: Parley Merrill; Camera Operator: Serge Martin; Assistant Operator: Charles Taffan; Production Manager: Frank Fly; Production Assistant: August Dolfis; Production Secretary: Tony Pitt; Soundman: Francis Grappian; Boom Operator: Corey Volpe; Makeup: Timothy Parson; Hairstyles: Cass Whyte; Sound Studios: International Recording/Westrex Recording System; Special Effects: CIPA; Animation: Charles Ramboldt; Editor: Cleo Converse; Music: Alessandro Alessandroni; Director of Photography: Richard Pallotin; Executive Producers: Harry C. Cushing, Humbert Case, and Jules Kenton; Produced and Directed by Mel Welles; Filmed at De Paolis Incir Studios; Copyright 1972 by Mel Welles and Condor International Film; Released in the U. S. by New World Pictures, Inc.; Running Time: 84 minutes (the publicized European running time of 99 minutes seems unlikely); originally released in Italy as *La Figlia di Frankenstein*; first announced in the U. S. as *Madame Frankenstein*; advertised in France as *Lady Frankenstein cette obsédée sexuelle*

CAST: Joseph Cotten (Baron Frankenstein); Sara Bay (Tanya Frankenstein); Paul Muller (Dr. Charles Muller); Peter Whiteman; Herbert Fux (Thomas Lynch); Renata Cash [Kashe]; Lawrence Tilden (Lorenzo Terzon); Ada Pomeroy [Pometti]; Andrew Ray; Johnny Loffrey; Richard Beardley; Peter Martinov; Adam Welles; "and Mickey Hargitay as Captain Paul Harris"

The Screaming Dead
CREDITS: Producers: Robert de Nesle and Luis Lasala: Screenplay: Jess Franco and Paul d'Ales; English Language Version: David Mills; English Language Version Director: Richard McNamara; Director of Photography: Jose Climent; Makeup: Lisa Vlileneux [Elisenda Villanueva] and Monique Adelaide; Special Effects: Manuel Baquero; Script Girl: Nicole Guettard; Assistant Director: J. M Loubarcl; Art Director: Antonio de Cabo; Musical Score: Bruno Nicolai; Music Publishers: Geneli; Color by Telecolor; Director: Jess Franco; a Co-Production of Interfilm (Lisbon), Fenix Films (Madrid) and Prodif Ets /Vaduz, C F.F.P. (Paris); Released in the U S. by Wizard Video; filmed in Alicante and Murcia, Spain; Estoril and Lisbon, Portugal; and in Paris, France; 1972; Running Time: 84 minutes; originally released as *Dracula contra Frankenstein* in Spain, with Dr. Seward's first name Emmanuel; originally released as *Dracula Prisonnier de Frankenstein* in France; first announced as *Satana contra el Dr. Exortio*, released as *The Screaming Dead* in Great Britain and the U.S.; released to British TV as *Dracula Prisoner of Frankenstein* in a 78-minute version; released in West Germany as *Die Nacht der Offenen Sarae*, with Dracula renamed Satana; released in Italy as *Dracula contro Frankenstein*

CAST: Howard Vernon (Count Dracula); Dennis Price (Dr. Frankenstein); Genivieve Deloir (Amira); Josiane Gibert (Cabaret Singer); Britt Nockols [Nichols] (Lady Dracula); Albert Dalbes (Dr. Jonathan Seward); Mary Francis [Pace Galbadon] (Maria); Fernando Bilbao (Frankenstein's Monster)

The Erotic Rites of Frankenstein
CREDITS: Producers: Victor de Costa, Arturo Marcos, and Robert de Nesle; Adaptation: Jess Franco; Producer Manager: Victor de Costa; Assistant Director: Jose Antonio Arevalo; Art Director: Jean d'Eaubonne; Makeup: Monique Adelaide and Antonia Nieto; Set Dresser: J de Alberto: Script Girl: Nicole Franco; Stills: Christian Hart: Music: H. Tical, Vincent Gemini, Robert Hermel and Vladimir Cosma; Musical Track Sound: "Musique Pour L'Image"; Director: Jess Franco; a Co-Production of Comptoir Francais du Film Production (Paris) and Fenix-Film (Madrid); filmed in Portugal and in Studio Balcazar in Barcelona, Spain; 1972; Running Time: 90 minutes (France), 80 minutes (Spain), 71 minutes (Great Britain); advertised before release in France as *La Malediction de Frankenstein* and *Les Exploits Erotiques de Frankenstein*; released in Great Britain as *The Erotic Rites of Frankenstein*; released in West Germany as *Das Blutoericht der Gequalten frauen*; released in The Netherlands as *De Verdoemnis van Frankenstein*

CAST: Denis [sic] Price (Dr. Frankenstein); Howard Vernon (Cagliostro); Anne Libert (Melissa); Albert Dalbes (Dr. Seward); Luis Barboo (Caronte); Daniel J. White (Inspector Tanner); Heather (Beatrice) Savon (Dr. Vera Frankenstein); Fred Harrisson [Ferando Bilbao] (Frankenstein's Monster); Doris Thomas (Abigail); Jess Franco (Frankenstein's Servant)

Frankenstein: The True Story
CREDITS: Director: Jack Smight; Producer: Hunt Stromberg, Jr.; Teleplay: Christopher Isherwood and Don Bachardy; Based on Mary W. Shelley's Novel; Associate Producer: Ian Lewis; Music: Gil Melle; Musical Supervisor: Philip Martel; Director of Photography: Arthur Ibbetson; Production Designer: Wilfred Shingleton; Editor: Richard Marden; Production Manager: Brian Burgess; Art Director: Fred Carter; Special Effects Supervisor: Roy Whybrow; Costumes: Elsa Fennell; Choreographer: Sally Gilpin; Sound: Don Sharpe; Filmed at Pinewood Studios; Running time: 180 minutes; 1973

CAST: Leonard Whiting (Victor Frankenstein); James Mason (Dr. Polidori); Michael Sarrazin (The Creature); David McCallum (Dr. Henry Clerval); Jane Seymour (Agatha/Prima); Nicola Pagett (Elizabeth Fanshawe-Frankenstein); Michael Wilding (Sir Richard Fanshawe); Clarissa Kaye (Lady Fanshawe); Agnes Moorehead (Mrs. Blair); Margaret Leighton (Foreign Lady); Ralph Richardson (Lacey); John Gielgud (Police Inspector); Tom Baker (Sea Captain); Julian Barnes (Young Man); Arnold Diamond (Passenger in Coach); Yootha Joyce (Mrs. McGregor); Peter Sallis (Priest); Dallas Adams (Felix)

Frankenstein, TNT, 1993
CREDITS: Turner Pictures Presents A David Wickes Production; Music: John Cameron; Editor: John Grover; Production Design: William Alexander; Photography: Jack Conroy; Costumes: Raymond Hughes; Special Effects Supervisor: Graham Longhurst; Special Effects Technicians: Dominic Tuohy and Ian Corbould: Effects and Models: Effects Associates Ltd.; Makeup: Alan Boyle; Special Makeup: Mark Coulier of Image Animation; Production Supervisor: Paul Tivers; Executive Producer, Writer, Director: David Wickes

CAST: Patrick Bergin (Victor Frankenstein); Randy Quaid (The Monster); John Mills (De Lacey); Lambert Wilson (Clerval); Fiona Gillies (Elizabeth); Jacinta Mulcahy (Justine); Ronald Leigh Hunt (Alphonse); Timothy Stark (William); Roger Bizley (Captain); Michael Gothard (Bosun); Marcus Eyre (Zorkin); Jon Laurimore (Sailor); Amanda Quaid (Amy)

Young Frankenstein
CREDITS: Producer: Michael Gruskoff; Director: Mel Brooks; Writers: Gene Wilder and Mel Brooks

(based on the characters from the Novel *Frankenstein* by Mary Wollstonecraft Shelley); Cinematography: Gerald Hirschfeld; Editor: John C. Howard; Music: John Morris; Art Direction: Dale Hennesy; Special Effects: Hal Millar and Henry Miller, Jr.; Set Designer: Robert De Vestel; Makeup: William Tuttle; released by Fox, 1974; 108 minutes; black and white; Academy Award nominations for Best Adapted Screenplay and Best Sound

CAST: Gene Wilder (Dr. Frederick Frankenstein); Peter Boyle (The Monster); Marty Feldman (Igor); Madeline Kahn (Elizabeth); Cloris Leachman (Frau Blucher); Teri Garr (Inga); Kenneth Mars (Inspector Kemp); Gene Hackman (Blind Hermit); Richard Haydn (Herr Falkstein); Liam Dunn (Mr. Hilltop)

Frankenweenie
CREDITS: Producer: Julie Hickson; Director: Tim Burton; Screenplay: Lenny Ripps (based on an idea by Tim Burton and inspired by the Novel *Frankenstein* by Mary Wollstonecraft Shelley); Production Supervisor: Tom Leetch; Associate Producer: Rick Heinrichs; Director of Photography: Thomas Ackerman; Editor: Ernest Milano, A.C.E.; Music: Michael Convertino, David Newman; Art Director: John B. Mansbridge; Unit Production Manager: Tom Leetch; First Assistant Director: Richard Learman; Second Assistant Director: Scott Cameron; Casting: Bill Shepard, C.S.A., Joe Scully, C.S.A.; Location Manager: Rolf Darbo; Script Supervisor: Doris Moody Chisholm; Still Photographer: Ron Batzdorf; Costume Dept. Supervisor: Jack Sandeen; Men's Costumer: Milton G. Mangum; Women's Costumer: Sandy Berke-Jordan; Sparky's Makeup: Robert J. Schiffer, C.M.A.A.; Makeup: Marvin J. McIntyre; Hairstylist: Connie Nichols; Set Decorator: Roger Shook; Property Master: Gary Antista; Lighting Gaffer: Ward Russell; Best Boy: Danny Delgado, Jr.; Key Grip: Essil Massinburg; Special Effects: Roland Tantin, Hans Metz; Special Electrical Effects: Ed Angel; Camera Operator: Doug Knapp; First Asst. Camera: Bill Waldman; Second Asst. Camera: Richard Mosier; Second Unit Photography: Peter Anderson, Rusty Geller; Visual Effects Animation: Allen Gonzales; Sound Supervisor: Bob Hathaway; Sound Mixer: John Glascock, C.A.S.; Re-Recording Mixers: Richard Portman, Nick Alphin, Frank C. Regula; Assistant Editor: Marty Stanovich; Sound Effects Editor: Al Maguire; Music Supervisor: Jay Lawton; Music Editor: Jack Wadsworth; Music Scoring Mixer: Shawn Murphy; Stunt Players: Bob Herron, Donna Hall; Trainer: Animal Actors of Hollywood, Christy Miele; Special Thanks to Dave Smith, Clark Hunter, Ed Nunnery, Marcia Jacobs, Chris Buck; released by Walt Disney Productions, 1984; 27 minutes; black and white

CAST: Shelley Duvall (Mom); Daniel Stern (Dad); Barret Oliver (Victor); Joseph Maher (Mr. Chambers); Roz Braverman (Mrs. Epstein); Paul Bartel (Mr. Walsh); Domino (Ann Chambers); Jason Hervey (Frank Dole); Paul C. Scott (Mike Anderson); Helen Boll (Mrs. Cortis); Sparky (Sparky the Dog); Rusty James (Raymond the Dog)

Gothic
CREDITS: Producer: Penny Corke; Executive Producers: Al Clark and Robert Deveraux; Director: Ken Russell; Writer: Stephen Volk; Photography: Mike Southon; Editor: Michael Bradsell; Music: Thomas Dolby; Production Design: Christopher Hobbs; Art Design: Michael Buchanan; Stunts: Roy Street; Costumes: Victoria Russell and Kay Gallwey; Makeup: Pat Hay; 1987

CAST: Gabriel Byrne (Lord Byron); Julian Sands (Percy Bysshe Shelley); Natasha Richardson (Mary Godwin); Myriam Cyr (Claire Clairmont); Timothy Spall (Dr. John Polidori); Andreas Wisniewski (Fletcher); Alec Mango (Murray); Dexter Fletcher (Rushton); Pascal King (Justice); Kiran Shah (Fuseli Monster)

Haunted Summer
CREDITS: The Cannon Group, Inc. Presents A Golan-Globus Production; Producer: Martin Poll; An Ivan Passer Film; Costumes: Gabriella Pescucci and Sartoria Tirelli; Associate Producers: John Thompson and Mario Cotone; Editors: Cesare D'Amico and Richard Fields; Music: Christopher Young; Production Design: Stephen Grimes: Photography: Guiseppe Rotunno; Executive Produc-

ers: Menahem Golan and Yoram Globus; Producer: Martin Poll; Makeup: Manilo Rocchetti; Special Effects: Ditta Corridori and Gino De Rossi; Based on a Novel by Anne Edwards; Screenplay: Lewis John Carlino; Director: Ivan Passer; 1988

CAST: Philip Anglim (Lord Byron); Laura Dern (Claire Clairmont); Alice Krige (Mary Godwin); Eric Stolz (Percy Shelley); Alex Winter (John Polidori); Peter Berling (Maurice); Don Hobson (Rushton); Gusto Lo Pipero (Berger); Antoinette McLain (Elise); Terry Richards (Fletcher)

Frankenstein Unbound
CREDITS: A Mount Company Production; Casting: Caro Jones; Visual Effects: Bill Taylor, A.S.C. and Syd Dutton; Special Makeup Effects: Nick Dudman; Music: Carl Davis; Editors: Jay Cassidy and Mary Bauer; Production Design: Enrico Tovaglieri; Photography: Armando Nannuzzi and Michael Scott; Associate Producers: Laura J. Medina and Jay Cassidy; Based on the Novel *Frankenstein Unbound* by Brian W. Aldiss; Screenplay: Roger Corman and F. X. Feeney (Ed Neumeir, uncredited); Producers: Roger Corman, Thom Mount, and Kobi Jaeger; Director: Roger Corman; Filmed on location in and around Milan, Bergamo, and Bellagio, Italy; 1990

CAST: John Hurt (Buchanan); Raul Julia (Victor Frankenstein); Nick Brimble (The Monster); Bridget Fonda (Mary); Catherine Rabett (Elizabeth); Jason Patric (Bryon); Michael Hutchence (Shelley); Catherine Corman (Justine)

Mary Shelley's Frankenstein
CREDITS: TriStar Pictures Presents in association with Japan Satellite Broadcasting, Inc. and The IndieProd Company an American Zoetrope Production: A Kenneth Branagh Film: Music: Patrick Doyle; Casting: Priscilla John; Costumes: James Acheson; Editor: Andrew Marcus; Production Designer: Tim Harvey; Photography: Roger Pratt, B.S.C.; Co-Producers: Kenneth Branagh and David Parfitt; Executive Producer: Fred Fuchs; Screenplay: Steph Lady and Frank Darabont; Producers: Francis Ford Coppola, James V. Hart, and John Veitch; Director: Kenneth Branagh; 1994; 128 minutes

CAST: Robert De Niro (the Creature); Kenneth Branagh (Victor Frankenstein); Tom Hulce (Henry Clerval); Helena Bonham Carter (Elizabeth); Aidan Quinn (Captain Walton); Ian Holm (Victor's father); Richard Briers (grandfather); John Cleese (Prof. Waldman); Cherie Lunghi (Victor's mother); Trevyn McDowell (Justine); Mark Hadfield (Felix); Joanna Roth (Marie); Sasha Manau (Maggie); Joseph England (Thomas)

Frankenstein and Me
CREDITS: Director: Robert Tinnell; Producer: Richard Goudreau; Screenplay: David Sherman, Richard Goudreau (based on a Original Story by Robert Tinnell)

CAST: Burt Reynolds; Jamieson Boulanger; Myriam Cyr; Louise Fletcher; Ricky Mabe; Ryan Gosling; Rebecca Henderson; Roc Lafortune

If you enjoyed this book, write for a free catalog
or visit our website at www.midmar.com

Midnight Marquee Press, Inc.
9721 Britinay Lane
Baltimore, MD 21234
410-665-1198

Lightning Source UK Ltd.
Milton Keynes UK
UKHW021449250719
346804UK00006B/1162/P

9 781887 664097